AS I SAW IT
BY BOB OSGOOD

COMPILED AND EDITED BY
PAUL MOORE

Published by Humbug Enterprises, 2017
Copyright © Paul Moore
All rights reserved.

ISBN-978-1539090984
ISBN-1539090981

On the Cover: Front – At the top is Bob Osgood's Logo. Below that is the title of his monthly column "As I See It," which has been edited to past tense. The picture is of the Cheyenne Mountain Dancers which graced the first edition of Sets in Order.

Back - Frank Grundeen drew the back-cover cartoons for all 444 issues of Sets in Order/Square Dancing magazine. This is the last one. The testimonials for the book are from a 'who's who' of square dancing.

CONTENTS

Appendices:

Introduction and Acknowledgments

Bob Osgood was a square dancer. And a square dance caller. He was also the publisher of the most widely read magazine on square dancing, Sets in Order, which changed its name to Square Dancing in 1969. He was the president of the Sets in Order/American Square Dance Society which provided funding and leadership for many square dance projects. He established the Silver Spur award which was given to people who made outstanding contributions to the square dance activity and he founded the Caller's Hall of Fame. He was a charismatic leader who attracted the finest in square dancing to his causes. It was largely because of his leadership that CALLERLAB and LEGACY were formed.

Bob was also a packrat. If you ever had the chance to walk into his office in Beverly Hills you would wonder how he could ever find anything. Then you would see memorabilia from his career scattered throughout the approximately 15 by 20 foot room. His interests outside of square dancing were prominently displayed: a World War I carbine, a World War II German helmet, proof sheets of stamps, and more.

Then as you tried to go from the doorway from the pool side of his patio to the opposite side where his desk was tucked into a corner with an IBM Selectric typewriter on it (he never did click with computers, though his staff certainly did), you had to squeeze between the banks of file cabinets that lined the walls and the eight file cabinets that took up most of the floor space. The tops of the file cabinets were laden with ongoing projects or things set aside to be properly filed sometime.

The file cabinets were stuffed with letters to (and from) the editor; column ideas he had, thousands of photographs, mostly taken by good friend and staff photographer Joe Fadler. There were several drawers with loose and carefully sorted and mounted postage stamps. A lot of the stamps came from his father's collection, but most were contributions to his collection from fans from around to world.

If you were brave enough, you could step through the door to the garage, turn right and open the first door to the right. That was the door to the first of three storage sheds Bob had added to keep old communications, old magazine articles, a vast collection of 16mm film (some just home movies, some of trips he made with square dancers), and last but not least, hundreds of audio cassettes and reel-to-reel tapes. Every meeting on square dancing he went to he taped. Many phone calls were taped so he could review the issues discussed. And there was a vast collection of tapes from friends and colleagues who liked to chat, and sending a tape was a way to hear the person as if he were in the room.

Amazing as it may seem, it was possible to locate anything you needed. Boxes were labeled, and every folder in every box was labeled. Heartfelt thanks to the staff of Sets in Order for keeping Bob organized. And more especially, after Bob closed the magazine, a big thank you to Gail Seastrom who reported to work a couple of days a week to file material, to hunt down material Bob wanted to use in a new article, and to take dictation (and thank heavens he did dictate – his hand writing was never very good, but it deteriorated badly in the later years).

Becky, Mrs. Square Dancing, who married Bob in 1958, also did a lot of the work of sorting stuff before she passed away in 1999. Bob died in 2003 leaving a houseful and office and sheds full of stuff for the family to sort out. Linda Anderson, Bob's daughter with his first wife, is as organized as anyone in the family. She undertook the job of making sure everything ended up in the right places. Becky's daughter, Wendy Hubenthal, though she lived far out of town, also was an invaluable aid in packing and shipping. All of Bob's square dance materials ended up in Linda's garage where she sorted through the massive accumulation of files and file boxes. She had had the idea of writing Bob's biography, but found it was overwhelming. She also was charged with making sure that all of this "stuff" arrived at the University of Denver, the archives that Bob chose. Linda passed that task on to me.

It was a bit of a challenge for me to fit a drive from Northern California down to Long Beach then locate a large enough enclosed trailer to haul the over 50 boxes back home – not to mention clearing enough space in my garage to store it all. The really good thing, from my point of view, is that I got to paw through every single box. Looking at pictures was definitely fun, but the real surprise was finding all the letters and Bob's answers to them. I don't think I mentioned that Bob saved every letter he received about square dancing; then when he answered the letter, he attached a carbon copy of his letter to the original.

Once the winter weather dried out at my home in Northern California, I rented another trailer and headed to Colorado. First stop was at Cal Campbell's house in Castle Rock just a few miles south of Denver. Cal and I had been in communication for years about adding the Osgood collection to the Lloyd Shaw Foundation archives at Denver. What could have been a really short detour took all night because: 1) it gave Cal a chance to see what was in all the boxes; and 2) I got to eat one of Judy Campbell's marvelous meals.

From Cal's it was back up to the University of Denver where I was met by Kate Crowe and a crew of students. Kate is in charge of special collections, which at DU is massive. She was overwhelmed at the time because the library was moving into a brand new facility, but she made me and all the boxes feel welcome. Everything was temporarily stored in the old library until the new facility was ready. Waiting the couple of years for the dust to settle at University of Denver just about drove us crazy, but it is now all organized and available. My thanks to Kate for all that work, and for the ongoing service of looking for documents or files as I needed them.

Whenever I head anywhere near Denver I have to stop in to visit with Bob and Allynn Riggs, dear friends who have provided room and board, friendship, and lots of good advice about square dancing. I must admit that I really take advantage of their hospitality. After several days in Denver I headed back home.

Linda Anderson had hoped to have the time to condense all of Bob's ideas from his "As I See It" columns into a book. Finally, she called and said the job was just too much. So I took another trip south to pick up the remaining 30 boxes. When I got back home it was to a discussion with my wife Mary about where we could possibly store that many boxes. That is when Buddy Weaver of Blue Star records came to the rescue…he took all of the cassettes and digitized them. That left only 15 boxes for me to store, but it took Buddy over three years to get the cassettes done. There are now four more boxes in my garage of reel-to-reel tape that I am working on. Amazingly, the tapes are not in bad condition; in fact, I have had very few of them break. It's that the people on the tapes are so fascinating. Digitizing the tapes is an immensely time consuming job because it is almost impossible to do anything else while the legends of square dancing are talking right there in my office.

Meanwhile, when not recording the tapes, I spent my time going through all the files that had been set aside for the book. I discovered that Bob had started writing a book…several times. There must have been at least 10 outlines and even more starts. There were some completed chapters, and there were pages of hand written notes (written with a Sharpie on notebook paper with no regard for the lines). The later notes became harder and harder to read because Bob's hand writing was getting progressively worse. Also, the World War II wound to his left eye had become infected, affecting his thinking processes. He remembered the years when square dancing was at its peak and he relived the times with Pappy Shaw and the callers from the Hall of Fame.

Working through the many outlines of the book that Bob had done, I finally came up with a working outline. It was time to start filling in the details, but I have a severe handicap when it comes to research; for example, if I look up one word in the dictionary I usually read the whole page. Compound that problem a hundred-fold and you will understand what I was up against. A real time saver was that all of the issues of Sets in Order/Square Dancing magazine had been digitized by Gardner Patton. Gardner, at the suggestion of Jim Mayo, also digitized all issues of *American Square Dance* magazine which are all available on line. That gave me reason to renew an acquaintance with Jim Mayo, the first chairman of CALLERLAB, indefatigable archivist and author for square dancing, and a driving force behind the square dance archives in New Hampshire.

Meanwhile, while going through Bob's boxes I found some real treasures. For example, a copy of the 12" RCA recording of "Soldier's Joy" and "Blackberry Quadrille." That two-sided hoedown album by Floyd Woodhull was one of the few decent recordings available as square dancing moved from live music to recorded music. I also opened up a large padded envelope that contained a reel of 16mm film. I had no way to see what it was, so I took a gamble and sent it off to a company that specialized in digitizing film. Within a few weeks the digitized film arrived. It was of Mildred Buhler's demonstration group from the early 1950s. By pure happenstance, Mildred's son was a neighbor of mine. You should have heard the shrieks of joy when Fred played part of the tape for his sister who had never heard her mom call. The film is on You Tube and is accumulating a lot of hits. The You Tube credit goes to David Millstone, the president of the Country Dance and Song Society. David manages the Square Dance History website on which he posts square dance history – documents, film, and recordings. David paid for the film by reading and criticizing rough drafts of this book.

There were a number of times that I came to a screeching halt – I just could not figure out where to go with the book. So in came some emergency help. Some of them were the regular troops like Jim Mayo and Cal Campbell, and of course Kate Crowe and her staff at DU. Mike Seastrom, one of the great callers and also a good friend of Bob's, was able to fill in with personal recollections. Larry Edelman, a superb musician and caller of traditional squares, heard about the project, and he could be relied on to pop into the University of Denver library and look things up. He also took the 16mm film that DU digitized and got it distributed.

There were also some unsolicited helpers, such as Stan Burdick, who had published *American Square Dance* magazine for many years, and who was one of the three founders of LEGACY. Dr. Bill Litchman of Albuquerque, NM, former president of the Lloyd Shaw Foundation, who provided a lot of help in how to get the Osgood materials stored with the LSF archives. Another surprise was contact with Jerry Helt of Ohio, one of the first inductees into the Caller's Hall of Fame, who could tell first hand stories of the founding of CALLERLAB.

One of the greatest contributors was my good friend Bob Brundage (brother of Al Brundage). On his own, and mostly at his own expense, Bob started the square dance oral history project. Bob traveled around the country hunting down the great callers from the past and interviewing them on tape. It is through Bob's efforts that we have the sound of the legends of square dancing telling their own stories. Of course I am thrilled whenever Bob gives me a call or sends a letter.

Well, I recently got a rough draft of the book done, but it was bad. One major problem was verb tense: I was using documents that Bob Osgood wrote many years ago, and I had to adjust the verbs to show the time difference. I was kind of proud that I made that draft sound like Bob was just sitting out by the pool and chatting. But Bob rambled and he had a hard time staying on topic. It was like any conversation with one idea suggesting another. The cavalry came to my rescue: Cal Campbell, who has written several books on square dancing, did a tremendous job of reorganizing, spotting redundancies, and generally making it readable; then Jim Mayo, with his long history with square dancing and being an author, provided help in spotting what Cal did not see, checking spelling, and other errors. One of Jim's major assets was that he had been there when a lot of the action took place. Then the computer whiz Gardner Patton was invited on board. I did not know that he also has written and published books. And Jerry Junck, former chairman of CALLERLAB and history buff volunteered. Jerry does the interviews at the CALLERLAB conventions called "Visits with the Legends."

You may wonder how we can call this the autobiography of Bob Osgood. It is easy. Bob left so much material - a lot of it in first person - that all I had to do was follow Bob's outlines (all fourteen of them), select episodes, and tie them together. As much as possible the story is in Bob's words. All anecdotes and opinions in the book are Bob's and not mine.

One last comment here: if Bob could write a dedication for this book, it would be to Becky.

So, to Bob and Becky with love.

Paul Moore

Chapter 1. It Had to Start Somewhere

Four or five years ago my granddaughter, Gayle, asked me to write down some of the things I recall of the days gone by. What were the things that I remember most about the early years? Here are a few:

I was born in New York City, April 28, 1918 - the same month that Pershing sent the first U.S. troops under our own flag into battle against Germany.

My father was an architect and a darn good one.

Among my early memories I must have been four, or at most, five years old for these first recollections of being taken to Grant's Tomb on Armistice Day...of going boating on the Hudson River and being alarmed at the lady who lost her hand as she was getting on the boat (recollections play tricks on us at times, certainly this woman who indeed was lacking one hand, had lost it prior to that boat trip)...of my dad taking me to watch a parade while sitting on his shoulders and of being taken to see the circus - I don't remember the circus but I do remember that while waiting for my dad to pick me up, my mother served me mashed potatoes with a soft boiled egg on top (why do we remember things like this after all these years?) And I do recall being part of a group of youngsters my age at Cherry Park. Miss Johnny was the leader (I can almost remember what she looked like). And I do remember this reoccurring dream of a stark landscape and a rather strange urinal.

While living in New York City my mother and dad's folks lived in Los Angeles and I remember talking to one of my grandmothers over the telephone. I know that the call had to be placed the day before, and that there was a good deal of yelling back and forth to be heard, let alone understood.

1

But that was almost 80 years ago - what a difference in telephone communications from then 'til now. In the summer of 1922 the folks moved to California. We took the train from New York to Chicago and then from Chicago to Los Angeles. I don't know how long we stayed in Chicago, it might have only been an hour or two, but I remember that it was HOT and somewhere in the picture while waiting for the train I can recall a cake of ice. I have no idea what that has to do with the story, perhaps I was sitting on it, or just wish that I had been.

Our first home in the Los Angeles area was a rental on Western Avenue. I can vaguely remember the day my sister, Mary, was born. It was 1923 (I think). First of all, a house across the street caught fire and I can still smell the smoke and the wet ashes. That evening my dad took me by street car to visit my new sister at a maternity home in Hollywood, and in the process was treated to, as I remember it, a gigantic parade. A movie, "The Big Parade" was opening at the Grauman's Chinese Theater that night and this was the prologue – a customary event for all grand openings. I don't recall much about my visit to see my new sister or my mother, but I won't forget that fire and the parade.

We moved into our new home in Beverly Hills (Dad was the architect) and it was Halloween 1925. What I remember most clearly was the wonderful aroma of fresh baked bread coming from the Wonder Bakery about a mile west of us. Other sounds and sights from those times included the occasional call from the newsboys who would come through the residential areas. One "EXTRA" that stands out was Lindbergh's successful crossing of the Atlantic. Others included the outcome of outstanding boxing matches - "TUNNEY DEFEATS DEMPSEY - Read All About It."

At this time our area was sparsely built. From our front window we could look to the east and see clearly some three miles away and watch for the streetcar bringing my dad home from his work in downtown L.A. We had no automobile - we didn't need one. The streetcar stopped just a block away and two grocery stores were in close walking distance. However, as things sometimes happen, my mother who didn't drive was left an automobile by an old friend, a very wealthy woman she knew in Inglewood. The car was something else. It was an electric - the kind that looked the same from either end. The interior was resplendent with cut glass flower vases in the two forward corners. As I remember it, the controls were limited to two sticks, one above the other. The top was for steering. The lower one was for acceleration (or it could have been the other way around). There must have been a braking pedal on the floor.

Dad, who at one time owned a Model T, knew how to drive. They somehow agreed that on a quiet Sunday afternoon Dad would take Mother out and teach her the tricks of driving. Getting the car ready meant at least 24 hours for charging the batteries. Dad backed the beast out of the garage and parked it in front of the house (so the neighbors could see) and Dad began to give Mother her first driving lesson. Being a new city there was lots of road construction going on, some of the streets were paved but many were filled with potholes. As it turned out Mother had some sort of a fixation about driving and she felt that it was important to
get over the gullies and rough spots as quickly as possible.

According to Dad, she didn't miss a one with the result that Mother's first (and last) driving lesson took perhaps a half an hour. The score - about half of the batteries were shaken loose and both Dad and Mother were sufficiently shaken themselves with the result that the battery chargers and the car were hauled away during the next few days - I've often thought how great it would be to have that car today - it would be quite a collector's item.

We owned a nice phonograph and a number of red label 78 speed records, and dad owned an Atwater Kent radio. I remember it took three different dials to tune a station in. Each dial had to be adjusted separately. I'll never forget dad waking up all of us early one Sunday morning to hear the Mormon Tabernacle Choir all the way from Salt Lake City - a bit of static, but what the heck, this was quite an achievement.

The Beverly Theater opened some time in the mid-1920's and featured a kid's matinee on Saturday afternoons. The show cost all of ten cents for a ticket and if we had an extra nickel to spend, we could buy licorice whips (not the short ones) for a penny, licorice-type candy hats, which we would lick and then stick to our forehead to have handy during the main feature. I remember having the winning ticket at the first of these matinees and being the proud recipient of two round-trip boat tickets to Catalina Island. The movies, though silent, always were quite thrilling, with an organist playing the accompaniment, not only for the main feature, but for the comedy, the coming attractions and the serial, as well.

There were lots of kids my age within a block or two of our house on Oakhurst. With several of them as good friends, and with a number of vacant lots across the street and behind the house, we had many places to play our kid games. Right about then, as the movies were changing from silent to sound, "All Quiet on the Western Front" became the epic of the day and also became the theme for endless hours in our own trenches, dugouts and battlefields. A trench would be a hole three or four feet deep. A dugout would be a "trench" covered over with a metal "For Sale" sign and covered with dirt and weeds. These fabulous homemade playgrounds occupied a good share of our out of school hours. 4th of Julys, in particular, with permission from our parents, allowed half a dozen of us to start out (as soon as it got light) to shoot off our firecrackers. Starting with the lady fingers and working up to the flash crackers and the bombs. A few of us owned "bangsite carbide cannons" which were supposedly just as noisy, but much safer than the flame activated explosives.

Getting back to the movie "All Quiet ... " it was billed as the movie everybody should see and, after having seen it no one would risk another war. My folks having read this in the paper decided that I should see it, particularly inasmuch as several of the performances were being given for the Boy Scouts. Mother bought two tickets, one for Dad and one for me, and we set off for a Saturday matinee by taking the streetcar down to the Cathay Circle Theater. Just a word about this particular showplace. It was truly the grandest theater in the area and for this showing a large display of World War I guns, equipment and uniforms were in the forecourt of the theater. Maybe you remember the film - I'll never forget it. It was in black and white and the sound, as I remember it, was amazing. You would almost get the idea that you were in a battle as the sound speakers gave the impression of shells moving back and forth across the theater. In watching the film (a number of times) over the years, the battle scenes had lost little of their intensity. The one thing I remember was that in several of the major scenes as a battle was starting the screen would open up to what seemed like twice its width (not unlike our wide screens of today, but a novelty back then). In watching the movie on television over the years I do believe that a good part of this film may have been lost due to forgotten methods of using Grandeur film.

At any rate, the combination of the audio and the visual effects of the film may have led my dad to suggest that instead of taking the streetcar home, it might be well for us to walk. Heading the two or three miles west on Wilshire

5

Boulevard, it wasn't until we had walked (unintentionally) past our street that we realized we were fully feeling the effect of the picture. (Sort of a semi-hypnotic shell shock, if you will). Another little side light on "All Quiet" was that following the making of the picture and before its release, our class (could have been in the 5th or 6th grade) was invited as a whole to go to the Universal lot and visit one of the sets - a French village that had been under attack in one particular scene. One of the girls in our class (named Miriam Schwartz, I believe) was the daughter of one of the executives on the film. It, too, was an exciting experience and added more to my ongoing interest in World War I.

We had many street games we used to play. Early on there was Kick the Can, Tap the Icebox, and Buck the Bear. I can describe any of these to you, if you want, but let me just give you a quick run-down on the last one. Two teams, usually best when each team had five or more participants, would be decided upon. One team would start being active. One of the members of the "active" team would stand up facing a line of his teammates. The next in line would lean over and lower his head to the side of the standing member and put his arms around the goalie's waist. A third member would then put his arms around the second player and lean over so that the "playing field" of one standee attached to a row of leaning over, locked together participants provided the "target" or playing field.

The second team, lined up single file several feet away from the "target," would one at a time run and jump up on the back of the target participants. If there were five members in each team, the attacking participants would, one after the other, land on those bending over until all members of the attacking team would be astride. Once all members of the attacking team were "on board" it would be up to those bending over to hold them for a pre-decided period of time; either a ten count or 15 seconds - whatever. Once the attacking team was successful, or had failed, the two teams changed places and repeated the action. That's how I remember "Buck the Bear."

Perhaps our most popular street game was touch football, which would range from three players on a side to as many as eight or ten. We played on the macadam paving of the street with the field length from a light pole on one side of the street to a light pole down the block a ways. The width of the field was between the curbs. It was usually easy to get a pick-up game and these would last sometimes an hour or so after coming home from school or until it was too dark to see the ball. Once or twice I can remember the football being kicked onto someone's property and breaking a window or two, but this didn't happen too frequently. Once Jim Cool's father came out to give us a lesson in place kicking (he was also pretty good as a drop-kicker). On this one particular instance he made a beautiful place kick, traveling, I don't know how far, and breaking the street light. I don't remember any of the others of us ever breaking one of the lights, but I do know that it cost him four or five dollars for the few minutes of fame.

Jack Kendig, a neighbor across the street, used to come out and give us a few pointers. He enjoyed kicking the ball a bit, also. It was in the Kendig 's front yard right by the house where the most wonderful guava bush was on display, and from time to time during the guava season invariably at least once during a game the football would "accidentally" be kicked up onto the Kendig's lawn and under the guava bush. It usually took as many as five of us to get the ball out from under the bush. Sometimes that appeared to be a good excuse to stop the game for a while.

7

I like to think of us as just a bunch of fun-loving boys, but sometimes, in looking back, I wonder how many almost-heart-attacks we may have caused. Our street just to the north was a dead-end which meant a limited number of cars would come by holding up the progress of the game. I don't know where the habit came from, but every once in a while when a rather well contested game was underway and a car would drive up, fully expecting us to hold up activities until it had passed, when one of the players, waiting until the car had almost passed, would take his fist and bang on a rear fender. Simulating a badly wounded contestant he would grab his knee and, with the assistance of several equally divisive co-players, would limp and be assisted off the field to the curbing. If and when the driver of the car sensed that he had hurt one of the players and would stop in a panic, the "injured" party and others of us would suddenly disappear. Thinking of it now it was a bit of a dirty trick.

Another interruption which we didn't mind too much, particularly during a hot Saturday football game, was the ice truck that would come by and stop. The ice man would get out, get to the back of the truck, pullout one of the large cakes of ice and begin to chop it up to the size the sign in the window indicated was needed. Invariably, there would be more chipping of ice than was absolutely necessary and while the man was making his delivery the teams would call a truce and enjoy a handful of ice chips. Bless all ice delivery men.

In thinking back to these times, not necessarily having anything to do with stopping the football game, I do remember when one of the houses on the block would be under construction and the roof men would be working with tar to use in papering the roofs, that we would enjoy absconding with a piece or two of tar and chewing it for the rest of the day. I don't remember that it tasted very good, but it was something to do and it was free.

The 300 block on North Oakhurst, Beverly Hills, was a wonderful place to be brought up. There were lots of kids in our area, many in the same grade in school, and we had fun times. The parents would see to it that we had a number of block parties each year and a progressive fun event at Halloween was something we always looked forward to.

While I was still in grammar school I got my first job selling the Saturday Evening Post door-to-door. Later, when I had started in high school, I got a job delivering the Los Angeles Downtown Shopping News. This was a hand delivered advertising paper operation. My first route included the area where I lived and ran between Burton Way and Wilshire from Wetherly Drive west to Maple. Each paper had to be folded ("boxed" we called it) and had to be delivered right to the front door of each house. It was free so it was not a case of getting subscriptions. When I first started it was delivered in the afternoon two days a week, and later, in the mornings starting at 5:00 a.m. In the beginning I recruited my sisters, my mother, and a few of the neighbors to come over to the house and help fold the papers before I went out on the route. Another reason to be grateful for a friendly neighborhood. These jobs allowed me an early sense of independence with income that eventually allowed me to buy gifts for birthdays and Christmases, and eventually to pay for my own dentist's bills and, in later years, my college education.

The neighbors next door had two young children and they bought for them an old motorless Model T chassis as a sort of toy that sat in their back yard. Somewhere along the line a number of the fellas had problems with the man who lived at the corner at the south end of our block. Come Halloween one year the fellas gathered all of us together with the idea of wheeling the old wreck down the alley up either

9

onto "Mr. Problem's" front lawn, or if luck was with us, onto the roof of his house.

Okay, are you with me? Halloween seemed the perfect time to do this and while it got dark early in October, we waited until about 8:00 on the target night to do our dastardly thing. There must have been twenty of us, all boys, the oldest perhaps 17 or 18. We had no trouble in rolling the car quietly out of the backyard and into the alley. Then, with one of them doing the steering, the rest of us on each side and behind began pushing. We had gone perhaps 100 feet when suddenly all Hades broke loose. Police cars with red lights flashing approached from both ends of the alley. Whistles blowing, voices shouting, "All right boys, stop right where you are!" The car movement stopped at once. I was aware of a lot of scrambling.

It all happened so quickly and, while it was some time ago, I do remember that I was suddenly all alone - me, the car and the police officers. Everyone else had skedaddled over back hedges and fences, through yards and out into the night. It ended up that the police (and I) pushed the motorless wonder back into the yard and, I suppose, to teach a lesson to the others, I was taken to the Beverly Hills Police Department, ceremoniously locked in until my parents could come and get me a short time later - my first tussle with the law (and hopefully my last).

My red-headed friend, Burling Ney, and I got real ambitious one summer. It was a time in the 20's when miniature golf was entering the scene. It was a fun recreation and people were taking to it all over the city. Well, Burling and I decided that we should have a miniature golf course so we went to work in our two backyards erecting five or six holes on his back lot and perhaps the same number on mine. Our joint courses really turned out quite well. I can't remember anybody paying to play on them. As a matter of fact, not too many people took advantage of our offer for a free game or two, except our sisters.

Every summer Burling and I managed to take on different projects. I remember we had discovered that you could get free samples of Hire's Root Beer extract so we set up a bottling factory in the washroom of his home. Going to and from school down alleys made it possible for us to accumulate from various trash containers a number of bottles which we washed and carefully stowed away until the next brewing period. Somehow, we had invested in a bottle capper and a number of bottle caps. I remember one particular session. I'm not sure whether we added too much yeast or not enough extract, but whatever it was the brew cured a little quicker than we had expected and along about 3 A.M. one day, the bottles began exploding. I recall that it took us the better part of the next day to clean up the mess and it was at least a week before that end of the block stopped smelling like root beer.

Beverly Hills was becoming widely known as the home of the fairly new-fangled industry - motion pictures. It was not unusual to see the stars and others you recognized from being in pictures at your local market, at church, or just walking down the street. One time my dad had heard that the mayor of Beverly Hills was going to be speaking to the citizens of this city and he and I took off on a Sunday morning and hiked a couple or three miles to the Beverly Hills Hotel, a center then of the Who's Who of this city. Running from east to west in front of the hotel was an impressive bridle path and on this particular morning many of the gentry had arrived at the hotel on horseback or in fancy carriages. In front of the hotel they had built a large speaker's stand and people had gathered on all sides of the platform waiting to hear the mayor. I don't remember much of what he said that day, but for an eight or ten year old youngster it made a lasting impression on me for our mayor, Will Rogers, was truly a favorite of everyone.

When Rogers died a number of years later as a result of a plane crash in Alaska, television was not yet in existence and even the radio was slow in getting out news broadcasts. So, helping out a friend who published a small newspaper in our town, I was out selling an "extra" about the tragedy and even though I had heard him and seen him but once, that day I had felt that I had lost a friend.

It's interesting how certain things stick vividly in one's memory. It was in 1928 or 1929 and we were suddenly, abruptly and unquestionably in the midst of a great depression. We heard that people were jumping out of windows and once strong businesses were closing. It seemed that everyone was affected. Ours was not a wealthy family, nor was it a poor family. Suddenly, and I do mean suddenly, my dad was out of work. That meant that construction work and architecture had stopped - no work. I remember distinctly that my dad who was a stamp collector (a hobby that was mine also and would increase over the years) let me sell stamps from his collection so that we would be able to buy necessities. On that score, Mr. Holloway, the manager of the Safeway store two blocks away where we did most of our shopping, took my mother aside on the day that the banks had closed and told her that she was not to worry but that anything that she wanted she could charge. This was a true friend.

And, speaking of the grocery store. I can still remember how it worked. I would go to the store with my shopping list and Mr. Holloway, or one of the other clerks, would stand behind a counter and take our order down and then go to the shelves and fill it. This wasn't too bad on a slow day. But, when the holidays rolled along or for some reason or other everybody was out shopping, it was a slow process. I don't remember much about the prices, but I seem to remember that because of the value of the dollar, most everything would seem to be giveaway prices at today's dollar value. I remember that those large dill pickles which sat on the meat counter in a five gallon jar would cost only a nickel apiece. For some crazy reason, I tended to enjoy them as much as a chocolate bar - I still think they're great.

I was never interested in architecture as a profession, but I admired seeing some of the buildings and homes that my dad had designed. At some point in the late 1920's or early 30's Stiles Clements, the firm for which my dad worked, had designed the new limit-height Richfield Building in downtown Los Angeles. We would get him to talk about it at the dinner table and the more I heard about it the more interesting it sounded. One Saturday he took me with him on the streetcar to a factory that had made a plaster of Paris model of the building and I oohed and aahed at the structure in its miniaturized form. Sometime later, as the building was under construction he asked me if I'd like to go down with him and take a look at it. I would. When we got off the streetcar and walked a block to the construction site, I looked intensely for that tall graceful building depicted by the model. There was no such thing. Just a tall wooden fence to protect passersby from the heavy equipment and windows to look through to see the huge cavernous beginnings. Obviously, noting my concern my dad smiled and said, "You expected to see the finished product, didn't you? Well, don't forget the stronger and more important the structure the deeper the foundation has to be" I was to learn that this was true of so many things that we build in our lifetimes.

We had earthquakes! I remember one in particular - I think it was back in 1932. We felt it in Beverly Hills, although I think the epicenter was in Long Beach or down south of us somewhere. One thing about earthquakes that makes them so different from tornadoes and hurricanes is that there is absolutely no warning; no rattling of pans ahead of time, no notice in the newspaper. They just happen when you least expect it. I remember that in a little lighter earthquake than the one in 1932 my mother was out shopping in Beverly Hills when a sizable quake jolted the area. It wasn't that the earthquake was all that strong, it may not have been. But, she was in a hardware store at the time and if you can imagine the saws and pails and other things all banging at one time, you can guess that my mother was relieved when the shaking had ended.

I remember one night while eating dinner that we heard what sounded to be a large flight of aircraft. As it drew nearer it sounded less and less like a group of airplanes. Running out to the front of the house and looking south toward Wilshire Boulevard, there, paralleling it and heading west was the most tremendous airship. I seem to remember that it was the Shenandoah, although both the Akron and the Macon, and perhaps other lighter than air craft took this route during the late 20's and early 30's. An amazing sight!

We lived in a time then when airplanes were more or less a novelty. And why not? Aircraft had only been around over the past 15 or 20 years, and movies such as "Wings," "Hell's Angels," and "Dawn Patrol" were depicting the World War I era that ushered in the aviation that was to come. I went to a number of air shows and was always amazed at the beautiful flying creatures. At one point, I remember that the papers out here publicized the fact that the air races at Clover Field in Santa Monica would feature the daredevil aerial acrobatic team known as the "Three Musketeers." This was an opportunity of a lifetime to see this amazing group, so Dad bought tickets planning to take me the following day. The morning we had planned to attend an announcement was made that the day before one of the trio while flying competitively and too close to a pylon crashed and was killed. This, of course, was a great disappointment. But, because we had planned to take the time and already had the tickets, we went anyway.

It was a fantastic show and when the time came and the program announced the next feature as being the "Three Musketeers," we checked to see what would be substituted. Suddenly, our attention was attracted by the sound of the roar of engines and as we looked up the public address system announced the appearance of the programmed "Three Musketeers." The announcement went on to explain that in place of the pilot who was killed the previous day, his position would be taken by Charles Lindbergh. Something else I'll never forget. As a boy nine years old when Lindy made his epic flight across the Atlantic (1927), having this opportunity to see this American hero in action remains as a big event. Years later, while visiting Hana on the island of Maui in Hawaii, I drove out to his grave site. The many thousands who visit this out of the way spot each year was a simple indication that Lindbergh was still a hero to many.

Not counting several schools while in the Navy, over the years I attended four, the first of which was Beverly Vista Grammar School. This, the second of the four grade schools to be built in Beverly Hills, had been constructed two years before I entered the first grade in 1925. Beverly Hills was quite a new community and, in walking to school some six blocks away, it was still a city of vacant lots. I have a photograph of my first grade class and our teacher, Miss Wilson, who by the way was quite an amazing person in herself. Some twenty years after being a part of her class and while still in the Navy and in uniform, I visited the school, went down the halls to the elementary section and there was Miss Wilson's door with her name. Looking in the window on the door there were some twenty or twenty-five current first graders – their backs to me and Miss Wilson (looking exactly as I remembered her some decades ago) was facing the door. Looking up, she smiled, got up from her desk, walked over to the door, opened it, and as though I had left it only moments before to go and get a drink of water, she smiled broadly and said, "Hello, Robert. How are you?" Teachers are amazing!

Walking upstairs and into the 6th grade section, I stopped by a room to see if Miss Florence Fedroff might still be there. She was, and it was interesting for me to recall years later when she, now Mrs. Florence Morrow, was a pupil in my square dance class at Beverly High Night School. Miss Irene Thompson, who I must admit was one of my favorite teachers, had me as a student in the 7th and 8th grades. A native of Hawaii, knowing that I was a stamp collector, she contributed several hard to get early issues to my collection - I still have them.

A momentary highlight in my eight years at the grammar school was when Jim White sold me his antique Rickenbacker (Hat in the Ring, symbol and all) touring car for $5.00. During the short time I owned it (one day) I don't remember whether it ran or not, but my folks had to remind me it would be several years before I could get a driver's license (I had to admit that they had a point), and while five dollars seemed like quite a bargain, these were Depression years and five dollars could probably buy quite a bit in the way of necessities.

A freckle-faced Jean Ruple was my first "date." I took her (or her folks drove us) to the Beverly Theater to see the musical epic (Dick Powell and Janet Gaynor) "42nd Street." It was about this time, as we were moving into our final year at the grammar school, that the parents of different students gave parties for us. We used to play all types of games and had "fancy" refreshments. But I remember that one of our classmates decided that we would have a party

16

where we would dance. I certainly wanted to attend, having been invited, but I didn't know how to dance, and the very thought of it was a bit awesome. Telling Jean that I probably wouldn't be able to go because I couldn't dance, she quickly came up with a suggestion. Her mother could teach me. For several afternoons before the big party I walked Jean home. Once inside the house Jean went to her room to do her homework while her mother and I rolled back the living room carpet, moved the furniture aside, and for an hour or so each session we danced. I think we had a session or two on waltzing, a bit on whatever was the popular ballroom dance of the day - probably the foxtrot. By the time the sessions were over I had a fair amount of confidence that I might at least be able to keep up with the others.

Finally, the big night rolled around and Jean's dad drove the two of us to the party. Not unlike the previous parties we played a few games and ate creamed chicken in patty shells. Then, to the tune of some popular dance band, the hostess announced that it was time for us to ballroom dance. Eager to show off what I had learned, I took Jean's hand and said something to the effect of "Okay, Jean, let's dance." "I'm sorry," said my hoped-for dance partner, "I don't know how to dance." That's life.

During these years at Beverly Vista I remember, sometimes briefly, people, events, and other bits and pieces. Sometimes I'll wake up in the middle of the night and think of an episode which, when morning comes, I've forgotten again. But I do remember Miss Collier, our extremely friendly principal. Unknown to my mother, I invited Miss Collier, along with Miss Wilson and a couple of other teachers to the house after school one afternoon for tea. Thank goodness for their understanding and my mother's quick action to put the kettle on, it all turned out all right.

I also remember that at the little church my mother and sisters and I attended I would sell the church newspaper on the steps before Wednesday evening meetings. The paper cost a nickel and I would get to keep one cent from each sale for myself. One cent doesn't sound like very much, but if I sold ten papers, that was enough money to go to the movies for a Saturday matinee. One evening one of the well to do members of the congregation bought a paper from me. Handing me a crisp one dollar bill I'm sure he could tell by my face that I didn't have the ninety-five cents change that would be required. "That's all right, sonny," he said. "Just keep the change..." pausing a minute while I reflected on my sudden wealth, then "...and put it in the collection next Sunday." I don't know whether I was grateful to him for the moment of bliss or angry at having seen this great wealth so quickly disappear.

Going to movies was always a great treat for the whole family. My favorites were some of the war movies, silent and in black and white. My mother was always impressed with how natural her favorite actors and actresses appeared on the screen, and was telling our company at dinner one evening what a great job Wallace Beery did in playing the part of a lady. When asked if he sounded like a lady, she said, "Oh my, yes. It would be hard to tell that he wasn't a lady if you didn't realize that it was a man playing the part." Sometimes these silent movies could fool people.

Fight! Fight! Fight for Beverly High! Win the Victory! My eight years of grade school were over. One moment a glorified senior, the next a lowly freshman. The beginning of four high school years was indeed traumatic. The high school was far enough away from home that it took $7.00 of my hard arned paper delivery money to buy a bicycle. Everyone had bicycles in those days. Few could afford automobiles and a large area down by the Men's Gym was filled with bike racks. The school, new since about 1927, was built

18

on a slight bluff at the west end of Beverly Hills. It over-looked a now-gone wooden race track where speedsters, the ilk of Barney Oldfield, displayed their stuff on a wooden plank raceway - long gone, but not quite forgotten. My 9th and 10th grades saw the high school as a part of the Los Angeles School District. Then, in 1935 the city of Beverly Hills took over the campus which would be my home for the 11th and 12th grades and brought in a brand new faculty.

That first morning, under the new regime, as classes were opening I remember wandering through the auditorium and being grabbed by one of the students I knew who asked me if I could play a musical instrument. Admitting that I knew nothing about music I remember him saying, "That's all right, we've got just the thing for you." Taking me by the arm he introduced me to George Wright, the brand new band master, who handed me a pair of cymbals and told me where to stand. I don't remember how it all happened, but by the end of that first week we had recruited some 30 members who could play some sort of a band instrument. I do remember that the first football game was just a week or two away and in that time we did a fair job on learning the school fight song, and one or two Sousa marches.

Marching bands always had a tremendous attraction for me and I remember sometime during my high school years that the local papers were filled with the fact that the American Legion would be holding its greatest meeting here in the Los Angeles area. Foremost of all of convention events was an all day parade, moving from downtown Los Angeles south and ending in the Los Angeles Olympic Memorial Coliseum.

This, I had to see. Even though the parade would be a long one covering a number of miles, the crowds were out lining the streets hours before the first marchers passed by. I somehow found a key spot and if I say I stood in that spot watching the parade for twelve hours or more it would sound

19

like an exaggeration. But, in thinking back, it was that long. From the best of my memory there were something like 160 marching bands and well over 200 drum and bugle corps. At one point there was a lull in the parade, perhaps two city blocks empty before the next band would pass by where I was standing. Off in the distance I could see the marching units. These were men who had fought in the First World War. What they wore was not unlike the military uniforms of 1918, except for their helmets. Silver in appearance, these chrome headpieces reflected the sun and it was as though some giant halo was over the entire group.

When the units were within a half a block away, it was easy to see that there was one person walking in the lead. The New York units boasted of a number of musical groups and it was a temptation to get out into the middle of the street and march with them. Suddenly, I could recognize the lone marcher who headed the contingent. It was Fiorello La-Guardia, mayor of New York City and an army Major, I believe.

A little less on the grand size, but a far more personal touch was my time with the Beverly High School Band. Most of our performances were at football games, although on a number of occasions we marched east on Wilshire Blvd. in an Armistice Day parade and later on after I had graduated, I was asked to serve as manager of the band on its two bus treks to San Francisco and the World's Fair where it participated in an amazing high school band competition.

I don't think I'll ever forget our first night game. We were to play Long Beach. Just before halftime the band filed out of the bleachers onto the end zone behind the goal posts, waiting for the quarter to end. We had been practicing in the day time for several weeks and we knew exactly what we were supposed to do. Although we had not performed at night, we had no doubt that we could make old Beverly proud. The gun signaling the start of the halftime sounded and being the guest team we were ready to go. Did I mention that in the final seconds of that first half a typical Long Beach fog settled in. And, I mean settled in! No matter. We knew what we were doing. The drums started the cadence (I was now the bass drummer) and we started off down the field. The percussion section was in the rear of the band and while our cacophony all but drowned out the sound of the brass, woodwinds and the reeds, we had no fear that we could handle the situation. Passing the 20-yard marker the fog had really gotten serious, but no fear, we knew what we were doing. Past the 40-yard marker and then it was even difficult to see the chalk marks on the field. Bravely, the snare drums were snaring, cymbals cymbaling and me banging away as though I knew what I was doing.

Because we couldn't hear anything but the drums we couldn't imagine that anything was wrong until suddenly we were crossing into the opposite end zone and passing the goal post at the other end of the field. Coming up to the edge of the bleachers a bevy of the faculty, plus two or three of the cheerleaders, greeted us with the information that we had been separated from the others who were proudly serenading the stands at the 50-yard marker. It was the sort of incident that was talked about for a considerable amount of time and for a number of years the drums in the band were referred to as the "lost battalion."

During those high school years my friend Burling held down a number of jobs. One of them was to run a parking lot across the street from the Fox Wilshire Theater. And, sometimes after school, I would go down and visit with him. On occasions tourists from out of state would stop by with questions about sightseeing in the area and occasionally when business was slow, Burling would accompany them for a half hour or so showing them movie star homes, some of the studios, etc. On this one particular afternoon the parking lot was unusually busy and as I was watching the process

21

of parking and moving cars, a car drove up and the driver asked my friend if there was anyone who could show them the sites. Apparently, I was the only one available and although this was a new experience for me I had lived in the area for a good number of years and felt that I could give them their money's worth. Just before taking off, Burling pulled me aside and said, "Give them what they want to see and there will be a good tip in it for you." That's all I needed to know.

They wanted to see Harold Lloyd's estate - fine, I knew where it was. Pickfair? "Turn right, go up this hill and it's just about a half a mile on the right." And, the Beverly Hills Hotel, sure, "just go left on this street and then pull a right on Sunset and you'll see it." Then they began asking about stars I didn't know and some that I did know but hadn't the foggiest idea where they lived. Remembering Burling's caution, I was able to show them the home of every star that they were curious to see. Cary Grant? "Right down this street and turn to the left." "Adolph Menjou, that's his home up there on top of the buff." Well, it was an experience. Not an altogether honest one, but if you could see the looks on the faces of the people in the back seat, you could tell that they were satisfied and happy. I don't remember what they paid me, but I'm sure it was more than ample.

Summer jobs are always important to high schoolers and college students. One summer I joined my friend, Bill Loy and went up to work in his uncle's apricot dryer in Hayward, California. Including all the expenses of the trip, I still had enough left after that three months summer to buy my first car - a 1929 Model A Ford, complete with rumble seat. Parents were always helpful, as were close friends, in finding interesting summer jobs. Sometimes you're liable to get more jobs than you can handle. In my 11th year in high school I managed to tie down a summer job working on the Palomar Mountain telescope site. It was a good opportunity though I knew that the work would be strictly on the tough side. Then, just before the start of summer vacation, I was offered a job at Lake Arrowhead, a mile-high resort about 100 miles from home. My work was to be an assistant at the bath house on the lake's swimming beach. Getting up to the lake on the first day after school let out I reported for duty. First of all, I found that I would primarily be renting out dressing rooms, handing out towels, etc., and keeping the area clean. Secondarily, the man who was to be my boss was the lifeguard. He quickly informed me that my secondary job would be to fill in for him when he wasn't on hand. The fact that I was not a very good swimmer didn't seem to matter to him and I can't tell you how relieved I was to get through that summer without any emergencies coming up.

By this time during the school year I had been advanced in the realm of shopping news delivery and was an inspector managing some twelve carriers, driving my Model "A" around Beverly Hills making sure that everyone did his job and then serving as paymaster. While I could never be considered a model student, I did enjoy my time in high school, particularly the drama sessions with Gene Nielsen, who later became the coach for James Dean. My stellar performances included the role of Tisby in *Midsummer Night's Dream* and the husband in *The Warrior's Husband* - neither of them speaking roles. In my senior year the city had just gotten around to discovering the mammoth damages that had been incurred in the school buildings during the recent earthquakes and consequently, the classes were moved into temporary Quonset-type huts. Our senior play was held in one of the four grammar schools in the area, and graduation ceremonies in another. With all the activities afforded by being a student at Beverly High, my fondest recollections were of some of the extracurricular activities.

A number of us who attended the same Sunday school were blessed by a number of parents who felt that we should have the advantage of learning to ballroom dance. So, taking advantage of the Ernest Ryan Studios, in our area about 200 of us close to the same age (16-18) took part in a series of lessons. It was truly a dress-up affair with the young ladies in long dresses, the boys in coats and ties. Not only were we taught some of the basic ballroom steps, but we learned what our parents felt we needed to know about proper etiquette. I remember in particular that a required part of the boy's costume was a clean, white handkerchief. This you put in your right hand as you put your hand in the small of your partner's back to insure that your hands, that were supposed to be clean, would not soil her gown. After a year of once a month classes we graduated and, having antici-pated this moment, the parents formed us into a social group we called "Los Amigos" with dances at the Beverly Hills Woman's Club every month. The dancing was fun. The ex-perience resulted in a lifetime of friendships, some of them still lasting after 60 years.

Goodbye Beverly High School - Hello Santa Monica Junior College. With no idea in the world about what life's work I would choose, it seemed like the best bet was to go the route of the junior college. Santa Monica JC was "just down the road a piece" so I enrolled. The campus was any-thing but fancy. All the buildings were of a temporary vari-ety. Not much different than the facilities I was leaving at Beverly High. Before long I managed to get involved in the school activities and wrote a regular column in the weekly college news magazine. I somehow became manager of the basketball team, an assistant cheerleader, as well as holding down a spot in the college band. Although not a German stu-dent, I joined the German Club and on several occasions went with the group to a local hofbrau house where dancing the schottische was my primary accomplishment.

In 1938 our French class teacher got several of us interested in making a trek to France and touring the country by bicycle. Two of us, Curt Anderson (who is still a friend today) continued our interest and along with our teacher spent several after class sessions planning our trip for the summer of 1939. Obviously, we had picked a rather popular time. That summer a Mr. A. Hitler decided it would be appropriate to start World War II, choosing the same areas we had selected for our trek. Obviously, the adventure was put on hold.

All this time the activities of our dance group, Los Amigos, continued with dances, dinners and parties keeping the group busy. One thing about those years in Santa Monica that will be hard to forget was the day before Thanksgiving 1938. Morning classes had just gotten underway when the word spread through the campus, "Fire!" Stepping outside the classroom and looking to the north toward the Santa Monica Mountains, we could see huge billows of smoke and flame. If you've ever lived or traveled through this part of Southern California, you'll know that the area is loaded with dry chaparral and trees and brush that are loaded with natural oil. While brush fires were not unusual, this one was obviously a biggie.

Faculty members who lived in the fire area were released and hurried home. Students who had transportation took off as quickly as they could. One of my fellow classmates came running up to me and said that other than his bicycle he had no way to get home and to his father, a semi-invalid whose home was on the Coast Highway at Topanga Canyon, and could I drive him home? We were on the Coast Highway in no time flat and after having traveled a short distance to the north we could see the smoke and flame approaching the roadway. By this time a fire storm had built up and increasing gusts of wind hurled blazing tumbleweeds several hundred feet to start new flame centers wherever they landed.

Homeowners on the beach side of the highway were spraying water on the roofs in hopes of saving what they could. As we were driving, the smoke was getting heavier. At one point we narrowly managed to squeeze through barricades being erected by the police. A little further on and we were near to the area where my friend's father would hopefully be found. Quickly working out a plan, I left my friend off. Quickly turning the car around I drove several hundred feet south back the way we had come. Parking the car in an area that looked safe, I raced back. Heading down a short hill in a mobile home residential area, on the side of the highway away from the ocean, I started looking. It was difficult to see very far because of the smoke. The homes that were fueled with propane gas were beginning to catch fire and at least one blew up while I was yet a short distance away. Suddenly, I came across my friend and together we began looking for his father. Coming to his home we were relieved to find the elderly gentleman, dressed only in skivvies and moccasins. He was pushing a wheelbarrow loaded with what he must have figured were his most valuable possessions - many volumes of the National Geographic Magazine.

SMJC had no fraternities, nor sororities. What it did have were a number of clubs created around a number of personal interests to which attendees to the college could join if they wished. One of these was a branch of the college Y.M./Y.W.C.As, a semi-religious study group that provided various types of meetings and recreational programs. Having a number of friends who belonged to the local chapter, I became a member. Some 20 or 30 campuses along the West coast also had chapters, and they jointly held a yearly conference between Christmas and New Years at a conference ground called Asilomar. Not having anything planned over the 1938 Christmas season, I signed up and offered transportation for several of our local members.

Located some 400 miles north of Los Angeles on the Monterey Peninsula adjoining Pebble Beach, was this fabulous section of land, owned at that time by the Y.M.C.A. Some 500 students from the area's colleges and universities attended. Located right on the ocean and surrounded by many miles of white sand beaches the facilities had been designed by Julia Morgan, the architect who had designed the Hearst Castle. The program, which lasted for six days, included class sessions with speakers gathered from around the world and covering topics designed to be of interest for everyone.

The first day I managed to take part in just about everything, but discovered I was fairly worn out from all the sitting and listening. The second day started out with more classroom sessions in the morning. Then, following a short conference after lunch, I decided I'd had all the sitting I could stand, so, for a much needed change of pace I took off to explore the area. Walking from the Administration Building along a path I could hear, off in the distance, music. It was a catchy folk tune, not unlike the music we did schottisches to with the German Club. Following the sound I found the music getting louder as I reached a large auditorium-like building. Stepping inside I found 200 or so of my classmates involved in a large circle activity of some sort. Ending a moment or two later, I became aware of a voice coming over the microphone. It was telling the participants to each take a partner (and with music playing in the background) it told them to promenade in the big circle. Then the people did all sorts of things following the instructions. Everybody taking hands with everybody else. Looked like fun. Then, as the man who did the announcing stopped, the music stopped, and everybody hooped and hollered and clapped - ready for more.

At about that time I found myself being pulled into the melee. This time four couples at a time were told to form small circles, which I soon learned were squares. And we danced, learning as we went along. The hour or two sped by. At one point, while taking a breather, I realized that this was the first time that the conference participants were getting acquainted. They were shaking hands, throwing their arms around each other, and laughing a lot. I don't know what all we did but I thought I would like to do more of it. The next day, and each day after that, I found my way up into Merrill Hall for what I had come to learn was square dancing. The staff member who called out the directions was paid by the WPA (President Roosevelt's Work's Progress Administration), and, traveling around the country from one place to another, this was his full time occupation. The dancing was great fun, of course. But how many of the several hundred individuals, most of whom had known no one at the conference except the representatives from their own campus, had now become friends with everyone else? From my point of view, the conference had, become a success.

For the remainder of my time at SMJC I managed to keep busy and for the last half year served as president of the graduating class. Having completed all the college I felt I needed, I was ready for the big world. I could, I felt, start to work in any number of places, and doubtless in no time would be running the business. My starting job was with Safeway Stores in the candy manufacturing department. The first two months of summer I spent making gumdrops. Then, for the third month I was promoted to marshmallows. Looking round about me one day I suddenly realized that I was not yet a CEO, the president, not even a department head. Was I a failure? What more did I need to know? Then, the answer came to me, perhaps a bit of training in the ways of business wouldn't hurt. I resigned from the candy department and applied for admission to the Woodbury College of Business Administration in downtown Los Angeles.

I found this to be an amazing place. I majored in foreign trade and for the next two years felt that I had made the right decision. The courses were quite concentrated, but the professors were most helpful. Along with the required subjects I found myself involved in a number of clubs and I enjoyed membership in the honor fraternity.

Going back, for a minute, to my first day in the college. With new students coming from across North America and from countries overseas, a Welcoming Party was planned for the afternoon of the first day. Interested in starting out on the right foot, I headed down to the auditorium at the time announced. In the hallway, outside the hall were a number of students looking in, making no effort to go through the entrance. Inside were members of the Student Council and representatives from some of the schools' clubs. Dance music was coming from a record player and a few of the hosts and hostesses were dancing. Although a few "come in" motions were made by the folks on the inside, no constructive method was underway to bring the timid newcomers into the hall.

This surprised and disturbed me a bit and later when the Student Council held an open meeting where those attending were offered the opportunity to ask questions and make suggestions. I took the opportunity to ask about the so-called "Welcoming Party", and expressed the opinion that it was not a great success. When I was asked what I thought could be done to make the first-timers feel more at home, I told them what I felt, based on my experience at Asilomar. Later on that first year I was approached and asked if I would make suggestions on how the next welcoming day might be handled.

The school operated on a quarterly program with new-comers entering the school four times a year and after having been a student for about nine months I found myself working with the members of the Student Council in planning the welcoming party. No need to go into all the details of the planning, but the party turned out to be a rather amateurish one-night-stand. Briefed beforehand, members of the Student Council were encouraged to concentrate on bringing the newcomers into the hall assuring them that they wouldn't be embarrassed. Realizing that most of the first-timers knew little or nothing about ballroom dancing, we concentrated on simple mixers and other ice-breakers. To everyone's delight the party was a success and became the model for future "Howdy Dances". I had discovered for myself that this old traditional, friendly method of greeting really worked.

Members and faculty representatives of one of the clubs that I had joined held an off campus party one weekend. And, in addition to party games, refreshments and the normal entertainment, I was asked if I would lead the group in a dance or two. Because of the small size and awkward shape of the room I found myself involved in calling a simple quadrille, or square dance. The folks seemed to enjoy it and I had discovered that this was something I could handle. For the balance of my time at Woodbury we had a number of parties at this home of the Berger's and called the area where we danced "The Corn Crib". All of this happened 60 years ago and a number of us still keep in contact and manage to keep our friendships current. The group itself eventually developed a name, "Fun Unincorporated."

Although the college had no chapter of the Y.M./Y.W. clubs, I got an okay to be a sole representative of Woodbury at the next Asilomar midwinter session and here, once again, had my batteries recharged with the social possibilities of square dancing. During the following year several of the friends that I had met at Asilomar had get togethers where we square danced and I had opportunities to try my wings with such simple calls as the Texas Star, Life on the Ocean Wave, Oh, Johnny and a few others.

Somewhere along the line a group of us were invited to participate in a folk dance happening on the new campus of UCLA in Westwood. Apparently someone had asked us to do a demonstration square which we felt required proper costuming. Basing our limited knowledge of what to wear on what we had seen in western movies, the men had no problem in getting blue jeans, turning up the cuffs and acquiring rather loud western type long sleeved shirts. The ladies had more of a challenge. Knowing that what they wanted were long pioneer-type dresses, they went to Sears and ended up buying floor length cotton dressing gowns with a zipper the full length down the front. I don't remember a thing about the demonstration, but I do remember it as one more step.

During these years that I was at Woodbury small groups of us would spend weekends together having parties and going places. On one occasion a half dozen of us drove down to Ocean Park to spend a fun evening on the amusement pier. One of the more impressive buildings was a dance hall that featured the western band that was most popular at the time. Outside was a sign indicating that this night was a reunion for people from Nebraska and other Midwest states. Stepping inside we saw a square dance in full swing. From the best of my memory there must have been 15 or 20 squares, all hard at it, apparently having a blast. The band was playing up a storm, but something was missing. There was no caller.

Then, watching more closely, I realized that each of the square dance units was doing something different. Looking more closely, I realized that one of the dancing members in each square was doing the calling for his particular eight-

31

some. Then, at some audible or visual signal from the band, the individual callers would manage to bring the dance to a conclusion calling for much hooping and hollering and clapping. As they took off on a second tip I noticed some familiar calls and others I had not heard before. Cage the Bird, Chase the Rabbit, Allemande Left, Grand Right and Left, etc., Everyone was having a ball. This, too, was indeed a social success.

The college, operating as it did around the calendar, had a three week break in the summer and I remember Sam Shrigley, president of Gamma Sigma Pi, my fraternity, asking if I would like to come with him to his home in Phoenix, Arizona, and then head up to the family cabin in the Tonto National Forest. Flattered to be invited, I soon realized that the invitation was based partly (or largely) on the fact that Sam needed transportation. By this time I owned a Ford V-8 and the day school let out we packed up and headed east. I was quite impressed with Arizona and, after a short visit with Sam's folks in Phoenix, we headed out past Roosevelt Dam and on up into the mountains. This was the area that Zane Grey had written about in so many of his western novels. These were the hills where the sheep and cattle wars were fought. Reaching a spot called Kohl's Ranch, we headed in toward the cabin. There was lots to see, places to hike, streams to fish, but there were also things we were supposed to do while we were at the cabin. One of these chores was to build a new outhouse and, of course, job number one was to dig the hole, a task I shared with Sam. In the course of removing the earth a rock fell from the side of the excavation landing squarely on my right foot and breaking a couple of toes. This had the result of putting me out of much of the action; the hiking, the fishing, and a lot of those good things.

But, one morning when Sam and a couple of his neighbors were to take off for a hike, they first drove me down to Kohl's store and left me off so that I could get the feel of the rural area. As luck would have it, I soon discovered that this was the wedding day for two of the local residents. The store had been cleaned up and ribbons had been hung from the ceiling. This obviously was to be the wedding chapel. In about an hour folks began to gather, some in cars, many in wagons or on horseback, and others who lived close by showed up in family groupings. Nobody paid much attention to me so I accepted the fact that I was just one of the neighbors. As people arrived they carried a strange assortment of articles. A new shovel with a ribbon tied to it, a 50 pound sack of oats, jars of preserves, an apple pie and so forth. These were gifts for the new married couple. As near as I could tell, the wedding came off rather well.

Afterwards everyone kissed the bride and shook hands with the groom and then started wandering over to the adjacent store building. This had apparently been cleaned up for the occasion. Two small boys had just finished dragging a bale of hay across the floorboards to extract the splinters. Alongside one wall was an old upright piano, minus a good share of the white keys. Two people were seated on the piano bench. A man facing the piano was playing a hoedown. Seated beside him and facing the opposite direction was a man playing a fiddle which he held on his lap. Facing him on a small stool, was a little old lady, which I found out later was the mother of the two brothers. She had, in her hands, two knitting needles, and with these she was rhythmically strumming a cadence. This, I learned later, was called "playing the straws".

There was room for two squares, just barely, and with a caller in each square, 16 members of the congregation had a bit of a dance. Finishing the square, the "band" struck up a waltz and the bride and groom were pushed out into the center of the hall and started to dance. A man and a lady cut in on the couple; the man pinning a piece of paper money on the gown of the bride, while the intruding lady dropped a silver dollar in a tin cup that the groom was carrying. Eventually, everyone got into the act and pretty soon the tin cup was fairly full and the bride's dress was nicely covered with the paper currency. This was the newlywed's dowry and this was a mountain wedding that I'll always remember.

One more thing before I leave Woodbury. In my second year I became a member of the Student Council and was given the task of being Commissioner of Assemblies. This meant that several times during the school semester we would have a speaker or some bit of entertainment. Here at Woodbury it had been the custom over a number of years for the school to adopt a certain number of needy families at Christmas time and see that they got food and other necessities. The money raising plan was based on a drive during the month before Christmas and usually was kicked off with an assembly for which a charge was made. This Christmas charity assembly was my responsibility in 1940. I had a rough idea of what I wanted it to do, but when I mentioned it to the other members of the Council I could tell that they felt I was biting off more than I could chew. Well, I encouraged, let's give it the old college try.

My early morning L.A. shopping news had enlarged considerably over the recent years and I had a fair amount of driving to do each delivery morning. During this time I had been a faithful listener to an early morning show host, Stu Wilson. Starting out with him, I called him at the studio and told him that I would be pleased if he would emcee our Christmas show. He accepted. One of the popular nighttime radio shows was called, "Witches Tales." The leading witch "Nancy" was an acquaintance of one of my neighbors and using that as an introduction, I called Martha Wentworth and found her willing to help out by appearing on the show. That was step two. For the third, I called the Los Angeles Police Department "Special Services" and, having seen them put on a pistol shooting show, asked if they would be willing to take part in our money raiser. They would. They also said that if I needed them for anything else in connection with the show to count on their help.

Now, I needed a headliner. One of the crowd pleasers during the 1930's was Rudy Vallee. He had made the Maine Stein song and a number of other songs extremely popular. Do you suppose that he would be willing to come down and for a fairly small college spend five or ten minutes? There was one way to find out. I sent him a letter and asked. In almost no time at all I got his positive answer with a provision. He would be arriving by train from the East that morning and, not knowing if the train would be on time or not, he said that if he could get to the campus on time, he would certainly be there. In the meantime, he would send his accompanist to the school and at least have that part of the appearance prepared.

Sensing the time element, I called my new found friends at the Police Department and told them the situation. "Don't worry," was the lieutenant's response. "We'll have a motorcycle escort ready and waiting at the station when he arrives."

Well, the show was a sell-out. Stu did a masterful job as emcee. "Old Nancy" was her delightfully scary self and the Police firing squad saw to it that nobody fell asleep. Early in the show we introduced Rudy Vallee's accompanist and explained that if and when our guest of honor arrived it might be a fitting honor for him if we all sang the Maine Stein song. We practiced it a time or two. That agreed upon, the show was reaching its final stages. Stu was making remarks about the Police Pistol Team and suddenly the sound

35

of motorcycles and sirens managed to get everybody's attention. The rear doors of the auditorium were opened and with red light flashing, two motorcyclists came down the center aisle with Rudy Vallee right behind them. At that point, everyone in the audience rose (something they hadn't expected to do, but it was spontaneous) and sang Rudy's theme song with great enthusiasm. Making his way to the stage you could tell that our guest was impressed. The two songs which he had said he would do before leaving brought on a third and a fourth and more. Finally, after the five minutes had been stretched to half an hour, he left, I'm sure a bit worn out, but impressed. And we were impressed, too.

August 1941 I received my Bachelors of Business Administration degree, virtually simultaneous with my induction papers into the U.S. Army.

Chapter 2. The War Years

Section Base San Pedro, which would be my "home" for the next couple of years, was part of the greater Los Angeles dock and shipping area - a natural harbor reinforced with man-made stone breakwaters and housing many wharves and warehouses. The entrance to the harbor had been fitted with a series of steel mesh nets, designed to keep out unwanted shipping and in particular, if and when necessary, enemy submarines. A fleet of net tenders were based on a peninsula nearest the harbor entrance, and it was on this peninsula, utilizing the warehouses as barracks, that the harbor entrance control post and the Section Base were housed. A number of mine-sweepers and other patrol craft were stationed at the base and I was now stationed there as part of the ship's company that managed the harbor control.

Recruiting into the Navy, and possibly into other services as well, was on a hurry-up basis. I had received my draft notice several months before and had been given a waiver until graduation from college. And, now that school was behind me, (and thanks to some help from family and friends), I was able to bypass the Army and go directly into the Navy. Like some of the other enlistees just coming onto the base, I had no previous introduction to Navy life, no basic training. I was issued my prescribed sea bag, dress blues, undress blues, whites, dungarees, white hat, blue hat, shoes, Blue Jacket's Manual, and a sea bag. I had no idea what some of the issued material was for but I figured that in time somebody would tell me. My starting rating was Storekeeper 3rd Class.

A 3rd class petty officer was comparable to a buck sergeant in the Army. The rating of Storekeeper meant that I would do some form of office duty and the powers-that-be started me out in the finance office. Navy life for me was not all that different from college. I did have to live on the base and, except for weekends when we all could dress in civies, I probably gave a fair imitation of a blue jacket (that's sailor, son).

In the few months before the start of the war things were happening quickly at the base as I'm sure they were at most of the military stations across the country. A major project in our area was to convince the residents of the greater Los Angeles area that the Navy was prepared for anything that might happen. In an effort to do our part, the Section Base became involved in an operation proving that we, at least, were ready to repel any enemy whatsoever,

So, for the *Los Angeles Times* and other area newspapers, our base commander decided to put on a mock invasion of Los Angeles and the press were alerted to observe while we "fought off" an insurgent group coming from other local bases. In preparation for all this they trained us, all our storekeepers, yeoman, welders, and virtually everyone else they could spare, on how to be fighting men. I (already a veteran of one month) became a part of a machine gun unit. Aiming for reality, it was decided our white uniforms should be dyed khaki. So, they collected all our "whites" and put them in a strong concoction of coffee and boiled them for about a day. Then they dried them out and gave them back to us. When dried they actually looked like khaki.

Fairly early on Saturday morning, with the press already gathered, we were positioned behind packing crates, concrete walls and other protective shelters facing the incoming "invasion fleet."

It was a rather mild October day when we started. After a couple of hours the sun came out and it began to get a bit warm. By 11 o'clock it was actually hot and we were still waiting for the signal to do whatever it was that we were supposed to do. Then, we started to notice a strange pungent odor. That's right. You guessed it. We were sweating coffee! I don't recall whether the details were reported in the *Los Angeles Examiner* and *Herald Express*, but it's something that's not easy to forget. War is hell!

At a time, almost three months before Pearl Harbor, we were running a fairly slack ship, which simply meant that time off was easy to come by and we didn't have to wear uniforms off base. This allowed for time at the Berger's "Corn Crib" and a little square dancing in the homes of friends. Sunday, December 7th at home, started out like any other Sunday – up in the morning, breakfast, reading the Sunday funnies, then off to church. Following church was a different matter. Word had just been received of the Pearl Harbor attack and it was all anybody could talk about once we gathered outside the church. Driving home and listening to the radio, we in the military were advised to get down to our bases, ships, etc., as quickly as we could.

Arriving at the Section Base, the roads were blocked and guarded by the Shore Patrol and fully armed military police. Getting onto the base was a little difficult. Once the car was parked, I found myself herded with others to a group of trucks that had pulled in from Fort MacArthur which was located up the road apiece. At this point, we lined up and soldiers stationed at the tail end of the trucks asked each one of us what weapons we were assigned during our recent "mock invasion." I answered that I, as part of the machine gun crew, had been given a Thompson submachine gun. And as far as I knew it was fully loaded. They then asked me if I knew how to fire it. When I said that I hadn't the slightest idea, they showed me a small switch that I was to push in order to make it ready for firing. They then switched it "on" and sent me on my way to join the others in a preparedness drill for the invasion program. Of course, everyone knows that the Japanese stopped at Pearl Harbor and we were freed from the ugly eventuality of an invasion which we were in no way prepared for regardless of the training in our coffee suits.

In the early months of the war I was serving in the Captain's office. Among other responsibilities, I prepared the "War Diary." This was a report sent daily to the 5th Naval District covering the action of the minesweepers assigned to the base and a number of other daily functions. One of the reports was to "log out" and "log in" each ship, as well as the anti-submarine patrols conducted by surface vessels and the Goodyear blimps loaned to the Navy for the duration. As the blimp would go out in the morning it would "log in" and then late in the afternoon when it returned from patrol, it would "log out." I particularly remember one day when the blimp did not return. A search was put out and the Navy and the Coast Guard looked for it in vain. Several days later the blimp limply set down in a main intersection of one of the small towns in Northern California; no crew, no indication of what may have happened. A case of a modern *Mary Celeste*, the 19th century sailing vessel that showed up under full sail minus its crew.

Even with the war in full swing, a semblance of pre-war activity managed to continue. One of the spots I would head for when I could get off base was Plummer Park in the Los Angeles area with a group called the Hollywood Peasants. This was largely a folkdance group where, during a two or three hour evening, 15 minutes or so might be devoted to a traditional American square dance. The rest of the evening would include Russian, Mexican, Dutch, and other dances. No one got paid and usually a different member of the group would program the dances for an evening inviting different individuals to call a tip.

Once, while working with the War Diary, several of us were looking through the November 1941 issue of the

New Yorker magazine and discovered an unusual series of advertisements publicizing a game that could be played in one's bomb shelter. When studied, there were enough indications that the ads were a warning of some sort about what would happen on the seventh day of the twelfth month of the year. It was quite amazing. The men in Naval Intelligence in San Pedro were not able to determine the significance and we never did learn any more about it. (I still have copies of the ads.)

Among the many jobs that I had while at the Section Base was editing the station newspaper *Section Base Sweepings*. I also inherited the job, while serving with the Public Relations officer, of organizing a base library. The books were collected with the volunteer help of a bevy of Hollywood celebrities, under the direction of Mrs. Daryl Zanuck, bringing Hollywood entertainers to the base and setting up a canteen for the men. Starting in the months before the war was the project known as "Bundles for Britain." The prime project, along with serving coffee and donuts to our sailors stationed on the base, was to collect needed items for the battle-involved English. Following December 7th, the canteen name was changed to "Bundles for Blue Jackets."

The entire base was reconstructed from long standing storehouses and other existing buildings. My quarters were in the group of Pan-American buildings, which originally was the point of departure for those giant clipper ships that flew to destinations in the Pacific and beyond. Working out of our office were several notable figures, like Victor Mature, the actor, and Oleg Cassini, the fashion designer. I remember that my bunk was just yards from the chain link fence that bordered the base and within hearing range of an all night restaurant complete with jukebox. On warm summer evenings, with all the windows open, I can remember hearing strains of "Spurs That Jingle Jangle" and "Praise the Lord and Pass the Ammunition."

My mother, bless her heart, was a bit slow in catching on to the Navy way of doing things. One week I had rated a liberty and somewhere along the line had managed to get a bit ill. (Actually, I was sick as a dog). Early Monday morning preparing to leave the house and return to the base, mother said that wouldn't do at all. She then proceeded to call the base, and in speaking to the medical officer, explained that "Bob Osgood wasn't feeling well and would be staying home that day." The response on the other end of the line was something to the effect that "You get Osgood down here pronto, or we'll send an ambulance to pick him up." Needless to say, I was back on duty by noon.

We still had plenty of reminders that the war was going on. Transports would occasionally pull up to our service docks and contingents of the military would board, sometimes with bands playing, sometimes not. Early in 1942 a freighter limped into the harbor, lumber spilling out through the huge holes in its starboard side. Somewhere along the coast it had been the target of gunfire. At one time during those early years a draft of men from our base was trucked up to the oil fields in Goleta, north of Santa Barbara, to assess the damage caused by shells fired from a Japanese submarine.

I managed during time off from Navy life to help organize a group called Fun Unincorporated in connection with local members of our church who had a reception desk in the main railroad station in downtown L.A. This was a "Welcome Booth" for military personnel heading through Los Angeles. Those men and women who signed in were invited to homes for dinner, to places to stay overnight, or parties that were put on by different groups. Our "spot" was the "Hut" located just one block north of where our office was later to be situated on Robertson Blvd. at Melrose Avenue.

The Boy Scout Hut, which charged $5.00 a night and easily held six squares, was often filled with more than a hundred men and woman. Shortly after the war started we had an ongoing roaring Saturday night one-night-stand. What we danced was primarily easy material with donated refreshments and all the trimmings.

I remember I owned my first sound system, which was a Concorde amplifier (record player) that had a turn table on top. It would only play one speed - too fast. It had no variable speed. I did own a few records - back then only a few were available. One was a 12" Blackberry Quadrille backed by Soldier's Joy. We did have a few schottische records, and a varsouviana or two. A nucleus of friends were building up and it was at these parties that I had met and eventually became engaged to Virginia "Ginger" Hunt. Ginger was a great dancer and a most talented artist. Many of our mutual friends, having met through square dancing, were finding their ways to the altar.

Over the years a number of men and women have played major roles in the twists and turns my life has taken. Gene Anthony was a case in point. I met him first in 1942 just a month or so after the War had started. Managing to get into the Navy before answering his draft call and not possessing any special talents needed by the Navy, he was alert enough to do a bit of checking with the Navy recruiting office. He found that there was a need for ship fitters (these were the men often required, among other things, to repair damaged ships). So, as Gene told me later, he went to a neighborhood automobile repair shop and spent part of a day talking to the workers, learning how to utilize an acetylene torch and several other major tools that would be handy to a ship fitter. Reporting back to the recruiters he was asked a few questions, then was told to light an acetylene torch. This he did. "That's fine," said the chief, "you're now a ship fitter first class."

So Gene, knowing no more about ship fitting than he knew about being a sailor, came to our base and was immediately assigned to the metal shop, where, except for a chief and another first class ship fitter, he found himself to be one of the department heads. Realizing he could get into some real trouble if he didn't work quickly, Gene, who in civilian life was a very fine artist, managed to get permission to take a photograph of the base commander. In a few days it turned up on the C.O.'s desk as a full color oil portrait. The Commander called Gene in to thank him for the piece of art, which was really very good. Gene, not one to miss a single opportunity, asked the skipper if he would like to have a large portrait of John Paul Jones to hang in the mess hall. "That would be great!" Commander Guinn agreed. "But," injected Gene, "I can start on it right away if somebody can cover for me over in the ship fitting department." "No problem," said the C.O. And that was the beginning of the Navy life for Gene Anthony.

The portrait of J.P. Jones was finished in a couple of weeks. (Gene told me later he could have done it in three days - but why rush things?) By that time Gene had let the executive officer and the morale officer and several others know that he, Gene, had a good deal of influence with the Hollywood crowd. It would not be impossible for him to contact a few friends and acquire releases of new films to be shown on the base. Within a short period of time Gene was spending as much time off base as he was on, getting films and lining up members of the Hollywood community to make personal appearances on the base. Needless to say, he had nothing to do with ship fitting from that point, and, as a matter of fact as near as I could tell, was not base-bound too much of the time.

I came to know Gene rather well and some weekends, when I was off duty calling a square dance for members of the military passing through the area, Gene would show up and join in the dancing. Really, the reason for bringing Gene Anthony into this story at all is that, some 20 years later, he would create the portraits of the callers who make up the Square Dance Hall of Fame.

Oh, one other little bit about my friend. Going gleefully about his business and living off base a good portion of the time while the War was going on around the world, Gene almost had it made. About that time the French fleet under the Germans had sunk a good number of its ships blocking the way for an allied invasion scheduled in a few months off the coast of North Africa. Salvage crews were urgently needed to remove the debris. Drafts of qualified ship fitters were being made up at Navy bases across the country. If I remember correctly, Section Base San Pedro had some twenty or thirty ship fitters and Anthony, being one of the highest rated ship fitters on the base, was to lead the group to a shipping port on the East Coast and from there off to the battle area.

There were a few problems. Nobody knew where Gene was and the order, which came in the night before, called for the group to be shipped out (Gene in charge) by 11:00 a.m. the next morning. The hunt was on. One of Gene's friends was able to locate him at a neighbor's home and gave him the word to get to the base pronto. When he arrived with slightly an hour remaining before the scheduled departure, Gene discovered that he had little of his original uniform and equipment allotment that he had been given when he enlisted. So, a hunt was put on by his shipmates to locate a sea bag and the different bits and pieces that were required while Gene rushed to the medical department for his health records and to the personnel office for his orders. When finally the trucks arrived to pick up the draft and take the men to the

45

train station, Gene was still calling out bits of unfinished business that needed to be handled.

That was almost the last we heard from Gene until I got a letter from England. It seems that, en route to the East Coast, Gene learned from his fellow ship fitters how he would be involved. He would be working with explosives, probably a good part of the time underwater, certainly most of the time in harm's way. It didn't take him too long to realize that the Navy had made a mistake. Acquiring a camera and some film prior to boarding the transport, once the ship was underway, he set out in a new direction. Singling out certain officers that appeared to have more than a little influence, he started shooting their pictures. Acquiring the use of a sick bay, he set up a darkroom, and Gene became the ship's unofficial photographer. That set the wheels in motion to transfer his rating from Ship Fitter to Photographer's Mate First Class. By the time the D-Day landings were held on Omaha Beach, Gene was a Chief Photographer's Mate, serving on the U.S.S. Ancon, command ship for the June 6 invasion. Anyway, that's about enough on Gene Anthony except to learn that "getting lost" in the Navy is not always a bad skill to attain.

After having served at the section base for a little over two years, I was transferred to the Naval Auxiliary Air Station at Camp Kearney, in San Diego. By this time I was a 2nd Class Yeoman, having satisfactorily completed my tests for 1st Class. My assignment was in the control tower keeping track of the steady flow of navy bomber units heading out to the South Pacific. It was good duty and I had liberty to drive up to Los Angeles and take part in the local square dance activities approximately every other weekend. While stationed in the San Diego area I did have an occasion to locate one square dance group made up primarily of folk dancers, where, if lucky, I might get an opportunity to call a square dance tip during the evening.

Up to this point I had never been aboard an airplane. But, suddenly all this changed, and on occasions I would catch an indoctrination flight to San Francisco or Seattle and back. Being a part of "ship's company" I would occasionally be involved in reporting a plane crash and found my duties quite varied and challenging. One day, after having served at the air field about a year, I got a call to report to the executive officer ASAP. Never having had anything but the best relationship with the officers, I was surprised to see not only the exec, but the skipper and several other officers, standing or sitting and glaring at me when I entered the office. Looking up from a paper on his desk, the exec said rather sternly, "We've got some serious business to talk over with you." Having no idea what he was talking about, I decided the best bet was simply to be quiet and listen. "We just got a report here from the Shore Patrol in San Diego that I'm afraid won't look too good on your service record. The parents of a girl down there are concerned about you keeping her out late at night. We don't know how far this goes, but we wanted to hear your side of the story." Somehow I managed, "I don't know what you're talking about." "Here," the exec said angrily, handing me the telegram, "read it yourself." The officers couldn't hold it any longer. The telegram from the 11th Naval District let it be known that I had just made Ensign and that further orders would be coming soon.

Wow! My life had changed again. My wedding to Ginger was just two weeks away. I called her and told her, then my folks. If all went well, my transfer from the base and receipt of my orders would not arrive until the week following the scheduled wedding. So, we went forward with the plans. By the time of the wedding my orders hadn't yet been received, but I had permission to wear my officer's uniform to get married in. It was a large wedding at the home of Ginger's mother. It would be outdoors in the garden and about 200 guests had been invited. At the rehearsal the day before the wedding itself, I was in my enlisted man's uniform, proudly sporting a 1st Class Yeoman's emblem on my sleeve. Then, the following day, complete in brand new officer's whites, managed not to look too proud. My dad, however, couldn't stop beaming. It seems that I was the first in the family to get a Navy commission. Dad's grandfather, one month from getting his commission, fell out of the riggings of a training ship, thereby forfeiting his Navy future.

During World War II, college and university campuses across the country were utilized by the government as training facilities. Normally, the greatest number of naval officers came through Annapolis or other accredited officer training facilities. But in the time of emergency, when the need for officers grew with the construction of additional ships, bases and programs, other specialized institutions were brought into play. This was the case for the University of Arizona in Tucson. Qualified individuals, most usually college graduates in the business world, and a number of qualified enlisted individuals were brought to Tucson for a crash course while learning to become "officers and gentlemen." We were trained in basic navigation, plus other shipboard and naval customs. We drilled a lot, had minimal firearms practice and cried a lot over the tear gas drills.

This was to be an interesting but strange honeymoon for Ginger and me. On several of the weekends we had an opportunity to hunt down what square dancing there was at the time in Tucson. Things were not all that different although the caller used no microphone and he did have live music of sorts (piano and drums). The dancing styling, too, was a bit different (the swinging was quite lusty and the promenade and other walking movements were done with a two-step, rather than a regular gliding walk.)

I must admit that my almost three years as an enlisted man made it only natural for me to get involved in duties (projects) that relieved me from other assignments. Every morning we had a parade from the campus some one and a half to two miles to a park area where we drilled and had physical training. I felt that the drum and bugle corps, which led the parade, needed me just as it needed some 25 other officers-in-training. So, I ended up in the drum section. Each day for eight weeks we would lead the two battalions off the campus and down the road. Half way to our destination we passed a group of buildings which housed a fairly large number of children being treated for various breathing problems. It was our custom each day to be sure to play a march or two as we passed and we could tell by the expressions on the youngsters faces that they looked forward to this respite from what could very well be a rather trying life.

At a cross street we would notice, as we passed, the extension of the building down the block with other youngsters from their yards doing their best to see and hear the passing parade. As our battalion was about to graduate and our members sent off to various duty stations around the world, we did our final parade. Coming to the intersection we could notice a block away the youngsters straining to see us as we moved past. For some unannounced reason our officer in charge - the drum major - ordered our corps to do a ninety degree turn to starboard and head down the side street. Following closely behind the 19th and then the 20th battalions followed us. Finally the entire two battalions of naval officers, marching quite proudly I assure you, pulled an "eyes right" as they passed the viewing youngsters who, by this time were clapping, waving, and calling out to us. What we had done was not in our orders but few of us, who added an additional ten minutes of marching time to the parade, will not forget the experience.

A couple of stints of writing on the station newspaper and taking an active part in producing the 19th Battalion Variety Show which included Dennis Day, of the Jack Benny Show, who was a member of our battalion, rounded out my officer training. Shortly before our graduation, each one of us in the battalion had been given our future assignments. Mine was to report to the amphibious training base at Fort Pearce, Florida. I knew little indeed about the amphibs until the Saturday when we received our diplomas and the same day read in the headlines that the gigantic amphibious assault on the landing beaches in France had started earlier that morning.

California has a number of excellent amphibious training schools. So, coming from the West Coast, where do they send us for amphibious training? Why, Florida, of course. Several months of training started out by getting the officers well acquainted with our landing craft, the LCVPs. These Landing Craft Vehicle Personnel (also known as Higgins boats), were plywood in construction designed especially for landings on unfriendly beaches. Each was powered by a Chrysler Grey Marine engine and designed to carry 35 fully equipped fighting men or one vehicle, usually a Jeep.

Next, we would be assigned crews. Each boat would be assigned a four man crew. Three enlisted men would be coming directly from boot training and the fourth, a motor-mechanics mate, from special training. Our daily routines would include practice landings on nearby beaches. Each officer would be assigned to six, four man, crews and by the time the drill sessions ended the officers and men were shaped up into efficient working teams. Finally, the training was done. So, what happens next? We get shipped back to the Pacific Coast.

While Ginger was able to catch a train for transportation, our naval contingent traveled by "fast" troop train. Regardless of the fact that we had been told we were needed as quickly as possible in the Pacific, our train, which looked like residue from some earlier war, managed to get side-tracked time after time, allowing more important trains to go through. Finally reaching the Bay area, we were housed temporarily in barracks until our transport assignment could be finalized. Requesting and receiving a three-day pass to visit the family in Southern California, I called Ginger, who had arrived home several days earlier, and told her my flight number and expected time of arrival.

Catching a limo out of San Francisco, I managed to procure a priority number on a flight leaving shortly after noon. Looking forward to getting home, if only for a couple of days, I reached the airport and was in line ready to board when I was rudely yanked back to reality and told that I had been "bumped" to a later flight because an Army colonel had designs on my seat.

Not too bad. The next flight on which I was scheduled would be leaving in little over an hour. No need to call Ginger or the folks. Eventually our flight boarded and we were on our way. A little after we had taken off the other plane, the one I was supposed to be on, had crashed, killing all aboard. Not realizing this at the time, I was more than a little surprised at the reaction I got when I called Ginger from the airport to tell her I was in. The radio had temporarily, at least (and thank goodness) put on hold a homecoming celebration I had planned to enjoy.

The short vacation once ended, I was back in the Bay area at the point of debarkation. The Coast Guard-operated, former cruise ship, scheduled to transport us to Oahu was a mammoth affair. I don't recall a great deal about our passage, but I do remember we celebrated Thanksgiving Day in convoy. And it was here that I had re-impressed on my brain the difference between being an officer and an enlisted man. My entire experience in the Navy up to this point, except for the past few months, had been as an enlisted man. Being a 1st Class Petty Officer certainly had some advantages over being 2nd class, and 2nd class over 3rd class, etc. But, comparing a 1st class Petty Officer (and even a chief) with that of ranking as an officer really hit home.

Somewhere around noon that Thanksgiving the officers went into the main dining area. There were so many of us that we had to eat in shifts. But, it was worth it. What a thanksgiving meal it was! Not just turkey, but turkey and roast beef, stuffing, mashed potatoes and gravy, sweet potatoes and both mince and pumpkin pie and all the trimmings, nuts, cigarettes, cigars, etc. Well, that was fine and I was enjoying myself enormously. Then I looked to the side of the dining hall where there were windows or ports allowing a view of the adjoining deck and I could see just the heads of the enlisted men in line waiting to get served their meal. Oh well, I thought, they'll be fed the same as we. Foolish thought. When I went out on deck there were four members of one of my crews, each holding a slice of bread topped by a thick slab of bologna in one hand and an orange in the other. Under normal circumstances, when assigned to a Navy vessel or on a land base, the situation for the enlisted man would be little different than this. But I always remembered the comparison.

We got to Honolulu the day after Thanksgiving of 1944. As we moved into Pearl Harbor the sobering sight of the USS Arizona and the bombed out hulls of once-proud ships sunk just three years before gave us a sad welcome. Soon after we docked we were driven to an advance amphibian training base at a place called Wianae. We were separated from the crews with whom we had trained and they were sent somewhere else. We were now working with sailors who had made amphibian landings in Tiawan, Saipan and other war zones. They were joining us as advisors and the stories they told made us pay attention to the details of the training. Every week a new group of infantry, either Marines or Army, would come through and we would put them through practice landings at Sunset Beach that at times had 18-foot waves.

Wianae is the small seaside village that encompasses the base. Located in the midst of a pineapple plantation the area, at that time, was primarily inhabited by natives of the island and little else. As a part of the navy training facility the government constructed a pier that acted as a mock-up debarkation point for troops boarding the LCVPs which came alongside. Nearby beaches lent themselves to ideal, though sometimes hazardous, practice landings. With a stint at the training base completed, orders came in for several of us officers to be transferred to our ship - APA 177 - the U.S.S. Kingsbury. The AP stands for Assault Personnel and as a troop carrier it was fitted out to take fighting units into the war zones and dispatch them to the beaches via the LCVPs that the ship carried on board.

Serving as an officer on an APA was not unlike one of the characters in Gilbert and Sullivan's *Mikado*, who, in addition to being the Lord High Executioner, served a host of other duties. For instance, I stood deck watches, was assistant gunnery officer and held down half a dozen other assignments, including that of morale officer. On one occasion the Kingsbury made port in Seattle, Washington, to pick up Army troops as replacements on Iwo Jima. Not needed for several days, a number of officers managed to get shore leave. I reached Ginger by phone and planned to meet her in Victoria, British Columbia. Later on square dancing would bring me back to this area, but seeing it at this time it reminded me very much of what I imagined England would be like. We had a great, though short, stay on the island and I remember we stopped at a small restaurant in Victoria and treated ourselves to a couple of five course dinners that were truly sumptuous. Getting ready to leave, I paid with a U.S. twenty dollar bill and received, in change, more than twenty dollars in Canadian money (of course), but it still gave us the impression we had paid nothing for a fine meal.

Back on the ship and on our way toward Iwo Jima we were loaded to capacity with Army replacement troops. Now time weighs heavily on shipboard, particularly when the pace is held back by the convoy precautions. Recreation was sometimes difficult to plan, but there were boxing matches and impromptu bands and amateur shows. One group of GIs decided they wanted to do a square dance as their contribution. So, being the only one aboard who had any calling experience, I had the rare opportunity of facing eight Marines, four of them with handkerchiefs knotted in the corners and placed on their heads (as ladies' bonnets), and battle jackets tied around their waists to let others know that they were playing the part of lady dancers. If I do say so, it was a very memorable square dance demonstration indeed.

By the summer of 1945 the war had ended in Europe and those of us out here on the Pacific were in the process of planning for the invasion of the Japanese homeland. At the time, I had developed an injury to my eye and was being treated by the ship's doctor. While tied up in Pearl Harbor, the doctor suggested that it was better for me to go to the hospital. I was temporarily detached from the Kingsbury and admitted to Aiea Heights Navy Hospital on Oahu for treatment. Within days after my transfer the bomb was dropped on Hiroshima and the war was over. Almost immediately they started sending the military back to the States. Loading transports, freighters, aircraft carriers and battle wagons to their capacity, it was time to go home. For some reason, not known to me, I, who was completely ambulatory, was put on a stretcher, carried out to a waiting ambulance plane and flown to a hospital in Oakland, California, then shipped down to Long Beach for a few treatments and then released. That was the end of my illustrious Navy career.

Somebody once said that out of the horrors of war, ironically, come many blessings for mankind. We see this in the development of aircraft, in communications, etc. Perhaps, if it hadn't been for the War, there may not have been the need for the form of friendly recreation that square dancing offered. Two major elements merged as a result of WW II that led the way to the future of American Square Dancing.

1) Being introduced to square dancing in its simplest and most friendly form during the war years, many civilians and military men and women remembered the part that the square dancing activity played in their lives. And they wanted more.

2) The post-war period saw the return to normal lives for thousands of men and women and the creation of many new neighborhoods that needed methods to bring the people together socially.

During the early war years I had met Carl Myles and Ray Shaw (older brother of Lloyd 'Pappy' Shaw) and these two men, along with a few others, represented the calling that I was aware of in our area at that time. There were perhaps a dozen calls, including the "Virginia Reel" that were being danced in those days. Perhaps a handful of couple dances (we didn't call them rounds) including the varsouviana, the schottische, polka and the waltz. There were a handful of dances we did in big circles similar to the Oklahoma Mixer and the Hokey Pokey. These were particularly good with the type of groups we worked with because they were mixers and were the easiest way to mold a group of strangers into a friendly unit. That's where things stood for me and others in the Fall of 1945.

Chapter 3. Pappy and the Big Boom

Once again I was a civilian - a married one at that - my first necessity was to settle down and look for work. Fortunately, there was no great rush, for I had accumulated three months leave time with pay. Friends would ask me, once the war was over, did I jump right into calling? Actually, no one at that time ever thought of making money at square dancing, let alone earning a living. It was time to get resettled, raise a young family and, in the course of getting used to a civilian life, find a local group in the area that did some square dancing.

I picked up rather soon on our Fun Unincorporated at the Scout Club on Robertson in Los Angeles which was still going strong. In the days immediately following the war, when people started coming back from overseas duty, all over Southern California, as well as throughout North America, thousands of men and women were becoming reacquainted with a peace time world. Families were being reunited, businesses were starting up (again) and those recently out of the services and released from wartime responsibilities were looking for homes and jobs. The rush was on to develop new residential areas. New communities were springing up everywhere and vacant areas and recent farmland was being converted into villages with thousands of homes, creating a natural search for friendships and sociability among the new neighbors.

Many of those men and women who were building new lives had experienced the friendship of square dancing at local churches, USOs, and service clubs during the War. It was natural for them to look to square dancing for friends and for a release from the tension of warfare. In the greater Los Angeles area there were about six of us who called. Before the war I knew of one caller, Carolyn Mitchell, who was a great encouragement to me, and before the war was over I had met Carl Myles and Ray Shaw and attended some of the folk dance meetings.

In those years when I had first been introduced to American Square Dancing - mostly traditional New England type, with bits and pieces of Western square dancing tossed in, virtually the only dancing in the L.A. area that came near to filling the bill for me was the international folk dancing that was growing in popularity. There were a number of groups in our part of the state that met with regularity once or twice a month, sometimes even on a weekly basis. At these sessions, the native dances from around the world were introduced, practiced, put to memory, and then just danced and enjoyed.

Festivals, if my memory serves me correctly, were usually held on a Sunday afternoon; quite frequently in a large gymnasium or on a park or football field. Here at the festivals the dances were simply programmed. If one knew the dance he joined the others and counted on the music and his memory to pull him through. At the club inter-weekly sessions, the teaching instructions were given. But, at the larger festivals, except for the announcement of the next dance to be featured, there was no teaching, prompting, or calling. With the exception that if a tip of American dancing was to be included, the caller or prompter would be a part of the program.

There seemed to be no standard style or system of calling. The public address system designed to amplify the sound of the caller's voice and the music were still in the early stages of development. For that reason, many of the calls were abbreviated to necessary commands (Circle Left, Allemande Left, Grand Right and Left, etc.). Where there were groups that specialized in American Square Dancing, the choice of calls was fairly limited, passed along from one caller to the next, and often as familiar to the dancer as to the caller himself.

In those days, before and during WWII, the job of calling usually became the responsibility of one of the braver souls who realized that if there was to be any square dancing it would be up to him to do the calling. He would simply learn by listening to another caller, and then, working with a willing group who appreciated his bravery, he would do the best he could. Seldom very knowledgeable, he derived his bravery by knowing that he was slightly more knowledgeable than the dancers.

There were no square dance magazines *per se*, and very few books on the subject. Attending a dance of another caller was virtually the only means of getting material. For that reason, most everyone who wanted to call carried with him (or her) a little black notebook. At the end of each tip one could expect aspiring callers to write out in their own type of shorthand the calls they had just danced. Or the newcomers would get together to share figures: "I'll let you have my version of Arkansas Traveler if you let me have your version of the Route." Some individuals with better memory power than others could be counted on to develop a pretty fair collection. While having done their best to retain accuracy, it was understandable that many variations of calls were being developed.

Most (but perhaps not all) callers were extremely generous with their material, even going so far as to leave their notebook out on the table for any other aspiring callers to make copies. These same callers were most willing to share any knowledge they had. Some mentored new callers, sharing their knowledge, then offering suggestions and criticisms that might prove to be helpful. This was virtually the only caller training available before, during, and shortly after WWII.

In the months right after we came back from the War

there was a folk dance group called Hollywood Peasants. If you went to one of their dances you might be the lucky one to get to call the only square dance in the whole evening: all the rest of the dances were Russian, Jewish, British, Mexican peasant, and other kinds of ethnic dances. When the time came for the square dance, one caller was chosen from the four, five or six of us that were there. That was the only actual training we had.

In 1940 there was an article in *The Saturday Evening Post* about Doctor Lloyd Shaw, a school master in Colorado Springs, who had trained a group of high school students in the western style of square dancing. There was much more known about the eastern dancing because Henry Ford had done a book with his dancing master, a man named Benjamin Lovett. There were few books available containing square dance calls, one of which was *Cowboy Dances* written in 1939 by Lloyd Shaw. I had read the article in the *Post*, but I knew very little until I realized that one of the leaders in our area who had helped me so much was named Ray Shaw, a former high school boys vice principal. Ray was the older brother of Lloyd Shaw. Ray Shaw was one of the early pillars of square dancing in our area, and when Lloyd Shaw was brought to Hollywood to do the calling for the dance sequences in Selznick's movie *Duel In The Sun*, Ray saw to it that his younger brother showed up at one of our dances.

I got a chance to meet Lloyd Shaw for the first time at one of the folk dance sessions. I was very impressed. As I remember after the dance he got a bunch of us around to talk. He had watched the dancing that night and saw that everybody was sitting around the side, with some getting up for this dance and some for that dance. But when they announced a square dance everybody got up. Of course I can't remember exactly what 'Pappy' said, but it was something like, "You folks shouldn't have to hide American Square

Dancing in the background. It's a wonderful piece of our heritage and it appears that you have enough enthusiasm, both among dancers and budding callers, to start a separate activity." The year was 1946, and that was all the encouragement we needed. A half a dozen or so of us started calling - mostly one-night stands. There were no classes, with newcomers learning as they went along, being helped by those who were veterans of the previous Saturday night session. Music was always "live" and thanks to the man named Shaw, square dancing had broken out into the open.

Those who knew a little about square dancing, perhaps from school experiences, suddenly found themselves organizing and calling. Recreation halls, schools, churches provided the space, and many of the new communities included buildings where recreational activities such as square dancing could be featured. A number of the local parks and recreation departments scheduled regular weekly dances in their halls, and I, along with Ray Shaw, Carl Myles, and Ralph Maxheimer, found ourselves in the middle of 1946 being paid ($7.00 per evening was my take!) for calling a two and a half hour dance. The playgrounds provided the promotion and paid for the orchestra. Admission was fifty cents per dancer.

With the growing popularity of this new/old American activity, which some had tasted during the war, there was a sudden demand for callers, with the result that most of us fell into the habit of trading calls.

Starting in 1946, following a dance or on a Saturday morning, a few of the new enthusiasts often corralled one or two of the veterans for as much time as was available. The more experienced among them would willingly share their knowledge and field the questions as best they could.

"What do you teach first, a right and left thru or a ladies chain?"

"How do you teach a couple swing?"

"What do you suggest your dancers wear for square dancing?"

And on and on. There were many questions, because a growing number of individuals were getting into the throes of teaching and calling. A number of differences began to arise that somehow had to be resolved.

Most local leaders shared what calls they had collected and efforts were made by the callers to get together as frequently as possible and exchange ideas. The only training of callers at that time was by apprenticing - a new caller attaching himself to a more experienced leader. As time went on the need for caller training became more and more apparent.

The callers' coffee klatches began to grow and a few of the veteran callers started Saturday morning callers' sessions in their homes. It was in Ray Shaw's kitchen and living room that the informal group adopted the title "Caller's Powwow" and continued to meet in this way until the number of callers interested in attending outgrew the limited space provided in Ray's small home.

As engaging as square dancing was, I needed to find a job to support me and my family. But what type of work should I look for? My college training four years before had prepared me for a spot in the export/import business, but this no longer interested me. In talking to friends and relatives no specific business tended to grab me. Then I got an idea. With a bit of help, I came up with the names and phone numbers of a dozen different fields of employment that seemed interesting. Calling each one and asking to speak to the person in charge, the company president, CEO, general manager, etc., (it took a bit of patience and insistence, but over a period of a week or so I managed to, in most cases, speak to the top man, or woman in person), explaining that I was not looking for a job, but that I hoped to have an appointment for a short interview. Explaining that I had been and was still in the Navy, I was looking for advice. "If you were in my spot, what field of work would you be interested in?"

Of those I reached by phone, seven granted me a personal interview, three took me out to lunch, and one offered me a job on the spot. This last one was Edward Mehren, President of the Squirt Soft Drink Company. Just recently out of the Navy himself, and extremely optimistic concerning the future of the soft drink world, his enthusiasm (and the fact that he was willing to take me on in his advertising department) was certainly the boost I needed.

The job was as a Public Relations and Publicity Manager for the home offices of the Squirt Company, a soft drink organization that was growing following the War. It turned out to be a great organization to work for and in a short time, in addition to my regular assignments, I was asked to edit their monthly newsletter "The Squirt Reporter." The art designer and printer was a Charles Dillinger, who turned out to be a great help for me in getting back into the swing of journalism. He was one heck of a nice gentleman and really talented, even though he was not a square dancer. I had lunch with him and we started talking about communications; maybe I could turn out a square dance newsletter or something. He said, why don't we think seriously about sometime putting out a magazine. I said that would be great, but that went on the back burner for the minute.

The soft drink industry suffered from price controls set during the War. The cost of producing a bottle of soft drink went up a couple of cents. Because the majority of soda pop was sold through vending machines, which could take single coins (a nickel, a dime, a quarter), the bottlers had to increase prices to the next whole coin. Ed Mehren came up with the idea of fractional coinage. He suggested a 7 ½¢ coin, which would make it possible for bottlers to recognize a profit and still not have to go up all the way to a dime. In the same campaign he figured that a 25¢ coin (two bits) could be split into one bit pieces, or 12 ½¢. He figured that these two additions to our coinage would not only be a savior to the soft drink industry, but to candy bars, and other vending items as well. So Ed Mehren set off on a crusade. He even got me on to the Lions and Rotary Clubs luncheon circuit, speaking about all of the advantages these simple changes would make. The company art department designed and produced hand-painted men's neckties with pictures of the fractional coinage.

"The Squirt Reporter" was an internal house organ intended for the employees of the franchise bottlers around the country, telling them how to do a better job with advertising, getting new customers, etc. A dozen or more companies of different types in the Los Angeles area had established an industrial editor's association and Squirt suggested that I belong to it. My associations with other editors, many of whom I had been in the publication business with for 13 years or more, were proving to be valuable. Getting involved apparently was a knack of mine: soon I was an officer in the local branch of this national organization, then eventually president of the local chapter. And within a short period of time I was regional chairman.

The company also had me do quite a bit of traveling to visit bottlers across the United States. The task involved my giving assistance in ideas for sales promotion, do stories on them, and give them suggestions on points of purchasing advertising and how they could increase their business. At times I actually traveled with some of the bottler's delivery trucks to gain an understanding that would allow me to write training books and get material for the issues of "The Reporter." The bottlers, as a rule, operated from 9 to 5 which

63

meant that when I was in another city, I would have the evenings to myself. At night I started looking for square dances in Wisconsin, Chicago, wherever I went; and I did find a square dance in almost every area. I not only found that I was welcome to visit these clubs, but I got an opportunity to talk a bit about square dancing in different parts of the country. Once the dancers learned that I was a dancer and caller in California, questions would roll in:

Dancers: "Do you folks out there dance the same way we do?"

Me: "Most of the dances I danced with you here are pretty close to the way we do them at home, except with a few little styling differences."

Dancers: "What do you mean styling differences?"

Me: "Well, you promenade with your hands up. We promenade with our hands held in front of us.

Dancers: "What do you folks wear when you're square dancing?"

Me: "Well, the men like to wear colorful shirts and blue jeans with the cuffs rolled up and inch or so at the bottom. The ladies go in for long dresses."

Dancers: "Where do the ladies buy their dresses?"

Me: "They don't. They make them."

And so it went. Folks were really interested in what was happening out there, but they could not find anything out unless someone came traveling through. I had noticed that there were seldom two areas where the dancing was the same. In one area the #1 couple faced the head of the hall, and they numbered the couples around that way. In the days before sound systems, if they had six squares, they had six callers. The number one man had to be able to see the fiddler so he could let the dancers in his square know when the fiddler was coming close to the ending. That to me was an education too.

I learned also that:

-There were umpteen ways to do a swing. I noticed everyone was swinging differently which didn't matter a diddle because everybody just danced in their own geographic area.

-In Texas there were different ways to walk; there was the regular shuffle or walk step and there was the double-step.

-In other parts of the country there were the Sweetwater lifts and other types of steps, depending largely on the speed of the music and the speed of the calling and the age of the dancers.

-This experience of asking and answering questions as well as my job in publishing certainly led to decisions I would make later.

Working for the Squirt Company provided me a number of unexpected "perks." For one thing, my dances at the Griffith Park playground, which started out without any refreshments, eventually became the one program in the area that provided ice cold Squirt. Along with my job description in the advertising/publicity department, I was in addition (for a time) in charge of "sampling." I found that it was no problem and it was strictly within my job responsibilities to have eight or ten cases or the soda delivered to the park on the Saturdays before the dances as long as I could return "sampling" questionnaires.

As mentioned earlier, I was elected one of the six regional chairmen of the International Industrial Editors Association, with a large membership of organizations scattered across the country. Members represented the airlines, major manufacturers, food producers, film studios, and just about everything else you can imagine. And so it wasn't too surprising to find that our government suddenly became aware of the promotional importance of somehow reaching out to the many thousands of readers of the house organs produced by these companies. As chairman of the Western Region of Industrial Editors, I received an invitation to attend a conference in Washington, extended by John R. Steelman (an advisor to the President) with additional supporting invitations from J. Edgar Hoover, the Speaker of the House, and representatives from the Treasury Department, Agriculture Department, and State Department. The conference would last for four or five days in the nation's capital. In looking back at this period in my life, I certainly must have been excited over the invitation. But the combination of all the things that were in the works for me at that time made it impossible for me to grasp the importance of the invitation and the memories and experiences that would result from it.

At any rate, I tossed the ball to management in the company and Ed Mehren, the President, seeing the possibility of a fortunate tie-in with his fractional coinage project, said that I should go, with the company paying all the expenses. Being a rather gutsy individual, I sent a cable to Mr. Steelman which went something like this:

> Mr. Steelman: Would be honored to attend the conference if I would be given the opportunity to see my white house. - Bob Osgood

Very shortly thereafter I received the following wire from Mr. Steelman:

> Of course, you will have the opportunity to visit the White House as my guest. Just give me a call when you get into your hotel and I'll give you directions.

With my personal invitation to visit the White House, Ed Mehren must have thought that this was a door opener for the fractional coinage situation. Well, to a point, it may have been. The handful of us representing the industrial editors were treated like royalty. We had a session with J. Edgar Hoover, meetings with several members of the Senate, and the dubious honor of firing a Thompson submachine gun (not at the members of Congress). We were busy every moment until it was time to head back home.

Oh no, I haven't forgotten the invitation to visit MY White House, or the bit about the fractional coinage. When I arrived in the capital city and got settled into my hotel, I called the White House and asked for Mr. Steelman. In no time at all, I was talking with him and he explained apologetically something I already knew, that the President (Harry Truman) had chosen this particular time for a visit to, of all places, California. So, I would get to see his office and the surrounding area, but unfortunately he wouldn't be there to say "hi" (humor). A time was set on my first full day in the capital area and I was told what time to go to the "Press Entrance," identify myself, and head in to the office section of the White House. Once inside the door, having been checked by several uniformed guards, I was met by this extremely friendly gentleman who shook my hand and announced, "I'm John R. Steelman." "And, I'm Bob Osgood," I needlessly informed him.

With an arm around my shoulder, he took me through what appeared to be a secretarial pool. It was a cheerful place and busy. I can't tell you what I saw and what I didn't see. I know that we covered a lot of the building and at one point I saw the lines of tourists wending their way through the various corridors and rooms.

He showed me his office and then said, "Come on, I'll show you the President's Oval Office." I didn't have to be invited a second time. I noticed that there were guards and uniformed police all over the place, but they didn't seem to intrude and I took it for granted that it was just part of the routine. What an amazing feeling to be inside the office of the President of the United States. I was about to ask Mr. Steelman a question while he was showing me the props on the President's desk, when an attractive lady entered the room and said, "Mr. Steelman, the phone, please."

My guide excused himself, saying he would be back in a moment, and left me all to myself in this wondrous room where so much of America's history had been charted. It must have been only seconds, but it seemed as though I was in the room for quite some time, walking across the emblem of the Presidency woven into the carpet, looking at the stack of daily papers and magazines on a table by the door, and breathing the same air the President would have inhaled had he been here instead of in California. Leaving the Oval Office, and stepping outside, I was shown the area which for the previous president had been an indoor swimming pool, now altered (I seem to remember) to a bowling alley.

Heading back to the office area, I suddenly remembered my fractional coinage mission. Taking the ties I had brought with me bearing pictures of the 7½¢ and 12½¢ coins, I gave them to Mr. Steelman, explaining that one was for the President, one for him, and the third for someone else. My escort seemingly understood about the movement, promised that he would see that they got into the President's office and had proper homes. He gave me a great smile, a warm hand clasp and I was on my way. This was not an experience that anyone in their right mind would take lightly; but then, was I in my right mind?

One other thing while in the area; I did attend a square dance. I can't remember the caller's name, what he called, or anything about the dance: my mind must have been somewhere else.

These were new times and new surroundings for so many in California, and we found in square dancing the opportunity for a social activity which proved to be a "natural." Up to this time we had perhaps only a handful of individuals who could do any calling. I had no trouble calling the Saturday night dances at the little Boy Scout Hut regularly. Old-timers Ray Shaw and Carl Myles, originally from Colorado Springs, served as mainstays within our area each calling on a regular basis.

In the years before, during, and immediately following the Second World War, square dancing bore little resemblance to the contemporary western club form being danced today. The way we danced here in California must have been quite similar to the way folks danced in other areas of the country but with a bit more of the Western flavor out here and influences of New England dancing evident further East. You have to remember that recorded accompaniment music and sound systems didn't enter the picture until well into the 1930s, and even late in the 1940s they were clumsy and rare. That meant that live music in one form or another and a different form of non-amplified calling was necessary.

My recollections of the pre-war dances were of non-complicated, one-night stands with an emphasis on social mixing. Each dance evening started "from scratch" with nothing taken for granted. Even the simplest Dosado and couple swing had to be explained. Dancing tended to be a bit rough - but most everyone seemed to be having a great time. This form of dancing was prevalent in our area during the war years when square dancing proved to be the natural way of entertaining the service personnel stationed in or passing through Los Angeles.

My dance at Griffith Park Playground on the first and third Saturdays continued to be a one-night stand not unlike the other half dozen or so "open dances" in our area. Run either by the callers or by the Parks Departments, they were attracting quite sizeable crowds, and although there were many faithful attendees, the brand new dancers made it necessary each time to start at the beginning. Because of this there was little opportunity to smooth out the rough dancing and move ahead. For the callers and the more experienced dancers this was a frustrating period. Except for Henry Ford's "Good Morning" and Lloyd Shaw's "Cowboy Dances" and one or two other collections of calls, we had very little available to us in the way of dance material.

In 1923 Henry Ford visited the Wayside Inn in Sudbury, Massachusetts where he participated in the regular dance program of gavotte, the schottische, minuet, and the Virginia Reel led by Benjamin B. Lovett. Ford enjoyed the program so much he offered Lovett a regular job to teach dancing and to train new dance leaders in Dearborn, Michigan. Lovett turned down the offer because he was contracted to the Wayside Inn. Ford, who had a personal wealth of twenty billion dollars (in 1920's dollars), simply bought the Wayside Inn and Lovett's contract. The contract was rewritten for Lovett to come to Dearborn for two months – he stayed for twenty-six years. During the Depression of the 1930s Lovett was paid $12,000 per year, plus a new Lincoln every year, a home, most of his meals, and all of his transportation costs. Ford and Lovett used the situation to promote American Square Dancing. Two hundred dancing instructors were invited to Dearborn to learn how to dance and to call the Virginia Reel. Lovett was also instructed to start a program for Dearborn public school children. The dances that Lovett taught were regularly printed in newspapers nation-wide. Every Sunday Lovett would travel to Chicago to call live on the radio the dances that had been printed in newspapers the previous week – with separate broadcasts to account for Eastern and Western time zones.

Benjamin Lovett became so busy that he had to train additional dance teachers. He developed a minimum staff of twelve to fourteen dance instructors to help him with his ever increasing work load. The program kept expanding due to the generosity of Mr. Ford. Any school district that wanted a dance program merely had to contact Benjamin Lovett, Mr. Ford would write a check from his personal account, and Lovett or one of his instructors would be sent to that school. Lovett, again sponsored by Henry Ford, was responsible for bringing square dancing and ballroom dancing to thirty-four institutions of higher learning, among them Radcliffe College, Stevens College, Temple University, University of Michigan, University of North Carolina and the University of Georgia...with no charge to these universities.

Because square dancing took more space than ballroom dancing, Ford built a dance hall in Greenfield Village, site of the Henry Ford museum. It was beautifully decorated with chandeliers and had a hardwood floor that would hold approximately forty squares of dancers. Ford even hired one man full time to polish the dance floor daily, whether the floor had been used or not.

In 1926 Henry Ford published an excellent book on early American Square Dancing entitled "Good Morning." The title page states: *After a sleep of twenty-five years, old fashioned dancing is being revived by Mr. and Mrs. Henry Ford.* In the archives of the Henry Ford Museum, several written accounts of former executives report that Mr. Ford invited all of his executives to take lessons in early American Square Dancing. He was quick to tell them that he wanted them to take these lessons of their own free will, and not under any pressure. However, an invitation from Mr. Ford was tantamount to a command from royalty.

Benjamin Lovett was a strong leader in early American Square Dancing. He was the personification of a gentleman. Regardless of the fact that most of his dancers were people of great wealth and position, he told them what they were to wear and what they were not to wear. He insisted that the ladies wear formal dresses and corsages. Men were told that they were to wear dark suits. The ladies were instructed that they were never to cross their legs at the knees, but only at the ankles. And no one could cross directly across the dance floor except Mr. Ford.

When Ford passed away Lovett could no longer afford the promotion of square dancing. In 1949 he announced his retirement and he left Michigan, never to be seen there again. He died in Massachusetts in 1951.

Ford and Lovett moved square dancing out of the barn and into the ballrooms, but the leader who had the biggest effect on square dancing was a school superintendent from Colorado. Through his student dancers from the Cheyenne Mountain suburban public school at Colorado Springs, Dr. Lloyd Shaw, an educator with the instincts of a showman and the zeal of a missionary, had spread the square dance gospel from Broadway to Sunset Boulevard. He loved square dancing for its color and lustiness, but his crusading spirit was born of the conviction that it fostered the spread of democratic processes

Many of us out here in California had heard the name of Dr. Lloyd Shaw because of an impressive article in the Saturday Evening Post which had pictures of the Shaws with the Cheyenne Mountain Dancers, a group of young high school boys and girls who were attracting attention across North America.

Most people in America had not taken up cowboy square dancing in the 1930s, but Lloyd Shaw and his Cheyenne Mountain Dancers were going to change the country. The dancers weren't professionals – just a bunch of kids that loved to dance because nothing yielded them more fun. They wore gorgeous costumes and did some amazing dancing, but that was not what got to the people who crowded auditoriums and gymnasiums around the country. There was an intangible quality that no professionals could achieve. These eight boys and eight girls romped through their dances with a complete absence of affectation or self-consciousness. The dancers had as much or more fun than the audiences. And Doctor Shaw gave them that confidence with love.

The performances of the Cheyenne Mountain dancers inspired the formation of innumerable square dance groups, which in turn inspired the formation of other groups. It was the vigorous personality of the smiling schoolmaster that promoted square dancing in America.

Cheyenne Mountain School, just outside of Colorado Springs in the Eastern foothills of the Rockies, was small and included grades from one through twelve. Nevertheless, prior to starting the square dance program, Shaw had organized and coached a football team of only fourteen boys (with one borrowed from eighth grade) that defeated all opponents, including the state prep champions. The school never played another game in interscholastic football competition.

"I was appalled at what I'd done to my boys," apologized Doctor Shaw, who became a de-emphasizer two decades ahead of his time. "The effect of the headlines and newspaper pictures was to make insufferable prigs of them. Just because Nature had made them a bit larger and stronger than the other fellows, they strutted about as if they'd really accomplished something.

"I'm an educator. The training of youth for adult life is my profession. The few athletes competing in football receive training useless to them in later years. Competitive sports that glorify punishment of a physically weaker foe have no place, to my way of thinking, in a civilized social order. Physical perfection and victory over one's own weakness should be the goal of civilized sport."

But what to replace football with? Doctor Shaw tried rodeo with bronco busting, steer roping, steer wrestling and all the trimmings. Shaw rode broncos and bulldogged steers along with the kids, before he decided the sport was unsuitable to a school because it was another sport for boys only. The girls could dress up in Western costumes and look pretty, but it fell short of the ideal recreation the young schoolmaster was seeking. Doctor Shaw had in mind an intramural sport that was appropriate for boys and girls and could be continued for a life time. Above all, it must promote the perfection of self rather than the humiliation of an opponent.

When Doctor Shaw was first hired at Cheyenne Mountain School he wanted to introduce ballroom dancing as a way to teach the students some social graces and rhythm, but parents did not want those kinds of dances at the school. He was, however, allowed to introduce folk dancing because it seemed more like a sport. The folk dancing did achieve part of his ideal activity, but it seemed to be unrelated to the lives of students in the middle of the country. While delving into Western frontier lore, he found that the old square dances still were being danced in Colorado cattle towns and mining camps. He was impressed by their likeness to the folk dances.

He introduced one or two of these dances to his students. The free and easy lustiness of the dances appealed to the youngsters. The gym resounded to the strains of *Wild Horse* and *Soap Suds Over the Fence*. While many of the boys had felt folk dancing was panty-waist stuff, these cowboy dances struck them as he-man entertainment. The calls were different – crude, sometimes, and boisterous, but touched with rangeland breeziness and humor they liked.

Here you twist and there you whirl
Right around that pretty girl.
Here you duck and there you dive,
Pep up, boys, and act alive!
Twist 'em right and twist 'em wrong,
Straighten 'em out and trot right along.

The cowboy dances became the heart of the program, but its variety was limited, so Doctor Shaw added dances from New England, the cotillion, waltzes, schottisches, and more. The people who settled the west had brought their dances from their homelands. The best of these dances were retained in the local communities, and these became freer, more flexible, more boisterous.

"The old-time dances are not coming back," Shaw said. "They've never gone."

Shaw determined to carry his message to the far corners of the nation with the gospel, "If people can play together, they can work together." Juniors and seniors were given priority to be on the team of 16 dancers. All students had to be up with their studies and willing to give up some vacation time for touring. Since the dancers had been learning the dances through all of their school years, there was not much need for extra practice time except just before the tours hit the road.

The students performed the dances at local venues, and then before thousands of tourists at Colorado Springs and at the Opera House at Central City, Colorado. Their fame spread. They were invited to appear at universities throughout the country. Eventually they performed from the Hollywood Bowl to Carnegie Hall to Royal Albert Hall in London.

However, the unanswered question was whether the dances filled the social need as well as the physical. Almost every argument in their favor applied equally to adult groups. Shaw believed that they were more earthy, more democratic than conventional ballroom dancing. In square dancing a group of congenial couples may retain their own set, but repeatedly exchange partners and from time to time mingle with all the couples on the floor.

Doctor Shaw rejected many invitations for each one he accepted. He arranged the itinerary with a magnificent disregard for the convenience of those who clamored to see his dancers, considering only the opportunity to provide new and enriching experiences for the kids themselves.

When asked if the publicity the youngsters received was more perilous to the adolescent ego than the sports page publicity that led him to abandon football, Doctor Shaw answered with an emphatic, "No. Sports writers publicize the halfback who makes the winning touchdown. Our square dancers are publicized, not as individuals but as a team, so they escape the ruinous hero worship of their fellow students."

Between engagements Doctor and Mrs. Shaw took the youngsters on sight-seeing tours. The boys, who danced with different partners at each performance, knew they must not show one girl too much attention. Doctor Shaw, whom they called "Pappy," was intensely proud of his kids.

Being accepted into one of the summer sessions was like being inducted into the top fraternity on campus. Many applied, but only those who could be fitted into the small cafetorium were accepted. This is where it was in 1947, when it all truly began for many of us. I wrote to Dr. Shaw and said I was just starting in calling and I'd been with it for a little while, but I really need some training. I would love to come back there and be with him. I got a note back a short time later saying that class was full because there was space enough for only a limited number of students and partners; maybe you could apply again next year. I was partially shook, but not entirely. I went to Ray Shaw and asked him "to help me out on this thing." Ray got in touch with his brother. A day or two later I received an okay to join the class.

This was the man we were to spend a week with. He had started his classes for callers in the 1930s but suspended them for the duration of WWII. When the classes resumed in 1946 requests for enrollment exceeded the space available.

I think this was the biggest turning point in my life: here I was with a start of a business career in a soft drink company which could have gone on forever and been very interesting, but I was getting more and more involved in square dancing. I was calling for a couple of groups in Los Angeles, with a group of about 200 dancers every time we got together (I think two Saturdays a month at Griffith Park). The ones who didn't know how to dance or had never been to a dance before came early and we would show them a few simple things to do. At that time it was not a matter of showing them a few basics, it was to show them how to react to music and how to move. They, of course, would learn an allemande left, right and left grand, and the essential basics because the evening was relatively simple, and they could learn them quickly, and they would learn from each other. But, at that point, things were just about ready to explode in our area. More people were getting interested in calling. My acceptance into Shaw's class made my life change direction.

None of us who waited outside the main entrance to the one building school house in Colorado Springs that August morning in 1947 knew what to expect. None of us had ever attended a callers' school before. As a matter of fact, I don't remember that there were any other schools for callers at that time.

Present in that 1947 class were callers from across the country. Many, notable leaders themselves (such as Herb Greggerson from Texas) attended, and all were present hoping to gather ideas to help build for the future. It was interesting that with all that talent on hand the great emphasis was placed on how to dance and to dance well. Imagine, if you can, a class made up of some of the most influential callers of the day, spending a good share of their time together - dancing. At first a bit rag-tag dance-wise, by the end of the second day the callers/dancers began to shape up and see the pleasure in dancing well - together.

Each day would start in the auditorium with a lecture. Shaw's lectures were the real meat for the messages he wanted to impart. It was obvious these talks contained the values he had developed and he hoped that those in the class would take them home.

Speaking to us, as he was, a few scant years following the end of the Second World War while the world in general and our own areas in particular were just pulling themselves together, Pappy explained the great enthusiasm for the emergence of square dancing in this way: "Perhaps it was the war, perhaps the atomic bomb, or perhaps all the unhappy rumblings from stress-born Europe, but people are a little frightened and they are sort of lonesome now. Modern science tore some of their simple, wholesome faiths to shreds. They have had enough suspicion and mistrust and unfriendliness thrust on them. They want to clasp a neighbor's hand again and laugh and sing and dance again."

Pappy had been talking to us that morning about the privilege of calling. Too many times the caller, having just completed a call and hearing the applause of the crowd, fancies himself the sole reason for the group's happiness. Pappy then went on to tell us the story of the late Admiral Richard Byrd who, as a young Navy Ensign, was directed to carry the flag at a parade in our Nation's capital. As he moved at the head of the marching units down Pennsylvania Avenue the people rose to their feet, men removed their hats, everyone applauded wildly. He was impressed with himself and his importance until he suddenly realized that it was the flag that was being applauded - not him at all. "This," explained Shaw, "was like the caller glorying in the reaction of the crowd following a beautifully called dance. He didn't realize that he was 'carrying the flag.' It was the dance, the great joy of dancing, that they were applauding. We should not let the applause give us the impression that we are something special. We, as callers," Shaw pointed out, "are privileged to be a part of this joyous experience and to be allowed to 'carry-the-flag.'"

In the first sessions of this first callers course following the war, Shaw took the necessary elements of calling, formed them into a tripod, which he explained was the sturdiest of mechanical structures. Then, adding the necessary ingredients, founded the structure on the elements of CLARITY, RHYTHM, and COMMAND. Just think about these three for a minute. If a caller does not possess clarity he simply cannot be understood. Without a sense of rhythm, the caller's delivery grates on one's nerves making it difficult, if not impossible, to move to the music. And, command. Without the ability to differentiate between the all-important directional commands and the frills of non-essential (though colorful) bits of patter, the caller is simply not in control. A lot has changed in square dancing over the years, but those three basics still hold true. Reaching out from this triad were pitch; coordination; pattern or judgement; tang or flavor; and participation or excitement.

He did not just talk about dancing, but also about history and about people and about fellowship and about all the things that make this movement what it is. He had the great ability to create moods and to stimulate dreams that no one thought possible. I recall one morning session when Shaw was talking to us about smooth dancing: "Rhythm is the essence of all true dancing," he said. "Without rhythm you are not dancing! And with poor, uncertain rhythm you are dancing very poorly indeed. It doesn't matter quite as much with beginners, but experienced dancers should become more experienced with each step they take. This silent seeking for perfect rhythm will keep you dancing all your lives and still seeking the truths that lie beyond it. But ignore the rhythm, make it purely secondary, seek for the outward forms of style only, and you will soon tire of the game and quit it forever."

This sentiment was impressed upon us as we left the auditorium that first morning and headed into the area that served the school as a combination gym and cafeteria. Although standardization of sorts was present in each of our areas, there was no universal style.

Picking up the microphone, Pappy put us into large circles. "Dance tall," he told us. "Raise your shoulders, pull your dining room back, tuck in your sitting room. Now you're beginning to look like square dancers!" Noting several six-footers among the class members, some of whom had a tendency to lean forward or slouch as they danced, he would say, "Stand tall. If you're a tall person, take your cue from the dancer who is short - stand erect, be proud of your height."

A major portion of Shaw's teaching was done by utilizing members of his Cheyenne Mountain Dancers who were with us during the week. By observing these high school boys and girls, the members of the class felt like teenagers ourselves and, as a result, danced as young people. Frequently in our practice sessions these sixteen and seventeen year-olds would take members of the class as partners consequently influencing our dancing ability. Using the same techniques that proved so successful with his younger dancers, Pappy would spend time with the entire class each day in learning the importance of smooth dancing. He would impress upon us that it was square DANCING and not square standing or simply moving around in a square. It was dancing to the music that counted and not just getting from point "A" to point "B".

Truly a high point in the after-lunch sessions was the opportunity for class members to call and/or teach for evaluation by Pappy - this was a traumatic experience for many who, perhaps, had never called for any other than their local followers. Here's how the experience affected the late Charlie Baldwin, former editor of the *New England Caller*.

"Nervous, knees knocking, stomach in a knot. I proceeded to walk the large group through the dance pattern. When finished with the walk-thru, my mouth was so dry I could not have spit if I had been offered a million dollars. Turning to Pappy I asked what one did in a case like that. Chuckling, he replied, 'Smile - that will relax everything.' Sure enough, I did, and the saliva returned and I called several numbers without any more trouble."

We were impressed with what Bobby Jones, one of Pappy's dancers had to say about him. "If Pappy sowed the seeds for the revival of American folk dancing, it was not for just fun or notoriety. It was because, to him, square dancing was a true folk expression of our country. Because he knew and loved this country and its people, it became his mission to bring this folk art, the art of square dancing, back to its natural place, with the people."

What was it about Shaw's school for callers that

helped so overwhelmingly feed into this big boom of square dancing? Primarily, it was a new attitude about Western square dancing. "This is the true dance of America," Pappy would say. "It comes from so many directions; it is the spirit of the West. It borrows much from its overseas ancestors who brought their dances with them when they came to this country. Like other things American, it mixes and borrows from the world and makes it purely an American dance." While emphasizing the importance of keeping the original customs of square dancing in mind, Shaw was quick to realize that within this class were representatives of many regions, and all would be dancing together. This emphasized the importance of accepting standards in styling, in language, and in attitudes that could be enjoyed, not just in a single community, but everywhere, so that square dancing taught and learned in one area could be enjoyed throughout the country.

A bell must have rung simultaneously in the minds of those callers who attended. We all wanted to share with our dancers the experience we had in Colorado Springs. In the way we'd been operating over the years, we had developed little or no continuity. With brand new members entering our groups each time we met, there had been no opportunity to "fine tune" the dancers, making it necessary to start all over at the beginning each time. While it was obviously not practical to round up a group of individuals in our home areas and work with them as we had worked eight hours a day for six consecutive days in Colorado, we could recruit a group of potential dancers, meet with them 2 or 3 hours once a week, and develop the whole class, without interruption, into a group that danced well together. In this way they would be able to enjoy the same satisfying experience their callers had experienced.

Within a short time after returning from the Shaw experience, a dozen or so new classes started up in our area as they doubtless had in other areas across the country. This was all very new. Lesson plans had to be developed and goals set. Our first classes which stressed dance attitudes and developed automatic reaction to the calls took seven lessons. Once having learned together, it was only natural that the group would want to continue dancing together and thus clubs, as we've gotten to know them today, were formed. This was just the beginning.

All of us had been influenced by the styles of square dancing that had been going on for many years: the traditional in the East and the developing Western or cowboy dances. We saw that much give and take was needed to be exercised to make even the smallest of decisions. For instance, there were a number of ways to promenade (hands in front - right hand on top, or left hands on top, varsouvianna style, open escort, closed escort, etc.) Much of the styling back in the late 40s was picked up from the folk dancers in the area. When told to "swing," the dancers might do it with hooked elbows or with hands loosely gripped around the partner's neck or waist, or any of a variety of other ways. The walk-around or buzz swing were often left open to the choice of the dancers. We saw that the callers would have to start making decisions together.

All of this was taking place over a year perhaps, with lots of experimenting. The unanimous feeling of those involved was that new dancers coming into the area should be able to learn from one caller/teacher and then dance to other callers in the area. Early standardization included these directions for ending a couple promenade: as they reached "home" the man would stop, raise the joined right hands, the lady moves forward under the raised arms and around in a clockwise direction. The couple would balance away and then swing once and turn to face the center of the square.

That was the method decided upon and it probably lasted for six months, or so, resolving itself into just a lady turning under the man's raised arm, a slight acknowledgment, then face the center. All of these things seemingly had to be done in the process of reaching a workable standardization.

Pappy had opened our eyes to what had been, what was, and what could come. He had told us that we did not have to depend on other programs to define square dancing. He taught us pride in our American Square Dance, and respect for all of the traditions it encompassed.

We had new attitudes toward square dancing as a stand-alone program, but we had not solved all of the problems. Some of the problems came from the outside. For example, the professional ballroom dancing teachers were trying to get legislation through our State Senate in Sacramento, CA to make everybody who teaches dancing (including square dance callers) join their association or league or union or whatever it was. This would have given the ballroom dance instructors a stranglehold on all dancing, because they could have regulated what halls were available. So, representatives from a number of the newly formed clubs got together and set out to lobby against this bill. Some of the representatives were pretty special: one was a lawyer for NBC, another was on the police board in Sacramento. There was a purpose in square dancers working together and they did defeat the thing. Out of that, the first associations were built. Associations were not formed just to perpetuate themselves. They were formed in order to help with square dancing.

Some of the problems came from the activity itself. At first dancing was built along the lines we had had in the past. Simple single visiting dances slowly grew into more challenging all-working figures. Most everything the dancer needed to know to get to the current mainstream was being taught to him in the limited number of class lessons. The couple dances at first were the traditional ones that had been around forever and the caller could handle these with little or no problem.

With all of this change in the involvement of the dancers it was only natural for the creative elements in the callers to cry for attention. In no time at all, callers had dressed up the old allemande left with a bit of flourish and presented 'Allemande Thar' to the dancing public. That excited the creation of a multitude of different allemande figures.

Early in the game, parts of other dances were separated into identities of their own. 'All around' and 'see saw' and 'cross trail' were born. This was fun and it was challenging for the dancers and inspired the creative juices of the callers. However, a trend was starting to take shape. Ed Gilmore, one of the activity's leaders, sensed what was happening. He pointed out that for every new titled basic movement added to the caller's vocabulary, three hours of class time had to be added to present, drill and re-teach until it could be handled automatically. Those in the clubs who had completed their class work were introduced to the new movements as a matter of course. Those now taking a square dance class, expecting to move smoothly into an existing club, needed additional class time in order to bridge the growing chasm between class and club.

Anyway, while that particular experience was a great one in my life, it only seemed to slow down the progress of planning all the things that were avocational – is there such a word? And my business? I don't think that the Squirt Company business suffered at all, but I was away from the office perhaps more than I should have been. I'd like to just mention that in our early classes the people who came to the classes always had bottles of Squirt as a refreshment and were often asked to fill out a little questionnaire about how they liked the drink. The business worked in with square dancing and vice versa.

Chapter 4. Starting Square Dance Classes

SHOOT THAT PRETTY GIRL

First couple out to the couple on the right
And circle four
Leave that gent in the middle of the ring
And circle three.
Shoot that pretty girl through to me
And swing, boys, swing'
Four hands up and here we go,
Around and around and a docey-doe,

RIGHT AND LEFT WITH A STAR

Allemande left and allemande thar
With a right and a left
And form a star.
Let that star through the heavens whirl
And a right and left to the second girl
And star again.
Shoot that star and find your own.
Swing her hard, and promenade home-

OH JOHNNY

A Singing Quadrille

All Join hands and you circle the ring
Stop where you are and you give her a
swing
You swing that girl behind you.
Now swing your own if you have the time
When you get through (and)
Allemande left on your corners all
And dos-a-dos your own.
And all promenade
With that sweet corner maid
"Oh Johnny, 0h Johnny, Oh!"

THE ROUTE
> *First and third, balance and swing*
> *Promenade the outside ring, half way around*
> *Right and left as you were before*
> *The ladies chain, and chain once more*
> *Same two couples out to the right*
> *And circle four in line.*
> *Forward eight and back you go,*
> *Forward eight with a dos-a-dos:*
> *Ladies chain across, ladies chain in line*
> *Ladies chain across, ladies chain in line*
> *Swing on the corner, etc., etc.*

Square dancing through the early 1950s was pattern dancing. We did not break dances down into separate movements – or, as they are called now, basics. We taught the whole dance, and taught steps as they showed up in dances. Also callers came up with patter, or poetry, to go along with the movements. Sometimes the doggerel was to keep the caller and the dancers in time, and sometimes it was just to add a level of entertainment.

> *All jump up and never come down*
> *Swing your honey around and around*
> *'Till the hollow of your foot*
> *Makes a hole in the ground.*
> *Promenade, boys, promenade.*

This opener was intended to be silly and to make the dancers act a little silly. Dancers often would see how high they could jump or what contortions they could go through while in the air. The truth of it was that dancers took only four beats of music to jump up and land again. By the time the dancers landed, the next command to swing your honey was given. The couples then would swing until the next command to promenade came. In the amount of time it took the caller to say lines three and four the dancers could comfortably swing two to two-and-a-half times. The promenade is just the command, but callers had a bookful of rhymes for promenading:

> *Promenade, boys, and home you glide*
> *Like a bowlegged man and a knock-knee'd bride.*
> *Possum in the road and a chicken on the rail*
> *Keep on goin' and home you sail.*
> *Two penny, four penny, six penny high*
> *Big pig, little pig, root hog or die.*
> *Promenade around and home you go*
> *Like a barefoot fella in the snow.*

The promenade was almost always the last part of any dance pattern. It gave the dancers a chance to enjoy the music, to move smoothly without solving a puzzle, to flirt. And you have to admit that courting is a major reason for young folk to dance. Most promenades were all the way around so dancers had sixteen steps to make contact with each other. That reminds me of another bit of poetry that led into the promenade:

> *Swing that pretty gal and pat her on the head.*
> *If she don't like biscuits give her cornbread.*

The last line was a code that everyone knew. Biscuits was a promenade with the man's right arm around her waist. But if the girl did not want to be that close, cornbread meant a two crossed hands in front style of promenade.

But back to the topic at hand, the dances. Dances that were done early in the evening before the new folk had gotten their feet under them were pretty simple. There may have been quite a variety of types, but they were simple. Most of them could be danced just by listening to the calls; and if you did not know the calls, get into the number four position, watch what everyone else did, and you would be an expert before it was your turn to lead the action.

TAKE A LITTLE PEEK

First couple out to the right -
Around that couple and take a little peek
Back to the center and swing your little sweet
Around that couple and peek once more
Back to the center and swing all four
Four hands up and here we go
Around and around and a docey-do

Take a Little Peek was one of the classics of the period and was quite easy to do. Oftentimes the call would tell the first couple to bow and swing before going out to the right, but the important part is the first couple just going to stand in front of the couple to their right. Nowadays we call that a lead to the right, but the simple wording made it easier for new dancers to be successful. When the first couple was facing couple two, they would step away from their partner, lean forward around the second couple, and take a peek at each other (another way to flirt, with permission). Then the first couple would back into the middle of the set and the two couples would swing. The first couple got a second chance to peek, or the caller might mix things up and say: "around the couple sneak a little kiss." That call would usually be saved for when the caller saw a young courting couple was in the lead.

I do remember one night in the late 40s when I was calling a dance to live music. It may have been one of those Griffith Park one-nighters, I really don't recall. I do recall what happened next. My brain was in neutral and I mixed up the calls and the consonants, so on the second half I called: "Around that couple take a little piss." The dance came to a complete halt and everyone was staring at me. I can't recall ever being so embarrassed in my life, but I was saved by the fiddler who just started up the melody again. The only way I got over that was when no one who was at that dance was still alive. For years people would come up to me and say: "I was there at Griffith Park when you called Take a Little (pause) Peek."

The dance patterns – I don't think that we really had basics in mind back in those days. A basic was just another call and you did a certain thing, just like if we said "turn left" you turned left. The first time we ever turned left we may have had to teach people how to turn left. But doing a Right and Left Thru was just taken in its course, because we did a dance and it had a Right and Left Thru in it. It also had a turn left and it had a forward and back, and all those things were just part of a dance. Every time I introduced a dance I had to walk the dancers through all of the steps in that pattern before we could actually dance it. Every night I had to teach how to hold hands, how to Dosado, and how to swing. The difference between new dancers and an experienced dancer, is one who could react automatically, not step on the calls, but to follow comfortably and dance with the music. We spent a lot of time in just moving to music.

So we came home from Colorado Springs ready to change the world of square dancing. Dances which featured just square dancing had been pretty much one night stands; that is, dancers show up and learn while on the floor; the callers have no expectation of knowledge on the part of the dancers. My Saturday nights at Griffith Park were great fun. There is no doubt that calling with live music to over 200 dancers each session was a thrill. But I could see no improvement in the dancing from week to week. Each session I knew that about 60-70% of the dancers would be repeats – people who had danced at least one session and some (bless them) who were regulars. But having 30-40% of the dancers being first timers meant I always had to start from the beginning.

The good part of that type of dancing was that dancers could drop in and out at will. And most dancers did not mind repeating dances. "Oh, Johnny Oh" was a hit no matter how many times you danced it. But callers got tired of teaching and calling the same dances over and over. In many places the callers did not teach at all. If a dancer had trouble in a particular dance, experienced dancers would coach him during a break.

Some callers, such as Ed Gilmore of Yucaipa, California, and Bruce Johnson of Santa Barbara, California, and Joe Lewis of Texas, saw that the steps of dances could be arranged in different ways to create new patterns. They wrote those patterns out, including the rhymes that went with them, and other callers began to use them. The sequences of these dances, however, were too complex for new dancers to dance smoothly. Dancers needed to have experience to understand them, and that meant classes

In 1946 following WW II, many thousands returning from the war settled into new communities where at first all were strangers to each other. Here the friendliness of square dancing saved the day and drew neighbors together

World War II was horrible, have no doubt about it, but many great things came out of the war. The technological advancements are too numerous to list; America took its place as the defender of freedom in the world; and the world envied the freedom and lifestyle of America. But we do have

to remember that not all of the war activity took place overseas. Many factories were converted to war production while new factories were built in other areas of the country rather than the Northeast. Military bases were built and expanded in every state and in some foreign countries. The people from the East Coast discovered that there is a West Coast besides Hollywood. After Pearl Harbor the nation was afraid that Japan would assault the US mainland at Malibu Beach or sail under the Golden Gate

After the War soldiers came home to families or sweethearts and they were desperate to build new lives. They needed to make contact with other people in a friendly, cooperative setting. The men who had been in combat were deeply scarred. They had seen things and done things that a normal person could not imagine and they did not want to remember. I, and other callers, noticed that most of the men who came to square dances did not share 'war stories.' Those men who could not block out those memories literally went crazy.

On the distaff side, many of the women who had been working in the defense industry now found themselves displaced by veterans. They had relished earning a living and doing work that was considered important. They showed the world that women could do the jobs usually reserved for men. These women needed an escape from the drudgery of housework and a chance to socialize.

Here is where square dancing came into the picture. Before the war, Lloyd Shaw had shown the country the joy of good, old American Square Dancing. After the War Shaw had his kids on the road again making two trips a year. The pure joy that the Cheyenne Mountain Dancers expressed in their dances enlivened the nation. Square dancing filled the need for almost everyone: the men had a place to socialize without talking about work, and the women could greet their men with dinner and outfits to go out to an evening of dancing.

Each person had his own reasons for coming into this activity. For me, square dancing helped to solve a major problem. I was attending a small college in California whose student body was gathered from all parts of North America. Coming into this institution of learning was a traumatic experience for many of the students. Attempts were made at the start of each school year to provide social functions that would bring the people together, but almost no one attended. Folks were shy and easily embarrassed. I remember watching this drama my first year at the college and wishing there was something I could do to help these people get together. The taste of simple, traditional American dancing that I had picked up at a conference provided the answer, and by the following fall, when classes started again, I got to try it out. In what today would be a one night stand we brought virtually the entire student body up onto the floor in circles, squares, and lines, holding hands, laughing, yes, and actually talking to each other. At that point we saw square dancing as a means to an end. It was a way for people to forget their concerns of the outside world and to enjoy movement to music in an atmosphere of neighborliness.

At one point in time (after the magazine was established) we had a project of asking square dancers, what brought them into this activity. Many of those we asked had by that time become avid enthusiasts and had to stop and think before answering. Here are a pair of typical responses: "We had recently moved into our neighborhood and we didn't know anyone. A local square dance class changed all of that and we suddenly found ourselves surrounded by friends." "We found ourselves trapped in front of the television set night after night. We'd get home from work, grab something to eat, and settle in for a night of viewing. We had almost forgotten how to talk to each other. We were simply watching as others entertained us. When we heard that a square dance class was starting in our area we both thought, here was our chance to break away, to become involved. And that's what we did." - The late President Kennedy once referred to us as "a Nation of Spectators." We watch as others perform. Just look at the sports section of the daily newspaper and see how many events are geared for us to watch as others do the recreating.

It seemed to us at that point that square dancing had gone just about as far as it could go. Each evening of dancing started from the very beginning for those people who were new. And while new dances were included at each session, and people were having a good time in general, the interest of the people could not be counted on as long as there seemed to be no real forward progress. What this meant to the dancers and callers at that time was really not known, but that's the way it was.

I think most callers, and I certainly know I did, wished we could teach our dancers to dance well and smoothly and just go through the patterns. We knew that there were different patterns being used all over the country, but we felt obligated to use the tried and true formulae. I was especially aware of what was happening in square dancing because of my travels for Squirt.

Years after the magazine was established, one of the great callers from the East Coast, "Decko" Deck, sent us an article entitled "What Ever Happened to My 'LEAD STEP'?" Decko's main point in his article is that the fun of dancing is built on the music and the enthusiasm of the caller. It is also the "fun" of sharing this musical/dancing sensation with others that propels us into group participation. As we share the feeling we, also, share a sense of togetherness. The music holds us together in a unified flow of motion, building self-confidence within ourselves as we find and give support within our group. Sometimes, the evening dancing is so captivating, we stay to savor the last dreg of joy and excitement we feel in the dance. It is a short evening and we hate to see it end. Other times, we find ourselves checking the clock about halfway through the dance. The evening seems long and we talk to our friends about doing something after the dance. We decide to leave early. What makes the difference?

Square dance music is expressed in a regular series of musical thoughts known as "eight-beat phrases." These phrases are instinctively felt and expressed by the dancer's body flow which instinctively follows the ebb and flow of the musical expressions. There is a tendency to want to surge and pause with the beginning and ending of each phrase. If we do not feel this, the sense of dancing degenerates to the level of a mechanical drill. In such case, it is more likely that the problem is not in our ability to dance, but in the fact that we were unable to find the musical phrase, which dictates the flow of movement.

The square dance caller, as the coordinator of the dance, has the responsibility of informing us of four things:

WHERE TO GO

HOW TO GET THERE

WHO TO SEE

WHAT TO DO

It is the caller's duty to let the music say "WHEN TO START." The caller who assumes this responsibility himself, does so at the risk of destroying the esthetic feel of dancing.

In other words, the good caller lets the dancers start moving on the first beat of each musical phrase. One of the real joys of contra dancing is that the calls are given ahead of time so the dancer can start each movement with the music. This innate desire to dance to the music rather than to the caller is something that needs to be learned – by callers and dancers. It was easier to achieve when we danced and called pre-set patterns.

The older, traditional forms of square dancing that existed through the Second World War essentially provided something for the newcomer who could come to a square dance early, learn the essentials that would be called that evening, then stay when the instruction period was over and be able to virtually do all of the squares. While at the same time the person who might come to the dance every month or more frequently would skip the learning session, join in on the dancing when it started with his ability increasing the more frequently he danced. It never seemed to matter if many of the same dances were repeated from one week to the next. The pleasure and ability of each individual increased with the frequency of his or her dancing.

When we came back from Colorado Springs, the callers from the Los Angeles area – Lee Helsel, Arnie Kronenberger, Ralph Maxheimer, Jack Hoheisal , etc. – came up with the same plan: we needed to start teaching classes. Unless we wanted to watch badly danced 'Birdy in the Cage' we had to teach dancers how to dance well: stand erect, feel the music, and respond to the calls automatically.

However, there were other hurdles to overcome first. For example, teaching a dance might have taken just a couple of minutes, and even the people who were standing during the instruction could do the dance. Then came the last two lines. As before couple one backed into the middle of the square and both couples Swang (Swinged, Swung?) their partners. Then they joined hands in a circle of four (four hands up). But Do-si-do? That figure has pretty much gone the way of the Dodo bird, but it was a fun and integral part of many dances of the period. As the two couples circle, each lady walked around the other, passing left shoulders, to end facing her partner. Her partner took her left hand in his left and led her around behind him (letting go of her hand as she goes around). The ladies then faced the opposite man and gave him her right hand, but this time she pulled the man past her. The two men then passed left shoulders (or back to back) to meet his partner on the other side. Then with left hands joined and the man's right hand on her waist, the couples turned as a couple with couple two going back to home and couple one going on to couple three to repeat.

Most of those who had gone to Shaw's school already knew Dosado and Do-si-do, but Pappy had a new one for us: Dopaso. You just saw the description for Do-si-do, which some dance historians say is a derivative spelling of Dos-y-dos, Spanish for two-and-two. Others say that is a mispronunciation of Dos-a-dos, French for back-to-back. And of course there is the wit who drew a picture of a deer in the woods and calling it Docey-doe. Dopaso was Pappy's way of preserving elements of Do-si-do but simplifying it. The new call had everyone turn partner with the left, the corner by the right, and the partner by the left into whatever the next call was. "Dopaso" opened up the creative side of many callers who then began to invent more new calls that could work into dance patterns. There were a couple of other figures we learned at Pappy's that are now modern square dance standards: Walk around and See-saw, and Allemande Thar.

Those were figures that we took home, but not always as we had been taught them. For example, if the dancers are in a circle or square, they can Walk Around the Corner, that is, step right shoulder to right shoulder and walk around the pivot point between the two dancers. The See-

Saw was the same type of action but left shoulders with partner. It was a very smooth flowing figure eight figure. Unfortunately, Joe Lewis, a well-known caller from Texas, had the shoulders reversed, so for him Walk around was left shoulders with corner. He taught that at home in Texas, and on a tour he took to Australia. It took quite a while to get a state and a continent straightened out.

Teaching Do-si-do was a challenge. Some people just could not picture what was wanted from the caller's instructions. So oftentimes we had to ask a couple of experienced dancers to demonstrate it… in slow motion first, then up to speed. That proved to be dull, stopping to teach Do-si-do at every session. Then I had to call it several times until people could do it automatically. The teaching was so repetitive and it took up so much time from the dancing that I became frustrated.

All of us who had been at Lloyd Shaw's caller's school in August were anxious to share what we had learned, but the one-night stand type of dances were not the setting to teach dancing well. We were lucky when the dancers got through simple dances in the course of the evening. We could not talk about posture, and styling, and timing. We could not include figures that were more complex than Do-sa-do or Do-si-do. The obvious answer was that we needed to teach classes. We understood that we could not teach everything about square dancing in a class, but we could introduce and get automatic reaction to the basic moves and dances. Then as the class people continued to dance, more could be added in the dance setting. The advantage was that we would not have to reteach Allemande Left every night.

In September 1947, I tried an experiment of teaching a class, just to see if it would work. I selected a number of dancers from my Griffith Park group and invited them to try out a six week session in which we would learn timing and posture and grace. I charged $5.00 per person for the entire set of six classes, payable in advance. The class was closed to new dancers after the first night so we did not have to re-teach anything. I had the money to rent the hall and pay for the band up-front. Where other groups were having attendance problems, we had no trouble with tardiness or absenteeism. We used the Boy Scout Hut up on Robertson Avenue in Los Angeles which held four sets easily. The rent was the right price too: $5.00 a night. The Boy Scout Hut is the kind of ragged looking log cabin that we had used before the War for 'Fun Unincorporated' and during the war for entertaining soldiers in transit. It is also where I met Ginger.

I planned to hold my first non-experimental class in the Fall of 1947. As I had learned from my experimental classes six weeks was plenty of time to teach people to move automatically to the calls and in time to the music. There was also time to work on styling and graceful dancing. I could also introduce some couple dances, such as the schottische and varsouvianna. In these classes, we tried to do the things we had learned from Pappy, teaching people how to dance first. We didn't teach basics unless they came in with a particular dance. We taught movements. In other words, there were only a certain number of movements as such, like facing right or left, forward and back, walking, swinging, turn-unders, and things like that; there were only a number of these things that would be involved in all the steps we would be doing in dancing. Our goal was not just to teach the people dances, but to teach them how to be good dancers and teach them something about attitudes and allow them to have fun.

Publicity for the first class consisted of an advertisement in the local little throw away papers here in Beverly Hills. The location for the class was the Beverly Hills High School gymnasium. The class was scheduled to begin at 7:00, so I planned to arrive at 6:00 to make sure the gymnasium was set up for dancing. Also, we used live music since there were few records available that were suitable for square dancing. As I recall I had a three piece band for these classes. When I approached the school I was amazed to see a line of people that went around the building and down the steps and the sidewalk to the street. All of the people were dressed for square dancing: The ladies in brightly colored long dresses and the men in the typical blue jeans with the cuffs rolled up, checkered shirt, and cowboy boots. There were no shops to buy dance costumes in so the girls improvised or made their own costumes. (I remember one lady who appeared in a dressing gown - zipper up the front and all. It was so tight that every time she took a step it slid about her knees.) Obviously there were too many people to fit into one gymnasium, so I called Arnie Kronenberger to help out. Arnie had been an active participant in Fun Unincorporated and was an outstanding caller. He also had been with me at Colorado Springs. We quickly opened the second gymnasium and hired another band. This was the start of our beginner classes.

At this time a caller was able to teach all a person needed to know in three or four weekly lessons - the balance of the time was spent in teaching "how to dance" – smooth styling, posture, etc. Everyone was taught the couple dances, such as the varsouvianna, the schottische, and the waltz. They, like the squares, were all part of square dancing. Much of the teaching was done by mixing the dancers. In a circle dance, a single sequence would usually end when the ladies (or gents) progressed or moved back to their partner - which in the short sequence dances might mean a person could dance with 15 or 16 other dancers in the course of just one dance. The mixing of partners was one of the significant teaching techniques because it would break up a slow learning couple and share the ability of a couple for whom learning was a simple matter.

Mixing also had the effect of breaking down any attempts at forming cliques. Within a short time after class had started, the group was a single unit rather than a collection of disconnected individuals. Within the squares such novelties as "scatter promenade" and "scoot 'n scat" would encourage the tendency to mix, and this was done more and more. In the early days of the class dancers found it natural to exchange partners on their own and to dance happily with anyone who joined the square. In looking back almost fifty years, we can see that the purpose of the class was to create, through circle mixers, etc., a feeling of friendliness. Mixing partners assured that dancers knew everyone else in the class and they bonded as a group. The goal of the class was not necessarily to see how much material could be learned as to learn automatic reaction. Once a dancer had learned to do even the simplest of patterns and movements without hesitating, then they were ready to react quickly to almost any teaching. The other benefit to mixing was the number of repetitions the new dancers did of a particular call or sequence of calls. Boredom was warded off by doing the repetition with different people each time. And with each repetition, the dancers smoothed out their dancing and began to move more automatically to the music. Most of these dance drills were designed to give the first beat of the musical phrase to the dancer.

The classes not only improved the quality of dancing, but they gave me friendships that have lasted a lifetime. I have already mentioned Arnie Kronenberger, but there were other callers in the area who worked together to improve square dancing. One of the first I should mention is Ray Shaw, Lloyd Shaw's older brother who was a school administrator. Ray also was the man who headed up the Callers' Pow-Wows which were often held in his kitchen. As you recall, it was Ray who got me into the 1947 class in Colorado Springs. Ray was an excellent caller in his own right, and had a large following of loyal dancers. He remained active as a caller right up to the end. One night he called an especially vigorous dance, and you could see by the sweat on his face that it had taken its toll on him. At the end of the last tip, Ray sat down on the edge of the stage and gave the usual caller's call that ended a tip or a dance: "Keeno, boys, that's all." He then set his microphone on the stage beside him, lay back, and quietly passed away. It was Keeno for Ray.

My square dance classes turned into two clubs. Those who had gone through the classes at Beverly Hills High School were welcomed into the Beverly Hillbillies (so named long before the TV show). Another club came out of the classes and dances held at the Boy Scout Hut: Rip "n" Snort, named after one of the traditional square dance calls, started in 1948. The first two presidents of RIPs danced with the club for years and were part of the demonstration group I used on television. Then along came Jones…Chuck and Dottie Jones (Chuck was an animator for Warner Bros. cartoons, specializing in Bugs Bunny and also creating The Road Runner, Wiley Coyote, PePe LePue, and others. The structure and the activities of the club brought them all closely together and while it was square dancing that brought us together in the first place, the many non-square dance activities were what made us friends.

The club continued to dance together through the 1980s, and though many were unable to dance in the later years, they still came to the special parties and outings of the club. One especially important friend and colleague came from the experimental classes: Joe Fadler. Joe was young and energetic, and was an outstanding photographer. Besides that, he was married to one of the most beautiful women I had ever seen. As soon as I began serious talk about starting a magazine, Joe was on staff - from the first issue to the last.

The mechanics of developing this square dance club simply evolved over the first one or two years. It was a custom of clubs back in those days to have a permanent caller, usually the one who taught the dancers in the first place. Chuck Jones, who as time went on became the unofficial voice of the square dancer, worked with me in an unbeatable partnership and the members of the club were much more than members only. The club members willingly took on duties, from being greeters at the door to being members of the refreshment committee. The program was typical of other club programs in our area and probably across the country. We danced from 8:00 until 10:00, and then enjoyed the following 15 to 20 minutes cooling off and enjoying an after party. Over a period of time, every club member in one way or another was involved in an after party. These ranged from relating business or wartime experiences to tales of a recently completed cruise or tour.

The second Home for Rip 'n' Snort following the learning period was located just a block west of its former home in the Boy Scout Hut and two blocks west of its next home on Robertson Blvd. This hall, Carpenter Hall, was used several days a week by a ballet class, and for this the hall was equipped with a large (5'x 8') mirror. In the course of setting up, or taking down equipment for one of the RIP dances, one of the speakers hit a glancing blow on the mirror, sending it crashing to the floor into billions of tiny pieces. Concerned about the cost of replacement, the dancers within hours had decided to put on a "Broken Mirror Dance," and sold tickets to raise enough money to pay back the cost of a new mirror. Over the next couple of weeks, funds were materializing quickly, and tickets were selling fast. At the same time, after two weeks, a check was received from the insurance company paying for the mirror completely. By this time the club members were having such a ball making plans for the benefit dance, they decided to go ahead with it anyway. The number of people planning to attend rapidly outgrew the size of Carpenters Hall, so Plummer Park, a large and more adequate facility was engaged. Live music, an overflow crowd with guests coming from as far as Laramie, Wyoming, made this one more example of the friendship of square dancers.

Rip 'n' Snort held a series of classes every fall. This indeed was a club project. All the members did their bit in actually bringing recruits to an Exciter Dance. This was an opportunity to project the friendliness that was in the club. The evening was a typical one-night stand. It included refreshments, some sort of a square dance involved show, or games. And the friendly atmosphere was natural, not put on. The result was that you could usually count on a good number signing up for the classes that started the following week.

Classes were a going thing all over the Los Angeles area, and around the country, and the square dance activity was growing beyond our wildest imaginations.

The increase in the number of square dancers led to an increase of the number of callers in the area. Each caller wanted to teach his own class and thereby start a club. The number of clubs mushroomed and joined the associations which helped with the organizing of clubs and sponsored large festivals every month.

Later we will discuss another consequence of increasing the number of dancers and callers: not enough musicians.

Chapter 5. Cheyenne Mountain Dancers and Sets in Order

In the months following Lloyd Shaw's institute in Colorado Springs I was determined to accomplish several things. All of us who had gone to Colorado wanted to share what Pappy had taught us, and we knew that the continuing "one-night stand" type dancing did not allow for teaching styling and smooth dancing. That meant that we needed to have classes.

Much of my traveling was being done in connection with my job at Squirt but I did get a chance to get encouragement from the different callers and dancers that I met for this magazine that I was proposing. In thinking back, so many things were happening at one time that, although some of the things may at that time have had little to do with square dancing they had to do a lot with me and my education in the world. My four years in the Navy by this time had pretty much quieted down to a time of working for a soft drink company and the great avocation of square dancing but I kept getting more responsibilities with the Squirt Company.

At this time our ideas for a square dance magazine were really jelling. Two of the local dancer associations showed enthusiasm for the idea, and people volunteered to help with circulation and distribution. We thought now this would be really great if 'Pappy' and his dancers could make an appearance in Los Angeles and we could come out with our first issue of the magazine simultaneously. With luck on our side, 'Pappy' said he could make the Fall 1948 tour with the kids to the West Coast.

I talked to Charley Dillinger, the printer and graphic artist who printed the Squirt magazine. Since he already was on the payroll at the Squirt Company and he had shown interest in printing a square dance magazine, it was logical to start with him. Charley and I did a mockup for a national magazine which we called Sets in Order because that was the call that every caller used to get the squares up on the floor to dance. So that was our beginning. Using Charley's rough mock-up we went out and sold some advertising – just on the basis of the rough with the idea that the first issue would come out in November, 1948.

Dillinger's Mock-up of SIO. We used this art work to start our search for advertisers. On the left is the design for the cover. The picture changed for the actual first issue, but we stuck with the font style for the life of the magazine.

We knew that Pappy's Kids would be featured in the first issue, so Charley put that article on page 3 of the mock-up magazine. We also knew that Frank Grundeen's cartoons would grace the back-cover, so Charley invented one just for this dummy issue. I still don't know what they are saying in the cartoon, but I certainly can imagine.

Well, all these things were happening at once. I was still working for the Squirt Company full time and travelling for them as well as doing my first travel calling. I had gone to New England and called and met Charlie Baldwin, and Ralph Page, and others. I had also made stops throughout the Mid-West

In this new magazine, I planned to publish new calls and figures, successful ideas about forming and running a club, and such other news of square dancing that was of general interest. Sets in Order was to report such news of the clubs as would interest other clubs - an entertainment novelty applicable elsewhere, an innovation in publicity, or a clever invitation. It was to be a how-to-do it magazine. Party ideas were especially important because the dancers get together for fun and friendship and they are always ready for a party.

Backing up just a bit. In high school I had worked a bit on the school newspaper and designed its masthead. In junior college I needed an English credit and ended up by taking journalism and writing a regular column on the weekly news sheet. At Woodbury College my class advisor was the journalism teacher from whom I took several classes, and who eventually became the circulation manager in Boston for the *Christian Science Monitor*. While in the Navy, along with my other routine service oriented jobs, I was assigned to edit the Section Base newspaper *Sweepings* Also, my first job after leaving the Navy was producing the house magazine for Squirt. This was my daytime job, but I spent evenings visiting square dance clubs. I was bombarded with questions concerning costumes, speed of dancing, styling, etc., in my area. This is what started my plans for a quality square dance magazine; square dancing needed a way to exchange ideas and information.

Most (but not all) callers were extremely generous with their material. These same callers were most willing to share any knowledge they had; some even took a new-comer under their wing and shared their limited knowledge. Some even went so far as to allow the beginner to call a tip at one of his dances, and then, after the dance, offered suggestions and criticisms that might prove helpful.

But back to the topic at hand, the dances. Generally, the dances that were done early in the evening were pretty simple. There may have been quite a variety of types, but they were simple. That gave a way for the newcomers to get their feet under them.

Please do not misinterpret this as a criticism of the type of dancing and of the callers of the time. The simple dances gave people who could not dance on a regular basis a place to go for a fun evening. And there were great callers across the country. One of the best – and most colorful – was Jimmy Clossin. Jimmy was a lean, cowboy style Texan. At the time Jimmy started calling, square dancing was quite regional. There were some similarities with dances from other regions, but a knowledgeable dancer could easily pick out a

Texas square from a New England quadrille or a Kentucky running set.

Jimmy was already an established caller when Lloyd Shaw started his research for *Cowboy Dances*. In 1920 he taught square dancing at Texas Technical Institute and in 1937 did a series of classes to train school teachers in San Pedro, California. He published *West Texas Square Dances* in 1938, which was revised and republished in 1940 as *Honor Your Partner*. [Editor's Note: The UNH Library identifies the Clossin book *West Texas* - as published in 1948 and as a revision of "Honor Your Partner" written by Buck Stinson in 1938.] He was one of the earliest callers to see the benefit of teaching basics, or the square dance steps, instead of teaching whole routines. Probably the main principle that Jimmy followed was to keep it simple, that way square dancing was available to everyone. Jimmy finally retired from calling in 1962, but on the way he influenced hundreds of callers and taught thousands of school children the joy of square dancing.

There is a story about Jimmy that is worth telling. He was known in the early 1900s for his calling experiences when he was a Texas Ranger, patrolling the border between Mexico and the U.S. at a time when the horse played the role later taken over by the jeep and later by the helicopter. Now Jimmy was considered one of the best in those days and if anyone was going to throw a hoedown or a barn dance you could bet that Jimmy would be invited. Today, of course we don't think a great deal about driving 15 or 20 miles for an evening of dancing. However, back in the range days that Clossin remembers, the working folks would stay hard at it until the sun went down and the chores were done.

And that's the way it was with Jimmy. After work he'd attach his celluloid collar, tie, and best coat, in a neat package to the pommel of the saddle and take off for the ranch some dozen miles away. He might pull up about 9:00, change into his respectable clothes and start calling. This would go on till maybe midnight when dinner would be served, then there was more dancing until about 3:00 or 4:00a.m. When the dance was over, Jimmy would change back into his work clothes, tie his bundle on the saddle and mount up. Jimmy said he'd just let the reins go, and give his horse her head. Sometime later Jimmy would wake up in his own corral. Such was the life of a West Texas caller.

Square dancing was not isolated to Texas and the West. New England was also fired up by the old time squares. One of the most famous callers was Ralph Page of Keene, New Hampshire, who labeled himself as the singing caller. How he got to all of his dances is somewhat of a mystery because he never learned to drive: he had to rely on the good will of friends or the train schedule. For 25 years he traveled to Boston every week to call a contra dance. Perhaps what is most important about Ralph was the mimeographed magazine *Northern Junket* of which he was the sole publisher, editor, and writer for 35 years. It was much more than a magazine about dancing: it was about the heritage of New England and its people. Before he was widely known as a caller, Ralph had served as a selectman in Nelson, NH, and he got a good education in dealing with people. He kept elegant notes on his time in public service. He also was an avid reader of just about everything (he had hundreds of mystery novels on his bookshelf), but his main interest was history, and that is what he featured in "Northern Junket." He made his debut as a caller in late 1930, and by 1938 he was able to call full time and leave behind his day job as a store keeper.

Charley Thomas, another one of the old timers in the calling business, was also a lawyer practicing in the state of New Jersey. Somehow with all of his responsibilities he still found time to start one of the country's first square dance magazines *American Squares* (today's *American Square Dance*). I can remember my first meeting with Charley back about 1946. Business had taken me to the East Coast and a phone call told me that I wasn't too far from the hall where Charley would be calling that night. In the true spirit of square dancing, Charley picked me up at the hotel and took me home for dinner. Then it was sound system, wife, baby and me into his car and off to the dance.

I can't remember all of the details but I do remember that with Charley a sound system wasn't necessary. That man had lungs and he let everyone in the hall and for several blocks around know it. He was loud! That was the reason I supposed that when he started calling, his six months old son started exercising his vocal cords right along with papa. But then the strangest thing happened. Charley picked up junior and, with the youngster in his arms, Charley continued to call. Wouldn't you know it, the baby fell sound asleep. The only time he woke up and cried was when Charley stopped calling. Then, when the calling started the baby went to sleep again, perfectly happy.

Another Charlie, this time Charlie Baldwin, originated and became first editor of the *New England Caller* magazine. It started as a pocket sized monthly and grew into the magazine we now know as the *Northeast Square Dancer* magazine. Charlie founded the Square Dance Foundation of New England now located on its own property in South Weymouth, Mass. with dance halls, meeting rooms and archives. *[Editor's Note: after this was written the Square Dance Foundation of New England (SDFNE) relocated to Manchester, NH*

111

where it continued to maintain a Library/Museum until 2016. The historical materials have now been transferred to the Milne Special Collections Library at the University of New Hampshire in Durham, NH]

In looking back at some of my earliest and most enjoyable class experiences, I'm reminded of one in particular where I discovered how many real bonuses come with being a class caller. It took place during the second or third night of a seven lesson course.

I had been noticing one of the class members in particular. During the breaks between tips he'd be sitting over on the sidelines, writing. At first I thought I'd gained a spy – someone who liked my last call and was wasting no time in getting it down on paper.

Eventually my curiosity won out and I wandered over to see what he was doing. Hoping that I wouldn't embarrass him, I looked at the pad he was working on only to see a sheet filled with sketches. Funny sketches, most of them. Drawings, or more correctly, caricatures or cartoons, depicting his classmates in all imaginable poses and predicaments. For example, we had a number of calls those days that actually couldn't be danced but were semi-humorous bits of patter. The dance I just finished calling had started out with a traditional opener that went: "All jump up and never come down (swing your honey round

This happens every time I call "All Jump Up!"

and round, etc...)." And, here on the sketch pad was his dancer's interpretation of how the call might turn out.

"May I see what else you have there?" I asked. "Sure. Help yourself," my talented friend said, handing me a small stack of paper. I was amazed. Here were pencil drawn illustrations of what the new dancer was going through, sketches of the life of a dancer, little insights that could best be expressed only in this way.

This happened in October of 1947, just two months earlier I had attended Lloyd Shaw's school for callers in Colorado Springs, and had returned home to find the 'big boom' period of square dancing moving into full swing. The newspapers carried stories about it, Hollywood was including it in the movies and classes were starting up all over our area. My alma mater, Beverly Hills High School, not wishing to be left out, added it to its adult education program and took me on as the caller/teacher.

Combining luck with a dash of clairvoyance, this seemed to be the appropriate time to start a magazine devoted to the square dance activity. I was at this time in the planning stages for the magazine when Frank Grundeen, the cartoonist I had just discovered, entered the scene. When the first issue of Sets in Order came out in November 1948, its back cover displayed the first of the Grundeen cartoons that would be a highlight of the magazine for the next thirty-seven years.

Many of the cartooned images featured by Frank were inspired by fellow members of the Beverly Hillbillies, the square dance club that was formed from the 1947 high school class. Frank showed little or no respect when he depicted a caller or someone teaching a round dance. Refreshment committee members were frequent targets of his humorous cartooned barbs.

The world of Grundeen, outside of square dancing, included daily syndicated Donald Duck cartoon comic strips for the Walt Disney Corporation. Together with his wife, Ethel, he managed yearly tours around the world, but almost above everything else, I would imagine the Grundeens' greatest pleasure came from the time they spent with their many square dance friends.

Three-and-a-half decades is a long time to work on a single publication. His cartoons probably received as much if not more attention from readers than any other single section of the magazine. So when Sets announced that it would stop publication with its December 1985 issue, the distress calls from Grundeen fans were overwhelming. Anyway, that final issue contained Frank's 444th contribution. He'd never missed a deadline even though searching for new ideas based on square dancing often proved to be a challenge. Within a month after that final magazine went into the mail, having completed his assignments, Frank Grundeen passed away.

As I recall I didn't have any money to pay for the printer, but Dillinger and I had worked on the Squirt Reporter and I think he just trusted us. Even though we didn't know if the magazine would last a year, Dillinger just liked the idea of being in on the start of a new magazine.

Learning to teach classes, calling several nights a week, starting a magazine, and being the focal point for the Shaw visit all came at the same time. Ray Shaw helped set the dates for Pappy to come – November 1948, but finding the dates was difficult. As mentioned earlier, there were more requests for appearances than they could possibly fill. Plus these were school kids who needed to be in class sometime. During the negotiations Pappy sent us his schedule for the Fall of 1947.

Several have asked about our Cheyenne dance trips. We have a very green team but we are working on them and hope to have a presentable program ready soon. According to present plans we'll start our fall trip at noon Friday October 21. We may play Laramie that evening. On Saturday night we'll play Jackson Hole, Wyoming. Sunday and Monday we'll sightsee through Yellowstone Park and through Montana to Lake Coeur D'Alene. Tuesday we'll probably play at Walla Walla; on Wednesday the 26th, we'll do a show at Portland; Thursday at Bellingham; Friday at Vancouver; Saturday we'll go by boat down to Victoria and do a show for them, then by boat on Sunday down to Seattle and our big show there Monday night the 31st. Tuesday we may show at Grand Coulee Dam; Wednesday at Pullman, and Thursday at Spokane. This will be one of our biggest shows, and Friday we'll head for home, doing a show that evening at Boise, Idaho, and getting home Sunday evening the 6th of November. A few of the details are not yet settled and the program is subject to slight changes, but that's about it, and we are terribly sorry for the other invitations we have had to refuse.

Next Spring we'll probably go to Chicago, and the Great Lakes Region, perhaps dipping up into Canada again for at least one show. We'll be seeing some of you all along on both of these roads, we hope.

Remember our plan was to coincide the debut of the magazine with the Lloyd Shaw appearance. We figured that the best way to get circulation was to expose people to the magazine, so we turned out 5000 copies to give away at the two Shaw performances; we also mailed sample copies out to dance leaders we knew in different areas of the country so that they could see what we were doing. I don't think I would be wrong if I said 1500 subscriptions sold at those two shows. I think that was almost enough to pay Dillinger. He wasn't particularly concerned since he was being paid by Squirt anyway. We were very fortunate in him, and he was our printer until our very last issue – 444 issues later. That was the start of the magazine. That was the big kick in the pants for square dancing if we ever needed one because square dancing was going great guns anyway and everything had fit into place.

It seemed at the time that everything in Southern California revolved around the Cheyenne Mountain Dancers show, and starting a new magazine added to the confusion. Things were going well, though: advertising was coming in, articles were being contributed, etc. The job of selling subscriptions was a gigantic one, but we had the help of the two local square dancer associations - Associated Square Dancers and Western Square Dance Association - along with the Folkdance Federation of California.

For prime efficiency and slick handling of the distribution of Sets in Order in the San Gabriel Valley Association area, we cite Harry Longshaw, our circulation representative there. Larry Shiffer was our Circulation Representative in the San Fernando Valley area, and a whiz at it, too. Magazines sent to him were counted, bundled, and Larry personally got around to as many dances as possible, delivering and selling Sets in Order. Larry distributed upwards of 800 magazines each month, no small chore. And as more dancer associations were formed, they joined the team to help provide material for the magazine and to promote square dancing.

It might be worth noting that we had to divide the staff between two locations. The editorial office was at Ginger's and my miniscule apartment on Burton Road in Los

116

Angeles, which also had to house Ginger's art studio and our whirling dervish daughter, Linda. The business office was on Palm Drive in Beverly Hills. The first issues of Sets in Order were created on the dining table of that apartment for a short time, and when we moved into the house on Swall Drive in Los Angeles, we had the whole business under one roof. We learned a lot from having various departments dispersed, so when we moved into "Sets in Order" hall on Robertson, we could run the record store and a dance hall there, but my office was at my home, and other folks worked out of their homes. We all knew our responsibilities and did not need someone looking over our shoulders to get the job done. And we did not have to keep tripping over each other, literally and figuratively.

Fun Unincorporated was more important than I could have imagined. Before and during the War, I spent a lot of time at the Boy Scout Hut, a log cabin-like hall that, crowded, could hold six squares. It was the home of the one-night stand weekly parties held during the war. Then for a short time, it was the experimental hall that would lead to our first classes. Friendships were built that would last for at least half a century. Arnie Kronenberger, the caller who helped out by opening the second gym at Beverly Hills High School, was part of Fun Unincorporated. It was there, also, that I met Ginger.

The Boy Scout Hut also gave the magazine its first staff person, Joe Fadler, who was the magazine's photographer from the beginning, and who remained a dear friend until long after the magazine closed. Joe has shot stuff for the magazine from all sorts of impossible places, including the rafters in the gigantic Orange Show building in San Bernardino during a big round-up. One of his more pleasant assignments was doing fashion pictures of a pretty little girl in her - well, camisole and pantalettes. Into every photographer's life a little sunshine should fall, Joe figures. He and

117

his pretty brunette wife, Barbara, are topnotch square dancers themselves, having appeared on television and for various exhibitions.

This postcard from Pappy in the Spring of 1948 added a little anxiety and refocused us on the up-coming show of the Cheyenne Mountain Dancers.

> *We just got back from our eastern trip which was one of the finest we ever had. And to add to the excitement we had a blow out and rolled the bus completely over in Kansas, and miraculously no one was hurt at all. Hope to see you soon.*

Keeping lines of communication open became increasingly important. Pappy had to be kept abreast of arrangements, as did Jack Hoheisal, who was taking care of the performance details, and Ray Shaw who was in charge of housing for the Shaws; and there were other people in the associations and clubs who were handling ticket sales. Here is a letter I wrote to Pappy just a short time before he would be leaving Colorado:

> *Just a hurried note to you with a sort of program report on our activities out this way… the time and dates have been all cleared for Hollywood High School and that the publicity program is in full swing.*
>
> *There's one little item here that may be of interest to you. For quite some time I have had in the back of my mind starting what I would hope to be a really good square dance magazine featuring the western style of the dance…Finally realizing that I had procrastinated long enough I drew up the first dummies during the last week and today found that the San Gabriel Valley bunch of square dancers would back the magazine wholeheartedly. ..Its present plan is to have the first edition ready for the two shows on November 7th and 8th so that at that time*

we may catch the greatest number of Southern Cali-
fornia square dance enthusiasts. It is my intention to
feature you and the Cheyenne dancers in this article
with the cover picture of action and the lead story of
two or three pages telling the story of you and the
kids.

Just days later I received the most glowing letter from Pappy.

"Congratulations! Your dummy is a knockout! You
are doing a much bigger and finer thing than I had
dreamed of. It should go over with a bang and be a
tremendous stimulus to the square dancers of the
whole country. All the success in the world to you.
And that's a lovely article you have written
about my kids and me, if I could only believe it all.
But I won't say a word but 'thanks'. We do appreci-
ate it."

The local Los Angeles press came through and built
up a great level of anticipation for the kids' performance.
One press release came as follows:

Pappy's Pupils
The effects of the Black Death had not yet subsided,
and the graves of millions of its victims were scarcely
closed, when a strange delusion arose in Germany...and
excited the astonishment of contemporaries for more
than two centuries... It was called the dance of St. John
or of St. Vitus, on account of the Bacchantic leaps by
which it was characterized, and which gave to those af-
fected, whilst performing their wild dance, and scream-
ing and foaming with fury, all the appearance of persons
possessed.

So wrote Historian J. F. C. Hecker of the great dancing mania of the 14th and 15th Centuries. By medieval standards, the square-dancing mania that possessed many a U.S. youth last week was pretty tame, but Schoolmaster Lloyd Shaw, its originator, observed hopefully that children, too, were beginning to cut loose…

(Dr. Lloyd 'Pappy' Shaw) is… known as the leader ("caller") of a troupe of high school square dancers who in the last few years have pranced from coast to coast. In their wake they left a host of square dancing clubs and a boom in square dance costume manufacturing…His dancers wear colorful costumes-silk shirts, dungarees and cowboy boots for boys; tight-bodiced, full-skirted dresses for girls. As caller, Dr. Shaw goads them on with cowboy verses:

> *Turn right back on the same old track*
> *And swing that gal behind you!*
> *Rope your cow and brand your calf,*
> *Swing your honey an hour and a half!"*

That article ended with the following paragraph: "Lately a few parents have complained against over-emphasis of dancing at Cheyenne Mountain, charging that girls have collapsed of exhaustion during practice, that Pappy's troupers are away from school too much. But when Mrs. India Magnussen, mother of three pupils, ran for the school board on a platform proposing less dancing, voters mowed her down."

For us, in the early 21st Century, it is hard to imagine the draw of square dancing to the students and to the public.

Erna Egender, one of Pappy's dancers in the late 1930s, recalled the experience for us. The Herb she refers to was her husband, another one of Pappy's dancers who went on to have an illustrious military career and to become one of the great callers.

"For several years, Pappy Shaw and his Cheyenne Mountain Dancers traveled throughout Colorado giving exhibitions for high schools, civic organizations, conventions, etc. At the time we were dancing, the exhibitions were usually two one half hour programs consisting of four sections. The Early American section opened the show with the girls dressed in hoop skirts and the boys in cutaway coats, high collars and bow ties. This section included quadrilles, mazurkas, line dances, etc. done as they were brought from England and Europe to the New England states. Then followed a group of European folk dances with the dancers costumed in colorful dress representing various countries. The third section was Mexican dances. Who could ever forget the beautiful Matlanchines done to the beat of a tom-tom or the equally beautiful Mexican varsouvianna? The fourth and final group of dances was the Western Square or Cowboy Dances.

"Needless to say, this was a lively finale with the cowboy boots, long pioneer-type dresses and fun. Many times, to alter a performance, Pappy would invite people from the audience to dance the squares with us. In this way, he was introducing square dancing to each area visited. And then came the opportunity to spread this fun activity even further...Pappy had several programs booked at colleges on the return trip to help pay expenses. The good people of Colorado Springs also helped before we left by attending some benefits, one of which was presented by

the American Legion, it was an evening of exhibition dancing followed by the crowd trying its first square dancing with us. The admission for the evening was a whopping 25¢. The bus we traveled in had been given to the school by a kind benefactor...

"We drove to Washington, DC. via the southern route, seeing any and every sight along the way that was of any historical value. We returned to Colorado Springs after three weeks and many miles of traveling. It was an exciting, fun trip but, in addition, it was quite an education for seventeen young people, most of whom had never been that far from home. Certainly it was one of many experiences Herb and I had as members of Pappy's dance team and as students at Cheyenne School which continue to enrich our lives.

"Herb's first summer at Central City (Colorado) was 1937; we were both there in '38, '39 and '40. At that time Central City was a true mining town. They had restored the Teller House Hotel and we were thrilled to see the "Face on the Barroom Floor" in the bar. The Opera House had also been restored to its original beauty and we really felt a part of history as we sat in the back row or stood watching the performances. Pappy, as always on any of our trips, made sure we saw and were aware of anything of historical value in the area. We visited old mines, panned for gold and took full advantage of the sights in and around Central City.

"Before the Opera performance, we would walk down the dirt road to Williams Stable in our hoopskirts with the boys in cutaway coats and very formal shirts. We were very dignified for this performance which included waltz quadrilles, mazurkas, etc. After the Opera it was a different story. Again we

headed down the middle of the dirt road but this time we were in square dance clothes and anything but dignified. We made an entrance whooping and hollering and immediately started our program of western squares. There was a varsouvianna, schottische and probably a Cowboy Weasel which the audience really enjoyed. After the performance, Pappy would invite the spectators to join us in our dancing and many of them did.

"What an experience! We all regretted graduating from school and having to work summers so we were no longer able to go to Central City."

I vividly recall watching the Cheyenne Mountain Dancers, and so did many others. All around the country callers built performance teams, some of them quite good. If you were one of the lucky ones to get in on one of the two performances of the Legend of 'Pappy' Shaw portrayed so well by the Washington Square Dancers at the recent convention, then you went away a little wiser perhaps concerning the history and background of this activity. You probably also came away chuckling a bit over one of the unplanned sequences.

As happens so many times, it's the little unexpected episodes that become the highlight of an experience. This happens to all of us in our everyday life. We go on an expensive tour, enjoying everything that had been planned by us and for us but what do we remember? It could be that unscheduled parade that popped up when we were in Malaga or the visit to a country market when we were in Vermont. The unexpected always last the longest in our memory.

In the Shaw show, the scene stealer was completely oblivious to the fact that all three thousand in the audience were watching her. The setting was supposed to be a playground at the Cheyenne Mountain School in Colorado Springs where square dancing began a revival in the 1930's. Several small boys on the "playground" were Indian wrestling. Some girls were jumping rope and in the fore-ground was a group playing leapfrog.

Apparently, in the practice sessions, the youngsters wore blue jeans, but here for the big performance, the young lady who caught our attention was dressed in a floor length gingham dress. All went well with the leaping until it became her time to be the leaper. Starting as she had practiced, her hands went on the shoulders of the young lad ahead of her and she leapt. One small problem. As her legs were about to go over the young man, the dress billowed like a parachute, catching the small hind-end of the boy in the skirt and virtually tipping him into a somersault.

Somehow she got by the first of her three hurdles. However, she had the same results with the second and the third. In one instance, it looked for all the world that the show would come to a complete stop. The audience, now watching only one portion of the stage, was in an uproar. Our young lady, feeling she had let the others down, was almost in tears trying to unhook herself from the hindermost part of the final hurdle. Needless to say, the act stayed in for the two performances and we're sure the heroine of it all discovered she was indeed the hit.

That adventure reminds me of the story they tell of one of the early performance of the Cheyenne Mountain Dancers, when, in one of their wild Western costumed numbers, the elastic gave way on the pantaloons of one of the girls. A showstopper in itself as the pantaloons reached the floor, but a professional in every sense of the word, the young dancer simply danced out of her underpinning, picking them up the next time around. Then without missing a beat, she stuffed them in her partner's pocket to the approving applause of the crowd.

In another instance with these same dancers, a highlight was a "Pop Goes the Weasel" sequence which we believe was a part of the old Rye Waltz. One of the exhibiting couples had just come to the finale, a point when the boy puts his hands on the girl's waist, flexes his knees slightly, then with the "pop" of the music, lifts the girl high into the air. Only on this occasion, the young man about to do the lift inadvertently stepped on the girl's skirt. Then, with all his might, he lifted her completely out of the yards of calico, letting her down to find her standing there in petticoats.

A quick thinker, or perhaps a slightly upset young lady, without wasting a beat of music, hauled off with a strong right open-palmed hand, slapping the young man with a resounding crack. Then, turning her back she huffed haughtily off the stage, dragging her skirt behind her.

Chances are in both these performances, little else will be remembered except the scene stealing, unplanned episodes.

At the beginning of 1948 everything was going great guns. We had the dates for Shaw and the kids to come out; we hired the Hollywood High School auditorium, which I think holds around two thousand for Thursday night, and the gymnasiums at Hollywood High School (the large gym holds about 200 people) for the workshops on Friday night, all day Saturday, and Sunday morning. Then we booked Monday at Pasadena Civic Auditorium which holds about 3000 – all tickets for the two main shows were sold out. Over the weekend, between the shows at Hollywood High School and the Pasadena Civic, there was a workshop for dancers to be held in the High School gym. We gave pairs of tickets for the workshops for the dancers to the Associations who had helped so much in hosting the events. There was so much demand for tickets to the workshops, everybody wanted to go, that it turned out it was either the President and his partner or Vice President and his partner of each one of the existing clubs were all that were given tickets. That was all the tickets there were.

I never have felt so strongly that square dancers could work together - tickets were sold to various events - I think we only gave a few complimentary tickets away - one to the Mayor of the City, one to the Chief of Police, one to the head of the Sheriff's Department, one to the supervisor of the School district - all the rest were sold - it was a complete sellout.

Shaw's kids had a show - I think it was Tuesday night in Phoenix, Arizona - then they came in and spent Wednesday night in San Diego. I don't know that they gave shows at those two places. Then early on Thursday morning, the day of the performance they started their drive from San Diego up to Santa Monica where they would be housed and they stopped in La Jolla so the kids could see the beautiful surf. It was the first time most of the kids had ever seen the ocean and they all went over to the place to look down. Three of the boys went down the walk - Tommy Collins and Bobby Jones and I forget the third one although I know him real well - they walked down to the water's edge to watch the waves break and a huge breaker came in and took two of the boys into the surf and it was a wild surf.

One of the boys pulled himself out but the other one drowned. This was a horrendous thing for the group. The Life Guards and the police did everything they could but did not find the body. When the kids got in the bus, Shaw called me and said, "Bob, we just had a terrific thing happen." He explained it and I said, "Pappy, we'll be prepared to turn back the tickets to everybody. We'll be at the box office so don't give it a second thought and let us know if there's any way we can help'"

He said, "Don't turn them back yet." He said, "I'm trying to reach Tommy Collins' folks in Colorado Springs and tell them what happened. We're heading back to Santa Monica now and I'll call you in a little bit and I'll see if I can reach them." Meanwhile Ralph Maxheimer and I decided we wouldn't tell anybody at all. We would just keep it to ourselves and we would play the thing by ear. But, in anticipation of the worst, we worked out what order we'd do it in if we had to return tickets and cancel the venue

About 1:00 Shaw called and said, "I've reached Tommy's folks and they said, 'We'd like you to go ahead and do the show for the number of people that are expecting it. We'd like it if you would dedicate it to Tommy.' So," Shaw said, "I took the kids - we were at San Juan, Capistrano - we went in and we spent about 15 minutes in the chapel of the mission there and we let everybody do his own thinking. We talked to them in the bus a little bit and Dorothy Shaw in her excellent way talked to them."

He said, "The kids all decided that in honor of Tommy that they would do the show." So he said, "Go ahead but don't tell anybody." We decided that just Ralph and I would know and nobody else. They came on in - one of the challenges was, Lloyd told his brother Ray "We have two of the dances that require all our people and we need somebody that can fit into Tommy's costume that can do this dance and one of the others. Ray immediately got in touch with this professor from USC, a Jack Reinhart who's a long time square dancer and a dance professor who had danced with the gypsies in Spain. They talked it over. Jack had seen the kids work in Colorado Springs but had never done these dances himself. He was 68 years old but he could fit into Tommie's costume. So, with a little talking and stuff - probably just a one-time walk-thru, Jack did it and no one even noticed that he was an old timer. Well, there was tremendous enthusiasm throughout the auditorium at Hollywood High School that night.

Many of the people came early - everybody was dressed up - it was really a fancy deal. We had half a dozen square dance couples dressed to the hilt at the entrance handing out free copies of the first issue of the new magazine. We had the press and the dignitaries there and there wasn't a seat empty. When it came time the lights dimmed and the curtain parted. Pappy stepped through the slightly opened curtain and said, "We're dedicating this show tonight to Tommy Collins." The curtain finished opening, the music started, and the show went on.

Joe Fadler, our photographer for many years, was told about what had happened and kept it to himself. Joe was back stage and was even in the fly space up above shooting down on some of the show. Later, after the show he said, "Those kids never touched the floor all evening. They danced a good foot and a half off the floor." The audience, you know, just raved about it, and at half time - when there was an intermission the word got out about what had happened. So for the rest of the show they were aware of it - of Jack Reinhart dancing in the place of Tommy. The show was a great success. And the dancing in the workshops over the weekend was superior. The people who were at the workshops were put through the kind of things that we had been put through in Colorado Springs. If any of those folks thought any of the training was silly, they had only to look up and see Shaw doing the same things - the posture and the smoothness and all the styling - for couple dances and squares and contras. The Cheyenne Mountain Dancers, dressed in regular clothes, danced the demonstrations, which gave an added impression. So the long and the short of it was a tremendous boost of square dancing in southern California.

Not only did the audiences love the show, but so did the press:

The opening curtain stills the 2,000 persons whose talking has filled the auditorium. The footlights brighten and the musicians start a lively hoedown tune. Onto the stage come sixteen of the world's most enthusiastic ambassadors of true Western square dancing. First one pattern, then another, a round dance, then a square; all so colorful and free from any evidence of unnaturalness or stiffness.

Suddenly the audience realizes that there is yet another person on the stage. His voice— booming above the music and the sliding of the feet—commands, cautions, jokes with, and applauds his dancers.

No ordinary kids these, for they are the Cheyenne Mountain Dancers. And the voice of the caller? That belongs to Dr. Lloyd Shaw. Square dancing, for many years, locked up in small barns, hidden in the confines of private homes, occasionally slipped into (and just as swiftly slipped out of) a "popular" dance, has once again come into its own. Much of the credit for its overwhelming success belongs to these Cheyenne kids and their beloved 'Pappy'.

Dr. Lloyd Shaw, an educator with the instincts of a showman and the zeal of a Missionary, has spread the Square Dance gospel from Boston to San Diego. He loves square dancing for its color and lustiness, but his crusading spirit is born of the conviction that it fosters the spread of the Democratic processes.

For he's primarily an educator—a school su perintendent and college trustee. His Cheyenne Mountain Dancers, high school students at Colorado

129

Springs, aren't professionals. They're just a bunch of kids who love to dance for the fun of it. They've been having this kind of fun all over the States—in concert halls, at festivals, and at universities. And now they're here in Southern California to share their fun with you.

Twice each year eighteen kids (two sets) leave their classrooms and together with Dr. and Mrs. Shaw and Mrs. Harriet Johnson, the pianist, set out for distant parts to carry the gospel of square dancing where it will benefit the greatest number of people. In the Spring the trip carries them East. Last year it was Chicago, New York and the New England States. This spring it will be the South, going as far as Florida. In the winter the kids climb into their bus and make the trek West to the Pacific Coast where in years past they have appeared before capacity audiences in Seattle, Berkeley and Palo Alto.

Truly, here is one person who believes in the great present and wonderful future for square dancing. As he explains it in his own words, "Here is the dance of true democracy. Joyously laughing and shouting, we can weave lovely patterns together. We can refresh ourselves together. If we can play together, we can work together. This old dancing is packed with hidden treasures of value.

Those steps and figures go back to our ancestors. They've come down to us through the very blood stream of our bodies—so-

'Around you go just like a wheel
The faster you go, the better you feel'.

Sets in Order included a program of the Cheyenne Mountain Dancers' first performance, making that first issue a valuable keepsake; as a result, at the performances and during the weeks to follow, we picked up several thousand subscribers - enough to continue. Because of the work to put on the Shaw show, running multiple classes and clubs, and a few unexpected events, we missed the deadline for a December issue – if we were to have one. Instead, we skipped December and started our initial year with January 1949. Several months into that year, we combined two issues, with the result that for all of 1949, we have twelve issues, a plan we continued during the time we stayed in publication. One thing that pleased us was the attitude of the advertisers who came to us requesting space. We were surprised to find out that setting up the mechanics of the magazine took much more time than the editorial side.

A special treat that we were able to give to Pappy and the kids was a package of photographs of the workshops and the show. Joe Fadler, Sets in Order staff photographer, made up a booklet including some of the pictures. Along with the booklet was a handful of 8 by 10 glossy photos of various phases of the Institute and Show which Pappy could hand out to the gang. We also included several of the poster sheets that were used for publicity, with the idea that they might make interesting souvenirs during the years to come.

So the magazine was born. But there are some major changes in square dancing and in Sets in Order to come.

Chapter 6. The Lone Square Dancer

"Seven over there."

We told you that Frank Grundeen was with us from the first issue of Sets in Order through the last of Square Dancing – 444 cartoons that remain fresh even now. For our 25th anniversary we ran the following column as a tribute to Frank. The response was so great that two months later we ran another column of Grundeen cartoons. The Lone Square Dancer (portrayed in the cartoon above) hoping for seven others to join his "square," became the most imitated square dancer of the "fad" years of the activity. You could scarcely attend a dance in the late 1940s without some comic moving out into the center of the floor, seven fingers raised, hoping to attract others who would join him.

Seeing the human and humorous side of the activity since the first issue of Sets in Order (SQUARE DANCING) in November, 1948, has been the assignment of Frank Grundeen, artist, family man, square dancer. This month marks the 300th Grundeen cartoon to grace the back cover of this publication, and over the years Frank has taken his share of "pot shots" at callers, round dancers, new dancers, ladies' fashions - you name it, Frank has undoubtedly covered it at one time or another.

Frank and Ethel started dancing with us back in 1947 in our classes at Beverly Hills High School. We still remember watching as Frank hurried over to the sidelines after a tip to pick up his sketch pad to record some event that seemed to him unusually titillating. When we started the magazine many of these funny moments became the subjects for a back-pager.

Because it's our anniversary issue, we thought that you might enjoy going back 25 years with us to view the funny long dresses and the fringed shirts and laugh with us at some of Grundeen's "best." We hope that we've included at least one of your favorites.

"We'd like an application...all he needed was a little persuasion."

"He had to do something...the problem of getting a baby sitter was becoming acute."

"That's my husband...I had to drag him to his first square dance."

These two say a great deal regarding Frank's views on ladies' costumes and refreshments.

"How's the lemonade tonight?

The youthful dancer gets his share, while round dancing is always a prime target for the Grundeen wit.

"I'd love to call at your festival, but I have to be in bed by 10 o'clock"

"Side behind...side front..."

"This new round of ours has one or two tricky spots."

Each month Frank Grundeen continued to appear as an important part of the magazine.

Somehow the callers that Frank and Ethel have known have been "hot" on new movements, "live" music and white (for the good guys) cowboy hats.

"Martha! I've got it. This one They'll never be able to dance, by gad!"

"Hold everything, folks. Here's a brand new figure from a small town in Kansas!"

Every once in a while somebody will write in and ask us how Frank keeps getting all the ideas for his cartoons. Perhaps the best way to explain it is that Frank just "tunes in" to the common little happenings on a dance floor and with that special knack of his, comes up with something both humorous and human.

135

Evidently you enjoyed going back in time with us via Frank Grundeen Cartoons (see the November, 1973 Anniversary issue of SQUARE DANCING magazine). From your letters we gather that you'd like another glimpse of the Grundeen humor so here's a collection that old timers may remember and newer dancers may find just as timely today as when they first appeared sometime during the last 25 years.

Don't get nervous, dear, but I think scouts from High-Level Squares are giving us the once over."

"Actually our altitude is only 4 inches, but the level of dancing here makes these mandatory."

Being an extremely "down to earth person, Frank tends to be a bit critical of snobbishness in both dancers and clubs. No written editorial even begins to accomplish what Frank can do with a single cartoon. This commentary on gimmick groups and "way out" badges brought in a lot of letters when it appeared in 1958.

Their leader, here with the microphone, says they're trying to qualify as idiots."

"Rough dancing," inconsiderate dancers. Frank tells it like he sees them.

"That's Carol-Anne...that's one gal who knows how to handle rough dancers."

After more than 25 years of dancing and working with us on the magazine, Frank and Ethel still manage some dancing. In addition, you may still notice the Grundeen touch with the daily, syndicated Donald Duck comic strip. "What would square dancing be if it wasn't fun?" asks Frank. We think we see him pictured in many of his cartoon creations. And, finally, some of our favorites are the "classics" that need no caption to tell the story.

Grundeen caricature

Yours Truly

138

Chapter 7. Sets in Order Evolves

As of November 9, 1948, we had more than a mock up and some advertising – we had a magazine. We gave away 5000 copies of Sets in Order at the Cheyenne Mountain Dancers shows, and we received over 1000 subscriptions. That was just about enough to pay Charley Dillinger, our printer and graphic artist.

After the initial presentation of the magazine at the Shaw events I began to build my first staff. An enthusiastic young lady, who had been busy handing out sample copies of the first issue, said to me, "I'm Helen Orem. I'm a writer. Can I help you with the magazine?" Helen became staff member number one. Then a moment or two later, I'm shaking hands with Helen's husband. "Hi. I'm Jay Orem. I sell things. Can I help?" Now I was in business for sure. I had a writing staff and a sales staff. Jay, a salesman for an auto parts company, and his wife, Helen, a movies news column-ist, came on staff soon after the first struggling issue was out in November, 1948. From then on, both were devoting all of their time to it. I don't know what became of Jay's auto parts business, or of Helen's column. Jay became business man-ager, and Helen became assistant editor. Eight of us – Helen, Jay, Ginger, Joe Fadler, Frank Grundeen, and helpers from the square dance associations - all specialists in some phase of our subject, worked together on Sets in Order. The edito-rial office remained in our apartment until March of 1949, while the business office was on Palm Ave. in Los Angeles.

We knew that square dancing needed a way to ex-change ideas and information. From my travels for Squirt I knew what square dancers in other areas in the country were curious about: tempo, dances, styling, costumes, calling techniques, etc. I planned to publish new calls and figures, successful ideas about forming and running a club, and such other news of square dancing that was of general interest. Sets in Order reported the news of the clubs in one area that would interest other clubs, such as an entertainment novelty applicable elsewhere, an innovation in publicity, or a clever invitation. It was a how-to-do-it magazine. Party ideas were especially important because the dancers get together for fun and friendship and they are always ready for a party.

Because the first issue was a hit we used it as a model for future issues. The cover, of course, featured the Cheyenne Mountain Dancers, then inside was an extensive article about "Pappy's Kids." We always featured the latest and best of the square dance records because, even in those days, "kitchen junkets" were popular. The first issue came out during the visit by the Cheyenne Mountain Dancers, so we included a special article on a youth club that started in Southern California. There was also the "Idea Corral" in which dancers and callers were invited to share ideas on how to improve anything in square dancing. Topics I heard about while traveling were the speed of dancing, how complex the dances were, the condition of dance floors, etc. So this first issue addressed the topic of speed – too fast, too slow, etc., and an article on the "Care and Feeding of a Square Dance Floor." We also started a regular column on what was happening around the country. This column grew in length and participation immensely over the life of the magazine.

And we got letters. In the second issue we published several letters from dancers mostly in Southern California. Soon we found out that people were sharing their copies of Sets in Order with friends, so letters started coming in from other states. Eventually letters would come from all over the world. In this second issue, the letters all complimented us on starting the magazine. In future issues we showed that dancers held some pretty strong opinions on all facets of square dancing, and they were not shy (though they were polite) about sharing their opinions. The letters gave us, at the magazine, a picture of square dancing in America that no one else had.

Thank heaven most of the letters were of praise for the magazine and included checks for subscriptions. Most of the letters, for the life of Sets in Order and SQUARE DANCING magazine, centered around just a few topics. One was tempo. I recall responding to a letter that complained about speed at a festival by saying the 142 metronome beats per minute was not too fast. Then later, after attending a special dance I commented that the dance, at over 150 bpm was too hectic.

The second most common topic was that too many figures were being introduced. We have to remember that in the late 1940s dancing revolved around complete dance patterns, not individual figures. Sets in Order tried to help the dancers out by printing the patterns to many of the popular dances. However, even we became overwhelmed to some extent with new dances. A complication was that the same dance had different names in different regions of the country.

We received the following story from a reader that vividly makes that point. Overheard: out of town guests to a local square dance the other night were noticed to be sitting out quite a few of the dances. Approached by one of the club members they were asked whether they did much square dancing where they came from.

"Yes," was the answer, "we dance about three times a week back home."

"Well," went on the host, "I imagine you dance quite a bit differently out your way than we do here."

"No, our style is almost identical to yours."

"Well, then, why aren't you dancing?" further queried the inquisitive Californian.

The out-of-towner looked at his wife, then turned and smiled sheepishly, "Well, I guess we're sort of funny but we wanted to be sure we knew the dance before we started it. But each time we ask the name of the dance somebody tells us that its "Forward Three" or "Back You Blunder" or "Four Hand Star" or some other name we've never heard before. We sit out so that we won't mess up the dance only to find out when it's started that it's one we do back home, only under a different name. Be kinda nice if somebody sometime sits down and either invents brand new names for every dance so that everybody can stick to them, or folks everywhere decide to call the dances by the same name. That way everybody would know what to expect."

We heard that story and took it to heart. There did need to be a way to make it so people could travel and still dance. In an effort to help solve the problems of non-standard dance names, we also had a column on the "Dance of the Month" which featured the calls to the dance and a short biography of a well-known caller who wrote or used that pattern. Within months we had a several page section in the middle of the magazine of just choreography submitted by readers.

Soon readers inundated us with letters, and even now, many years later, we still appreciate the letters complimenting us on the magazine. In spite of the general positive stories, some readers told us stories of bad experiences at festivals or when visiting other clubs. An important theme was the lack of courtesy. All too often dancers would get on the floor with pre-set squares, so there was no way to join them. One couple told of being invited by the president of another club, but when they arrived no one greeted them because everyone was already in line for the pot luck. On the other hand, there were many readers who were elated by how warmly they were welcomed no matter where they traveled in the country. This avalanche of letters proved that we were on the right track. People around the country did want to know what was going on in other places, or they wanted to share experiences that other dancers might experience also. Our job of providing communications in the square dance world was working.

For the first several years of Sets in Order, American square dancing was pattern dancing. Most people could do the dances to the calls. And if they did not know the dance, they simply got into the number four position, and by the time it was their turn to lead they had seen the pattern three times. For example:

BIRDIE IN THE CAGE AND SEVEN HANDS 'ROUND

First couple balance and swing,
The gent leads out to the right of the ring.
Swing the lady on the right with a right hand 'round.
Partner left as you come down.
Turn the opposite lady with the right hand 'round.
Leave her in place and return to home.
And back to your partner with a left hand 'round.
Now the lady on the left with a right hand 'round.
And a left to your partner as you come down.
Now it's birdie in the cage and seven hands 'round.
The bird hops out and the crow hops in.
The crow hops out with a left allemande.
A right to your own and a right and left grand, etc.
Continue with couple two leading.

It was very easy for the #4 couple to be confident when it came their turn to lead.

Not all the dances were as simple as "Birdie in the Cage." Some of the dances which still used a very limited number of Basics could be much more confusing. The pattern of the dance below is not too different from "Birdie," but without having had a walk thru it would be a challenge. Notice that this is not a single couple visiting pattern but has all dancers active. That in itself would have presented a challenge to new dancers.

FOUR GENTS STAR

Four gents star in the center of the square.
Turn the opposite lady and leave her there.
Star right back in center of the set.
Turn your own, you're not through yet.
Star right back in the center of the town.
Turn the right hand lady with the left hand 'round.
Star right back in the center of the floor.
Turn the left hand lady or she might get sore.
Star right back and you should know.
Meet your own with a do-pas-o.
It's partner left, corner right, partner left with a left
*   all around*
And promenade your corner when she comes down.

Four Gents Star was a fast moving dance, but the pattern was learnable and predictable. Most dancers (after a single walk-thru) were able to dance it.

And there were dances with such arcane language that dancers had to know the dance to be successful. This next one needs to be set up so that either the head men or the side men are in lines of three with partner on the right and corner on the left. It is not hard at all, but dancers will need to have danced it before to be successful. The first trick is to set up the lines of three with dancers all in the proper sequence. Perhaps the common way was to have the head couples lead to the right and circle to a line, then the head men leave them there and head for home. The square then was in position to do the triple duck:

Forward six and back you blunder
An elbow hook and the left lady under
A triple duck and go like thunder
And form new lines of three.

I can hear almost everyone saying, "Huh?" The lines of three have the side men in the middle with his partner on his right and his corner on his left. The lines step forward and the two men hook left elbows and keep hold of his partner's hand. The couples move around the men's elbow while the corner ladies duck under with everyone moving forward. The triple duck is the ladies ducking under the arch made by the side couple three times. Then all of the ladies join the head men, in the same type of formation. Rhyming was an important feature of pattern dances and unfortunately, the rhymes did not give much help in dancing the figures. For example, "Texas Star" starts off:

ladies to the center and back to the bar
men to the center with a right hand star

Nobody knows what the bar was, but it rhymed with star. The phrase "go like thunder" and its variations was very popular, but rhymes were scarce, so "thunder" and "blunder" paired up.

Sets in Order printed these dances with the most common name for them so dancers could successfully visit other clubs.

Well, the Southern California Caller's Pow-Wow continued to operate, but it outgrew Ray Shaw's kitchen. We wanted to complement groups like the Southern California

Callers' Pow-Wow. With square dancing becoming so popular, we found we had close to a hundred callers in the Los Angeles area who wanted to form a caller's association. Sets in Order gave a voice to the callers. (In 1948 we started with that 100, and by the time the Southern California Caller's Association folded in 1980 something, it grew to over 3,000 members from all over the country.)

Jack Hoheisal, a member of the standardization committee, and I grabbed onto the idea of standardization and worked up a list of twenty-three most popular calls and published it in a separate booklet. Here is the advertisement Sets in Order ran in July 1949:

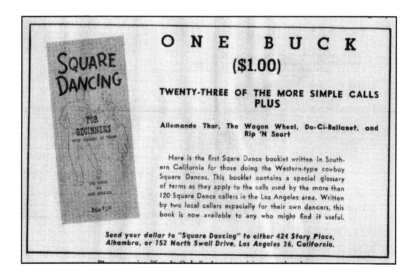

And then in October of the same year we came out with:

That same session of the Southern California Caller's Association came up with another first – a caller's code of ethics. I think these were adopted as guidelines to new callers so they set off in the same direction as the rest of the callers in Los Angeles. Some of the rules are to remind all callers to treat dancers and clubs fairly.

THE CALLERS CODE

(The following ten points are incorporated into a code agreed upon by many Southern California callers on June 2, 1949).

The ideal Square Dance caller will:

1. Aim primarily to give his group enjoyment.
2. Promote good fellowship.
3. Discourage cliques.
4. Help beginners.
5. See that proper decorum is observed at a dance.
6. Maintain a professional attitude towards other callers.
7. Cooperate with the other callers in exchanging calls.
8. Adhere to uniform nomenclature.
9. Maintain a good reputation for personal integrity.
10. Keep scheduled engagements.

At about the same time the Callers came up with their standardized list and Sets in Order published the square

147

dance booklets, we decided it would be good to leaven everything with a little humor. So our always serious staff devised a list of Dopeynitions:

Sets Out of Order or DOPEYNITIONS

ALLEMAND LEFT:	The first movement in a caller's attempt at creating mass confusion.
BALANCE:	What you wish you still had in the bank after buying a new square dance outfit.
BREAK:	Sometimes pronounced "Broke", (see balance).
CALLER:	Maniac with a sense of humor and desire to mix everyone up and say it's all their fault.
DO-SI-DO:	Depending where you're from. In New York they mean do-sa-do. In Texas they really hope you'll do a do-pas-o and in California it's a ladies' figure which is the same thing as being caught in a revolving door.
FIRST COUPLE:	Show offs who think they know what the caller is going to say.
GENT GOES WRONG:	Polite way of saying "Brother you sure messed up that dance".
HONORS LEFT:	What little honor you have left after forgetting to "Turn right back" in a Grand right and left.
KEENO:	That's all, bub, you can rest now. Okay, sister, your feet are killing you — take your shoes off.
ODD COUPLE:	The funny looking people across the set.
ONCE AND A HALF:	See "Single Elbow".
OX BOW LOOP:	A convenient manner of dislocating your left shoulder.
OPPOSITE COUPLE:	The odd couple as seen from the other side. (see odd couple).
PROMENADE:	Act of each couple taking a tramp home, to music.
ROUND DANCE:	Anything that isn't a square.
SASHAY:	Double talk meaning, the perfume is in the top bureau drawer.
SINGLE ELBOW:	See "Once and a Half".

I probably should remind you that in 1949 we were still dancing patterns, and the Basics were taught only in context of a dance. In an early issue of Sets in Order we published a list of the recognized dances used in Southern California – there were 138 dance titles listed. Then shortly after we printed that list, we got a letter from a dancer telling us of another 40 or more dances we had missed.

No wonder that visiting couples had trouble dancing in Southern California. As we have mentioned several times, most callers learned their material by going to dances then writing down the figures in their "little black books." Oftentimes the caller worked so hard to remember the sequence of calls in a dance that he completely forgot the name, so he gave it a title just to help him remember what the dance was. A particular dance could have a dozen different names. At least the approach of the Southern California callers was to standardize the Basics. This thinking of Basics, or individual dance steps, will have a profound effect on square dancing in the later years.

The magazine, certainly kept us (Ginger and me) out of mischief. With the enlarged staff, we began to see that the apartment Ginger and I shared with our young whirling dervish, Linda, was awfully small to publish a magazine and keep a family. That one bedroom place had developed into Ginger's studio, my office for Sets in Order, Linda's nursery, a practice hall for square dancing, and more.

Somehow we delivered the first regular monthly edition (the second issue) to the printers in December to be published in January. We were surprised to discover that setting up the mechanics for the magazine occupied far greater time than setting up the editorial end of the job. Charlie Dillinger, our printer and sketch artist, was a miracle from the mechanics part of publishing. Somehow he managed to convert our mock-ups to printing plates and get the magazine out on time. He also did a lot of the filler art that covered up

It's something new - square dance record

white space. But one thing that really pleased us was the attitude of the advertisers who came to us requesting space. As a result we were able to maintain our original standards as to the type of advertising we included.

They say that a fellow can only do so much, and I'm convinced they're right. But, back then in the late 1940's while Ginger and I were still young, I felt that there was more that I personally wanted to do for square dancing. I found myself dividing my interests among so many different activities that no one of them was drawing my undivided attention, consequently everything was suffering to some extent. My experiences at the Squirt Company had been outstanding. Each day brought me some new experience and I enjoyed my day job immensely. However, I never had any job more enjoyable or more exhilarating than my activities (my hobby) in square dancing. I certainly didn't know where it was all going but I did think that I wanted to put out a better and more helpful Sets in Order. The problem was that if I were to leave Squirt at that time, Sets in Order could not by itself pay my way, even with the income I was making from calling at night.

The question was, then, how to increase the income from Sets in Order? The first, most obvious answer was to increase circulation and advertising. Both of those concerns were being taken care of. We had great people in the office working on circulation, and Jay Orem was a salesman with a capital "S." But as investment advisors always tell you, diversify. And that was the direction Ginger and I decided to go. As a result of the endless number of queries we had received: "Where can I buy some good square dance records?" "Where can I get Lloyd Shaw's books?" "Where can I get some help about finding a caller or a place to dance?", we decided that perhaps here was a good opening for somebody who knew the field backwards and forwards and could be of service rather than a hindrance.

Many people would go to their local record store ready to spend anywhere from fifteen to fifty dollars on albums and records only to find that the calls were New England style and quite foreign, and the round dances, particularly numbers like varsouvianna, were not ones they were familiar with. The result so often was a discouraged and disillusioned square dancer. So many times the folks told us, "You tell us to get a certain book or a certain record and we have an awful time finding a place that carries it." Others said that they go to one of the few places to buy such-and-such a record only to be discouraged by the clerk who knows little or nothing about the subject.

When we considered how many dancers and callers lived in the greater Los Angeles area, we saw a huge potential market. The answer was to open a small record and book shop that specialized in square dance materials. Jay Orem provided crucial information on how to run a retail business. We knew little about how to build an inven-

More picturesque than commercial is the actual store location of Osgood's Record Square. The country style Sign in front is the only identification from the street

tory, that is, how many of each record or book to purchase. We especially wanted to market Pappy Shaw's *Cowboy Dances* and his recently released *Round Dances.* Also square dance music record companies were mushrooming, but unfortunately many of the labels knew nothing about square dancing, and they produced squeaky fiddle music that was undanceable. However, there were quality labels too. For years we had had *Soldier's Joy* and *Blackberry Quadrille* on the RCA label. Now finally there was quality dance music being produced by people who understood square dancing. Many of the new producers were callers who were filling their own need for good dance music. But the ordinary record store clerk could not keep up with the number of titles and labels showing up.

Inventory for "Bob Osgood's Record Square" was a minor problem compared with where to put the inventory. We could not run a store out of our apartment, and we could not afford to rent a storefront. So, in March 1949 we bought a house at 152 N. Swall Drive just outside of Beverly Hills in an easily reached location and in a part of the city where it was permissible to run an open business. The house - which had four bedrooms - was changed into our store and offices. One large bedroom was used for the SIO office as well as my square dance headquarters. Then we lined the large living room with shelves and two listening systems for shoppers to hear records before they bought them. There was ample space between shelves to try out that new schottische or to walk through one of the dances listed in the Round Dance book. The house was also large enough for Ginger to have a separate room for her studio, and Linda got a bedroom of her own.

During the time that our Swall Drive home shared space with the growing office needs, including the business staff, we held a first Anniversary celebration for Sets in Order. It was an open house that attracted several hundred dancers and callers. Each night a different bunch of callers added their bit to the fun. One night alone there were more than 43 Southern California Callers and their wives on hand taking part in the squares. Advertisers put up special displays and there were many photographs of square dance activities in the area. The open house became an annual event.

Still an employee of the Squirt Company and calling several times a week, I had truly stepped into a hornet's nest. Being reasonably young helped us get over the growing pains, even though sometimes the challenges were almost too much. I still remember one Sunday morning - it must have been around 9:00 a.m. and I was still in bed having done a calling thing the previous night. Waking up, I suddenly realized that I was not alone in the room. Some unknown individual was sitting on the edge of the bed, using the telephone. The voice, which I did not recognize, was asking somebody about a dance later that day. When I finally managed to open my eyes, I realized that my guest was a complete stranger. That experience, and a number of others, and the fact that all this time we were getting larger and busier, made it evident that we had outgrown our current venue.

In those days we subscribed to a news clipping service, and imagine my surprise when this article came through.

BILLBOARD, CINCINNATI, OHIO Oct 15, 1949
Merchandising pays off: L. A.'s Osgood Makes
Career Of Square Dances, Disks
By Lee Zhito Los Angeles Oct. 15.

Selling square dance disks is for dealer Robert Osgood a career as well as a retail business. The owner/operator of The Record Square in the county strip between Hollywood and Beverly Hills, Osgood publishes a hoedown magazine, sells nothing but square dance disks and is a caller in his own right

The interior is decorated with knotty pine paneling and good display use is made of the colorful album covers. Osgood's monthly publication, Sets in Order, is his strongest sales promoter. The magazine offices are

*located right in the store. The magazine has a circula-
tion of 6,000 a month and sells for 25 cents a
copy...One of Osgood's biggest events as a caller was
the recent Hollywood Bowl All Western night. An un-
told amount of business is directly attributed to this
event. In any event specialization in so limited a field of
recorded music has turned out to be a lucrative venture
for Osgood who learned about square dancing when he
attended a serviceman's party while a Lieutenant in the
Navy."*

Because of the extreme growth of the magazine we
came into some criticism that we were trying to take over
square dancing. But what I was trying to do, along with the
people who worked with me, was not saying the magazine
was the leader in the field, or Bob Osgood or anyone else
intended to be king, we all realized that Lloyd Shaw was the
leader. He had the ability to promote the activity and to see
that it got off on the right track; he taught as many caller
leaders as he could, who in turn went home and taught leaders. Eventually there were fourth and fifth generation people
who had never met Shaw and never really knew a great deal
about him that were teaching new dancers and teaching
caller classes. So, in the magazine we tried to keep abreast
of what was happening. In the magazine we promoted the
best caller/teachers of the time, who shared the Shaw vision.
There were the Ed Gilmores with their vast experience with
caller training; there were people like Bob Van Antwerp who
led one of the largest recreation departments in the country.
We went after the people who were masters of some facet or
other in square dancing to write articles. One person who
believed one way and wrote a caller article was balanced
with an article from another point of view. We recruited people from all areas of square dancing to write articles – to
share their knowledge and expertise, as long as it wasn't
against principles we felt were important. So, the magazine

154

became more than a disseminator of news, it became a communicator. We never attempted a leadership position in the role that we thought only Shaw could handle. But we liked to get what Shaw did and other leaders have done over the years into the hands of other people and we were able to do it through the magazine. But I soon became aware that square dancing was taking a different path.

When Sets in Order originally started, classes emphasized not how well you danced but how much you knew. (If I know more than you I am a better dancer.) That was what we grew up believing. The opposite happened as well: people who did not know as many figures felt they were inferior dancers. We much preferred Dorothy Stott Shaw's definition that a good dancer was one who danced what he knows well and smoothly, and makes other dancers feel comfortable dancing with him. At the same time there was an increasing gap between what one learned in class and what it took to be a club dancer. About 100 callers in the Los Angeles area got together in May 1949 to discuss some kind of standardization so that dancers could move about more successfully. We did not make a list of dances because we did not want to stifle any caller's style or imagination, but we did want callers to have approximately the same list of Basics used in the dances. We came up with a list that was relatively short but still left room for creativity. The list included such Basics as: Allemande (with all kinds of notes on styling), Arch over or under, Balance, Grand Ballonet, Birdy (or Crow) in the Cage, Do-Si-Do Kentucky style, and Turn Back. There were some 35 Basics on the list from which callers could create dance patterns. Not all dancers learned all of the same Basics in classes and the list was designed to give some uniformity throughout the LA area

As said before, there were complaints that this small group was trying to take over square dancing. We thought that there needed to be some way for dancers and callers to

155

dance or call in other settings than their home clubs. We tended to go along with the following philosophy taken from a publication on engineering standards:

It has often been feared that standardization will retard development and cramp initiative in design. Standards should, however, always represent, and often do represent, the best-known way of getting something done, and should be used until a better way has been developed. When this has been done, the standard should be changed appropriately. Standards should not be static but progressive in character. If a progressive policy is adopted towards standardization, there need never be any fear of retarding the development of new ideas, and the many advantages of standardization can be enjoyed to the full. It is hoped that leaders in the standards field will fully evaluate the potential of this method.

Anyway, in addition to the names and descriptions of dances, we began a regular series of photographs of square dancers doing the dances. We sincerely hoped that this approach to filling the class/club gap would work.

From the mid-1950's on through the 1960's callers felt that the way to notoriety was to be known as a choreographer. Too many of these dances were just changing the order of basic figures and then giving the combination a new name. The names of dances soon out-paced the ability of callers and dancers to learn them. To simplify the system, callers began calling "hash," or combinations of Basics with no name to the sequence. Later we will deal with the effect of this hash calling on square dancing in general. But in the early 1950's we were dealing with pattern dances and the problem of too many of them being called. One way we tried to slow down the avalanche of figures was polling the leaders who cooperated in the project to see which of these movements should be on a list. A lot of callers from around the country worked to build what we thought was a fairly standard list of dances being used on a regular basis. For several years SIO published dances, usually three to six per issue. Then we added the Workshop section in the middle of the magazine so that more choreography could be presented.

We came out with our first lists in the magazine in the late 1940's. Then in July 1949, with the help of Jack Hoheisal, we published a 2" x 3" size little book that was our first Basic movement handbook. We put out three or four editions of those, and eventually they became a Basic list of dances. So, we put out a book in the center of our magazine that had the Basic lists all illustrated. Then not long after that we came out with the Extended Basics, and these handbooks were printed as a center section of the magazine. If we ran a magazine and say we had a 20,000 run of the magazine with these in the center section, when the magazine run was through, we kept the presses running just for the insert, and some of the press runs were better than 200,000. We figured at one time that we had several million of these books printed over a period of thirty years. They sold for the astonishing price of 10 cents each. But they got out into the hands of people and they had a description of the dances which were illustrated with photographs taken by Joe Fadler.

But I have gotten ahead of myself. Just the magazine and the Record Square had grown to the point that the house on Swall could no longer house us. The experience of the unknown caller in the bedroom, and a number of others, plus the fact that the magazine was growing and we were constantly getting more involved, convinced me that somehow we needed to separate the business and whatever private life still existed. For a while we thought of selling the Record Square to provide some space for ourselves and the growing office needs of the magazine, so we had an "open house" that attracted several hundred dancers and callers to our Fall Festival.

The reaction to the notice of the store being for sale created such an overwhelming response that we reconsidered selling the going business. To our chagrin, and to the disappointment of several readers, we had to run this article:

YOU CAN'T BLAME US FOR CHANGING OUR MIND

Following our little notice in the February SETS IN ORDER about wanting to sell the Record Square because it was rough trying to run a business and a home under the same roof, people in Texas, San Diego, Phoenix, Chicago and Spokane wrote in saying they were interested and wanted more information. Other folks came into the store or telephoned us to get the low down. We began to wonder, maybe if this many square dancers were anxious to get into this sort of thing it might be well for us to think the thing over a little bit before rushing off and selling the business.

Then there were a lot of people who wrote in asking if we wouldn't consider keeping on as we had because the store was giving the kind of service square dancers needed. We did a pile of thinking and finally ended up by moving the Record Square away from our home into brand new quarters in a large, modern, new building. We've made a good move, we think. There's lots of room (enough space for nine squares right here in front of the counter). We have ample space for packing and sending out shipments

much faster than ever before. There's much more el-
bow room, two listening rooms and a corner for
browsing and looking over the newest books and rec-
ords.

We're eager to have you see the set-up. Never
feel obligated to buy, just come in and look over the
new releases and be assured that we're going to do
our doggonedest to make our selection the most com-
plete in the country.

So just a year after the move to Swall we moved "Sets in Order" and the Record Square to the upstairs part of a building on North Robertson in Los Angeles. The building was just a couple of blocks south of the old Boy Scout Hut. My club Rip 'n' Snort made this its new home. By this time the staff had worked together enough that we did not have to be in each other's back pocket, so much of the staff did their work from home. We coordinated our work with phone calls, letters, and occasional staff meetings. Soon the place was known as the "Sets in Order Hall," and even when we changed the name of the magazine, the front door was still labeled "Sets in Order."

In November,1950, we celebrated our second anniversary for Sets in Order. In those two years we had published 156,000 copies of the magazine. It was mailed to all but four states (Delaware, New Hampshire, North Dakota, and South Carolina); we also had subscribers in Alaska, Canal Zone, Hawaii, Guam, Canada, Mexico, Iceland, Denmark, Bolivia, England, and Japan. Between seventy-five and a hundred high schools, universities and libraries throughout the country got Sets in Order every month, as well as city and state recreation departments and park districts.

We continued to expand our printing business. We were already printing the Basic Handbook, and we added an

Intermediate/Advanced booklet as well. Because of the popularity of round dancing, we got Frank Hamilton to write a booklet on rounds, which included photos of how the dances were done. Even Ginger got in on the act, and we published two round dance books that she wrote in co-operation with Virginia Anderson and Grace Hoheisal. We expanded the size of the Basics book and had twenty-three Basics fully illustrated.

The Sets in Order Hall was busy. The editorial offices took up some of the space, and a large area had to be left open for dancing. The Record Square carried a larger inventory of records and books. We also developed the "Corner of the Square" for retail products. That line started off small: belts and belt buckles, ties, ceramic figurines, graduation diplomas, and the like. Then we devoted part of the space for our advertisers to display their items. We did not sell them on site, they were mail order only, but dancers could come in to see what the products looked like. So we had several lines of square dance dresses and shoes, men's shirts and slacks, not to mention boots.

Sometime around 1955 an inspired flash crossed the orbit of the business division of Sets in Order. "Why couldn't we," said they, "reward the initiative, energy, determination and interest of people who sell Sets in Order subscriptions by offering some nice gifts for this selling?" They cast about for gift ideas and came up with some beauties, among them a shining 50-cup coffee maker that would be really useful to any club or class.

Very carefully the Premium Plan was set up after hashing and rehashing, thinking on and discarding many different ideas concerning it. It had to operate smoothly; be handled accurately both by the agents and our office and offer as little chance for "goofs" on either side as possible.

Once a workable plan was adopted, the next thing was to tell the story in the magazine and see what happened. What happened? It was a deluge. Queries flooded in from all over the United States and Canada and soon agents were "beavering" diligently to earn their coffee pots. Or their electro-voice mikes or badges for their clubs or books or decals. The way the idea was picked up was startling and gratifying.

First club of all to win a Premium, in this case a coffee maker, was the Merry Go Rounds of Kalispell, Montana, with Millie Christiansen as the spark-plug. The Premium was sent out in May, 1955, and was enjoyed, not only by this club but by other clubs to which it has been loaned on occasion. Since that time several dozens of these popular Premiums have whisked their way to diligent clubs. Some have even earned two and three of them.

Not everyone was thrilled at the success of Sets in Order and the Record Square. They were even less thrilled with our publication of lists of dances and Basics. We tried to cool down some of the criticism by defining "amateur," "professional," and "commercial." Still some people saw us as in the square dance business just to make money at the expense of square dancing. In May 1954, in my "As I See It" column I tried to explain what we were doing.

From 1948 until the late 1960's Sets in Order stayed pretty much the same. The magazine underwent some changes in format and content, for example, we started a center section for those who wanted a larger selection of choreography. We called it "The Workshop" and it was part of the special caller's edition of the magazine. It cost callers an extra few cents per month to get this supplement. The selection of items at the Record Square changed some, but most to meet changing tastes.

As I said before, we built a staff starting in 1949 and they stayed with us through the mid-1960s, but there were some other changes worth noting. From the first issue through 1951 the masthead showed that I was the editor in conjunction with Western Square Dance Association and Associated Square Dancers. That changed in 1952 when I became the sole owner as well as editor. Jay Orem was listed as business manager.

During that time we had extended our reach to selling records, clothing, square dance memorabilia, and more. We had also started the Vacation Institutes at Asilomar, and it seemed that we would get more and more involved. Being the sole owner of the magazine with a subsidiary foundation left me vulnerable to legal action. In 1954 we changed the legal set up so that "Sets in Order," a corporation, was the owner while I was listed as publisher, editor and managing editor, and the business manager was still Jay Orem. I was the sole stockholder in the corporation (that changed when we sold a handful of shares to Chuck Jones, though he was never listed as a shareholder). As time went on the government wanted more information published in the annual statement, so not only owner, publisher, business manager, but also post office and average circulation. In 1960 we distributed 17,000 copies; by 1964 circulation had increased to just a bit over 23,000 copies per month.

In March 1967, we bid farewell to Jay Orem. There is nothing more comfortable or more difficult to learn to do without than a pair of old shoes or a business colleague of many years. In no way would we refer to Jay Orem as an old shoe, except for the simile that working with him has been a pure comfort and a rich and rewarding experience for almost 19 years. In his resigning from Sets in Order to go into a business operation of his own, we had the feeling that we were losing a strong right arm. Jay had endeared himself to many members of the square dance family in all parts of the world, in Canada, and in the United States. He had been instrumental in bringing various elements of the square dance recording activity into a closer alliance with each other. It was with his assistance as business manager of Sets in Order

163

that we have grown from a small idea to an important position in the square dance world. Jay went on to found Scope records, and took with him some of our favorite recording callers.

Helen Orem, too, cut down on her responsibilities although she continued to be a link in Sets in Order activities. Readers noticed her fine hand in the writing department of the various features and special research articles which have benefited so much from her enthusiasm and knowledge of the activity over the years.

[The other major change in this period was my divorce from Ginger and marriage to Becky. This story will be told in more detail later on.]

At the time Sets in Order started a full scale war against drop-offs and started working on a dozen or so projects I had in mind to help improve and strengthen the magazine. We believed that the square dance recording field was adequately covered by quite a number of outstanding recording companies. For the time being, at least, we put all our recording efforts into educational square dance recordings. Along that line we developed the new series of school teaching records with the help of Bob Ruff and Jack Murtha.

In May 1969, I initiated the big change in Sets in Order. I sent out a long letter to the staff explaining the direction I wanted to take and why. For the previous two years Sets in Order had turned out more constructive ideas for square dancing than it had in its 21-year history. We had established the Gold Ribbon Committee and published its report on the status of square dancing. We could point to that report, the hand-book on One Night Stands, the manual for the Basic Program, and more to show that our place in the square dance community was well established – not just as a magazine but as an important facet in the direction and stimulation of the activity as a whole. In spite of all of this, our circulation had remained status quo flat for the past four or five years. Somehow we had to find a way to maintain our current subscribers and attract new readers.

I felt that what we were doing contributed to a worthwhile project, and therefore our circulation should be increasing, not standing still. We needed to find a way to perpetuate our activities and ideals into the future. At that time the magazine and its content rested on the efforts of a relatively few individuals, and the editorial policy was entirely up to me. I was obligated to catch the pulse of square dancing and reflect it in all we did.

But we were not looking to the future of the company and its beliefs. If I were to retire, for whatever reason, Becky and one or two others might have been qualified to carry on for a bit. However, we needed a tangible plan. Becky and I thought of a complete retirement from this activity in five years to coincide with the time that our daughter Wendy would have completed her college education. At that time, we thought that the ideal situation would be to turn over the entire organization to an individual or group of individuals, confident that it would be perpetuated.

In 1955 we had formed a Sets in Order Foundation with the prime purpose of establishing the Silver Spur Award to be given for meritorious unselfish service to this activity, square dancing. What we proposed was to enlarge the activities of this Foundation, to invite and encourage involvement and participation by inviting membership. In a way similar to the National Geographic Society, the Sets in Order "organization" would not be selling subscriptions to a magazine. It would be offering memberships, and a benefit of membership was a one-year subscription to Sets in Order, as well as other privileges.

We had been accused of wanting to take over square dancing by calling Sets in Order "the official magazine of square dancing." We hoped that setting up the new organization as a "service organization" would lift the "commercial" stigma, thereby making our projects more effective.

For three days Becky, Marvin, and I manned a booth at the National Square Dance Convention in Seattle where 13,000 dancers attended. We were thrilled to see so many subscribers to the magazine; many of these people stopped by to say that the work of The Gold Ribbon Committee was just what the activity needed. Many indicated that the stand on leadership taken by Sets in Order was one of the most important happenings in the square dance world. We were somewhat overwhelmed by the recognition that Sets in Order received over local television and in most of the key spots during the 3-day meeting. If ever we needed our "batteries charged" that was indeed the time and place.

Since establishing the magazine, Sets in Order had been involved in far more than simply publishing a magazine. Asilomar Institutes with courses in Leadership for callers, two university leadership conferences for callers and teachers, a series of school-teaching records that were being very well received, the first in a series of four caller/teacher manuals, a motion picture on square dancing that has been circulated throughout the world, a series of almost a dozen specialized handbooks on various phases of square dancing were a few of the great number of additional responsibilities we had undertaken. I felt that some of the effectiveness of these activities was jeopardized by being sponsored by a magazine. We needed to find a way to increase the positive view of Sets in Order. We also had to consider just the economics of the situation: increase in printing costs, increase in postage, increase in salaries for staff, etc.

Perhaps we were being a bit cynical, but there was a lot to be said for "snob-appeal": people all over the country were joining organizations, charitable groups, fraternal organizations, and so forth, just to feel they were "closer to the action." We could change to a membership without having to change much of what we were doing.

People who joined the Sets in Order "organization," would receive the magazine as a benefit. We also set to work on additional benefits such as a membership card, eligibility for group charter travel to many spots in the world, group insurance, participation in leadership training and possible seminars and conventions, or opportunity to purchase Sets in Order textbooks at pre-publication prices, or an opportunity to receive Sets in Order yearly premium records for a cost and handling fee (perhaps $1.00), etc.

There were many details we had to work out, but most of the changes seemed to be of great value. One change was going to a calendar year membership, so all dues were paid at the same time – we no longer had to keep track of due dates on subscriptions. We made that date at the height of square dance season so more people would be sure to keep their membership up to date. The two issues of the magazine before the renewal date contained the most interesting and colorful articles to inspire interest.

Over time the task of putting out a monthly publication had become more and more complex. We found that we were spending many hours each week in answering questions from dancers, callers, and teachers from all over the world. We were writing and publishing books and collections of calls, conducting callers' courses, setting up institutes, organizing University Leadership Conferences, advising, helping, directing — in short, we were swept into the mainstream and we found that we had become in fact a nerve center of American Square Dancing.

Whatever the circumstances, we looked upon all of this as both a challenge and a responsibility. For Sets in Order this had never been less than a total involvement program utilizing the efforts of virtually every leader in square dancing at one time or another. The opinions expressed had never been just ours alone, but had been composite ideas felt by many and expressed editorially in the pages of Sets in Order; for example, The Gold Ribbon Report had involved fifty square dance leaders for more than three years. It had been our belief that the unselfish contributions of ideas and directions of many individuals can do much to lead this activity intelligently.

We changed our facade from that of a magazine to a service society so that we were in a better position to accomplish these goals. The end result of all this was a society dedicated to American Square Dancing. We invited people to become "a part of the action," a "member of the family," so that what we did became a part of the dancer's world of square dancing.

We tried to lay the groundwork for a continuing service society. To plan successful programs was of great importance, but to be assured that such work would be perpetuated in the future was just as vital. So, along with all the other reasons for the formation of The Society, the part about making it a permanent part of the square dance scene had been put in place.

Nineteen-seventy was perhaps our most important year. First of all, we had assembled a group of our friends here at home (where we could meet with them frequently), to serve as *pro tem* members of a steering committee to help formulate plans for the future of The Society. In October 1969, shortly before the announcement went out to the public in the November issue, we wrote up a progress report on each of the committees to give everyone a chance to see what Sets in Order the American Square Dance Society wanted to accomplish. The report was addressed to the committee members:

Thank you all for agreeing to take a look, as pro tem members, at the first task force groups we have set up for The Society. Undoubtedly, there will be additional projects later on, but, this is a beginning.

- *Achievement Recognition: Of all the projects we've tackled over the years the ones that have allowed us the opportunity of "saluting" deserving individuals for the part they are playing in the activity have given us the greatest pleasure. Being able to spotlight a "Caller of the Month," a round dance couple and a feature caller in the magazine has probably been the only national recognition some of these people have ever received. The Silver Spur award has paid tribute to a few outstanding individuals over the years. A "Square Dance Hall of Fame" has been set up and we should consider some ground rules for its continuation. Perhaps there are other ways to encourage and honor deserving individuals and this is the purpose of this particular module. (Pro tem chairman: Joe Fadler.)*

- *Caller Leadership Training: Perhaps, in this section lies our greatest urgency. The fact that many of our callers today are neither leaders nor teachers. The attitudes possessed by some of our well established and proven caller/leaders is quite frequently not passed on to young callers just entering the field. We are in an excellent position to help establish an "academy", to encourage a convention of just the professional portion of this activity and possibly discover some way to bring the recognized top leadership closer together so that it is in a position to help direct leadership training in the future. (Pro tem chairman: Arnie Kronenberger.)*

- *Finances: Even if our needs are fairly uncomplicated to begin with, we are going to have some expenses and we are immediately setting aside a small percentage from each membership in The Society to help with scholarships and various other expenses that may be incurred. We will also look toward future budgets that will tie in with the plans of the various modules. (Pro tem chairman: Ralph Hartley.)*

- *Magazine Coordination: Since the publication is now a part of the society instead of being the sole entity, it is important that a program be established that will relate the monthly editions to the activities of The Society as a whole. (Pro tem chairman: Helen Orem.)*

- *Membership: Just how to go about reaching the square dance public with the new Society is the purpose of this particular module. If the various projects can be of service to a few, they can certainly be of equal service to many others. To be effective, we need to find a way to reach more members. (Pro tem chairman: Ray Jensen.)*

- *Motion Picture(s): There is a need for a public relations film establishing American Square Dancing in all its color and appeal as The Great American Dance. Prints of this, used by square dance associations throughout the country, can help to answer many questions brought up by non-dancers. In some areas square dancing is still a "dirty word" and the right story line with a well-produced professional film could be a great help. At the same time, there is the need of an educational film that can be used in schools along with our training records. This film could also be used by caller/teachers during the new dancer's learning period. A byproduct of this phase would be a series of short 30 second and minute announcements that can be used in different areas as television "spots". We are also in the position where we are asked to advise other groups making films or organizing exhibitions of square dancing and we should have good answers for all of them. (Pro tem chairman: Leif Hetland.)*

- *Round Dance Projection: Following the Gold Ribbon Report on round dancing we have had quite a lot of "feedback" and recognize that there is a need for a study of round dancing in the square dance picture today. We hope to update our present round dance "tools" and see if we can determine what help is needed and what we can do to put this particular segment into focus. (Pro tem chairman: June Berlin.)*

- *Scholarships: A few callers' courses exist today, but it is appalling sometimes to realize how few avail themselves of such outstanding caller coaches as Ed Gilmore, Lee Helsel, Bob Van Antwerp, Earl Johnston and others. If we might assume that the reason for this apparent apathy might be lack of personal finances, then perhaps we are in a position to assist by making a few scholarships available. Perhaps this section can also cover the needs felt in various areas of the world where no callers exist at the present time and where we might be able to make it possible for a caller or teacher to travel to an area and be of service. One present challenging project would be to bring a young Japanese caller, who is doing an excellent job in his country, over to the United States where he can attend a course for callers. This segment will endeavor to study these possibilities. (Pro tem chairman: Elizabeth Jensen.)*

- *Special: If ever there were a "catch-all-eight" division in our little endeavor, this would be it. We know we are speaking in broad generalities with all of these sections, but we have to start somewhere. Among the many things we do at present and plan to*

171

continue in the future is to produce guides and direc-
tories, traveling callers lists, etc. There is a museum,
as a matter of fact, there are a number of museums
of square dancing started throughout the country.
There are some needs that will eventually be placed
into other categories, but they can be placed here
temporarily for initial study. (Pro tem chairman:
Milt Zabaro.)

- *Square Dancing in The Schools: While it is not a sim-*
  ple matter to look past the commercial implications
  of supplying the needs for better square dance pro-
  grams in the schools, we should look closely at what
  is being done across the country and determine how
  we can, not only supply more "tools", but help other
  groups doing similar work. (Pro tem co-chairmen:
  Bob Ruff and Jack Murtha.)
- *Textbook for Callers: There are literally dozens of*
  books on the subject of calling but none are directed
  to the brand new caller who needs to know, first of
  all, that "one plus one equals two" before he tackles
  advanced calculus. This is one phase in our program
  that is now under way, and the first chapter of the
  new book will appear in the January issue. (Pro tem
  chairman: John Kaltenthaler.)

January 1970 the first issue of SQUARE DANCING,
the Official Magazine of the Sets in Order American Square
Dance Society rolled of the presses.

Publication of the magazine rolled on smoothly for
several more years. When CALLERLAB was established we
used Square Dancing Magazine to inform dancers and to
promote square dancing. Much of the story from here is
wrapped up in my involvement in CALLERLAB.

Chapter 8. Chuck Jones

In the late 1990s Becky and I joined 17,000 other folks at the Hollywood Bowl for a tribute to a great film director and a good friend. There was a huge movie screen suspended high above the stage of the Bowl over the full Los Angeles Philharmonic Orchestra. As our friend's best movies were projected, the Orchestra played the musical background and a sound effects man filled in the various noises. The first half of the program featured about eight of his films, as did the second half. In the middle, Chuck Jones, the director of many animated films featuring Bugs Bunny, Porky Pig, Elmer Fudd, and more, came on stage and entertained the crowd as he had done numerous times for the Rip 'n' Snort square dance club.

In the late 1940s, Chuck and his wife Dorothy discovered square dancing, and he became an avid supporter. But before we knew Chuck, he had already had an illustrious career in film. His career had a modest start in 1931 as a cel-washer at the studio of noted animator Ub Iwerks. A cel-washer was the person who literally washed the transparent sheets of celluloid used in cartooning so that they could be used over again on the next cartoon. After all, those cels cost about seven cents apiece in those days. No longer are cels just disposed of or recycled because cels by well-known animators now sell for four figure prices.

Chuck moved to Warner Bros, where he slaved (except for a one-year stint at Disney) until the studio's cartoon division was closed in 1962. The atmosphere at what the animators dubbed "Termite Terrace" was strictly free-form, and the cartoonists worked in small groups uninterrupted by management - as long as their cartoons continued to make money.

This was the perfect creative environment, but it also stimulated the naturally mischievous nature of the employees. One time the wacky animators decided that their latest creation needed a special voice to set him apart from the other characters. So  they copied the distinctive lisp of their supervisor, Leon Schlesinger. The animators, realizing that their boss would be the first person to screen the new cartoon wrote out their resignations in advance and stood in the back of the screening room waiting to turn them in. But their boss laughed uncontrollably throughout the cartoon and never noticed the voice had a familiar ring. The resignation letters were quickly and quietly torn up.

The cartoons created at the Termite Terrace were distributed by Warner Bros. The animators never cared for the two brothers, Jack and Harry Warner, who ran the studio, and the feeling was mutual. The animators believed that Harry Warner, in particular, couldn't have cared less about his own cartoon division. One of the team of animators who was fond of relating Harry Warner stories told this story over and over again and swore that it was true: Harry Warner always thought that Mickey Mouse was one of Warner Bros. cartoon characters, and the day he found out that Mickey was a Disney creation, he closed down the animation studio.

Warner Brothers did not know that their animators were the creators of some of the most popular cartoon characters ever. In 2002 TV Guide did a survey to discover the top toon characters of all time. Seven of the top fifty belonged to Warner Bros., and more specifically, Chuck Jones. The Merrie Melodies/Looney Tunes folk inherited the stock characters of Bugs Bunny, Porky Pig, and Daffy Duck (whose voice was based on Jones's boss's voice at the Termite Terrace), but Jones defined the characters and never broke the rules of those characters.

Jones understood the heart of all great comedy was the controlling power of character to locate disaster, on screen as in life. Whether we pity misfortune or laugh hysterically at it depends upon its source. If it strikes from without as bad luck, we pity its victims and fear its randomness.

 But if it grows from within the certainties of character, we suspend compassion and laugh at the beauty of its logic, knowing that we are safe from its pain. An article in the *Wall Street Journal* entitled "The Existential Dilemma of the Coyote" claimed that Wile E. Coyote was a tragic character (note the depths of *Angst* in those sorrowful eyes!). The author of the article saw Wile E. as Sisyphus, the Texans at the Alamo, and Cool Hand Luke all rolled up in one. Another author said. "In nature's humorless order, a coyote chases a road runner to eat, not to kill. But it is the repeated failure of this Coyote to catch his prey that brings out the human in him. As the redemption of his honor surpasses his need for food, he not only becomes human. He becomes a fanatic one - a fanatic being one who redoubles his effort once he has forgotten his aim." Warner cartoons have endured because they are characters in search of action, not action in search of character. The laws of physics may be negotiable, but never the laws of character.

Mr. Jones's understanding of his animals followed from his understanding of people, and therein lies the difference between a cartoonist and a literary figure. Daffy Duck, for example, made his debut in 1937, not as a knock off of Disney's Donald Duck, but as the screen proxy of Mr.

Jones's boss, Leon Schlesinger, whose company supplied all the early Merrie Melodies and Looney Tunes characters for Warner Bros.

The *Wall Street Journal* article continues: "Warner cartoons radiate intelligence, sophistication and a bracing absence of sentimentality. If Disney's appeal aims at the inner child in every adult, Mr. Jones knows there's an inner adult in every child. He goes for that, which explains why one never outgrows his work. A poll of 1,000 animators and producers once named the 50 greatest cartoons, and four of the top five were Chuck Jones films. And in a recent appreciation called "Chuck Jones: A Flurry of Drawings" (University of California Press) critic Hugh Kenner, whose 25 other books have dealt with such literary as James Joyce and Ezra Pound, wrote that no single figure in animation 'had so literary a conception of character as Chuck Jones.'"

He told me that he's felt like the luckiest man on Earth because people paid him to draw.

Characters upon whom Mr. Jones has set his stamp include Bugs Bunny, Pepe Le Pew, Marvin Martian, Henery Hawk, Elmer Fudd, and Michigan Jay Frog, the singing siren of greed whose appearance in "One Froggy Evening (1955) has been twice canonized: first as one of those five greatest cartoons ever created, and more recently as the logo of the new WB television venture. He also won three Oscars for his films. He produced and animated "How the Grinch Stole Christmas," "The Dot and the Line," and the "Phantom Tollbooth." During World War II he was part of a department the Army created to produce training films. Working with Ted Geisel (Dr. Seuss), Chuck created Private SNAFU – the ultimate klutz of a soldier. Many episodes of

Private SNAFU were created, but the war ended before they were released. We may not know about the films, but the name of the private went into ordinary speech.

In its prime the old Warner Bros. cartoon unit of the '40s and '50s was so taken for granted it didn't even rate decent office space on the Burbank lot. Today it has become the cornerstone of a burgeoning Warner retail empire that is mining coin from Fifth Avenue to Beverly Boulevard. Forget Cagney, Bogart and *Casablanca*. It's 10-foot statues of Daffy Duck and Sylvester that welcome customers at the Old Orchard store near Chicago.

"All art is working under the deprivation of freedom," Mr. Jones told a newspaper reporter. "Running in all directions is not art. Art is choice, not chance. The more restriction there is, the more possibility there exists for creativity and ingenuity. Character is the most severe restriction. Every great comedian obeys rules consistent with his comic persona." Mr. Jones himself adheres to one basic principle in all his work. There is both pleasure and instruction in watching animals behave like people.

Chuck's understanding of human nature and his ability to portray it through cartoons attracted the attention of *Psychology Today* magazine for which he did a joint interview with his good friend Ray Bradbury. The subject, of course, was fantasy.

Chuck explained that "You must build an entire world that is believable. Everything about this world must ring true, and the facts of the imagination must become as acceptable as the facts of reality."

Fantasy and poetry are horribly underestimated by people who don't realize that the toughest, the hardest thing in the world to write is poetry. And the second toughest is fantasy. People think there is one set of rules for every form of literature and another set for fantasy, and that's where most mistakes in analyzation are made. The rules are exactly the same. You make sure that both intuitive and sensual logic are involved, not just intellectual logic. We believe only that which is proved artistically.

The animator is lucky. He is the only artist who actually creates life. He must give the absolute illusion of reality to something no one has ever seen before. He deals with the utterly impossible. That means no cutting corners. Chuck told the story of when his daughter was little. "She told me that Terrytoons were 'the ones where the water disappears.' I checked to find what she meant. When water was spilled or a wave washed into the shore in those cartoons, the water would disappear. It didn't remain because it was cheaper to film by having it disintegrate. That shattered the reality of believable fantasy. All my daughter remembered about those cartoons was that the water disappeared." There must be a wedding - or at least a liaison - between the logic of reality and the logic of your fantasy.

Chuck told us what he believed: there are only two things that matter in life - work and love. And only the love should show. That line about love was a constant in Chuck's life as we will see later.

Much of what Chuck has been recognized for happened before we met Chuck in 1948 when Chuck and his wife Dorothy joined the Rip 'n' Snort (RIPs) and soon became Presidents - the club managed somehow to lose the club's constitution so we had no way to get them out of office. We did know that in the years prior to and during the War he had created those marvelous characters and put them in cartoons – six minute shorts that everybody enjoyed.

We loved Chuck for his work in the movies, but even more Chuck and Dottie were square dancers who made our lives richer. RIP dances ended about 10:00 and then we had refreshments, and as long as Chuck and Dorothy were Presidents there was an after party. As part of his show, Chuck would draw creatures and tell captivating stories about them. I remember he did the one of the Red Breasted Fly Catcher that had caught his fly. Well, that didn't come out quite the way I wanted – but it was very funny. Eventually everyone in the club was involved in some skit or song.

Chuck and Dottie exuded love for life, and that love drew the club more and more into being a family. The following is a longish story, but it shows a lot about the effect the Joneses had on the RIPs.

Somewhere in here around the early 1950's my life began to change. Ginger, whom I had married during the war, and with whom I had a young daughter, Linda, and I decided to go different directions. She as a rising artist, and me as an enthusiastic square dancer, magazine editor, caller, etc., were divorced. Under the best of conditions, if there ever is a best condition in a situation like this, the world tends

to fall apart. My full time employment was now editing and publishing a square dance magazine, calling several times a week for classes and clubs, planning and managing several Asilomar vacation institutes each year, and finally in the midst of summer 1956, heading to places like Banff in Calgary, Canada, to direct their initial vacation square dance institute.

Up to this time, most of what I had done in square dancing was with Ginger. Now, even surrounded by square dance friends, it wasn't quite the same world. Getting through the week up in Canada was a challenge. Finally it came time to head home and the time for the blues. Then, Bob and Babs Ruff and their children, who were on the staff, offered to drive me to the airport in Calgary, and they stuck with me until I had boarded the plane. The first leg of the voyage home was to Vancouver. Getting off the plane, I knew I had to head for the airport waiting room and stick around for a couple of hours waiting for the next flight, when I suddenly found myself in the arms of Norma and Al Berry, who had come to keep me company while I waited. (Aren't square dancers great!)

It wasn't a long flight back to Los Angeles but I did have plenty of time to think about the relative loneliness awaiting me. There were distractions during the flight to lighten things. The plane not only was filled, but among its passengers was a basketball team from one of our local colleges, along with its rooting section and enthusiasts. The sounds of a happy basketball team, just coming off a successful game in Vancouver, led me to realize that not all was doom and gloom.

As the plane landed and taxied up to the gate area, I could hear what were obviously the fans of a collegiate welcoming ceremony prepared to greet their returning champions. Once the door was opened, the welcoming sounds became more intense. It took me a minute or two to gather my records and garment bag, and celebration sounds were still going strong when I got up. As I reached the cabin door, one of the stewardesses smiled and said, "Well, it wasn't for them. It must be for you."

Stepping out onto the portable ramp I began to look a bit more intently at the crowd who had gathered. Hey, there were the RIPs headed by Chuck and Dottie.

Good golly, it was midnight and the whole club was here to greet me. Suddenly, the desperate feeling of returning home alone disappeared and I was hustled off to one of the homes for a true Welcome Home Party!

As square dancing grew and as people began to know that he was a square dancer, from time to time Chuck was invited to talk to folks at some of the square dance conventions and festivals and things like that. He became a regular feature at a square dance festival in Laramie, Wyoming, and other locations. With his gained confidence on stage Chuck was a captivating speaker/entertainer/MC. His daughter Linda remembers that when she was young – six years old – her dad would come home from a long day at work and start to tell stories of what happened at work…"and can you guess what Daffy Duck did next…?" Chuck's life revolved around telling stories, but prior to square dancing, his story telling was in the studio, and his audience was the other animators.

In 1950 Chuck sub-mitted his first of what would be many columns about square danc-ing to SIO. It was called "A Car-toonist Takes a Look at Square Dancing," and in typical Jones style, he poked at some of the cen-tral foibles of square dancing, espe-cially among the women. Then, due to popular demand (started by his wife) Chuck followed up two months later with equally funny and biting satires of the men.

Remember that we had Frank Grundeen doing the back cover cartoons and some illustrations for articles in SIO. We also had Charles Dillinger, a superb graphic artist in his own right, who was also our printer from the first issue on. One day Chuck asked if he could do a cover for us. Imagine Chuck Jones *asking* if he could do a cover. I thought about it for a half second or so and said "Absolutely." His first cover art was of a deep sea diver, with helmet, weights, and air hose, dancing the varsouvienne with a Mermaid. Chuck did several more covers for us, and even got Warner Bros. to give us permission to print Bugs Bunny on the cover. In 1954 the cover of SIO featured Bugs cartoons in sequential months: in April Bugs is perky and packed to go the national in Dallas; in May Bugs is exhausted and disheveled heading home from Dallas.

Eventually Chuck said, "Would you like some of these things that I talk about at the after parties put into a column?" The outcome of that was, "Of course," and he began doing one every month…and they are funny, so if you get any back issues of the magazine going into the 50's dig them out and read the Chuck Jones parts. The columns ranged from the serious to the humorous to the outrageous. You can tell that while writing a column something went through Chuck's mind and he could not resist telling about it, with an illustration. Still Chuck kept to his description of what he was going to write about: the same type of stories he told at the RIPs after parties. For example, "Back in the old days before deodorants and things like that, they used to use a bag full of pine needles to sweeten the sheets because there was a shortage of soap powders and water and washing facilities they didn't wash the sheets as much as they used to so they used these sweeteners. As the beds got down to a smaller size they found out they didn't have to use a big bag of pine needles or potpourri or whatever they used. They finally came out with the Murphy bed, and the Murphy bed evolved into a portable bed which you could roll around on rollers. They found out that they could get away with a bag just about half the size, and this was the origin of the call 'Rollaway With a Half Sashay.'"

Another story Chuck did for a crowd of us that made its way into the pages of Sets in Order was the story of "Jerry Tates, who was an inventor that not everybody has heard of certainly; but, certainly, you folks have heard of him – but he was quite famous. He did a number of fantastic inventions, but the one he worked on so long was the compass. He had an idea for a compass that went like this. Take a look at a standard compass and see the marks for North and South. Well, he just mixed them. He just turned those two around and then on the East/West he traded those two and the in between things he changed them for the benefit of this theory that he had. Well, the thing didn't really go too well. Well, it became known pretty soon that 'he who has a Tates is lost.'"

Before and After National Square Dance Convention covers by Chuck Jones ©Warner Bros.

One night in 1957 we were in Beverly Hills at the home of Alan Reed. About half way through the evening a group came from the house across the alley. The group had just come from a wedding rehearsal. With them were the best man and the maid of honor. They had come over to share the news and we all got to meet each other. They square danced a couple of times, then the best man and the maid of honor asked where they could learn to square dance. We gave them the name of a caller and they started to take lessons but then the caller stopped. The lady's name was Becky Smith and I found out that she was a divorced young lady with a little girl five years old. Becky then joined a group that I was teaching. We had several dates and then I kind of decided if Becky would have me she would be a great one to be my wife and do some of these things with me.

Our Rip 'n' Snort square dance club was most friendly, so while I was dating Becky, I brought her to the club. She had not done much in the way of lessons, but the group said, "That's okay. We'll teach you." So one night for three hours, seven members of the club brought Becky up to the level which was moderate at that time for that club.

At this time the club was getting ready and had plans in the works for a trip to Hawaii. It was probably one of the early club trips we've taken together, and we had been planning this for a while. I might just indicate that our club president was Chuck Jones. One time, Chuck and Dotty and I were talking about things that the club might do that they had never done. We had done a lot of visitations in the area and we thought it would be possible to take

Great Hairy "No" Discouraging Tender Young "Yes"

the whole club with us somewhere and do something big. It would be more than just an overnight. We decided that what would be fun would be going to Hawaii on a cruise ship that went directly. We knew we would have quite a job of selling these people, then Chuck said, "Why don't we try what we do in the studio? When somebody has an idea for a cartoon the group of writers and producers sit around a table and they discuss what they've got. Everybody can give his idea, but nobody can say anything wrong with any of them. This is the period of the big YES. We'll all go away having a chance to think about it. Then we come back maybe a few days later, and we go over the thing again. If there are enough things in favor of the idea we'll do it. If it doesn't seem like a practical thing, we'll drop it. But in the period of the big YES nobody can have a negative opinion. It just does not work."

In the instance of our club, the members were gathered together and told that all were going to participate in a venture. D-Day for the event was some two years in the future, and for that reason no one should consider any reasons why he might not be able to take part. Instead, he should think immediately in terms of the possibility that this great event (which was about to be announced) would be something he could become personally involved in. This being understood by everyone, the bomb was dropped and the club members as a whole understood there was no question about it, each one was going to be a part of this club tour to Hawaii. Back in those days this was like announcing a proposed rocket tour of the moon, but members of the club took it in stride, and accepted the challenge. The "period of the big YES" was on. The whole trip was already planned when Becky and I were married and Becky became part of the club. (I often say the reason Becky married me was so she could go to Hawaii.)

Our club was divided into four geographic teams, with each unit given an assignment of things to do relative to the trip. Everybody in the club was given the opportunity to bank any money they wanted with the treasurer as a savings for this thing. We had 60 members in the club at that time, and all of them, even the ones who were sure they couldn't go, were planning on going and having the fun of planning the trip. Becky and I married and shortly afterward the whole club went on our honeymoon with us. Out of the club of sixty, fifty-three went, which was kind of amazing at that particular time.

We had square dances on the ship and I remember there was one night we had a square dance in the main lounge and we were doing round dances. It was a little bit rocky, but not bad enough to make anybody ill or anything. We were doing the dance "Blue Pacific Waltz." This is a dance where the man rolls the girl from his right side to his left side as he moves behind her to his right. Well, in that action, depending on which way the ship was rocking, it was very easy if you didn't grab quickly to lose the gal. And while she probably wouldn't go off the ship, she could go clear across the room. We had no casualties but we did have fun. When the pilot boat came out before we were docked, square dancers came out with leis for everybody on the ship. As far as I know, no other groups were doing these things. So this trip was another "first" experience and it was wonderful. While we were in Hawaii we did have one dance that we put on for all the Hawaiians, and then they put on a dance for us at the YMCA. So, it was just one more experience that was a first and absolutely great.

Since then our club has found that the "period of the big yes" works wonders, and we've noticed other clubs approaching similar "moments of truth" with a positive attitude.

The trip went so well, that after we wrote it up in Sets in Order we were buried in requests from people who wanted to join the next tour. It looked like Becky and I were going to be travel agents. RIPs and Sets in Order hosted several trips to various places around the world.

Unfortunately, Chuck and Dottie could not join us on one of the planned trips. Close friends of the Joneses who had traveled with them on the other trips sadly told us that we would just have to give up on Joneses joining us. This was the time when television was going full blast and utilizing all the animation shorts that could be developed. This, of course, involved Chuck and Dottie.

But, when it came to the day of our departure, all 90 of us gathered at the Los Angeles Airport and there were Chuck and Dottie at the boarding entrance, shaking hands, and kissing each person as they left. A few tears, of course.

Finally, as the last of our co-travelers had boarded, Chuck announced to the few that were left that he and Dottie had permission to get on the plane to see us off one last time. Unusual, but not unlike something the Joneses would do. Walking up and down the center aisle and saying good-bye, somebody hollered out, "Chuck, you and Dottie better get off. They're beginning to close the doors." At that point, one of the stewardesses came up to them and said, "You better sit down, and get strapped in before we take off." It was only then, when the plane began to taxi, ready for take-off, that the group got wise. Chuck and Dottie had already checked in their luggage and had made plans to be with us. Of course, Becky and I had to be in on it. But, it did add to the fun and success of the entire venture.

Although Chuck and Dottie joined us in only that one overseas trip, their hand was very visible in other tours. At one time they headed a group to see us off and just as we were boarding the aircraft handed us a 10-gallon container of ice cream. (I have no recollection of what we did with it.) And, on another occasion, they made a presentation just as we were boarding the plane of a watermelon.

With what Chuck had done with RIPs and his column in Sets in Order he was in demand nationwide as an MC. Then in 1958 Pappy Shaw had passed away, just months before 'Pappy' and Dorothy Shaw were to present a cavalcade of square dancing at the National Square Dance Convention in Denver. It never occurred to Dorothy to cancel the show, but she did immediately contact Chuck to help out. Over the years the Shaws and the Joneses had become quite close. Chuck wrote in a letter remembering back on his experiences as a dancer: "The greatest dancing figure of all could not dance at all, but I remember sitting at Pappy Shaw's useless feet at Cheyenne Mountain School (the Sistine Chapel of western dancing) in Colorado Springs and hearing him dance with words like music, and the lovely loving eyes of Dorothy endorsing his gallantry."

The participants in the cavalcade came from all over the country, and each group had a section of square dance history they had prepared. They never saw or rehearsed with the other troops until the morning of the show. Meanwhile, though, Chuck and Dorothy worked together to create a script for the whole extravaganza. At the end of the rehearsal Chuck spoke to all of the dancers. "We have not rehearsed this together, but I know that all of you have put in a lot of work and love into this. In the end, let only the love show."

Chuck became the voice of the dancer. He had a unique way of looking at square dancing that gave everyone a new perspective. Perhaps I should end this chapter with Chuck's love song to square dancing.

Is Square Dancing Coming of Age?
By Chuck Jones

I can remember the last time I fell In love.

I can remember that I married the girl I fell in love with. But I cannot remember why I fell in love, nor can I conjure up the feeling, the emotions that arouse young love. I do know this, they are not the same reasons that I love that girl now. I have, over these twenty-two years, climbed a long ladder of experience and I now love her for what I know her to be - not what I suppose her to be, or what I expect her to be.

I think this may be the difference between adolescence and maturity. An adolescent loves what he dreams, an adult loves what he knows. I  *can remember a little more clearly the hot rush of my first love for square dancing. Callers were God-like creatures, experienced dancers had omniscience far beyond the realm of mere human beings; the grace of their movements, their easy familiarity with the strange garments, billowing petticoats, teetering boots. I moved in a happy haze, unreal and delightful, satisfied that I had found a way of life, almost a religion. Square Dancing! I looked with pitying contempt on my earth-bound friends, with the surprise of a religious convert for the ignorant masses.*

The reason why Dottie and I are still dancing eight years later, is because we still love dancing, but for different reasons than those given above. I believe that today we are adult square dancers. We love it now not for what we hope it to be, or require it to be, but for what we know it to be: a happy adult recreation. We love it, because like books, or music, or art, or just conversation, it increases our knowledge of mankind and of each other. It develops our tolerance and our understanding and broadens our horizons immeasurably. We know its faults to be the simple history of all human frailties and that we are a part of that history. We like square dancing because the people in it are fun and we are happier when we are with them.

How does the square dance picture look to me today? It looks healthy. Why?

Because the attitude of those in it is healthy. I think most of us have long since found what square dancing can do for us; we are now concerned with what we can do for square dancing.

Chapter 9. Square Dance Music and Records

"Say there, Sonny, you may call that thar stuf you're doing square dancing, but it shor ain't the way we used to do it back in the good old days."

The little man who has sidled up beside you at the Square Dance looks as though he knows what he's talking about. The "Old Days" probably take us back to the time when our grandmother and grandfather were a courtin' before movies, television, radio, and the automobile when the biggest entertainment was square dancing.

No, sir. Square dancing isn't just like it used to be. Gone for the most part are the leather-lunged, blood and thunder yellers of yesteryear who, sans microphone and public address systems, hollered in sometimes unintelligible screams to be heard over the roar of the crowd. The dance figures were different too. The advent of modern travel has inter-mixed the dance styles from different portions of the country until western calls are just as common in Vermont and Maine as some of the eastern "singing calls" which in turn, have left their influential mark of the dances of the west.

With hundreds and perhaps thousands of up-to-date phonograph records from which to select our square dancing accompaniment, it's difficult to imagine a time and place where there might not have been any square dance music available as we might know it. For example, could you imagine a square dance activity surviving where there were not only no records available but no musicians? In one part of New England square dancing was kept alive for many years with just the accompaniment of men, humming. That's right - just the music made by humming voices. Feet could move to the sound, and callers could call and folks enjoyed themselves.

It's all told in a little book we received a while back called "I Hear Ringing Reels." It isn't a large book but in its 15 selections are invaluable bits of true Americana written by William Dudley Laufman, a man who loves New England and loves square dancing. Here's the little prose song that tells about the lilting or humming form of accompaniment.

MOUTH MUSIC

Lived on a farm he did, up Cape Breton way,
back from the sea a bit, but with tide.
Said they dragged the river bottom each
spring to bring up the sludge you know
for to spread on the fields.
Did you know Don Messer the fiddler, I says.
O sure says he, and many's the time I
tuned up a dance too. Tuned up a dance,
says I, what do you mean by that? You
went around and tuned up the fiddles?
O hell no he says, I tuned up the dance.
We hummed the tunes don't ye know, mouth
music we called it, some call it lilting; our
fiddlers were in Germany or at sea for the fish.
Well, I says, how would you tune up a dance?
Do one for me now like you was up north.
Here's Miss McLeods Reel for ye. Deedle di
de didle di dum deedle dum; see now how it
goes. We used to dance out on the weather
gray wharf in the salty inlet, spruces by
the rock shore and gulls above wheeling
and mewing. Four old men with white beards
sat in the first row, they were the first
rate tuners. (One of them always held my
sister on his knee.) We younger chaps stood

in the second row, being second raters, and
suntanned fishermen with their wives and
girls danced and tapped on the smooth boards
above the salt tide.
O we made those folks dance, I'll tell ye,
there's a power of music in the tongue,
makes toes itch.
*I Hear Ringing Reels And Other Prosesongs and
Verse, by Dudley Laufman

If you're trying to find just how much old time element remains in the dance, however, you'd see that many things haven't changed. I think the greatest hangovers from the good old days are fiddle tunes synonymous with square and round dancing. The technique of the creaky sawing out the necessary rhythm could remind the old-timer of his early days.

"Mississippi Sawyer," "Uncle Joe," "Climbing up the Golden Stairs," "Golden Slippers," "Flop Eared Mule" are just a few of the better known tunes that every orchestra nowadays has on its "must" list. More important than the tune, however, are technique and rhythm of the dance. So different from the conventional piano or violin tunes, the cadence of the orchestra can make or break an evening and perhaps one single all important necessity for a successful square dance is the choice of the right music.

Not all groups are fortunate enough to be able to afford the live music and, even if they had the necessary means, chances are they would run into the same difficulty many entertainments are finding today – the lack of good square dance musicians.

Some callers have taken it upon themselves to train musicians, while some of the better musicians themselves have taken under their wing novices who wish to take their chances in this sudden boom.

One caller, interested in training two new musicians who had much promise, found his duet unable to read music. Solving this problem by means of a wire recorder, he travelled throughout various parts of California, Arizona, New Mexico and Colorado, adding a hoedown here, fiddle solo there, a varsouvianna and an occasional waltz or schottische tune so typical of that particular area. Bringing the tape back and playing it before his musicians, he soon added a large sized library to his musical menu.

Back in the early days of this present 'rise' of square dancing, a neophyte caller was faced with a very limited number of recorded danceable square dance tunes. Especially for the western square dance caller the task was difficult because the few records that had been issued in the East had a much slower tempo. As recently as four or five years ago a caller could call for an entire dance using two, perhaps three, recorded square dance tunes during the entire three hour period.

Today, however, the picture is considerably changed. More than a dozen recording companies, including the top name companies, have pressed into wax some of the nation's most outstanding square dance tunes. Today a caller has a choice of many varieties of square dance albums without calls. Over the years several companies have released complete albums of the more popular singing calls and other companies have travelled out into the field to find the best orchestras to record them in the time and tempo that the people who are square dancers expect and demand.

Frank Harper, who played on a number of our records, and for us at our club dances, played with a number of bands, and he always managed to smile as he played, giving the impression that he was having the time of his life - which he probably was. I always remember Art Dickies, who switched between fiddle and mandolin. He would invariably bring me a package of homemade sausage every time we worked together. And, then there was Jack Barbour, certainly one of the most popular and prolific square dance band leaders. Jack had a phenomenal fiddler, who loved to rattle caller Arnie Kronenberger by alternating "Tico, Tico!" with "Stars and Stripes Forever" insisting that these were true hoedown tunes. An unbeatable combination was Lounette Brazell on the piano, Clyde Lindsey on fiddle, and Jack Hawes on banjo. They appeared on a number of our SIO records. A few other bands were in constant use in our area, but with hundreds of classes and clubs entering the picture, the demand was far greater than the available groups. Imperial and a few other record companies primarily producing folk dance recordings came to the rescue in the late 1940's. Carl Myles and Bill Mooney came into the picture as some of the first "usable" callers to record.

There are certainly points to be made for each side - live music or recorded for square dance accompaniment. The big advantage of recorded music is the wide selection of music that is available on one form of recording or another. In listening to the past 50 years of records, not only do the size of the musical groups change, but the arrangements and the instrumentation allows the caller just about any variety he's looking for. Lloyd Shaw in his tours with the Cheyenne Mountain Dancers got just the sound he wanted from a single piano. "Teach," his lady at the keyboards for many years, played for us at the summer sessions in Colorado Springs. Here in Southern California there seemed to be an unlimited number of bands, the majority ranging from two to four or five pieces. It seemed to me that the majority utilized a piano, fiddles, guitars, mandolins, drums - you name it, somewhere at some time most every combination imaginable came into the picture. In contrast to the single piano was our experience of calling to the 96-piece Holly-wood Bowl orchestra.

It always amazed me that I could go in to call a dance with a band that I had never previously worked with, and find them able to adjust to anything I needed, whether sing-ing call or patter. One exception to this was the feature spot calling for the Nebraska yearly festival at the Aksarben (Ne-braska spelled backwards) Auditorium. Contracted to arrive in Nebraska a day early, a couple of hours was spent together with the members of the band going over the music. This is one calling assignment where the hosting group made up the program based on what they wanted and liked and having little or nothing to do with the caller's personal desires. I had been sent the program and before arriving at the rehearsal I had the program down pretty well. It was when I met Mary, leader of the group and the pianist, that I found out that one of the numbers which I felt I could handle had been replaced by a popular singing call - just out - and I'd never called it. Surprise!

These Nebraska festivals occurred on two nights. The first caller, in this case Bob Ruff, called on Friday night. And it was my turn on Saturday, with the governor of the state present to handle the microphone. The rehearsal did lit-tle to restore my confidence in the newly added singing call. (I was what you call a slow learn). At any rate, Bob Ruff who had finished his chores the night before and was scheduled to do a guest tip on Saturday night with me, realizing the problem, stood with his head just six or eight inches behind my ear. The 100 squares of dancers couldn't hear him. But, if ever there was an Edgar Bergen/Charlie McCarthy act on a square dance stage, this was it. Bob managed to cue just a beat or two ahead and I fortunately got through the evening in good shape.

Early in the game during the big boom period of square dancing in the late 1940s and early 1950s, it soon became apparent that we were running out of live musicians who could accompany our dances. A solution came in the form of square dancers making their own records. A number of record companies sprouted up overnight; C.P. Mac-Gregor, Windsor, Imperial and Sets in Order, were among the several that jumped on the train.

Like many another birth, that of Windsor Records was wholly accidental and not at all planned. Early in 1950, Doc Alumbaugh felt the need of supplemental learning material for home use by members of his huge square dance classes in Arcadia and Monrovia, California. The demand for classes was so great at that time, and time and facilities so inadequate, that it was necessary for him to break up beginner and intermediate classes into two and three groups. Meetings were held every second week and dancers forgot material during that time. Doc thought that recordings which had elementary and secondary steps and figures called on them would serve a useful purpose for home practice. Accordingly, he made the Beginner and Intermediate Square Dance Practice records and offered them to class members. They were immediately popular and very soon other callers, teachers, and schools wanted them for like use.

Along about this time several singing calls came into popularity such as Alabama Jubilee, McNamara's Band, etc. Records weren't available for these tunes so Doc decided to record them, more for his personal use than for general release, but, again, other callers and many dancers wanted the records. The first thing he knew, Doc was head over allemande in the record business

Several months before starting the Windsor Co. Doc had "retired" from a busy career in the business management field and looked forward to a more relaxed way of living by calling just a few times a week. In retrospect, he says now that he's never worked so hard in his life as he has since he "retired" and constantly threatens to go back to work again so he can get some rest.

The name "Windsor" was selected as it was a family name and Doc started the business in his garage, doing all the production, shipping, and selling himself. The firm eventually occupied a rather large building and owned its own pressing, printing, processing, and warehousing facilities. Some 35 distributors serviced hundreds of record dealers in all parts of the United States and Canada. From an extremely humble start, Windsor gained top position in the square and round dance recording field, and Doc told me that the responsibility of the position has made him lose a lot of hair.

When Jay Orem, on our staff, and I got together with Ed Gilmore in the late 40s to discuss the possibility of starting our own record company, we knew absolutely nothing about what we were going to do. Jay found a recording studio down the street on Robertson Boulevard. Ed Gilmore latched onto his sister who put together a four piece band (including "Bunky" on the fiddle) that agreed to be a part of our experience. Jim York, Ed Gilmore, and I were to be the three callers. Each of us would record two patter calls. The band would play the same music a second time for the flip side of the record so that each of the six tunes would appear on six records; one side with calls and the other without. Figuring loosely that it might take a half hour for the 'with' and 'without' calls records, six units could probably be done in three hours.

How quick we learn by doing! In the first place, it took a little time to get set up so that the microphones and everything tested out to our satisfaction. Not being aware of how things could be done with a lot less difficulty, Jim York started out with the music. In a very short time he made a flub, so Jim and the music started a second time ... another flub, and then another time. Finally, after four tries our first vocal side was completed. Then it was time for the band to do the music only version. At least another half hour.

By midnight (the recording session had started at 6:00 in the evening) it was my turn and it was almost as though I was trying to make a world record, at least for the Guinness Book of Records. After 19 "takes" with the base player's hands covered with band-aids that were in turn covered with blood, the session was completed. Except, of course, for the music only portion and this, just out of sheer desperation, was done satisfactorily in a rather short period of time.

When we listen to 3 minutes and 20 seconds of what sounds like a common, everyday record of square dance music and square dance calling, we think—"Now there's an easy way to get famous—just a few minutes of calling and the work's all done." True, once a satisfactory "take" is recorded, the caller can stop worrying, but he's probably too tired to worry by that time anyway.

The caller's experience might look like this. For at least three weeks the caller wondered about what to record. (Actually, what hasn't been recorded already?) Then came the problem of fitting the call into less than 4 minutes. (He never worried too much about time before— maybe a call would last 4 minutes—maybe 5 or 6—who cared? Then came the big day. How can your throat be dry all the time, when you just had a drink of water? (You don't twice make the mistake of drinking a carbonated beverage before a session.) One set of dancers is in the studio, sock-footed so the sound of their shoes won't make any noise. The director behind the glass window says, "Record 4721—take one," points a shaking finger in your direction and off whomps the music. You're so scared by the sudden sounds behind you and by the impressiveness of the whole set-up that you just stand there—shaking and soundless. "Cut."

"What happened?—Well let's try again"—the voice laughs—it's not funny—"Record 4721— take two" —Ah— the finger again and — that would be the music. This time you start —only too soon—"Cut."

"Record-4721—take 3"—this time the fiddle loses an A string—time out— . . . "take 4"—

Dancer trips on carpet-2 men start swinging each other—they're rattled, too! You go to pieces—"Cut!"

"Take 5" . . . "Take 6" . . . "Take 7" . . .

This time you're 3 minutes 10 seconds into the record. Almost over. You make the mistake of thinking about the next record—your voice says, " . . . Bow to your cartner—porners too . . . !"—"Cut!"

"Take 8-9-10-11." Finally, 43 minutes and 18 tries later—"That's a good one! Take time out—then we'll catch the next three sides!"

In listening to these first recordings of ours, though they left much to be desired, we figured they were a part of "history." Over the years there must have been 40 or 50 different special square dance record labels organized to feed the activity. Goodness knows how many individual tunes have been recorded. At times, and without controls, the same tune was recorded by several different record companies. And there must be thousands, if not tens of thousands of different recordings on the shelves and in the record cases of many callers. Among the major record releasing companies - Victor, Capitol, Columbia, and several others - got in on the act only to find that the "market" was not there for them and while gold records represented a million pressed records in the normal field, within square dancing they could represent anything from a thousand to five thousand records pressed in order to be so honored.

The caller today has an almost unlimited supply of recorded instrumental accompaniment at his fingertips. The advantage of recorded music was that there must have been a couple of dozen different bands playing on the records, so that there was no lack of variety when it came to the sound. While the early recordings were a bit amateurish, over a period of years, they became very professional featuring some of the pop bands top musicians. There must be hundreds, no - thousands or tens of thousands of records recorded especially as background/accompaniment music for square dances.

All of that having been said, and I think most callers will agree, and I'm sure dancers will agree as well, there is nothing like the thrill of dancing to (or calling to) a live band, particularly a good one, even though many times just the idea of dancing to live music is a thrill within itself.

Following WWII a few record companies began to spring up. To this time all square dancing was done to the accompaniment of "live" music. Some of it was pretty good. All of it was what was available. For regular dances I would usually have two musicians, quite frequently a piano player and a fiddler. I'll always remember one couple that I had: two ladies, one on the violin and the other on the piano, and noting from time to time the music seemed to slow down. I would reach with my hand behind me and move it up and down to indicate I'd like it a little faster (please). On this one particular evening, in turning and looking around, Mimi Paxton, our piano player, who was well up in her years, was bent slightly over the keyboard and as near as I could tell was virtually sound asleep. It turned out that she had been in such demand for her band music that she had been playing six nights in a row.

201

This was not always indicative of the accompaniment that was available to us. We had some pretty good bands including one with Jack Barbour and his four or five musicians who recorded for us on Capitol and played along with another band at the Diamond Jubilee in Santa Monica in 1950. When it came to topnotch recording musicians, Cliffie Stone was hired for a number of our early festivals and round-ups and was great fun to dance to, let alone to accompany the caller.

I got a call from the Tempo Recording Company asking for me to assist in putting together a record for Mr. Kitzell (Jack Benny "A Pickle in the Middle and Mustard on Top"). Working with Kitzell I came up with two calls; one "Life on the Ocean Wave" and the other a patter call. I wasn't present for the actual recording and I think somewhere along the line I did hear the record. Mr. Kitzell never called a live dance, but his recording sold far beyond the square dance crowd because of his "Brooklyn-Jewish" accent.

I received a call one day from RCA Victor Recording Co. asking if I could bring a group of dancers while Roy Rogers called four sides of a traditional type patter call. It had to be done after Roy and fiddler Spade Cooley had finished a night gig. I think the session started at 1:00 or 2:00 in the morning and lasted a couple of hours. We were all amazed at the excellent patter and the old time calls, but I don't remember ever getting a copy of the record when it was completed. But I mark the experience as something I'm not about to forget.

In the mid-1950s Bill Miller, a producer for Capitol Records, called asking me to do four sides for them. The session, which was recorded during the day time, featured Cliffie Stone and his band. Besides the band and the technicians, there were four squares of live dancers in the Capitol Record studio on Melrose in Hollywood. It must have gone pretty well because Capitol asked me to line up a couple of callers for a couple of more sessions; we brought Herb Greg-gerson in for four sides and Paul Phillips in for four sides.

The industry wasn't without its problems. A new western pop tune would come out and more than one of the producers would rush to produce it, trying to be the first to come out with the release. Oftentimes dancers would buy the latest square dance records and hold dance parties at home, which was a great way for the dancers to practice the figures on the records before they went to an open dance. I think it is safe to say that callers always used the figure that was on the record (there were some problems with that which I will get into later). In the 1950's a big hit was "McNamara's Band." It had the sound that just said "square dancing," and a number of labels rushed to be the first one out with that tune. All of a sudden there were a dozen versions on the market.

Not so much a disaster as one can imagine, the resulting calls and patterns for some of the dances, were delightful indeed. In fact, two of the calls, when interchanged, have proven to be a very satisfactory and delightful combination. Here are four versions of McNamara's Band, all from different parts of the country, all different, but fun in their own right:

This first version was written by Walt Byrne of Altadena, California,

> Opener and Chorus:
> Everybody swing your honey, swing, 'em high and low
> It's allemande left your corner, boys, and round the ring
> you go.
> Sure it's grand old right-and-left and then you take your
> lady's hand

And promenade around the ring to McNAMARA'S BAND!
      Figure:
The first old couple to the right and circle to the North.
And when you've finished circling: Balance back and forth!
Now take your corner by the right and pull that Colleen
      through
Then turn your partner with a left and circle when you're
      through.
Now, pick up the next old couple and circle to the North . .
      (Repeat as above and circle six)
Pick up the last old couple and circle to the North .
      Use the above figure for each of the four couples
      with the chorus after each complete figure.

The next McNamara's Band which proves quite interesting when alternated with the verse shown above, originated in the East (by Lou Harrington) and is used quite extensively by "Jonesy," and other California Callers.

      Verse:
Oh the first couple out to the right and circle hand in hand
And start that chain a rollin' you chain 'em cross the land
      (3 ladies chain)
You stand right in the center *(active gent)* and I'll tell you
      what to do
You chain those gals across the set till your own comes
      back to you.
Now to the odd couple.
On you go with a right and left thru it's boys your doin' fine
Right and left back in the same old track keepin' the gals in
      time
Do-sa-do your opposite do-sa-do your own
Give your girl a little whirl and on your way you roam.

On you go to the next old couple and circle hand in hand,
    etc.

      Volume III, No. 1 issue of *Rosin the Bow* (a popular regional square dance magazine) had a version which is really one of the variants of the Western "Docey Doe" set to a singing call. Here is the way this publication shows the dance:

    Introduction:

Left hand round your corner girl, right hand round your
    own

Docey with your corner girl then docey with your own (1)

Swing your corner ladies now, swing them 'round and
    'round;

Then put your arm around your own and promenade the
    town.

    (orchestra plays chorus for the promenade.)

    Figure:

Oh, the first couple out and circle four, circle four hands
    round;

Left hand 'round the other girl, right hand 'round your own

Now left hand round the left again and right hand round
    your pal ;

Step right up and swing with the other fellow's gal.

      (orchestra plays chorus for a long swing,

then the visiting gent with his new partner goes on to the
    next couple, etc., around the ring.)

      The last version came from Marvin and Margie Smith of Denver, Colorado, and goes like this:

The figure is done twice for the heads and twice for the sides – there is no break.

> Oh, the head two couples center go and opposites do-sa-do
> (The first and third couples go forward to the center
> of the square, while Gent No. 1 and Lady No. 3 will
> do-sa-do as well as Gent No. 3 and Lady No. 1.)
> Then swing the other fellow's girl, as homeward you will
> go (They swap partners and swing new girl home.)
> Oh, the left hand out, turn 'the lady left, the lady on the left
> Then do-sa-do your own girl, your own girl do-sa-do
> (Allemande left and a do-sa-do.)
> Now the left hand out, turn the lady right, the lady on the
> right (Do-sa-do partners again then left arm 'round
> right hand lady.)
> Then on back home and swing your own, the fairest of
> them all.
> Oh, promenade one, promenade all, you'll promenade the
> hall
> Pull down your vest, throw out your chest at McNamara's
> Ball.

All the versions of McNamara's Band were danceable, fun pieces of music. The only problem was that dancers were not always taught to respond to calls on the fly. Once they danced a singing call, they expected the same figure every time. Multiple versions of the same tune caused some confusion at the time. In the future, it will become common for callers to change the figure every time through the tune.

In September, 1953, we asked "Doc" Alumbaugh, one of the truly colorful characters in the boom era of the square dance picture, and founder of Windsor Records, to tell the story of a typical recording company

The process was quite involved, and always started with an idea of what to record. Often we got the idea ourselves, but many dancers sent us requests for their favorite tunes. The first part of the job is to sift these ideas carefully and select those that show some slight promise for national acceptance and popularity. Later we recorded a "working dub" of the music with a skeleton band, so that we could have music for developing a suitable dance figure. When the caller had developed a dance that he believed to be fairly simple, yet had some originality about it and flowed smoothly, he sent it to us for criticism and possible revision. We used orchestras made up of top-flight instrumentalists picked from several nationally famous orchestras, from radio and television studios and from motion picture studios. We gave the caller the job of calling the dance and a taped copy of the instrumental music was sent to a Seattle recording studio where he dubbed the calls over the music. Then came all the technical work of making a master and pressing the individual records.

Not all recording companies took the care that Windsor did. Walt Cole, a master of timing, made a study of records that were produced over a ten year period. He found that less than half the records had the correct number of steps in the figure to match the 64 beats of music. The number of steps ranged from a low of about 48 beats to over 80 beats. Callers tended to use the figure from the called side of the record, and that led to a lot of dissatisfied dancers who could not come out even with the music.

There was a brief attempt to regulate the industry. A number of recording companies got together to help with record distribution and to make sure that not too many versions of the same song were produced. The company, "Continental Corsair," even produced a handful of tunes of their own, but the system did not last too long. At the time I was quite enthusiastic about some help with keeping up with the industry – I did not have to do my own research into what tunes were being recorded, etc. As I said in Sets in Order in 1958, the establishment of a one-stop square dance record service had been announced by a group of leading square dance labels to provide better service to the distributors and thus to the dancers themselves.

And so it went with the recording companies. The principal interest of many of them was to sell records. Many of them did the best they could, but they did it all on their own without the advice or help of any particular individual. At the same time, the consciousness of the country went for four different types of records for our field. You know them: The record for accompaniment, the record with calls for dancers, the record for round dancers, and the record that was strictly for instruction. With the introduction of different types of records (LP-33 1/3-and 45) it became a lot easier for people to use them at home. There were more than fifty companies in those days putting out square dance recordings: Jubilee, Old Timer, Windsor, MacGregor, and all the others. Then there are the big ones: Decca, Capitol, Victor which bring in people from the field for advice. In 1954 the Record Square listed its entire collection of square dance records in Sets in Order – it went on for 12 pages, with approximately fifty tunes per page.

At about this time Capitol Records contracted me to record several sides to the music of Jack Barbour. I also was to be the artistic advisor for the label. Capitol became a major player in the square dance record industry. Sets in Order started the Premium Record plan to produce one brand new instrumental hoedown record for callers at the beginning of each month during 1952.

At about that time the large record companies made surveys that indicated that a tremendous proportion of the square dancing public danced only to records with calls. Many of these areas have never experienced dancing to "live" callers. With round dance recordings and instrumental records for use by callers running second place. Therefore SIO chose to emphasize the calling of the nation's top-flight do-si-do experts.

There were many experiments done in terms of recording. A common complaint from callers was that they could not use a particular tune because it was not in the right key...that is, it was too high or too low for his voice. Variable speed record players helped some, but as you varied the speed to adjust the pitch, the tempo of the music changed also. Marlinda records tried an experiment of putting the same tune twice on each side, the vocal on one side and the accompaniment on the other. The tracks were recorded in different keys to accommodate the vocal range of most callers. The records were still 10 inches, but they were recorded at 33 1/3 rpm to fit more music on each side.

Another problem with records in the 1950s was breakage. The material records were made of was stiff and heavy. It was all too easy to let a record slip out of your fingers only to find it in pieces all over the stage. Those 78s also had to be "cut" individually.

In the 50s we saw great advances in the use of various types of plastic. Most 45s were made of a flexible plastic that could be "pressed" instead of "cut." These new records were much lighter and less susceptible to breakage, but they did scratch easily.

Sets in Order had an advantage over most labels – we not only had access to the top musicians and the top callers, but we had the magazine to promote the records. As a gimmick to promote the magazine we had offered premium gifts to clubs that got the highest percentage of club members to subscribe; there were a number of prizes offered, but the most popular one was a large coffee maker. In 1952 we got the idea of the record of the month club. People could join the club and receive two newly released recordings on the Sets in Order label each month for six months. This was the beginning of the "5 minute hoedowns" from Sets in Order. Later, when the magazine reorganized, the premium records took birth.

The same technological advances that revolutionized the making of records were made in playback systems as well. My first set was not intended to be variable speed. It was a turntable that I set on top of the amplifier and it ran at whatever speed it wanted. For example, its mood depended on the electrical frequency in the building. I called one dance adjacent to a saw mill, and whenever the saw was turned on the mill drew most of the power in the neighborhood, and my turntable dropped almost to zero speed until the saw was up to full speed. Then when the lumber cut was finished the record would jump back up to full speed. In another incident, I was to call a demonstration out of doors in winter. When I got the PA set up, it wouldn't even shiver in the cold. The motor was not powerful enough to overcome the sticky grease in the gears. Somehow we got it warmed up and made it through the demonstration.

I think most of us used patched together equipment which meant a lot of heavy stuff to carry into a dance hall. I had the turntable, amplifier, speakers and stands, microphone, and boxes of records. We all carried several metal record boxes that had a handle on top and could hold about 25 ten inch 78rpm records and an index to what was in the case. I felt that my record cases got heavier for each dance.

Since this was the time before variable speed turntables, we had to use the music at whatever tempo it was recorded at. Some of my records ran at 150 metronome beats per minute down to about 120 bpm. Few of the record producers really understood the needs for square dancing.

But just as the quality of recordings got better as more knowledgeable people got into record production, so the sound systems got better. One of the biggest improvements was to make the units smaller and lighter. One of the major manufacturers in the 1950s was Califone, which introduced a set in which the amplifier and turntable were one unit, and the lid to the unit was a speaker. Califone also put in connections for more than one microphone and had tone control for the mikes. It also had three speeds so callers could play any of the commercially produced records: 78 rpm, 45 rpm, and 33 1/3 rpm. Several other companies began to produce quality PA systems. Newcombe seemed to dominate the square dance world for a while, but Frank Kaltman of Folkcraft records also made a compact unit, as did Clinton. In 1959, Jim Hilton of Oakland, CA, came out with a sound system designed for square dance callers

The Ultimate in Caller's Sound Equipment

Soon the Hilton system surpassed all other units in sales to callers.

Technical advances did not solve all of the problems with sound. Have you ever wondered just what you'd do as a caller if your public address system suddenly went out on you in the middle of a large dance or if you arrived for an engagement a long way from home, only to find you'd left behind some important piece of equipment? Equipment failures and "forgetfulitis" are not uncommon occurrences for the busy caller, and quick thinking and ingenuity have saved many a dance. Take one particular Southern California caller who, completely equipped, rushed into his dance, set up his gear and was ready to go on time only to discover that in his haste he'd picked up an album of popular records rather than the hoedown tunes he had ready for the occasion. In this instance the caller was fortunate and found he had several not-too-jivy tunes without vocals and managed to last a good portion of the night calling to "White Christmas."

Perhaps the most common "forgotten item" was the phonograph needle. Those not blessed with a player-arm fitted out with a permanent needle are always faced with the possibility of having their temporary needle jar out on the way to a dance and at the last minute, with aid of a borrowed pair of pliers change a straight pin into a sort of record-torturing device that will get them through the evening. Some callers make it "standard equipment" to have an extra pack safely put away in the glove compartment of their car. To a modern caller the problem of needles for records is a truly arcane issue. But in the 1954 catalog from Record Square (which was then located in Santa Barbara, CA), there was a notice on the first of the 12 pages pointing out that if a caller used a needle designed for the old 78rpm records he would destroy the newer 45 rpm records because the grooves on a 45 were narrower and the records were made of a softer material.

A good idea is one adopted by a caller in Seattle, Washington. He's made up a regular check-off list for each dance which he always consults before leaving the house for the evening. On it are such items as: P. A. System, Mike, (extra mike), three-way plug, extension cord, records, fuses (for house current and for his speaker equipment), needles, program for the evening, and some twine or heavy cord for fastening his speakers to the wall.

Good old imagination and stage presence have saved many a square dance party from going on the rocks. One caller, over half way through the evening, suddenly had a tube go out in his amplifier and was faced with the choice of stopping the dance at that point or struggling along the best he could. Fortunately the crowd was not too large and the lack of microphone did not make it impossible for him to be heard. He turned the balance of the evening into a work-shop, improving the style of the dancers, conducting a question and answer period that brought to light many problems that needed clearing up, and in general turned what might have been a "flop" into a most successful night.

In the mid-1950's Stereo broke onto the scene. Some of us remember the demonstration records, such as Tchaikovsky's *1812 Overture* with the orchestra balanced as if in the concert hall and the cannon shots came out of only one speaker. Or the sound of a train going from right to left through your living room. Stereo became the standard in the general recording industry, and there was a short lived experiment in stereo square dance records. The problem with those records is that on one side of the hall you heard only the calls and on the other side you heard only the music.

Just remember, when things look the darkest and your sound system begins to fall apart on you, that the old-timers still brag about calling for dances that lasted from 5 to 8 hours with five and six hundred persons, without the benefit of any mike or voice aid. Guess maybe we are a bunch of softies but somehow it's pretty sound reasoning that the callers' greatest hero is the guy who invented electric amplification.

Since those days we have seen callers shift from the heavy 78 rpm records to lighter weight 45 rpm records that had thinner grooves so they carried as much music. Then we hit an era where some callers were using reel-to-reel tape recorders. A single tape could hold many tunes, but there was the problem of finding the exact starting position on the tape. The next innovation was the audio cassette which came in various lengths, from five minute capacity to ninety minutes. Many callers found they could transfer their music to cassettes and have two tunes per cassette. The other benefit was that you left your original record at home so it did not get scratched. Further advances in technology gave us compact discs, mini-discs, mp3 players etc. In the current period, many callers are putting all of their music into the hard drive of their laptop computer. Add to that technology the advent of "powered speakers" that are very small and light but still put out a lot of sound.

Just as we had discovered the regulations by unions for TV and movie production, we found out about the music licensing organizations, particularly ASCAP, The American Society of Composers, Authors and Publishers. On June 6, 1951, Otto Harbach, the president of ASCAP, sent a letter to Leo Hublou, the proprietor of Saturday Night Square Dance at the Culver City Hall Auditorium. Essentially the letter said that ASCAP was happy that Saturday Night Square Dance was using music in its programs, but many of the songs used at Saturday Night Square Dance were copyrighted. That meant that composers were encouraged to continue to write music and have it performed as long as they received compensation for their work. Since it would be an onerous task on both sides – the venues and the composers – to make sure that the composers were getting paid, ASCAP was formed to collect the license fees and pay the composers. For ease of obtaining a license to use copyrighted music, there was an application with a fee schedule included with the letter. Until such time as Saturday Night Square Dance received its license, it was barred from using copyrighted music.

We became aware that the use of copyrighted music was a problem, not just in the U.S. but around the world. We received letters from clubs and callers from Germany to

Australia. My thoughts had been that calling square dances as educational sessions instead of entertainment might slide around the issue. I also thought that square dances used more public domain music than copyrighted music. But the problem remained when dealing with recordings of newer songs or with round dance music. Some of the ASCAP representatives realized that monitoring all of the square dances for copyrighted music would be far too costly.

The issue really came to a head in the mid-1980s when BMI and ASCAP discovered how widely spread square dancing was, and that they could locate the dances through our own publications. CALLERLAB stepped in and negotiated a deal whereby the individual clubs and halls did not have to be licensed but that the callers would be licensed to use copyrighted music for square dances. That agreement then extended to round dance teachers and line dance leaders. The exception was that large festivals and national conventions needed to carry their own music licenses, regardless if the individual callers were licensed.

The issue carried beyond music at live performances, though. Record companies had to be licensed to change the format of registered music. There was a very fine border between public domain and registered music. The difference was largely a discernment as to whether the final product showed enough difference from the original as to be considered a new creation. If the tune still felt like the original in terms of melody, rhythm, lyrics, etc., then the tune was considered to be copyrighted. No doubt some callers and record producers continued to pirate music, but for most of us, the agreement was satisfactory and put us on the legal side of the music business.

Chapter 10. TV and Radio

Sometime before the Cheyenne Mountain Dancers show I added one more activity to our busy schedule. While I was attending a United Nations' television program as a United States representative, one of the technical directors for KFI television asked if I would put on a series of six square dance instruction/demonstration programs on television. The idea seemed to be a good one. There would be no money in the project but it would be sustained by the radio-television station.

KFI was the oldest TV station in Los Angeles, one of the oldest in the country outside of New York. Though the TV networks of NBC and CBS existed, KFI was an independent, run by Earle C. Anthony, the owner of a used car lot. "KFI" stood for – the K for west of the Mississippi – FI was for Farmer's Information. Both the TV station and the radio station would interrupt its regular broadcasting to tell farmers about impending weather situations. Perhaps the largest crop in the KFI area was citrus, and those growers needed to know about possible low temperatures. With sufficient warning, the growers could get crews out into the orchards to protect the fruit.

KFI was aware of the square dance boom and wanted to get in on ground floor. The show would be only 20 minutes long, but it was at a decent hour. I had to provide the music and the dancers, still I thought it would be marvelous exposure to modern square dancing instead of the "hay bales" sets seen in the movies. The really good thing about the deal was that I would have control over the type of dancing.

In those early years I had a number of exhibition teams, one being the 'Rip and Snorters', members of my club. They became the pilot group on a series of television

217

shows: one at the old KFI-TV Channel 9, on Vermont Avenue in Los Angeles and later on at NBC when its studio was at Hollywood and Vine; and then again on Channel 4 when the dancing area was a drained swimming pool. From the beginning we had excellent viewer response. And to encourage this we produced (with the channel's help) a series of dancer notes, which encouraged the dancers in their living rooms to join us on the screen as we did one "teaching" session with each program.

Remember that this was in the early days of television and the medium was just learning about itself. Cameras were bulky and were not particularly mobile. Therefore the type of programming was pretty limited. The most popular shows were ones with a single set, or maybe two, where a camera could be set and the cast moved. The first sport program was professional wrestling because the ring was small and one camera could cover the whole match.

Square dancing seemed to be an ideal activity for TV except that it is somewhat boring if the camera is at the same level as the dancers. To really see the patterns the camera needs to look down on the dancers. At KFI there was a prob-

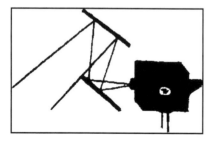

lem with getting high shots. There was just one studio and one camera (There may have been two). We explained to the director that close-ups on the dancers would not tell the story of the beauty of the patterns and we needed a high shot. But they had no dolly and elevating the camera seemed to be out of the question. Then the director and the floor manager came up with a solution - build a frame and mount a large mirror at an angle at which the camera shot up - thereby providing the illusion of a high shot 12 or 15 feet up, looking down on to the dancers.

It almost worked... but as we watched the experiment in the monitor, we noted something was wrong. The men were dancing the part of the ladies and the ladies that of the men. Why were the dancers circling right when the caller said left? Of course! Shooting into only one mirror put everything in reverse. The next week they had set up two mirrors angled one above the other so that the camera when dollied up slightly would shoot into the second mirror. Its 45 degree angle caught the image picked up by the top mirror and this double reflection set things straight. At best it was awkward. In our third session, they had rigged a series of risers and managed to hoist the camera and cameraman to an elevation suitable for our needs to show some good angles.

We put on our first show in the middle of November and then the show was on every Thursday for 20 minutes. Of course, 20 minutes isn't very long but we wanted to teach one square and one round and then to do approximately two demonstrations of squares in the time that remained. A few words of explanation, a little humor and just plain naturalness resulted in a surprisingly good acceptance of the show. After our six weeks were over the station asked us if we would continue. The response in letters was amazing. Our first show alone brought in 120 pieces of mail and then the letters came in regularly. We sent out copies of the calls and round dances we used, and we heard, through the letters, that people in their living rooms were joining in right with us in the dancing. The station was more than cooperative with us and allowed me to use the 20 minutes freely as I saw fit. I wrote and directed the show, put in whatever announcements I liked and disregarded all the normal rules for television procedure, I am sure.

Before we started shooting for the TV show we got some really good advice from one of the directors: "Whatever happens, smile. And, you ladies – lift your head up and shake your curls!" The director was giving us last minute tips on how to look well in our performance. "Keep your dances short," he suggested. "Leave the viewers wanting more. Make the dancing spontaneous. Show it like it is – if somebody makes a mistake, just regroup and keep on going."

Bob Osgood and Andy Divine on TV

After a few weeks, the dancers and I got the feeling that we were doing too much of the same thing. We were having fun, but we thought maybe the viewers were getting tired of so much instruction. We brain-stormed a bit and came up with the idea of having a guest on the show. We all agreed that Andy Devine would be about as good a guest as we could get. Andy had presence and we thought his size and his gravelly voice would really add something to the show.

To our great pleasure, Andy agreed to join us. We did not let the viewers know that Andy would be on the show. I started with a little bit about what it takes to be a caller, then asked for a volunteer to help demonstrate. At that point Andy walked onto the set to the surprise and delight of all. He called a bit of a square – Texas Star, I believe – then he danced in a square. We also had a great time interviewing Andy.

Stu Wilson, a popular MC of KFI and ardent square dancer, wanted a program to show what square dancing was really like. For a long time Stu had been irked at the Western variety shows that would have three minutes of cloggers (called square dancers), and the rest of the time was filled with yodelers, singers, and even a tightrope walker. Stu scheduled his program to start on Labor Day 1949 with Fenton 'Jonesy' Jones. The timing of Stu's show was to be on the air after my show had completed its run.

We learned something early in the game. To us, variety in square dancing was doing a singing call, then a patter call, and then maybe another patter call - that's variety for us. But, variety to a viewer, we discovered, was seeing different forms of dance. In other words, if we did a half hour show on television, and hoped to get our audience, we certainly wouldn't do it by doing five or six different square dances. Because to the viewers, who were mainly non-dancers, the dancing would appear to be just repetition. You would be doing equivalents to things like Right and Left Grands and Ladies Chains, and hand pull-bys that would look the same in all of them.

But, if you were to do a square dance then were to do a different dance, perhaps a couple dance, then you were to do a contra, and finally a dance done in fours like a mescolanza, that would hold interest. I had one of the men, a radio personality just getting into television, that came up with a great idea but it never sold. It was a combination of Americana and American dance. So, that in the course of a half hour show you would have several different spots of different types of square dancing. You would also do things that were part of American heritage. It might be 'how to spin a top,' or 'how to bake a cake,' anything that goes back in time. Things we used to do, like the games we used to play, marbles,and things like that. And it would be the dance of America, keeping it sort of traditional.

April 14, 1949, after twelve weeks on KFI, I signed a contract for a thirteen week series of square dance programs with KNBH (NBC outlet). For the handsome sum of $200 per show I agreed to the following.

(1) Artist hereby grants NBC the right to make live television broadcasts of the programs to be broadcast here-under over such stations as NBC elects and to make or cause to be made television recordings thereof, and to use or cause such television recordings to

221

be used for reference, file and audition purposes and for broadcasting over television stations.

(2) NBC may require additional rehearsals, subject to Artist's prior contractual commitments,

(3) Artist grants NBC the right to use and license the use of Artist's name and likeness for the purpose of publicizing such programs .

(4) Artist indemnifies completely NBC and all others against liability arising from any unauthorized act of Artist or the use of any material ad lib or otherwise, furnished by Artist.

(5) In the event Artist fails to sign this contract, performance by Artist at first rehearsal constitutes acceptance thereof.

We were getting into the Big Time - including makeup! We even had a little on camera rehearsal from 5:00 to 6:30 with air time at 8:30. The scene was a typical living room, rugs on the floor with a record player and a stack of records near at hand. The dancers (a group made up from members of the Rip 'n' Snort club but called the 49ers for the program) are doing the varsouvianna while I described the scene:

This is a typical American home – it could be your home today or it could be the home of your grandparents 50 years ago. The activity you see going on is just a neighborhood gathering of folks who like to do the real American Square and Round dances that have been so popular ever since our country got its beginning. We'd like you to join your living room with ours for this brief period and just let your hair down and have some fun with us. Don't worry about not knowing the dances because we're going to take everything real slowly. Just remember the main idea behind Square dancing is FUN! Let's join the bunch while they finish the varsouvianna. (Then I was given the cue that the titles for the program were cleared and the camera came in on me.)

That's your cue, ladies and gentlemen. You can't square dance in a room full of furniture so let's roll up the rugs – move back the vases or anything breakable and get ready to do some dancing. Now get four couples into a circle – that's right – join hands and make a square – that's square with the walls in your room, (ad lib).

We lasted for about six or eight shows, had a great mail response, but we didn't pick up any sponsors.

Our next stop was at KLAC. The studio site was an old motel that had been converted to a TV studio, but they did not have a sound stage that could accommodate the dancers. But they did have the old swimming pool that had been drained. It became our slightly tilted dance floor.

The boom in square dancing itself sort of indicated that everything was happening. Classes were filling as soon as they were opened up, and newspapers were carrying stories. We had worked for about thirteen weeks at KFI, the first station and had a lot of fun with it. I think we got paid an astounding amount of something like $0.00 for the whole square-and-a-half of us. The orchestra, of course, got union scale. But, we had a lot of fun and we learned a lot. We did get a lot of mail on that early show. Then NBC decided they wanted us to run a series with a possibility of network exposure. Well, at that stage of the game there was very little network television. I think this was going to be our first color show, and we ran this twelve weeks maybe a little more. Our time slot was right between the Dennis Day Show (Jack Benny's sideman for years – "Gee, Mr. Benny") and a news broadcast. An added treat was that Dennis and I had been in the Navy together. We received a lot of good mail, and the station did get a sponsor for part of the time. But, unfortunately, there was no interest by a long term sponsor.

The thing that brought this to mind was that on at least one occasion we had a non-dancing guest sitting on the sidelines and making notes. Not at all secretive, he had informed the club officers that he represented one of the local unions that checked on the live music in the area to make sure that all band members were a part of the local. Because no problems ever grew out of the experience I had imagined that possibly the fiddler, piano, and bass player belonged, or, that square dancing was simply too small pickings for the overwhelmingly large labor groups to mess with. This was only our first contact with the unions.

And this reminds me of the episode concerning a square dance round-up being planned in Northern California in the early 1950's, I believe. At any rate, the sponsoring association had rented the largest hall in the area and gone about making its plans for the dance. Most of the individual club dances met at the time in school gyms and private halls. The majority made use of three or four piece orchestras. The combinations varied among fiddle, banjo, bass, piano, etc. But for this big festival plans had been made to utilize a 7-piece band - a favorite in the area. Few clubs could afford this band because of its size.

The band had been contracted for and at a meeting of the planning committee, three members of the local musicians' union showed up. Upon learning the size of the band to be utilized, the union officials informed the somewhat startled executive committee that this particular hall was rated for a 25 piece band. The make-up of the band (how many fiddles, how many guitars, etc.) was, of course, left up to the sponsoring group. But it was important that 25 union members be hired

The sponsors tried the best they could to explain that no square dance had ever used any band of 25 pieces; there were simply no experienced square dance bands of that size; plus the cost would be unthinkable.

The square dancers pleaded their case, but the union executives were unmovable. Then, taking a little time to think out the situation and realizing that not only was their festival in jeopardy, but that their local dances which often used non-union musicians (they were excellent and were paid well, they just simply were not union members), were also in trouble. After several meetings they came up with a solution.

Meeting again with the union leaders they explained that they understood the situation and were ready to co-operate, also it could be handled in a way that would not disturb the use of the best experienced square dance band. The union required the hall where the dance was to be held to build an enlarged callers stage. On the rear of it would be constructed a large arch with positions for 25 musicians and their instruments. The union would then furnish 25 harpists who were capable of furnishing the type of music that would fit the particular audience.

Prior to each brace of squares and each round dance, the harps would play fitting selections as background music for the evening. In addition, on an easel in front of the stage, a large sign would announce that the 25 harpists were required (and furnished by) Local such-and-such Musicians Union.

A bit nonplussed, another time out was called for. The musicians' union, finding themselves a bit behind the 8-ball, acquiesced and the round-up went on with just its standard, high quality, western square dance band.

The television industry was indeed just emerging at that time. I remember I was an early member of the Television Artists Actors Guild. At first there was no money to be paid to the dancers - all were amateurs and there were no

225

restrictions. The caller would sometimes receive a minor amount of money which might offset the fact that he could not be calling a dance for a club that same night.

It wasn't long before the unions took hold, however, and dancers could not take part without joining the union. This never materialized for us at this stage because we didn't want to become professionals. However, one group, the "Y-Knot Twirlers," having joined the union appeared frequently on a number of shows. I believe it was Homer Garrett who was their caller and their dancing was pretty much acrobatic, with somersaults, "flaps like thunder", etc. They did a lot to send square dancing back to the barn with Li'l Abner/Daisy Mae costumes.

Somewhere along the line, I believe it was Senators Taft and Hartley who came up with a bill that made it possible for a one-time appearance of an individual without being a member of the union. At first I think there was a requirement that that individual would be paid the same as if he were a union member, but this changed. At least we experienced a change. Our ABC channel here in the San Fernando Valley produced an hour-long show featuring Merle Travis and a western cast. The writer/producer, Hank Richardson, decided to incorporate square dancing as a part of his one hour Variety Western Show. Merle Travis was to be the western star and I was to be "Mr. Square Dancing." We worked around the union problems by having a different club (six squares) and their caller, appear as guests each week. I would be the co-star with Merle Travis and my job was to bring on the different groups of square dancers. This presumably got us away from having to join the union. We would select a different caller and a club of his choice and he would bring to the show four squares of his dancers, appropriately costumed and rehearsed enough so that they were prepared for the two or three dancing tips on that show. In lieu of what I seem to remember as a required payment for the group as a whole, we would determine what gift for the entire club could be presented on camera during the performance. I remember such gifts as a 78 cup coffee maker and year's supply of coffee as being a gift. I can't remember the others, but I do recall that on one performance, just before Thanksgiving, a turkey was presented to the visiting caller by one of the lady singers in the cast. What we didn't realize was that the turkey was very much alive…and big. It was a noisy bird and awkward as all get out. Almost on cue, the turkey made a break for it and during the balance of the last dance (over titles) the bird ran amok, adding his unique sounds (and presence) to the dancing.

A real "grabber" at one of the performances was when we invited a caller and his group of wheelchair dancers to participate. It went over quite well, especially during the second number (which they had preplanned with the orchestra). When the music stopped, each of the dancers slid out of their wheelchairs onto another chair and presented their wheel chair to one of the able dancers who were also sharing the stage that night. Then for a rather raucous 30 seconds or so, these "experienced" dancers demonstrated their inability to handle a wheel chair.

One of the first things a packager of TV shows thinks, when he talks about square dancing, is contests. "First we'll have regional contests, then national. We might be able to stretch this out for thirteen weeks."

"Contests," you explain to him, "are not a part of contemporary square dancing. When they have been tried, they have destroyed the friendly atmosphere of clubs and erased the spirit of cooperation among the callers." And that's usually where the discussions began to fall apart.

Regional or local television shows and the educational channels seem to offer the best promise of allowing attractively costumed, happy dancers to give a faithful exhibition of square dancing. After NBC it was ABC that picked us up and they too hoped to go coast to coast. This was a western format. The producer of it was a friend of Meryl Travis's, so he put the show together as a vehicle for both Meryl Travis and for me.

Unions were just becoming aware of the square dancing and saw the connection with TV. Now, I can't really complain too loud about the unions because they were trying to protect their members from unscrupulous producers who would have replaced expensive union labor with free volunteer labor. We had started out by having the same square or two on our regular programs. We could no longer do that unless the dancers belonged to the union. And then we came across the clause in the Taft-Hartley Law that would allow us to have amateurs on the program if they were paid the regular rate. They didn't have to belong to the union and could only be on once.

In our ABC television series with Meryl Travis, we opened with square dancing. We closed with square dancing, and we had two spots in between. The visiting club would not be paid. We got by it by making it a contest - not in dancing. Because we're very strong against having any competition; we believed that since square dancing was a cooperative type of activity competition among dancers or callers would work against our ideals. But, instead of dancer competition, one time we had a greased pig run through the deal - with the pig itself going to the person who caught her. We had different word games. Something like that took very little time and didn't involve competition in square dancing or calling. It was fun to watch and it got us through with the Taft-Hartley deal. Every week we had a different caller and club featured on the show. That pretty much sums up our experience with producing a square dance oriented TV show, but it does not end our experiences with TV.

Sets in Order ran an article about a caller who was called in to do a segment "live" on the old Dinah Shore Show. Flattered and not unhappy by the description of what was to take place he said "yes" he'd do the calling - but, he added, it had to be a good representation of square dancing.

Once at the studio he discovered that the show had its own choreographer who had his own ideas about the professional dancers involved and what they were about to do. The caller was to look at the contrived routine and then call what the dancers were doing. It all happened so fast there was little time for discussion and reasoning. It wasn't bad enough that the dancers would be doing a parody ridiculing square dancing but there were only two couples not four - who would be doing the dancing. To make it worse, the introduction the star rehearsed gave the impression that this was the way it was in today's square dancing circles.

By this time the caller was getting a little panicky. What had he gotten himself into? What kind of an impression would this make on more than one million viewers, most of them non-dancers?

With less than 15 minutes to go, the answer became apparent. It just couldn't go on! But how to get this across? The star was busy with last minute make-up and a final script check with the director. The concerned caller moved in, wondering just what to say and how to get his concern across. Miss Shore stopped her talking and turned to the caller, "Well - what do you think of it?" she asked.

Caught a little off guard, the caller thought quickly. "I guess it will go over all right – that is if you don't mind stepping on the toes of several hundred thousand square dancers."

The director was interested. "What do you mean?"

"Well, sir," our hero was off and running, it was now or never. "If you let this performance go on - with just one half of a square projecting a corn-ball image that square dancers have been fighting for the past ten years, the folks at Chevrolet (sponsors of the show) are going to get so many irate letters they won't know what hit them. Sorry, but that's the way it is."

"It's that bad, is it?" the director asked.

"It's bad," said the caller.

"Let's kill it," said Dinah. "We don't want to offend anyone. And, anyway we have that extra vocal number we can run in to fill the slot." And so that was why that a million housewives across the country didn't see a square dancing demonstration that would have been a sheer disaster.

The caller was not identified in the article as it ran in the magazine, but it is time to admit that I was the caller. You know, sometimes you learn a lot more from your failures than your successes. I certainly learned a lot about asking all the questions before agreeing to make a TV or radio appearance.

Caller Earl Johnson of California had a similar experience, but he did not get the luxury of bailing out. The nationally syndicated Merv Griffin show managed to make a shambles of square dancing. People who saw that show must be wondering how disasters of this type are allowed to happen. Recent exposures on the tube have not all been this weird. As a matter of fact, most shows in the past five or six years have been good, showing square dancing as a friendly and exhilarating activity. Earl had felt secure in accepting what promised to be a good opportunity. "Never again," said

Earl, who adds, "my sincerest apologies to all square dancers and callers throughout the United States for the terrible display of what was supposed to be square dancing in the telecast. It will ease my shame and embarrassment a little if you understand that I did not know until I walked on stage that the people I was to call to were not square dancers."

Not all square dance bits on TV were disastrous. In fact, one show in particular was extremely courteous and supportive. We take our hat off to Phil Donahue who underplayed his role as master of ceremonies, fielding appropriate questions from the audience and portraying the typical first-nighter in a demonstration of introductory square dancing. Foregoing the temptation faced by many high caliber TV personalities in a similar position, Phil in no way ridiculed the activity nor in any way did he overextend his role as anything but "just one of the family." His opening statement "I have never met a depressed square dancer" set the theme for the entire program.

We were impressed with the ample, though plain, stage setting. Camera angles were excellent. For the most part, the viewer looked slightly down on the dancers from a vantage point that allowed him to separate the patterns and see clearly what was going on. A camera situated directly overhead allowed the opportunity for some excellent high shots, but these were not overlong, nor was the overhead angle used too frequently.

Close-ups on the studio audience were well selected and the temptation of doing close-ups on faces, feet of the dancers, or on the caller were handled with restraint. From our standpoint there is an advantage to letting the camera focus on an entire square, allowing the viewer to watch the kaleidoscope of color and motion.

Caller Lee Kopman did an outstanding job in his role of commentator, teacher/caller. Not overbearing, not trying to be humorous, he told it like it is while providing the type of information that Mr. and Mrs. Average Television Viewer would be apt to ask. It is obvious that Lee had done his homework well, for the variety of questions coming from the audience were most adequately answered. We couldn't help but feel that all the viewers were ripe subjects for a future beginners' class. In fact, when it came time for the brief exposure of the audience to a "one night stand" type of dancing, there was little or no hesitation in getting the volunteers up on their feet.

Doubtless, this single program had an influence on the coming crop of new dancers and we have little doubt that we'll be hearing more about the need for shows of this type in the years to come.

Radio and television have been very much in evidence ever since the present phase of the hobby was young and TV screens were but seven inches across. There have been "one-shot" square dance TV shows in Brussels, Belgium and two in Germany. Current TV regulars in the States and Canada include the perpetual favorite called by John Shadoan over local TV in Bozeman, Montana, the Earle Park Show on CKOS-TV, Yorkton, Saskatchewan, and another over WJCT, Jacksonville, Fla.

One quick word about radio. Radio shows have dotted the U.S. for some time, but one of the "hottest" areas for this type of show was in Canada. Regina, Saskatchewan, featured a regular weekly show with Noreen Wilson that beamed across Canada. In another market, Bill Savage covered a wide area with his weekly show over CTOC in Lethbridge, Alberta.

Stateside there was the Sunday morning program with Mildred Buhler from Redwood City near San Francisco. "Calling All Folk Dancers" mixed squares, rounds, and folk dances. Mildred called the squares and introduced the rounds and folk dances, which were then danced by folks who were live in the studio. Mildred often featured guest callers, such as Ray Smith, Jack Hoehisal, Cal Golden, and Rickey Holden either live in the studio or on tape. Initially the show was broadcast from the radio studio; the program was so popular that it moved to a local restaurant and the dancing came from "Breakfast at Bondi's." The program always opened with "Ragtime Annie," then Mildred would come on with:

> *Everybody in your places, straighten up your faces*
> *And get ready for another long pull.*

People set up their squares every Monday evening at 6:15 on Vancouver Island when CJVI went into a half hour square dance program that covered not only the Island but also the lower mainland of British Columbia and parts of Washington, USA. "Square Dance Party" was produced and aired by Dawn Draper, a square dance enthusiast, and Keith Thompson, radio time salesman. In accordance with the station's "good music" policy, a format of easy listening was mandatory not only for the dancers but for the radio audience as well. A guest caller was featured each week, either "live" or recorded. The format was pretty well set: never more than three sets of squares intermixed with round dances and information about square dancing in the local area.

Our cover of Square Dancing Magazine for April 1977 showed that we had been thinking about square dancing and the image it projected on the screen. Certainly, the brief glimpses of traditional dancing and the caller (or shouter-outer, as some old timers still refer to him) could do little to woo the non-dancers into the field of contemporary square dancing. And yet these brief exposures reach large audiences and they do create a certain awareness of the activity.

In the years since WW II, as square dancing emerged as a dance form and as a recreational hobby for six million or more men and women around the world we have seen it depicted on the screen and on the TV tube many times; occasionally in a complimentary manner, but frequently disjointed and unsatisfying. We have come to realize, relative to its portrayal in fictional movies that square dancing, as far motion pictures are concerned, has always been and, in all probability, always will be window dressing. No more, no less.

Picture is from "Bound For Glory" a bio-pic of Woody Guthrie. David Caradine as Guthrie plays the fiddle while Bruce Johnson calls

We wish that it were not so but after watching any number of films featuring square dancing, (always starting out in high hopes and usually ending up disappointed) we're more or less resigned to the facts.

The scene on the giant screen is a country farm. The neighbors have gathered for the town's annual barn dance (the setting). As the men and women arrive, unload from the assorted carriages and go into the barn, you hear the clapping of hands, the shouts of the crowd, the squeak of the fiddle and the commands of the caller (all this you've come to realize is window dressing).

Now, as you move inside (with the camera, of course) you notice a shy young country-type watching from the sidelines. What's he looking at so intently? (The plot thickens.) Aha, the camera is about to help us out again. It moves across the floor of happy, smiling, arm swinging dancers to a pretty banker's daughter who seems to be oblivious to everything but the tall, handsome man with whom she's promenading.

She is unaware, of course, that he's the shady character who plans later that same evening to rob the very bank owned by her father. We turn again to our hero who shows little interest in the Virginia Reel now in progress (the camera takes a quick pan of the happy dancers and even moves in for a brief close-up of the caller to convince the viewers that nobody expects the wild fight that in just moments will disrupt the whole panorama, call a halt to the dancing and bring the picture to fever pitch). And so the movie and its square dance sequence unfolds.

Most disconcerting to those of us who view these things in hopes that one may someday let the good guys (the square dancers) win—is when the caller is calling one thing and the dancers are doing something else.

"How can this happen? Can't they get someone knowledgeable enough to tell them that when the caller is saying 'swing,' the dancers shouldn't be doing a promenade?"

The answer, of course, is a simple one. The square dancing is relatively unimportant to the story line and simply serves as a lively backdrop to the action. A good example is the dancing that took place in the motion picture, *Giant*," shot at Warner Brothers a number of years ago. The setting was the patio area surrounding the home of a wealthy Texan. The neighbors are involved in a square dance. One of the principals in the film is calling. The dancers are going through a perfectly respectable Texas Star (what else?). In comes the lady of the house (portrayed by Elizabeth Taylor). From the other side of the patio enters her husband (Rock Hudson). All this time the square dancing is going on in the background.

"Ladies to the center and back to the bar," barks the caller (and he really barks!). You look closely at the dancers who appear to be doing a grand right and left. "Everybody swing!" Now they're doing ladies to the center!

All this time the plot unwinds in the foreground. The daughter is about to marry some out-of-town character. The mother frets. The father fidgets. The band plays on.

What happened to the dancing? Let's take a look. It all started weeks ago, working with the caller, rehearsing the dancers, pre-recording the calls. Finally the scene is to be shot. They dry run it a few times to establish camera angles. Then on go the lights—the music starts up again and in two minutes the dance is over—it's a take. The cameras are moved and they take it again—and again. Seven times they take the dancing—moving in for close-ups—then up for the high shots - the dancers doing the exact same routine over and over for two days.

Now it's time to bring in the stars. As the dancers start their action once again, the cameras pick up the story with the stars front and center and the dancing action going on in the background.

Once the shooting is completed and the actors have all gone home, the job of cutting begins. And here is where the square dancing comes in for a face lifting. We see the finished film. The scene starts with a high shot, perhaps as the dancers, the orchestra and the caller all start together. Then the camera moves in for a shot of Miss Taylor and over her shoulder we see the dancers dancing whatever it was they were dancing at just this moment. The sound track of the calling isn't at the same spot so the caller and dancers are out of sync. All of this is unnoticed, perhaps, by the non-dancer who is deeply caught up in the story line, but nonetheless it's tremendously frustrating to the dancer who views this and realizes what is going on.

Perhaps what we as dancers want most out of motion pictures is a true portrayal of our hobby. After more than 30 years of watching and waiting, it's doubtful that we're going to get it from Hollywood or on TV

TV is a strange medium. The color and sounds of square dancing come across beautifully on the tube, particularly when the directors will stay clear of close-ups and allow us to see the patterns made by the squares. Television is expensive and the union scale paid to dancers, whether they are union members of not, is quite awesome.

Producers are overly cautious when it comes to using square dancing. To be sure, a spot on *To Tell the Truth* or one of the other quiz shows or a quick segment on a late night telethon, squeezed in between vaudeville acts, is always exposure. But is it what we're hoping for?

As you can imagine, we've been getting letters for the past twenty years asking why square dancing can't have its own coast-to-coast network show, or at least be featured regularly on the Lawrence Welk show, or something of that nature. Quite often it boils down to the producer who asks, "How spectacular is square dancing?" Frequently this is interpreted to mean a type of square dancing that is not as we see it in our clubs and at our festivals.

As for the movies—perhaps the route of the documentary is the best bet. Such films may have to be purchased by square dancers but then the opportunity to represent this activity as we would like to see it will be well worth the responsibility and the expense.

What happened to the dancing? You'll find out in the next chapter as we move on to square dancing in the movies.

TV did give square dancing an unmatchable bit of advertising: The Tournament of Roses Parade from Pasadena, CA. More detail on this in the chapter on Exhibitions. I just can't resist putting in the designer's rendition of the 1981 Float.

Chapter 11. Square Dancing in the Movies

The appearance of an elegantly clad square of dancers in a short TV commercial raised the cry: "Why can't we have more square dancing on the tube?" Of course, the question doesn't stop there. "How come we don't see square dancing in some of our feature films – like we used to?"

The answer, as far as TV is concerned, has to a point, to do with cost. The dancers, even though they might be willing to donate their time and ability, must still be paid an amount commensurate with union scale, as we discussed in the last chapter.

The question of square dancing in today's motion pictures is something else. A great bulk of films that featured square dancing as a part of the story line of the film were shot during the square dance boom period in the late 1940's and early 1950's. Square dancing was really the BIG news back then. Everyone was doing it. Classes were filled the day they opened. Newspapers and magazines were loaded with stories of square dancing, and it seemed that the rich and famous were all, in one way or another, involved in it. It was the thing to do.

That eminent Thespian, Ronald Colman, noted for his many and mostly dignified portrayals on the silver screen, was also somewhat of a square dance caller. He and a group of other Hollywoodites used to be in a club called for by Paul Pierce, and Colman himself took over the mike, on special occasions, British accent and all. He and Mrs. Colman had the very popular NBC radio show, *Halls of Ivy,* and during one of their broadcasts, Colman, in the character of Dr. Wm. Tod-Hunter Hall, a college professor, is prevailed upon, in the script, to do a little call — "Birdie in the

Cage" to be exact. Mr. Colman as Dr. Hall says, "I must confess I enjoyed myself hugely. I think square dancing is a social release ... it gives otherwise shy and retiring people an opportunity to kick up their heels, bow from the waist, curtsey and sashay. In mock-seriousness they are 'acting' as pioneers and, at least for a brief time, regain the mutual shoulder-to-shoulder, hand-in-hand group spirit of their frontier forebears..."

Another star, Bing Crosby, sang "Country Style," in the 1947 film *Welcome Stranger*. The song is catchy and works in the calls for "Texas Star" pretty well. Bing seemed to really be enjoying himself as he danced and flawlessly, kept a line of patter going. Most likely, though, square dancers will bristle a bit when Bing dances with his partner on his left.

Famous cowboy icon, Roy Rogers. called square dancing in some films. But not surprisingly. Roy had started as a musician (a member of the *The Sons of the Pioneers*) and had learned to call to pick up some extra cash. In those days he went by other names, most often by his birth name Leonard Slye. After several roles as the fictional Roy Rogers, he legally changed his name. Perhaps the most interesting square dancing Roy did on screen was in *My Pal Trigger* – a fictionalized account of how Roy got the first Trigger. The square dance was a short sequence of mounted riders taking their steeds through some reasonably simple patterns, but it is a lot of fun to watch the horseback square dancing.

Some folks wondered if Roy could actually call a square dance. Contemporary caller Nate Bliss shared this story of Roy:

In 1965, while I was the caller for the Mach II Squares at George AFB, Victorville, CA, Roy came to a special dance that we had called "Welcome Home from Viet Nam!" Roy was a fairly new resident in Apple Valley at the time.

We had invited him to make an appearance, and offer a few words to the Airmen who had just returned from South East Asia. When he arrived, a couple of our old timers said, 'We've seen you call in the movies. Would you call something for us?'

He was very gracious about welcoming the Airmen back. However, he was reluctant to try to call as he had heard me calling as he came in. He apologized to the dancers by saying, 'You've seen me call in the movies. But, we had rehearsals.'

The dancers still wanted him to call some-thing. So, he did for about 3 minutes. The calls were very traditional, and no one could do it. We all got a good laugh about it. Roy stayed to sign some autographs and left before the dance was over. I would say, "Yes, I've heard Roy Rogers call at a Square Dance."

Undoubtedly, the appearance of square dancing in some of the fine (and not so fine) Hollywood films helped the activity gain the popularity among the public that it did. For the most part the "dancers" in those films were actors, or extras, many were members of the Actors Guild, or Screen Extras Guild. They were selected for the film, not so much on how well they could dance, but if they looked like square dancers (in the minds of the casting crew). They were taught

to do just enough square dancing in order to fill the require-
ments of the script.

Fortunately, some of these films utilized the knowledge of experienced square dance callers and teachers. Others, unfortunately, did not and, as a result, some of the studios were all but inundated with letters of outrage and dis-
pleasure. To follow up on the idea of square dance in movies,
John Brandt, a member of the Valley Trailers square dance
club from the San Fernando Valley in California, made a list
of movies that included square dance sequences. According
to John, 62% of the pictures were made in the 40s and 50s.
"Of course," John writes, "our nation was locked into a fascination with the "old west" way of life, mainly fueled by
Hollywood. Hundreds of western films were produced in the
40's and 50's. The early days of television were also dominated by westerns. The cowboy image was in, and the old
time dances portrayed in the films were popular with the
public. Square dancing fit the Hollywood image of the time;
the western wear, the music, and the dancing all fit the concept Hollywood had created. It was what the public wanted."

Here then is the list. Perhaps you've seen some of
them, or you may still get the opportunity late some evening
after your club dance to catch one of these old-timers.

The Great Train Robbery – 1909
The Old Barn Dance – 1938 – (Gene Autry)
Gone With the Wind - 1939 (Clark Gable. Virginia Reel
    played very fast.)
Destry Rides Again - 1939 (Jimmy Stewart and Marlene
    Dietrich)
Drums Along the Mohawk - 1939 (Henry Fonda, "Circle
    Dance and Reel")
Pride and Prejudice - 1940
The Westerner - 1940 (Walter Brennan and Gary Cooper)
State Fair - 1945

Sheriff of Cimarron - 1945 (Cowboy hero Sunset Carson dances)
Christmas in Connecticut - 1945 (Barbara Stanwyck)
Duel in the Sun - 1946 (Lloyd Shaw)
My Darling Clementine - 1946 (Henry Fonda)
My Pal Trigger - 1946 (Roy Rogers, square dancing on horses.)
Welcome Stranger - 1947 (Bing Crosby)
Square Dance Jubilee - 1949
Roseanna McCoy - 1949 (Farley Granger and Joan Evans)
Summer Stock - 1950 (Gene Kelly and Judy Garland)
Square Dance Katy - 1950
Copper Canyon - 1950 (Ray Milland with Les Gotcher calling.)
Hillbilly Hare - 1950 (Bugs Bunny calls)
Louisa - 1950 (Charles Coburn and Spring Byington)
Wagonmaster - 1950 (Ward Bond)
War of the Worlds - 1953 (Gene "Bat Masterson" Barry)
Seven Brides for Seven Brothers - 1954 (Jane Powell, Russ Tamblyn)
Oklahoma! - 1955
King and Four Queens - 1956 (Clark Gable)
Giant - 1956 (Elizabeth Taylor. Rock Hudson, James Dean)
Pardners - 1956 (Dean Martin and Jerry Lewis - Note: Square dance sequence was cut before release of the film.)
Searchers - 1956 (John Wayne)
Indiscreet - 1958 (Cary Grant and Ingrid Bergman) – (Cary does a side-splitting Eightsome Reel)
McClintock - 1963 (John Wayne)
Barry Lyndon - 1975 (Ryan O'Neal)
Bound for Glory - 1976 (Bruce Johnson does the calling.)
Comes A Horseman - 1978 (Jane Fonda, James Caan , Ja son Robards)
Square Dance - 1987 (Jason Robards, Jane Alexander, Winona Ryder, Rob Lowe)

My Cousin Vinny - 1992 (Joe Pesci)

Son In Law - 1993 (Paulie Shore, Ernie Kinney calling)

Ethan Frome - 1993 (Liam Neeson)

Barbarians At the Gate - 1993 (James Garner, modern style square dancing with Vern Weese calling to the music of the Ghost Riders)

Four Weddings and a Funeral - 1994 (Dashing White Sergeant – three face three)

Perhaps the earliest film with a square dance scene was *The Great Train Robbery* of 1909. It is a silent film and the plot is as simple as it gets: gang robs train, citizens are outraged and form posse, gang is wiped out by citizens in gun battle in the woods where the gang divided the money. It just turns out that the citizens were involved in a square dance in town when they were told about the robbery. Surprisingly, the dance is in the foreground of the action, and it stops only when the dancers are told of the robbery and all the men head for their horses.

In 1938, Gene Autry made *The Old Barn Dance,* which begins with men on horses singing. Gene hopes to sell his horses at Grangeville. The blacksmith's forge is turning into a gas station because tractors are more efficient. The bandwagon rolls into town for a barn dance. Gene advertises a big barn dance at which he plans to sell horses, but horse sales are terrible. The bad guy is the tractor salesman who writes fraudulent contracts that start costing the farmers their ranches. Sally, the radio station owner, wants to hire Gene for a radio program, but the tractor man owns the station. There never is much of a dance; mostly we see Smiley Burnett pushing the barn dance. Roy Rogers has a bit roll.

No doubt there were other films in the early years of the century that had square dance scenes in them, but generally they are forgettable. 1939 brought some remarkable dance scenes to the big screen. *Gone with the Wind,* with Clark Gable and Vivien Leigh, is probably one of the most popular films of all time, and part of its attraction is the grand ball scene. The Civil War has been raging for much longer than anyone predicted, and as the dance scene begins, the South is feeling very optimistic because General Lee has crossed into Yankee territory. The couple dancing is pulsingly emotional. The cap to the dancing is the Virginia Reel, as announced by the Master of Ceremonies. The dance could not be more appropriate because it is named for a Southern state, and it was loved by the Founding Fathers of the nation, and has become a symbol of independence. The dance is very fast, yet formal, and does not last much longer than Southern independence.

A more traditional square dance showed up in *Destry Rides Again* with Jimmy Stewart and Marlene Dietrich. Stewart plays a somewhat bumbling lawman opposed to the criminal element headed by saloon owner Dietrich. Inevitably the banjo and fiddle show up and there is a square dance in the bar. The dance figures are recognizable, but, as usual, the dancing we see does not fit what is being called at the time. But this one is just about as good as it gets. It fits into the plot and represents some decent dancing on the part of the star. Also in 1939 *Drums Along the Mohawk* was released. I think the purpose of the film was to build up feelings of American patriotism as the conflict in Europe intensified. The story deals with a young Henry Fonda, who brings his society raised wife to the backwoods country of upstate New York. They face the hardships of building a home, raising crops, and worse yet, Indian attacks, led by an unscrupulous British agent. At a barn raising, the folks break out into pretty decent versions of a circle dance and a reel that would have been popular at the time.

Nineteen-forty saw a couple of good dance sequences also. The seriously simplified version of *Pride and*

Prejudice with Laurence Olivier and Greer Garson was released. Since the plot deals with different levels of society, a big social ball must take place, with the English style of dancing. A much rowdier film of the year was *The Westerner,* with Walter Brennan as Judge Roy Bean (the hanging judge). Gary Cooper manages to be in the wrong place at the wrong time and ends up in Bean's courtroom. Through some clever negotiations Cooper is not hanged, but he is drawn into Bean's world – a barroom. The inevitable square dance breaks out which gives Cooper a chance to speak quickly with a number of other characters. There is some especially good by-play between Cooper and Dietrich in the square dance.

A number of films from the mid-1940s worked square dancing into the mix. Most notable are *State Fair* (1945) and *Duel in the Sun* (1946). You would think that a film about a State Fair would include some real square dancing, especially with Iowa as the setting, but the dancing is actually a stage number put on by the big band that was hired as entertainment for the fair goers. It is a huge cast number in which the dancers move through a variety of formations (never a square) that are reminiscent of square dancing – lines and concentric circles. But it is all lively and colorful.

Earlier, in the chapter about Dr. Shaw, we talked about *Duel in the Sun* because Pappy Shaw did the choreography and calling. It is still about the best mix of story and accurate dancing...and not just square dancing but also the perennial favorite varsouvianna (Put Your Little Foot).

In 1949, *Roseanna McCoy"* made its debut with a lot of hoopla. There were many articles and advertisements in Los Angeles newspapers and magazines about the film. But, there was almost as much about the Square Dance Jamboree that would precede the premier showing of the movie at the

Pantages Theatre in Hollywood. The major push was, of course, to get people to buy tickets to the movie and see the love story of Roseanna McCoy and Johnse Hatfield. The feud between the families is in full swing, but all it takes is for the young Hatfield to see the beautiful young McCoy at the square dance to get the tempestuous romance going. Johnse falls immediately in love with Roseanna, manages to get her away from her family for a moment, and tells her that she is his and always will be. From that moment, the romance builds in spite of the feud. The cast of the film is outstanding, including the 15 year old ingénue Joan Evans who plays Roseanna. Here is how a Los Angeles newspaper reviewed the premiere.

THE MIRROR-LOS ANGELES,
SAT., SEPT. 17,1949

"More Romancin' Than Feudin' in 'Roseanna'"
By DICK WILLIAMS
Somehow Hollywood has previously never gotten around to the fabled feud of the West Virginia Hatfields and the Kentucky McCoys. But Samuel Goldwyn's 'Roseanna McCoy,' which opened with a Pantages premiere last night rectifies the omission.
The result is a pleasant if not exceptional mountain love story with more emphasis on romance than feuding.
Young Roseanna (played by 15 year old new comer Joan Evens) is content enough with her pastoral life until she meets dashing Johnse Hatfield (Farley Granger) at a country fair.
When he totes her off to be his bride, all hell, as the saying goes in the hoss opera circles, breaks loose. The hard working McCoys drop their hoes to even the score with the lazy Hatfields who hole up in a fort across the Big Sandy river. In less time than you

247

can do a square dance promenade, rifle bullets are whining through the pine woods as the rival clans clash...

The premiere was preceded by some fancy square dance proceedings on the stage called by Bob Osgood, 'Jonesy', and Ted Roland. The 48 dancers set a colorful mood for the film which followed.

The last paragraph tells you my connection to the movie. The promotion work for the live square dancers was pretty heady stuff, but I could handle it. It was advertised as a "Square Dance Jamboree."

The premiere of 'Roseanna McCoy' will be accompanied by a square dance jamboree next Friday night at the Pantages Theater. All seats will be reserved. Under the direction of Caller Bob Osgood, 48 experts will demonstrate the intricacies of the dance craze on the stage of the theater prior to the showing of the picture...

Oh my, those Hollywood advertising people really laid it on thick...at times I thought I was the star of the movie. For example:

Bob Osgood, One of California's Favorite Square Dance Callers, has many open as well as invitational clubs in the Southern California area. A nationally-known Square Dance figure, (Originator and editor of the National monthly magazine for Square Dancers, "Sets in Order," which has a circulation covering more than 40 States and foreign countries. In addition, he has co-authored two books on square dancing for the beginner and the intermediate).

248

First caller in the country with a weekly Television Square Dance program (over KNBH and KFI-TV for 33 weeks. Huge following of "Living-room square dancers").

One of the first five callers in this area (there are now more than 150) Osgood began calling and teaching in 1940. During the War (Navy) he called square dances in different States and Hawaii. During the last year he called in Washington, D.C., Milwaukee, Wisc., Colorado Springs, Santa Fe, Chicago, Houston, and San Francisco.

He recently gave up a position as Director of Public Relations for a large national soft drink company (Squirt) to spend all his time editing "Sets in Order," teaching and calling for Square Dances, running a Square Dance book and "Record Square" which he set up in his living room 5 months ago.

As an instructor for Los Angeles State College he is training a group of 32 Park and Playground directors to become callers and teachers. In June he was on the faculty of the College of the Pacific folk-dance camp, instructing callers and teachers from all over the country. He has been a member of Dr. Lloyd Shaw's summer Square Dance classes in Colorado Springs for the last 3 years.

Well, at least the publicity people also gave some credit to Fenton 'Jonesy' Jones, one of the most popular callers in the country.

All the square dancers in this area, and all those in different parts of the country who dance regularly to his records, believe that 'Jonesy' is just about TOPS as a singing caller.

While not exactly a rarity, patter calls with him are not nearly as typical as the Western singing calls that he uses so frequently. A "native prune picker," 'Jonesy' was born in Los Angeles in 1907 and has been in the entertainment field, playing his guitar, singing, and yodeling since 1930.

A feature artist on the Hollywood Barn Dance program over CBS for a year, then a 15 minute program on KIEV, introduced him to Southern California long before the present Square Dance "gold rush." Jonesy, who started calling in 1937, says, "I just learned four calls, and found me a club to call to and started in."

He loves the singing calls - not as an Eastern caller calls but as a cowboy does in the Western style with an increasing tempo. "One highlight in my calling career," says Jonesy, "was when I was asked to call a dance for 200 teenagers. However, I didn't know until I arrived at the dance that the teenagers were all Chinese. They ate hot dogs and drank pop just like any other Americans, and thoroughly enjoyed themselves with the Square Dance so I figured they were truly American. It was one of the best evenings, I have ever spent."

We really did have six squares of dancers on stage for the show. A number of the dancers were called the "Forty-Niners," which was actually an exhibition group formed out of my Rip 'n' Snort club. They were the dancers I used in the TV shows on KNBH and KFI and in the live square dance show at the Hollywood Bowl. We also had the "Old-Timers," another spin off from Rip 'n' Snort. Some of the Old-Timers appear in the movie. They really were the old-timers because the youngest member of the group was about 20 years older than the combined ages of all of the members of the third group, "The Tiny-Tots," whose average age was six. Jonesy and Ted Roland also had members of their groups perform during this Square Dance Jamboree. I understand that there were live square dance shows before the movie in other parts of the country.

Between my visibility through the *Roseanna McCoy* opening, the magazine, the TV shows, and the square dance show at the Hollywood Bowl (more about that later), I began to draw the attention of the Hollywood moguls. In 1950 I received a phone call that should have made me jump. But, coming as it did right in the middle of all the excitement of the start of the Contemporary Western Club Square Dancing - a new magazine, calling for classes and clubs almost every night, etc., the phone call probably didn't make the impression on me that it would have in a less tumultuous time.

"Hello, my name is Nick Castle, I'm with MGM motion pictures. Are you the square dance caller, Bob Osgood?"

"I am."

"Well, we're about to do a picture that includes some square dancing in the script. I don't know diddle about square dancing. What I do know about is choreography of almost any other type. My question is, would you be willing to come in and train our dancers for a picture we're about to do?"

I was calling at nights, and by that time, was full-blast into square dancing. I had given up my job with the Squirt Company. I was interested and said I would like to come in for an interview. The voice assured me that it wouldn't take too much of my time, and he would have a guest pass at the main gate when I arrived.

Mr. Castle met me at the gate, and while walking me to one of the large sound stages, explained that this new picture called *Summer Stock* was to take place in a farm town in New England in the late 1940s. He said they were going to do a picture with Judy Garland and Gene Kelly, and he mentioned some of the other actors and actresses who were going to be in it. And he introduced me to the director, whose name I don't remember. The story was about a group of amateur actors going to do summer stock. They found a place with a barn they could use - it's a ranch or a farm run by Judy Garland. The head of the actors' troupe is Gene Kelly. The catch to the story is that every Friday night, the local people come in and have a square dance. Even though the show is in full rehearsal, everything has got to stop because the people must have their square dance. Mr. Castle told me he would like dances that would be done in that era, and could I help him?

I thought to myself, being a Southern California western type of square dance caller, I hadn't done a great deal of the Eastern stuff, but why not take a crack at it. I knew some dances that would have been done at that time or before.

"No problem," I told him.

"We'd need you for several days to plan the dances, work with our music department, and train our dancers so that the dancing, the calling and the music fit the picture."

I said that would be fine.

"We'll pay you $100 a day, is that satisfactory?"

Callers back then were lucky to get $15 or $25 for an evening's calling. One hundred dollars, as compared to my regular $25 for an evening, seemed like a real bonanza, not realizing that the work I was to do would normally draw a much larger paycheck.

The way the movie folk work is to have the principals that dance and two lead couples which are professional dancers work together. These people don't know diddle about square dancing, but they learn the dance action. When the director and choreographer are content, they bring in the extras to be taught. We worked out "Portland Fancy" and I also showed them half a dozen things that I thought might have been done during that time period in the way of couple dancing. Once things were settled on the dances, we taught the lead people, and a piano player. The piano player went with the orchestra, and they recorded the music. It was interesting that in "Portland Fancy," we used a figure that was in public domain, so we had no trouble doing that exactly. But the tune for "Laces and Graces" was too much like a copyrighted tune, so they used the counter melody. They underplayed the strong melody so it didn't sound like the music we used, but had the exact tempo. It was great music.

From such experiences as this come the special moments one will always remember. There was one point during the rehearsals when Nick Castle, Gene Kelly, the several dancers who made up the pilot group, and I were in one of the practice rooms running through the couple dance.

"Here's how I see it played," said Kelly, taking one of the young ladies in open dance position, "We'll move counter-clockwise around the room then turn to face - like this." As the two turned and started to back away,

Barn dance in Summer Stock

a voice, loud and clear, shouted from the back of the hall. "NO, no, no! You look like a couple of farmhands. Here, let me show you how it's danced."

The voice had moved up to where we were and, literally shoving Kelly aside, Fred Astaire (unexpectedly visiting the set), took his place and, regardless of the fact that he had no idea of what the dance was that was being rehearsed, set off in a wild polka which required his thrilled, but apprehensive partner, to hang on for dear life.

So, we went ahead and worked with the lead extras for a day. Then they brought in all the townspeople, all ages, but mostly older people, who they thought would be typical of the old timers in the community. We taught them "Portland Fancy," and "Laces and Graces." Then I had to teach one of the actors to call, and he did a good job. Anyway, the long and the short of it was it was a very successful deal. In watching the movie now, you would think these people had been doing "Portland Fancy" all their lives.

An interesting side story is that one time, while I was watching them move the sets around, change the electrical, and other things, I was sitting on a bench when Gene Kelly came over and sat down beside me and said, "I just wanted you to know that I just think this is so great. Our family watches the television show you've got on. America is made up of a lot of people who spend a great deal of their time sitting and watching 22 people bash their heads in football, or a bunch on the basketball court, or whatever it is. And we're a nation of spectators. Square dancing is allowing people to get out and do it, and find out what fun it is to be a dancer. You don't have to be a performer. You're just a dancer."

All in all, *Summer Stock* turned out to be a pretty good movie. The dance scene, which starts out with the town folk at their square dance, gets upset by the young actors. Here is one review from a Los Angeles paper:

YOUNG HOLLYWOOD:
New Dance Routine Has Atomic Bounce

by Reba and Bonnie Churchill

The year 1950 has started with a bang! There's a brand new dance epidemic that's already cornering the younger set's interest, It has an "atomic" bounce that makes the revival of the Charleston resemble a minuet.

Gene Kelly and Choreographer Nick Castle have taught Nita Bieber, Carleton Carpenter, and a dozen young Metro players how to do a swing square dance. It has proved so much fun and so gay that the dance has been incorporated into MGM's musical, "Summer Stock."

The dance starts out like any ordinary square - "All join hands and circle to the left," but here the similarity ends. The caller, whose tongue looks as if it's on a yo-yo, keeps up with the mounting tempo by changing a few directions. Instead of doe-di-doe-ing by your partner, the caller instructs, "Lindy across;" in place of turning in place, you "shag on the spot," and replacing promenade back home, you "Balboa to place."

Carleton Carpenter, who debuted in "Lost Boundaries," confessed he'd attended many a farm hoedown in his native Beddington, Vt., but never danced at such a peppery tempo.

255

In October of 1950 I was contracted to do the choreography, train the dancers, and do the calling for a film with the working title of *December Bride.* It was released as *Louisa,* and starred Ronald

Spring Byington & Charles Coburn

Reagan, Spring Byington, and Charles Coburn. Spring Byington (as Louisa) is the elderly mother of Ronald Reagan and has moved into her son's house so she would not be alone after her husband passed away. She desperately wants to do things right and to be helpful, but her help is seen as being disruptive to the household. She meets the local grocer, who is a widower. They date, and find that they are compatible. However, Reagan and the family have trouble with his mother dating a "mere" grocer. To get some work done for the company, Reagan's boss (Charles Coburn) comes to the house and is immediately smitten by Louisa. There is a rivalry between the grocer and the CEO which is settled at a square dance at the local country club. The dance is set up so that Louisa dances with the two primary rivals and another 10 men. The square dancing is traditional, and the calling and the dancing coordinate. The scene devolves into a "limbo stick" dance with Louisa and Coburn winning the contest by eventually sliding under the bar on their backs. I take pride in the fact that the dance is accurate, and it advances the story, a very rare occurrence in Hollywood films.

Also in 1950 another western, *Copper Canyon,* starring Hedy Lamarr and Ray Milland was released. Lamarr is the female crime boss in town who has hired Milland as a trick shooting entertainer. She

Ray Milland & Hedy Lamarr

does not know that he is actually an undercover agent. Our interest in the movie is the square dance held in the saloon. As usual, the square dance allows major characters to circulate and talk about business or make social arrangements. The dancing and the music are creditable, thanks to Hall of Fame caller Les Gotcher, who did the choreography and calling. As was so often the case, people who did side roles in movies in those days were not credited, so Les did not get screen credit. But, if you look fast, you can see the camera pan across the face of the caller – that's Les.

You may not think that a science fiction film would lend itself to a square dance scene, but that was exactly the case with *War of the Worlds* (1953) with Gene Barry. Barry is a scientist who has gone out into the country to investigate the crash of something from outer space. Since he has to stay over to complete his study, he asks what the town folk do for excitement. The pastor jumps in saying that there is a square dance that night. The dancing does not last too long, and it is acceptable. There is some dialogue that plays over the dancing.

I think most people have seen *Seven Brides for Seven Brothers.* It is a comedy where the somewhat uncouth brothers abduct the town girls they have fallen for in order to

marry them. One scene has the men involved in a barn raising, which is actually a competition between the country
boys and the city boys. Once the barn is up, it is time for a
barn raising dance. It starts off nice, but then Hollywood
takes over by changing the action to a competitive dance. It
is one of the really exciting dance scenes to ever come out of
Hollywood.

As far as dancing goes, *Four Queens and a King*
(1956) with Clark Gable comes as a real surprise. Gable is a
charming con-man who weasels his way onto a ranch run by
an older woman and her four beautiful daughters. He sort of
convinces them all that he loves them, but really he just loves
the gold that is hidden somewhere on the ranch. One scene
has everyone feeling spirited, and Gable dances with each of
the four daughters in a playful "square dance," one lady on
each side and Gable in the middle.

One day in 1954, I received an SOS from a gentleman by the name of Elmo Williams. He was a top film editor
out here in Hollywood (he won an Oscar for editing "High
Noon") and, on this occasion, he was just finishing a documentary film on the American Cowboy. While shooting one
of the sequences in New Mexico, he had taken about three
minutes of a typical square dance. He suddenly realized that
he had no sound track for this portion of the movie. Could
we help? You never know until you try just what you can or
can't do, so I took Arnie Kronenberger over to the studio to
have a look. In the small projection room, we were quite
thrilled by the color of the several sets of dancers doing a
beautiful job with some square, but for the life us we had no
idea which one! Because we didn't even know what music
was used, we had to guess that this was a patter call. Working
backwards from the finished dance to come up with the call
was a new challenge, but by watching the film over and over

for two days, we finally wrote calls that seemed to fit the movements.

Next we had to record the calls and music so that they could be added on to the film. Using a special editing viewer called a moviola, we took a blank piece of film and, noting each time the dancers would take a step, we would punch a hole in the corresponding blank. This blank, when played at regular speed, gave us the metronome count of 136 beats per minute. This was how fast our musicians would play. After practicing our calls with hoedown music that our band had worked out, we moved to a large sound recording studio and were able to deliver the needed sound track.

The movie was a documentary on the life of the American cowboy, and this segment was about a Saturday night when there was a dance in the next town 20 miles away. The cowboys clean up, then ride the 20 miles on horseback to get to the social. Some folks are already up on a raised stage dancing while others are crowded around the refreshment table. The dance scene is really pretty long for a Hollywood movie, and thank heavens, they did not zoom in on the caller. It was tough enough to get the music and calls to fit what the dancers were doing, and I did not want to have to lip synch with an on screen caller. Even when the camera goes away from the dancing to follow a couple walking in the shade of the trees, the music and calling continue. You will easily be able to identify the calls and match them up with what the dancers are doing. I never did find out where the dancers came from, or who the original caller was, but that is my voice as if I were actually there.

We have already taken a look at the making of *Giant* (1956) with Elizabeth Taylor, Rock Hudson, and James Dean. The story is obviously ripe material for an article in Sets in Order. Here is how I wrote it for the magazine:

SQUARE DANCING in the MOVIES
By Bob Osgood

[Editor's Note: For years now Osgood has been pestering me to let him write a first person article on square dancing in the Entertainment World — as he sees it. He believes that square dancing can be presented correctly in the movies and on TV and he's doing what he can to campaign in that direction. Here is the first of two experiences in motion pictures. The second will appear in a couple of months. Bob Osgood, Editor]

Bob Osgood with "Giant" director George Stevens

HERE are your 100 dance extras, Mr. Osgood. You are to pick out 60 and have them rehearsed and ready to shoot day after tomorrow." The 'dancers'are all over the great sound stage on the Warner Brothers lot in Burbank. Most of them have been in pictures all their lives — all are listed at Central Casting as "Square Dancers" and all are members of the "Guild." They're all shapes and sizes. Most of the men have cowboy boots. All are eager to be chosen.

I am told that from this group the ones I select must be trained to dance like Texans circa 1945. The picture is Edna Ferber's, "Giant." The director is George Stevens. My job as Technical Director — get them dancing.

For the last week I've been working with Actor Bob Nichols who will do the calling on the screen. He's never been to a square dance but as an actor he earnestly tackles the job of learning the square dance calls I have put together with plenty of long distance telephone assistance on Texas styles from Bertha Hoick (Foot 'n' Fiddle) in Austin, Texas. The music selection was another big step. With help from

Square Dancer Hal Findlay in the Warner Bros. Music Department and with direction by Academy Award Winner Dimitri Tiomkin the score was arranged and the music and the calls pre-recorded.

There's only one way to select the dancers — watch them dance. They respond quickly to my request to make a large circle. Now for the simple calls and we'll work up to something more difficult. "Bow to your partner — Bow to your corner." Whoops! They're all over the place. Try another — "Swing your partner." It's a madhouse. Some men are still bowing; there's a bit of elbow swinging going on; some right, some left, some impartial. Here's a 2-hand swing, and this couple's promenading.

Not really much else to do but find the ones that look most like square dancers, and can hear and move to the music, then teach them from the ground up. The sixty are finally selected and told to come in at 8 the following morning for a full day's rehearsal.

We get started at 9. I have a pilot square picked out and they learn the routine first. No basics here. Just teach what they need for the scene and nothing else. (They'll look like experts doing this one number, but let a caller give them one figure out of sequence and wow!). Finally it's 10:30 A.M. and all the squares are learning the routine quite nicely. Another six hours and we should be fairly passable.

"All Square Dancers over to Make-Up and then to Stage 9 for shooting this afternoon!"

It's an assistant director on the P.A. system. Only two hours' practice and they're going to try to take this! I'm told not to worry (pshaw, I never worry!).

Stage 9 is really something! A giant swimming pool and a garden. Hundreds of extras in bathing suits and western attire to lend atmosphere. The stars; Elizabeth Taylor,

Rock Hudson, James Dean, and many more are all over the place. How are they going to make this look convincing?

Bit by bit the scene is rehearsed and little by little it shapes up as if by some magic. The cameramen get the scene ready for shooting all that afternoon. The following day it's shot some more. Every conceivable angle is covered.

Hudson, Taylor, and Osgood

"Giant" Caller Bob Nichols

The miracle of moving pictures transports the actors and scenery back 10 years and 2000 miles to Texas. It all looks so real yes, even the square dancing!

Several years after *Summer Stock* and the same year as *Giant*, I got another call from Nick Castle. "This next film," said Nick Castle on the phone, "will be a bit different than the one you did for us before. Starring Dean Martin and Jerry Lewis, it will be a comedy and we'd like you to create the choreography and teach the calls to both Dean and Jerry. We can probably wrap up your part in three or four days. Will you do it?"

This time the action was at Paramount Studios. The set was western, and the story had to do with the two men somehow getting involved in what might have turned out to be a fight, but instead became a moderately wild square dance. The director and Nick Castle wanted the calls to be legitimate, but what would be happening during the dancing, and with the two men sharing the calling, would be nothing short of mayhem. Figuring that all of this would not set square dancing back, I said okay.

For this film there are hundreds of extras, plus an entire team of dancers, not square dancers, mind you, but folks who had appeared in such films as *Oklahoma* and *Seven Brides for Seven Brothers*. As choreographer, Castle's job was to blend in more than a dozen musical numbers, the dancing and drama action, and, of course, the endless bits of comedy that Martin and Lewis injected into the script. My job, Castle explained to me, was to provide an authentic series of square dance movements that could be worked into the one big production number in the picture.

"I don't want to make the same mistake twice," Nick explained to me and to the group of dancers on the rehearsal stage. "A few years back I did the dances for a movie on the life of a famous pioneer. The script called for a square dance in one of the scenes, and I put my best efforts into what turned out to be a rather Hollywood version of a Hoedown.

263

I didn't just get dozens or even hundreds of letters. I got thousands from ardent square dance fans all over the country suggesting that I portray their hobby with a bit more care in the future. That's why I want to be sure that these scenes are authentic."

The three weeks I spent with Nick and the dancers and working closely with Dean Martin and Jerry Lewis provided me with an unforgettable experience. When you see the picture *Pardners* you'll witness about seven minutes of square dancing such as you've never viewed before. Actually, the dancing steps and the calls are pretty straight – but when you turn Jerry Lewis loose on the center of the dance floor and expect him to call while in the middle of a Rip 'n Snort or Texas Star, you're in for something unique.

Jerry Lewis on the set of "Pardners"

A square of experienced dance extras worked with me until we created a workable routine. The next step was to work with each of the actors, which was the fun part. As it turned out, this was Dean and Jerry's last film together and you could sense a strain between the pair. They indeed were professionals, and took to learning the calls in as serious a manner as they did the balance of the script.

In working with the three or four squares of dancer extras, it soon became apparent that I was not teaching any of them to dance. My job was to teach them a routine they would be doing in the show.

264

Two little side lights: I mentioned a while back that I called for a small group of movie and theater people in their various homes on a once or twice a month basis. One of the most enthusiastic dancers was Ed Demetrick, and over a period of time, we had a number of conversations about the activity. At one of the breaks, while the electricians were setting up the lighting, Ed showed up with Spencer Tracy. The two were working on the picture *The Right Hand of God* on one of the other sound stages. While there was a break in their shooting, Ed figured it was a good opportunity to introduce Mr. Tracy to "his caller." I was impressed!

Unfortunately, after *Pardners* was released, I had to write the "Wha' Hoppened Department" article for Sets in Order. "I wish I could explain what hoppened over at Paramount Studios a month or so ago, just prior to the release of the picture *Pardners*, but the whole thing is a kind of a mystery. Some of the folks around here managed to attend preview performances of the new Martin and Lewis extravaganza and said the square dancing looked real great. Finally the day of the beginning of the regular run of the picture arrived and whambo! The phone started ringing. "Where's the square dancing?" "Were you feeding us a line?" Well, sir, it appears that the picture was just five minutes too long and the economics of the motion picture industry dictate that if a picture goes longer than a certain number of minutes it steadily loses its viewer appeal. So what gets pulled? The square dancing. Natch. Kind of a disappointment. I think you would have enjoyed the rather unique display of square dancing talent. Oh well, it might have set the whole activity back 20 years anyway (but I did have fun). - Incidentally, if you look real closely at the coming attraction trailers for this particular picture they tell me that you'll see some of the square dancing.

265

A film I was not involved with, but I think is worth mentioning is *Indiscreet* (1958), with Cary Grant and Ingrid Bergman. It does not have a traditional American square dance, but it has one of the funniest dance sequences I've ever seen. The "Eightsome Reel" is a traditional Scottish country dance, which is done in a square formation, and there's an occasional grand right and left that you'll recognize. The figure involves each dancer showing off his/her skill and style by going through a set pattern with each of the other dancers in the square. Grant's enthusiasm is strongly contrasted by Bergman's disgust with him at the time.

Jumping ahead several years, David Carradine did a really creditable job of creating Woody Guthrie in the 1976 film *Bound for Glory*. It is about Guthrie's early days in

Carradine on fiddle as Guthrie: Caller Bruce Johnson on right

the Texas dust bowl during the Great Depression, to his time riding the rails, and to his gaining some fame with his songs. However, Guthrie was always in trouble for supporting the union movement. In the film, Guthrie was the fiddle player in a square dance band with Bruce Johnson as the caller. Bruce was known for his showmanship, musicianship, and big voice, as he shows in the film. He shouted out the calls with no microphone or megaphone and was heard over the sound of the four-piece band. Given the technical difficulties

of matching sound and action, the dancing is quite creditable. Bruce also got a couple of more lines in the movie.

For something absolutely silly, there is a square
dance scene in *Son in Law"* starring Pauley Shore. Shore is
a city kid who gets to spend some vacation time on a farm.
He is set up to be a contrast with the previous year's high
school football hero who still believes that he is exempt from
the rules. Shore goes to the square dance and cannot quite
believe how square it is, so he takes the microphone and
jazzes the style up a lot. When he finishes he has all of the
young folk at the edge of the stage, so Shore dives into the
mosh pit and is supported by the kids. The caller, the famous
Ernie Kinney, gets his microphone back, calls a bit, and decides it's his turn for the mosh pit. But as he leaps, the people
all stand back and we see Kinney falling into empty space.

And one more film worth mentioning is *Barbarians
at the Gate,* with James Garner as a ruthless, ambitious cor-
porate CEO (the movie is based on the story of RJ Reynolds
Tobacco and Nabisco Foods). To create a scene where Garner has to meet all of the principals in the stock negotiations
in the same place, there is a society, dress-up western square
dance. Garner has to move through each of the movements
and is face to face in conversation throughout the dance. The
calls were all legitimate, but as usual, Hollywood did not
care if the dancing fit the calls. Kudos to Verne Weese who
called and to the Ghost Riders Square Dance Band which
played for the scene.

(Just a little aside: I was walking through the halls at
a National Square Dance Convention with Paul Moore when
he stopped to chat with someone I did not know. Paul then
introduced me to Dan Bright, the lead guitar player for Ghost
Riders. From Dan's reaction you would have thought I was
the President, or someone important. Next I found myself
tagging along with those two back to the main hall. A tradition of the Ghost Riders is to have famous callers sign the

guitar, and even though I had never called to them, or even recall having listened to them, Dan found the cleanest most protected spot on the guitar for me to sign. I wonder where that guitar is now, or if he went home and cleaned it.)

There were many more films made that included clips of square dancing, but I was not involved in most of them, I haven't even seen many of them. But, my big foray into film was the one I produced for Sets in Order.

In 1951, When Sets in Order was barely two years old, square dancing had reached "fad" proportions not only in our own area, but in many places across North America. We had several exhibition groups in those days, and spent quite a bit of time in traveling to meetings and conventions showing the non-dancing public what square dancing was all about. We began to find ourselves in the recipient spot of receiving kudos and complaints about the activity in general, and some parts of it in particular. Accepting the spot of un-official ombudsman, we were able, in some situations, to lend a helping hand, and a bit of optimism where it seemed to be needed.

One complaint frequently voiced was about the image square dancing was getting from magazines, newspapers, and especially, from motion pictures. Square dancing of sorts was portrayed in many movies. Most of them were Westerns, where a bunch of pioneer types would get up and, in the course of telling the story, do somebody's concept of a square dance.

Many times these cinematic views involved knowledgeable individuals, real callers, or dancers. But many times, the dancing depicted tended to irk the new dancers just coming out of class, and the callers whose responsibility it was to steer clear of the old barnyard feeling.

Fully aware of this, we started early in the game looking for some individuals or organizations who might depict square dancing in a favorable way, and make it available on film. We weren't too successful.

During a conversation with our staff, Joe Fadler (our photographer) started us thinking. "Why not put out a film of our own?" With a number of exhibition groups around the area it shouldn't be too difficult to round up a few dancers. But then, who would we portray in the film as being the typ-

Opening credits for SIO Film "Square Dancing"

ical age and appearance of today's dancer? In the process of attempting to solve that question we came up with a solution. Let's use four available groups depicting four different age blocks and have each group in turn demonstrate one of the prime square dance forms of the day. Once having done this we should be in a position to see what, if any, route to take.

Fadler said that he could handle the photography, Chuck Jones (of Bugs Bunny fame) helped with the script, and local caller, Leif Hetland, helped to organize the myriad details involved.

With the help of Dorothy Martin, one of our strong supporters, a group of youngsters of grade school age could fit in nicely. And a second group she had been working with, youngsters in the one to ten year old bracket could work out

269

very well. We had been doing exhibitions around the area with a group of young married men and women, the Rip 'n' Snorters, who were typically costumed. They would be our pivotal square.

Then, for our fourth and final unit, we thought back to a group of old timers who came and danced with our club on occasions. These were folks, grandparents and even great-grandparents ranging from mid-60's to high 70's. A quick check with the group at the dance one evening proved that this would be a great choice. Later we learned that these "old-timers" were experienced square dancers and showed up in a number of the old westerns.

So now we had the dancers, and we had the photographer. Coming up with some sort of a script would be no problem. But where will the shooting take place? Because it would be occurring on Saturday mornings over a period of two months, we started looking at my home on Swall. It was a not-too-large stucco bungalow separated from Beverly Boulevard by a gas station, and it had a long concrete driveway leading up to a one car garage at the back of the property. It didn't appear that we had a great deal to work with. That's where our friends in square dancing came in.

Take a Little Peek

With the help of a couple of club members, who were also involved in screen writing for the local studios, we put together a script. Fadler went out and managed to get the use of a commercial 16mm camera, and we somehow scraped together enough money to buy film. Each one of the four groups

270

would take care of its own costuming. But then, what about the scenery?

That too was apparently no problem. Early one Saturday morning a large truck from one of the Hollywood studios brought a load of bits and pieces, which in no time at all, thanks to the volunteer square dancers and members of the studio crew, the not too attractive garage front became the front of a country barn with large barn doors. On the side of the property along the driveway, hiding the gas station and the traffic on Beverly Blvd., they set up a backdrop of blue sky and white clouds, a wooden picket fence, and bales of hay.

This was great, and it began to look very realistic. But, it then occurred to us that the very thing we were trying to get away from was the barnyard feeling (the bales of hay, the pitch forks and horse collars, etc.). Then, we realized that all of this was being done as a labor of helpfulness designed to get across an idea, while at the same time making a rather unattractive area fun, and not un-American to look at.

In looking at the area that Saturday afternoon it was not without a little amazement. And yet, even with all of this, there was still one problem to be fixed. The driveway, like most driveways, was old. Although it was in pretty good shape, it was scarred by oil spots.

"I wouldn't worry about that," said Tom, the dancer responsible for bringing over the studio sets. "If we won't be in the way tomorrow (Sunday) morning, we'll have the answer for you."

It was no later than 9:00 that next day, and another crew showed up. This time we recognized most of the volunteers as local dancers. Armed with buckets and paintbrushes, this crew of local square dancers soon had the aged cement driveway appear to be an adobe-like surface. No more spots.

271

What dress rehearsals we held were on the following Saturday, and a week later, we started shooting. Joe Fadler was on the roof of our kitchen with his camera, and the dancers came in units, so were shot one set at a time. We prerecorded the music and calling ahead of time in a studio. Once the shooting was done, the project moved indoors with Joe doing the cutting and sound editing, and I added a commentary.

When we were finished several months later, and our first print was "in the can" as they say we had a fifteen minute, color and sound motion picture. We thought it was tremendous - especially because it had cost us the astounding amount of $998.

During the ensuing years, more than 400 prints of the film were made and circulated to school districts and various square dance associations. We never knew how it happened, but somewhere along the line the U.S. State Department got their hands on a print and wanted to use the film in their embassies around the world. They bought the non-exclusive rights to overseas use of the film with plans to translate the commentary (not the calling) into a dozen or more foreign languages. The film was such a success that, five years later, the State Department extended the rights for another five years.

Times have changed. Styles of dancing have taken giant strides, but most of all the costumes we wore then - with the lovely, long, floor-touching dresses and the elaborate embroidered shirts are not typical of today.

Well, now you have had the 25¢ tour of square dancing in Hollywood movies, but before we leave Tinsel Town, I need to introduce you to a man who represents the best of the movies and the best of square dancing.

Chapter 12. Diamond Jubilee

Nineteen-forty-eight was a remarkable year, and as I look back I can't understand how we got it all done. I was still working for Squirt as the national campaign manager, which introduced me to the industrial editors' association, which led me to a trip to Washington, DC, to promote Squirt but also to meet at the White House to propose the fractional coin idea. On trips such as that I kept meeting square dancers who wanted to know more of what was going on nationwide. Charlie Dillinger and I discussed the idea of starting a magazine more seriously, and Charlie came up with the logo/art work for Sets in Order. Meanwhile, Ginger and I were working with Ray Shaw and callers and dancers in Southern California to have the Cheyenne Mountain Dancers come to the Los Angeles area. Three of the largest events in my square dance life happened in November 1948: the Cheyenne dancers performed and the first issue of Sets in Order came out the same weekend. Then just a week or two later, I got the offer to host a square dance television show.

Something that became quite common in those days were demonstrations, or exhibitions, of square dancing. Just a little lesson in semantics: a demonstration is when amateur dancers get up in front of a crowd to show what square dancing is. An exhibition is when a well-rehearsed set of dancers show not only what square dancing is, but also show how well their group can perform the dances for an audience. So, for example, if you see dancers in a shopping mall, they are probably doing a demonstration, perhaps to build interest in their square dance club.

Here are some examples of exhibitions:

On July 30, 1949, the Hollywood Bowl - world-famed outdoor showplace - included square dancing as a portion of its "Symphonies Under the Stars." Representative

Southern California Callers and Dancers occupied a major portion of the All Western Program.

One hundred years ago the first California settlers brought with them in their prairie schooners the energy, foresight and ambition to form a new frontier out of the Western wilderness. With them they brought their folksongs, their couple dances and their quadrilles. Today, in celebrating the hundredth anniversary of California, the great extravaganza planned to depict the State's history, and produced in true Hollywood style, include goodly portions of square dancing. Hollywood Bowl's five-day gala presentation included exhibition sets from the Southland area, with caller Ralph Maxheimer at the helm.

For the first time in the history of the Hollywood Bowl a large portion of the "Symphonies Under the Stars" was given over to square dancers. The intricacies of the moving bodies, the swirl of the lovely costumes, helped only in part to make this portion of the show the highlight of the evening. The great significance in the square dance picture was put across to some 20,000 who witnessed the performance when they realized that one square of old-time dancers included two Great Grandmothers, and they were equally moved when they learned that the youngest member of that "old-timers'" square was 20 years older than the combined ages of all the people in the youngest square.

We were pretty impressed that square dancing was presented to such a large crowd. But the biggest crowd was just a few months away.

Perhaps one of the: largest "live" audiences ever to watch one single square dance was the one that viewed the spectacular presentation during the January 2, 1950 Tournament of Roses Parade in Pasadena, California. An estimated million and a half eager spectators lined the several miles of pavement that marked the route of march for this spectacular and colorful pageant. They applauded the antics of the "Hoop and Holler Kids," and the calling of Jack Hoheisal on the specially designed square dance float sponsored by the Western Square Dance Association of San Gabriel Valley. Another million or more spectators watched the float over television. Others throughout the country saw pictures of it in their newspapers and saw it in their newsreel theatres.

In 1976 Sets in Order had this article about the Rose Parade.

The Subject is Roses

Speaking of persons who deserve square dance Oscars, we'll have to place high on the list those who were involved in putting together the square dance float in the January 1st Tournament of Roses Parade in Pasadena.

The dream of a float has been with a number of the veteran square dancers ever since 1950, when an entry featured the late Jack Hoheisal and a square of youthful dancers. Attempts at having a square dance float in recent years were foiled at every turn.

"Sorry, but all of the floats have already been assigned for this year" was a stock phrase.

"We began to get the idea that they really didn't want a square dance float," explained Charlie Naddeo, one of the prime movers on this year's project. "Somebody on the committee had the old-fashioned idea that square dancing was still in the barn and we were determined to prove them wrong."

Finally, after almost giving up the idea for another year, John Fogg, another of the prime movers, learned only in October that one of the accepted sponsors had cancelled its float.

"That was our cue," said John. "With some inside help and some fancy talking we said we were a sincere group of citizens and that we could produce a top-notch product." Evidently that did the trick and the square dancers were given the go-ahead.

Now, most of the floats for this New Year's Day extravaganza are planned many months, sometimes a full year into the future. The square dancers had a scant three months to go and this included not only designing the float but the actual construction and raising $35,000. Undismayed, they rolled up their sleeves and started to work.

Professional float designers working with the float committee came up with a display that combined floral dancers in action along with a group of musicians also fashioned out of flowers. Pictures depicting a number of phases in the history of square dancing from the mid-1600s to the present formed a border across the top of the float. Other than the professional construction, all the labor was donated by square dancers in the Southern California area. Their job was primarily to put the finishing touches, including the flowers, on the float. According to pageant requirements, everything visible on one of these mobile displays must be some form of plant life. For this reason, the dancers and musicians fashioned out of paper maché were covered with petals. Their faces and the portraits along the sides of the float were covered by different colored seeds and much of this was put together more than a week before the parade.

Work got a little hectic as the final hours drew near and literally hundreds of dancers worked around the clock placing the thousands of camelias, orchids, roses and mums on the steel constructed chassis. Finally, just hours before parade time the most fragile of the blooms were attached to the float and the work was completed.

"The Great American Square Dance" A band of Floragraphic scenes depicts various eras of the square dance. Over 30,000 Roses in Springtime Pinks, Yellows are in the gardens, hanging baskets.

Once it was over those who shared in the work, as well as the many hundreds around the world who contributed their dollars to the project, could understandably give out

277

with a sigh of relief. It was a big undertaking but it was indeed a labor of love a job well done.

The square dance float had a good run, but word from both John Fogg and Charlie Naddeo, founders and promoters of the annual tournament of Roses square dance float, is that there would be no square dance float in the 1986 New Year's Day gala. At the moment, no explanation in the change of signals. But the fact that this annual event brought square dancing into the homes of millions of TV viewers around the world indicates that its absence will be a disappointment to many.

Both John (who mortgaged his home a number of times in the past to finance the project) and Charlie are to be commended for their years of dedicated work on the float. In addition, the many square dancers who put endless voluntary hours in building and decorating the float and the dancers who danced on its moving floor along with the thousands over recent years who contributed to the project should not be over looked. The square dance world thanks them all and says "well done."

This was the beginning of the square dance boom era. More dancers meant more clubs, and more clubs meant more associations. The associations all wanted to produce festivals or hoedowns, and the bigger the better. Venues from Chicago to Texas and from Florida to Washington State were bragging how big their square dance festivals were. Then, toward the middle or end of 1949 I got a call from the President of the Junior Chamber of Commerce of Santa Monica, California.

"It's our city's 75th anniversary in June next year, and we would like to have as a part of our celebration the world's largest square dance! We wonder if you would come down here and have lunch and talk with us tomorrow, and we can answer any of your questions.

"Oh," was the only response we could think of.

"What has been the largest square dance to this point?" was the first question. After thinking a moment, we said that we didn't really know, but we had attended one in either Texas or Oklahoma that was said to have as many as 2,000 dancers. "Well, that's fine," said our Santa Monica enthusiast. "We would like to aim for 4,000!"

"Where are you planning to hold it?" Living most of my life in nearby Beverly Hills, and attending junior college in Santa Monica, I wasn't aware of any building in the area that could comfortably hold that many squares of dancers.

The next day three of the JCs - business suits and all - met me at the corner of Wilshire Blvd. and Second Street. It didn't take long to get their story. Their plan was to have the square dance, a giant "street dance," right there on Wilshire Blvd, right where it ends forming a huge "T" at Ocean Ave. "We don't know anything about square dancing (understatement of the year), but, will this work?"

Spreading Spangles to smooth the road

"Well," we started out, "to begin with, streets don't make absolutely the best dance surfaces, and Wilshire Blvd., here, is pretty rough with a few potholes. And Ocean Ave. with its streetcar tracks and bricks would be next to impossible to dance on."

The men huddled together for just a moment, then, "We can fix that. They're not using the streetcar tracks on Ocean Ave. anyway. So, we'll get them to take the tracks out and on Wilshire and Ocean we'll get them to completely re-surface the whole area. Will that do it?"

"Well, not quite. The women's shoes – almost like ballet slippers - would wear out dancing on the asphalt in no time at all."

"Well, what can we do then?"

Not too familiar with street dancing at this point in time, I must have said, "Well, I know that you can use the small rubber ball bearings that result when automobile tires are retreaded. You can just throw these on the macadam sur-face to make a thin layer. I also know that they have had success with a product known as Spangles, made by the Bo-raxo Company you might use. "

"Okay, we can use them both. We would need a caller, wouldn't we? Who would you suggest?"

"Well, there are close to a hundred in the area and you would proba-bly do well to have more than one for an event this large. Let me think about it."

Jack Barbour and his orchestra

"What about music?"

"You'd certainly need live music, and we have a number of square dance bands in the area."

"Well, let's consider having two bands. What else would we need?"

I mentioned a sizable callers' stand if they were going to have two bands, as well as the callers on it. Also, the lighting for a nighttime event and sound were no small items that needed to be considered. And, parking: if there were going to be 4,000 dancers, that's a lot of cars.

Their response to every hurdle I placed before them seemed to have an immediate positive answer. By the scheduled morning of the dance they would have a large stand built that could hold two bands. The sound system would be furnished by one of the motion picture studios and they already had assurance from one of the Army anti-aircraft batteries for a number of units of Klieg lighting.

For the parking, they would shut off a several block area, so that only cars with square dance identification could enter. And, as for traffic control and as caution against any violence, they had the assurance of loans of a number of teams of police officers from the surrounding beach areas, who would take care of the law infractions that might come up.

By now our conversation had drifted us into a nearby restaurant and we continued the discussion while we had lunch. The JCs wanted to know where the dancers might come from, and they indicated they wished to have representatives from throughout the state. We indicated that there were some eleven newly formed square dance associations within California. They wondered if it would be possible for the President of each association to come down to Santa Monica for a lunch at the Miramar Hotel in order to see the area, and get a "sales talk." I explained that it was not impossible.

They asked me to make a suggestion regarding the callers to be featured, and I said I would.

"We were thinking," said the spokesman for the group. "We have pretty good assurance that we'll have at least one or two from the motion picture industry, and our governor, Earl Warren, has said he would try to make an appearance. Can you suggest any celebrities that would add to the attraction? "

I told them that government bigwigs and Hollywood celebrities might make an impression on the non-dancing crowd, but in order to make points with the square dancers, someone who would really make an impression would be Dr. Lloyd 'Pappy' Shaw.

"If you'll give us his address we'll see that he gets an invitation and we'll pay for his expenses."

By the time I left the JCs and returned to the office, we had a fair start on a venture that a few hours earlier would have seemed impossible.

During the coming weeks the planning was underway. The heads of the eleven dancer associations here in California indicated that they would come and be represented at the planning meeting. The city of Santa Monica had removed the streetcar tracks on Ocean Ave., and the six blocks on Ocean and Wilshire were soon to be repaved.

We had figured that the three and a half hours of dancing, with three minute tips of three callers, and with one round dance in between each tip, would allow for 35 callers to be on the program. The slightly more than 100 callers in our area had voted and selected the 35 who would represent them.

Square dance car identification cards were printed and sent out to those requesting them. Shaw said he would be on hand. Teams of square dancer volunteers to help spread the rubber pellets and spangles across the six block paved area were lined up. The two orchestras were arranged for and all the details we could think of were in place.

The day and night before the big dance the sound system and the lighting were checked out and everything was in place.

The morning of June 13, 1950 saw the usual Santa Monica fog over the area. The bandstand had been constructed. Someone had put together a signal system of three lights. One minute into his call, and the caller would get the green light. After two minutes, a white light and just before his three minutes were up, a red light would flash telling the caller to "wrap it up - now!"

A bit unnerving - that morning the banner headline across the front page of the Santa Monica Outlook, the newspaper, which only a couple of months previously told everyone to expect a record of 4,000 square dancers, now, blatantly told the world it could expect 8,000 (8,000! wow).

Squaring up on Wilshire Blvd.

By early afternoon the volunteer square dance workers began to show up armed with shovels, brooms and rakes, and the job of spreading the rubber pellets and the Spangles on the street started.

By 4:00 p.m. costumed dancers started arriving. Police officers from Ocean Park, Venice, and Redondo Beach had closed off the neighboring streets and it appeared that everything was in place.

6:30 p.m. and the bands were ready and everything was set to begin - when the typical Southern California coastal fog rolled in.

6:50 p.m. as the combined bands played a lively tune, the color guard began its march toward the stand - the show was under way...and, on cue, the fog lifted.

The National anthem was played and scores of colorfully clad dancers poured into the streets. At 7:00 p.m. (on the dot) the first caller, having been introduced, started his call and the Diamond Jubilee was underway.

Arriving at the speaker's stand and introduced to the throng of dancers, the Governor said, (and how proud we were of him at that moment) "I'm not about to interrupt a fantastic event like this with a poor political speech." (The Governor and his party, who had said they would just drop in and maybe spend ten minutes or so, stayed the entire evening.) Another half hour into the dancing there was a second planned interruption. East on Wilshire Blvd. again, another white convertible, a second bevy of motorcycle policemen, red lights and sirens blasting worked its way through the crowd. This time, as the cavalcade moved toward us, a sea of dancers surged in, moving closer. They knew who this man was. He was 'Pappy' Shaw, a man responsible for so much of the fun they were having, and with him his wife Dorothy Stott Shaw. Finally, reaching the stage, Shaw joined in sharing the master of ceremonies duties and apparently loving every minute of it.

Wheel chair dancers
at Diamond Jubilee

284

An hour or so into the program and the Chief of Police came up to tell us they had released all the neighboring city police, keeping only their own on duty for traffic control. There just had not been the problems they had anticipated. (We could have told him this!)

The Jubilee went on - right on schedule. I seem to remember that it ended at 10:31, just a little less than a minute over schedule. It was a real "happening" for the activity...We slept well that night.

15,200 dancers dance on the streets and 35,000 spectators fill the grandstands and line Wilshire Blvd.

The next morning I drove to Santa Monica to see the clean-up, thank a few people, and pick-up the morning paper. And, there it was – in bold headlines:

An association that had been deeply involved with square dancing for years was the Folk Dance Federation of California (I was on staff at their summer folk dance camp in Stockton, CA, in 1950, along with luminaries such as

Lawton Harris, Ralph Page, and Herb Greggerson.) The Federation published "Let's Dance," The Magazine of Folk and Square Dancing and the cover story for August 1950 was about the world's largest square dance.

Diamond Jubilee from Let's Dance
by Bill Castner and Dan Allen

In the late afternoon of Thursday, July 13, Southern California citizens who have poo-poohed the popularity of square dancing began to sit up and take notice - something was definitely going on!

Busses by the dozen rolled out of San Diego, jammed with men and women dressed in western clothes; thirty chartered busses roared out of the San Bernardino area filled with a similar throng; trains from as far as Bakersfield and Fresno were loaded with dancers and every highway leading to the Pacific was crowded with carloads of laughing folks in fancy boots, loud shirts and blue jeans.

Ten thousand of these citizens were members of the seven Southern California square dance associations the Associated Square Dancers, Cow Counties Hoedown Association, Tri-Counties Square Dance Association, San Diego County Square Dance Association, South Coast Association of Square Dance Clubs, Western Square Dance Association of the San Gabriel Valley, and the Northern San Diego County Square Dance Association. Five thousand were not members of any organization but were determined to join the fun as spectators. All had one goal in common - the jamboree at Santa Monica which was to climax that city's Diamond Jubilee celebration.

Santa Monica was ready for them and then some. For weeks the city fathers, the police and fire departments and the public works department had been as busy as a hoedown fiddler's fingers. Special stickers had been printed for the 37 callers and their families who had been invited; extra parking areas had been roped off, refreshment stands and bleachers erected and a four block area along Ocean Avenue and a two-block area down Wilshire Blvd, had been repaved and treated to several tons of a combination of soapstone, corn meal and borax to make the dancing pleasant and easy.

Under the watchful eyes of John Danley, chairman for the City of Santa Monica, and Bob Osgood, master of ceremonies and co-chairman, special spot lights had been erected on both sides of the giant T and carefully checked loud speakers bristled from dozens of lamp posts. At the point where the T joined there was a huge platform to accommodate the callers and their wives, the two orchestras and the visiting VIPs.

At six-thirty the streets in the special area were empty. One hour later there were over 1,000 sets in order and every inch of standing room along the streets and in surrounding buildings and houses was taken up by spectators. Every now and then a red cardboard square would bob up above a set as one of the 40 uniformed Boy Scouts on duty signaled that another couple was needed.

After greetings from city officials, John Danley and Bob Osgood, 'Pappy' Shaw of Colorado Springs, who had flown out for the event, took over. On the spot to say something nice about each caller he introduced, 'Pappy' solved the problem by a running gag. Beginning with Ray Shaw, his brother, he told the crowd that he had been talking to the caller's wife - or girl-friend - and understood, from this source, that he was the best caller in the U S.

In spite of the crowd there was no confusion as to patterns. This was due to the sound system which brought the calls clearly to each set, to the high caliber of the callers and to the careful planning on the part of Bob Osgood and John Danley, who selected only well-known or relatively simple patterns for the program - yet did not sacrifice quality and variety. No walk-through was given as has been the general practice in the past.

In the middle of the program dancing halted as Governor Earl Warren's car was escorted into the area by four police cars. Smiling, the Governor pushed his way to the callers' stand and made a tremendous hit with one of the shortest speeches on record. "I don't want to spoil a good party by a lot of talk," he said, waving and grinning, "and I'm not going to try and call either. But I'm proud to be known as the governor of the best square dancing state in the Union."

Screen Star Leo Carillo was then introduced and, taking his cue from Warren, said he had no intention of saying more than "thanks" for being invited to the party. The callers then took over again and, with two orchestras - Jack Barbour and the California Clippers and Grace and the Cow Counties Boys rotating - and each section of three tips broken by a folk or round dance, the jamboree rolled on. A cool breeze began to roll in from the Pacific, keeping the dancers fresh and putting new vigor into their steps; the huge palms along Ocean Ave. and the Palisades ducked in and out of the glow from the giant spot and flood lights; music, calls and the laughter and shouts of the dancers blended with the gentle roar of the ocean in a setting that only Southern California could produce.

Sharply at 10:30 the program ended with the Black Hawk Waltz and, within a half-hour, the streets were empty as the 10,000 dancers went out for something to eat, caught busses for the long trip home or gathered in homes and private halls to continue dancing into the small hours of the morning.

A small portion of the crowd of dancers and the full bleachers for spectators.

The next day there was none of the usual litter of civic celebrations – no broken pop bottles, bags and paper napkins. The Square Dancers had proved that, perhaps more than any other organized recreational group, they could gather without bringing down the town. All that remained to be done was to clean the streets to make them safe for traffic again.

No one who attended the Jamboree failed to be impressed by its color, friendly, atmosphere and basic American feel. And everyone from Governor Warren to the newest dancer agreed that Santa Monica's Jumbo Jamboree was the biggest, most exciting, dancingest and goldangest square dance ever held - a credit to a beautiful city and a tribute to one of the finest recreational movements in the U. S. today.

It is still hard to believe that there was such an event, and I have to look over photographs of the Jubilee or re-watch the newsreel film of the event. But we have more stories to tell.

Chapter 13. Exhibitions and Demonstrations

In the last chapter I talked about some of the really big dances and shows I was involved in, and I used some specific terms that I would like to clarify. Two of the terms "demonstrations" and "exhibitions" have been used interchangeably for years, but I like to differentiate them.

A demonstration is used to show how something works or what it looks like. For example, when you go to the vendors' building at the county or state fair, there are a lot of demonstrations: the latest in vibrating chairs or hand held food processors or scalp massagers. In square dance classes we use demonstrations to show the new dancers how to do a movement because many people process visual images much better than they do word descriptions. For some calls it just takes two people, and for others it may take a full square of eight dancers.

We also use demonstrations to attract new dancers to our classes. We round up a square or two, or even fifty squares, and put on a bit of a show for the public. Many clubs around the country put on demonstrations during square dance week to show folks at a shopping mall how much fun square dancing is. Sometimes we can even get the local newspaper or TV stations to cover the demonstration so we get wider coverage.

If the purpose of a demonstration is to tell others that square dancing is fun, then we certainly miss the boat when it comes to the groups executing complicated figures that result in grim-faced dancers. The impression that to be eye-catching an exhibition must be complicated is a fallacy. It's one thing to feel the challenge of dancing as a participant; it's another to view a group and to feel a response to the grace and motion so typical of this activity. The spontaneity and extemporaneous qualities of square dancing are frequently lost when exhibitionists memorize their routines and plant their patterns into sixteen and thirty-two measure segments.

What makes a good square dance demonstration? Many things. Among them good variety, contagious happiness, pleasing costumes. Should demonstration dancers necessarily be children? Certainly not. When a majority of demonstration groups is made up of teens and pre-teens, it is easy to give the impression that square dancing belongs only to those under the age of twenty years. And the same holds for senior citizens. A demonstration group should not be made up of all septuagenarians. This is, of course, not true, and if we are not careful an over-emphasis on the young people (or the old folk) in dancing may give an impression that the activity is not for them.

No, the best demonstrations we've ever seen have been groups of the ageless individuals who make up the greatest portion of the square dancing population. They have been able to dance well, but when they goof they allow this to be just as natural as all the rest of the demonstration.

At the same time, demonstrations should not be amateurish or even small scale. But neither are they filled with complicated choreography and fancy matching outfits. The goal is to show the non-dancing world what square dancing is. There have been some really big demonstrations that did not attempt to be flashy or slick. For example, in September, 1950, square dancers all over Southern California received a letter from the American Legion inviting them to participate in the "Cavalcade of California," a "tremendous and spectacular pageant" to be held at the Los Angeles Coliseum. The dancing was to be a relatively small part of the pageant which was going to portray the history of California to Legionnaires from all over the country who were assembling in Los Angeles for their national convention. We drew in 2,000 dancers to fill the field of the Coliseum. Jack Barbour and his orchestra provided the music while I got tapped to do the choreography and the calling. Here is an excerpt from the publicity that hit the Los Angeles papers in October.

> *Just how big is square dancing in California? That's the question thousands of folks are asking these days, and that's one question about 96,000 Legionnaires expect to have answered for them the night of October 11th in the Los Angeles Memorial Coliseum.*
>
> *Unable to get out and see a Jamboree or Roundup for themselves, American Legionnaires from all over the United States and the Territorial possessions, together with others who will help fill the 106,000 capacity Bowl will watch the 2,000 representing Southern California do several hashes and perhaps a round dance as one of the main features in the gigantic pageant, "Cavalcade of California," designed to portray the story of our State to the visiting Legionnaires.*
>
> *More a demonstration of what is being done, the dancers will only dance for but a few minutes of the great show, but all those participating will blend into the other acts, ride the horses and buggies, the old automobiles, the covered wagons, and will have "their day" as actors during the balance of the show.*

Square dancing made several appearances on the sports fields. During halftime of the NFL Pro Bowl in 1952 dancers filled the grid iron. In 1978 the South Eastern Massachusetts Coordinating Association sponsored the half-time entertainment at the New England Patriots vs Kansas City Chiefs football game at Schaeffer Stadium in Foxboro. Some 600 dancers came onto the field and danced for a crowd of 40,000 spectators. It was a fun time as the dancers had their box lunches, watched the game for free with their friends, danced for an hour after the game, and the weather was perfect. 75 squares covered the entire field. Jim Purcell directed the show and called for the dancing. Forty-seven clubs participated, with the dancers traveling in car pools and chartered buses from over 135 cities and towns in the south-eastern part of the state. (The Patriots won 24-7.)

An exhibition, on the other hand, is a carefully choreographed and rehearsed performance that is designed to entertain the viewers. 'Pappy' Shaw's Cheyenne Mountain Dancers did exhibitions for large crowds. They went through a selection of dances from different eras and wore the proper costumes for each era. Then, oftentimes, the kids turned into just dancers or demonstrators. For example, when the kids were in the Los Angeles area, they did two shows for large audiences, but on the days between the shows they helped 'Pappy' teach the local caller and dancer associations what the dancing was all about.

There are other remarkable instances of exhibitions. No one would think that square dancing at a county fair or state fair was

Herb Greggerson's Blue Bonnet Dancers

unusual. But how about at the World's Fair? There are a couple of instances where square dancing made a big impression. In 1939-1940 the World's Fair (or The International Exposition) was held in New York. Now I know that the New York Fair did not gain the notoriety of Chicago

(The White City) or of St. Louis ("Meet Me at the Fair"), but it has a kind of fame in the square dance world. Herb Greggerson – I think I mentioned him before as one of the great callers of Texas style square dancing, and as the author of "Bluebonnet Dances" – trained a troop of dancers and then took them all the way to New York. A couple of things were true about square dancing in those days that we have tried to overcome: competition and the barn dance image.

Herb used both of those to his advantage. There were all kinds of dance contests at the Fair, but I do not think there was another square dance group. Most of the dance groups showed off swing or tap, or things of that sort. Herb's dancers took home just about all of the awards in the dance competition, including costuming which was straight out of Dog Patch. Men were dressed in Texas-type western boots and costumes, while the ladies floor length dresses and bonnets were blue - the presentations were well received for the only square dancing most of America knew about was what they saw in the old motion pictures.

The 'Pappy' Shaw heritage was continued through his wife Dorothy who, as we have mentioned before, choreographed a magnificent spectacle of the history of dance for the NSDC held in Denver in 1956. But as the Cheyenne Mountain Dancers drifted on to new places and new experiences, 'Red' Henderson gathered a superb troop of young dancers who showed the world what 'Pappy' had done with his dancers.

Nationally known for the gay, interesting, instructive entertainment they offered, Spokane's famous teenage dance group "The Silver Spurs" gained more and more friends for square dancing as they crossed and re-crossed the country on their annual summer vacation tours.

In Spokane schools, as part of physical education work, some instruction has long been given in square dancing, but many youngsters became enthusiastic about the program and demanded more advanced work. In 1948, a Saturday afternoon recreation program featuring these dances was organized, jointly sponsored by the Spokane Public Schools and Park Board. From the most talented and interested of the boys and girls attending, the Silver Spurs group was formed. Edwin S. 'Red' Henderson of Spokane was the driving force behind the group's success.

A two-hour show, completely professional in presentation and costuming, consisted of nicely varied group dances, with solo, duet, and quartet numbers featured as interludes. The group dances included rollicking cowboy squares, colorful Mexican numbers, authentic Early American and English folk dances, graceful formal waltzes and perfectly executed examples of the Tango, Samba and Rumba. Also included was the tricky Filipino Bamboo Dance, a gorgeous ''black light" number, and the Indian Hoop Dance.

Another great exhibition of the history of square dancing was at the Fiesta de Quadrilla held in San Diego in November 1953. Produced outdoors in a huge amphitheatre, the Cavalcade traced the progress of square dancing up to the present. Next came a group of round dancers showing the basic polka steps that influenced so many of the later dances. Then once again back into the square formation for a demonstration of an old time prompted quadrille. Then came an assortment of dances typical of the '49'er gold rush period.

"Distances were great in the west," explained the commentator, "and dances could not be the affair of one small community. From a hundred or more miles in every direction dancers would come. Some had just moved into the country from Iowa, some had drifted up from Texas and some had followed the herds down from the summer grass in Montana, They could not do a precise and measured quadrille, they needed something simple in pattern that could be learned quickly. Thus developed a true Western dance built on the New England square framework. It is believed that the origin of this western dance stemmed from two main sources: that of the New England quadrille and the Kentucky running set, with perhaps the Mexican contributing some-thing in the way of steps."

We Americans have a unique contribution to make to the world-wide cultural scene. However, the majority of our citizens are unaware of the richness of the art forms which have originated here and are unique to our land. The California Heritage Dancers of San Diego (carrying on the tradition of 'Pappy' Shaw and 'Red' Henderson" and Herb Greggerson) are dedicated to preserving through exhibitions, the rich heritage of what has become known as American Square Dancing. In order not to lose these old time dances, the California Heritage Dancers was organized in 1986 recruiting members from various square dance clubs in Southern California. Extensive research has resulted in a large repertoire of varied dances from the 1700's to 1996. The dancers have created authentic costuming and music to complete the picture.

The distinction between a demonstration, an exhibition and a dance must not be drawn too finely or exactly. Sometimes it is almost impossible to tell them apart. For example, when WWII started, the World's Fairs took a decade and a half off. In the hiatus a number of venues claimed to be hosting the world's fair, but they were not associated with the international body that owns the trade-mark. For example, in 1949-1950 New York held another large fair – they even called it a world's fair - but it was sponsored by another group. However, there was square dancing in 1950 in New York. Al Brundage, one of the most popular callers in the country, brought his demonstration group down from Stepney, Connecticut, and put on a well-received show. [A quick aside: Al appeared as a mystery guest on the old TV show "What's My Line?" He fooled all of the panelists.]

The first official World's Fair after New York in 1940 and after WWII was held in Brussels, Belgium. I was tied up state side, but a handful of people went to the extra effort to make sure that square dancing was represented in Brussels. U.S. troops had been stationed all over Europe, and those troops included some outstanding callers and a lot of enthusiastic square dancers.

Margo Baughman who was involved in making the arrangements for the square dancers tells the story:

July 2nd, 3rd and 4th, 1958, were designated as American Days at the Brussels World Fair and what could be more typically American than a square dance. The European Association of American Square Dance Clubs and the European Area Square Dance Leaders Association, with the approval of United States Forces in Europe undertook the job of demonstrating to thousands of Fair visitors what square dancing is really like and how much fun it can be by including an audience participation dance in each of the nine one hour dances which occurred during the three days.

The under taking of this project was made doubly difficult by the fact that negotiations had to be made with the Belgium Government, approval was required from the United States Army and Air Force so that the dancers could participate, billeting, transportation, and etc. The administrative headaches which at times seemed insurmountable were overcome.

To sell square dancing to visitors at the Fair a bilinguist who was also a caller was the next requirement. Fortunately, Joe O'Leary, a well-known caller to square dancers in Europe, was available. Joe was selected to act as M.C., and in his very best "Texas French" conducted the audience participation dance.

As time was of the essence and approval from U.S. Forces was given less than two weeks before the scheduled date of departure to Brussels, only ten hours were available for final rehearsals. The dancers had to be gathered from many locations in Germany and France. This meant that neither precision dances nor intricate figures could be used. Merle Basom, the Program Chairman, developed a pro gram based on a typical square

Callers: Cal Golden is 3rd from right

dance club's activity. In retrospect, this probably was one reason for the success of this event, as precision square dancing was not emphasized but friendliness and fun was the theme. As a result of the friendliness shown by the dancers each time the audience was invited to participate it *became easier to coax them onto the floor. By the second day it was no longer a problem to encourage the spectators to participate and by the third day some spectators came back just to participate at each performance, and people stood 8 to 10 deep to watch 90 dancers gaily perform to the calls of Merle Basom, Dick Baughman, Bill Brocket, Betty Casey, Cal Golden, and Joe O'Leary. Cal Golden was the featured caller and his colorful costumes and overwhelming personality lent a gay atmosphere to the entire event.*

American Forces Radio Network commentators at the US Pavilion agreed that the square dancers drew exceptionally large crowds. This was quite evident by the fact that the overflow of spectators made use of the steps and balcony of the Russian Pavilion as a vantage point to observe the six performances at the U.S. Pavilion.

The square dancing at Brussels really went over the line – thousands of people watched the dancing, but also thousands had a chance to do it for themselves. It was shows like this that helped spread square dancing throughout the world. Square dancing had been introduced to Europe before the war, but with the presence of so many military personnel the activity really took off. As mentioned above, it was square dance clubs and callers in Europe who put the show together. In 1952 Mildred Buhler of Redwood City, CA, and her husband, moved to London for business reasons. She figured that her calling career was over, but she was warmly welcomed by British callers who were just starting out and they wanted someone knowledgeable to help train them. Mildred founded the British Association of American Square Dance Callers and trained some callers who became known throughout Europe

Square dancing returned to the World's Fair when New York again hosted it in 1964. This time a group of dancers from Upstate New York put on the demonstrations - the Cattaraugus Cuttarugs heard that June 22 was Cattaraugus County Day at the New York World's Fair, so for eight weeks these folks practiced under the leadership of Earl

Cuttarugs dancing on the map

Geiss, and they performed marvelously. As we said, the Cuttarugs put square dancing on the world map, which was literally true, because the dance surface had a map of New York State painted on it.

The next world's fair that featured square dancing was in Knoxville, Tennessee, in 1982. The theme of the Fair was energy, which at times was very technical, but the mainland Chinese said that their energy came from their people. To show that, they brought pieces of the Great Wall, a couple of statues from the terra cotta army, and a marvelous restaurant which featured the cuisines of the various areas of China. And square dancing? We were in the birthplace of mountain music. It seemed that every few feet there was another live band, and there were constant demonstrations of clogging and traditional square dancing.

There have been some truly unique square dance demonstrations. Some of them are different because of how they were done and others because of where they were done. So here comes a kind of strange mixture of stories about square dance shows.

This story, which comes from Jinx Weskie of Lakewood, Colorado, starts out by saying, "Through the past months, SQUARE DANCING Magazine has covered a number of articles on the history of the activity, i.e., what went on before and after World War II. But what went on during World War II?" She then tells the following story.

There was one command performance that occurred during the height of the war in the very heart of Germany. The location was a prisoner of war camp just a few miles south of Berlin. Jack Bennett, a square dance caller from Denver and a prisoner of the Germans, along with other prisoner/officers were frequently requested to attend a performance of the imprisoned English officers of the RAF who were barracked in the same camp. Eventually it came time for the imprisoned American officers to perform and Bennett came up with the idea of putting on a barn dance and inviting the English prisoners of war to be their guests.

But where were the girls? Naturally there was a shortage (an actual dearth you might say) of lady prisoners, so, on orders of the commanding officer, a group of the American officers were selected and persuaded to dance the part of the ladies.

Jinx's story reminded me of when I was stationed in Hawaii in 1944. Somehow, I always tend to associate dates of holidays in terms of square dancing. When it comes to Christmas, I remember some of those wonderful Christmas square dance parties that the clubs and groups have had in the years past. In thinking back, the most unusual square dancing Christmas to me was in 1944. Thoughts of Christmas were pretty grim for a bunch of us who were stationed at an amphibious training base in the Hawaiian Islands. For a lot of the men it was the first Christmas away from home. And for all of us, home and loved ones seemed so far away.

301

Making the most of the situation, the recreation officer and the C.O. of the base decided that the boys should have a party they wouldn't soon forget. Calling in the Chief Petty Officers and some of the others who seemed to have a lot of ingenuity, plans were made for a gigantic square dancing Christmas party. Chief Carpenters Mate Simpson from Tennessee and his gang went to work on an old Japanese school house just outside of the base. A crew of other boys and drivers working with the local YWCA and USO managed to recruit several truckloads of Hawaiian and Japanese high school and college coeds for dancing partners. The party was a dilly.

And, Louise Roundtree of Florida tells of the most exotic square dance she and her husband, caller Bill, had been in. Let's have Louise tell the story:

> *Our most memorable experience in our 10 years of teaching and calling was on the evening of February 9, 1961, when we took 14 square dancers to dance at Mrs. Herbert May's estate in Palm Beach when she was entertaining King Saud of Arabia and his entourage.*
>
> *Upon arriving at Mrs. May's 129-room estate we were escorted to her secretary's bungalow, a separate establishment from the "Big House," where the Taws and Paws were assigned separate rooms for dressing rooms. After dressing we trouped across the big, beautiful spread of lawn to the magnificent ballroom with its lovely parquet floor and orange and cerise drapes, all matching the Arabic decor of the room. A perfect sound system was all set up behind the attractive stage with its backdrop of an Arab horseman astride a handsome white stallion.*
>
> *After a delay as the guests finished their dinner, we were told that it was time for us to go on. We were to enter the ballroom in single file, caller first,*

*pass the couch of honor upon which were seated
King Saud, his host, Mr. May and the King's two
sons, the Princes. As we passed the couch we were to
curtsey to the King. This went quite well except that
I was the second one in line and, not being sure
which man was King Saud, hesitated in front of Mr.
May. As he motioned me on, I did a sort of grapevine
step ending up in front of the King as I was meant to
do.*

*After that we squared up and danced for
about 15 minutes while the King tapped his feet in
time to the music and the young Princes tittered with
their hands over their mouths each time the healthy
swings showed an exposure of colorful pantalettes!
Incidentally the guests were all men; not even Mrs.
May was present, as befits an Arab gathering.*

*As we promenaded off after our last number
the King stood up, the rest of the company immediately following him, and away they went. We were
told that we could stay in the ballroom and dance
awhile, which we took advantage of, while men serv-
ants served us coffee and sandwiches.*

Square dancers also headed east across the pond to
Eastern Europe. There have been many phrases and slogans
I attached to square dancing over the years, all with positive
emphases, and perhaps now a new one should be added,
"Square dancing bridges national barriers." A few years
back, The Georgia Square Dance Caravan, 168 strong, visited Russia and Poland. Conceived by Bill and Ruth Starnes,
with assistance from Mac and Virginia McDonald and callers Rod Blaylock and Bob Bennett, the vision became a reality in an invitation from the two countries. The American

dancers enjoyed the sightseeing but the group's unique reason for traveling was to dance — and dance they did, with spectacular results. Rod Blaylock writes, "I think both countries were a little stunned at the performances we put on and the reception from the viewers. We had one estimated crowd of 10,000 in a market place in Krakow. We had 4,000 in an outdoor theatre in Wroclaw. Moscow was a full house in a tremendous ballroom in a hotel. Leningrad and Minsk were in Student Centers and Club houses, packed to capacity. Polish television taped one show.

Each program started with introductions all which had to be interpreted to the audience: the dancers represented more than six million square dancers who enjoy the activity as a hobby in the United States. Next came a Grand March, followed by square dancing. Two rounds, with cueing by Tom and Lib Hubbard, were included at each show and the Clogging Squares, directed by J. C. Jones, took their turn. The shows generally lasted about an hour and fifteen minutes.

As a grand finale the audiences were included in a mixer, a simple round and finally were brought into squares. They would dance "Texas Star," "Birdie in the Cage" and other simple routines. The locals caught on quickly to the clogging with a natural feel for the exuberant music and dance steps and they always enjoyed dancing "Cotton Eyed Joe."

And square dancers went to the West, that is to the Far East, Japan to be exact. On an American Square Dance Workshop tour, seventy-six square dancers traveled to the Orient where they were feted at a dance in Tokyo. Planned and executed by the Tokyo Callers Association and the Far East Square Dance Association, the event was held at the Meguro Park Lanes bowling alley. Over six hundred dancers from all parts of Japan were on hand to welcome the Americans. Tour escorts Wally and Maxine Schultz and Don and

Marie Armstrong joined with Masaru Wada, Tac Ozaki and Motoza Asanuma to call the squares and contras for the evening program. The group was also honored by the presence of Prince Mikassa who participated in the dancing with the Japanese and Americans.

Prince Mikassa was not the only royalty entertained by square dancers. Before she was crowned, Princess Elizabeth made a tour of the domain, including Canada. She was royally entertained by Canadian square dancers who wrapped her up in a square. From the smile on her face in the pictures, she had the time of her life.

And a little closer to home, there was Sam Queen, Sr., of North Carolina, a colorful figure in square dancing whose life was snuffed out by a prowler in his home. Now Sam's fame as a square dance caller was entirely built around his ability to train some of the finest Appalachian exhibition dancers going. Emphasis was on smoothness and ultra-precision but at a fast tempo - and later he added another element, the clog. So he had two groups - Smooth Dancers and Cloggers, all going at a furious pace. There was one especially grand spot in Sam Sr.'s life. During the Roosevelt administration Eleanor Roosevelt dreamed up a party for the King and Queen of England when they visited the White House. It was to be an all-American program but one that showed the British Isles background. Lawrence Tibbett and Marian Anderson sang. So did the Coon Creek Girls from Renfro Valley in Kentucky. And - you guessed it! - Sam Queen brought his Soco Gap Dancers from Haywood County, N.C., in the Great Smoky Mountains and they danced for the White House party. And, believe it or not, there were some society people who complained loudly about such a rag-a-muffin group being allowed in the White House at all.

Another time, but the same place: the White House. The night of January 21, 1977 marked a significant first in our square dance lives. That was the night that the first Presidential Inaugural American Square and Folk Dance was held with more than 6000 dancers from all over America in attendance. The dance took place in the National Visitors' Center, Washington D.C. and provided an opportunity for Square Dancers to salute our new, Square Dancing President and his Lady. It was truly a "grand night for dancing." The Inaugural Square and Folk Dance evening can be counted as a great success in many ways. It was a night that saw square dancers overcome less than acceptable sound and some measure of confusion in programming and still have a wonderful time.

The evening started with a First Nighter which introduced more than 2000 non-dancers to the joys of our activity. Music for the evening was provided by an excellent lineup of bands from all over the country. Leon Sash and the Midwesterners provided the majority of the square dance music with bands from North Carolina and Vermont playing for the New England Style Square Dancing and Clogging demonstration. In each segment of the evening, the dancers were encouraged to join those on stage and try other forms of dance. After segments by the New England Style, Cloggers and American Sioux Dancers, the dancers were really charged up for a "mini-diehard ball" to close out the evening. Modern western square dancing enjoyed the segment from 7:30 till 8:45 and from 10:30 until midnight. Included among the callers was Rod Blaylock from Albany, Ga., who taught President and Mrs. Carter to dance.

We were able to identify some of the dancer contingents who came from all over the country. There were more than 1000 dancers from Georgia, 200 from Minnesota and groups from West Virginia, Florida, Wisconsin, Missouri, Arkansas, Texas, North Carolina and Indiana who shared the evening with dancers from the nearby Maryland and Virginia clubs. I am sure that we missed recognizing some of the dancer contingents but we do know that those who shared the evening made possible its success.

Not the White House this time, but still an eminent building. Canada's Annual United Nations Ball one year was highlighted by some rousing square dancing, participated in by notables from many nations. The U.N. delegates proclaimed this one of the best parties of the season. To quote the Ottawa Square Dance Assn. news-sheet: "The Ball started out with the usual waltz, fox trot and Latin music. Then suddenly, to the astonishment of all, a fellow in square dance attire got up on the stage and started instructing the U.N. diplomats and their lovely ladies in the intricacies of the Canadian square dance. He was Jack Zoubie of the External Affairs Dept., who makes square dancing his hobby when he isn't handling Canada's foreign policies.

Whether the U.N. people were attired in tuxedos and ball gowns or the national costumes of their countries, Zoubie soon had them dancing to a definite Canadian beat. On the ballroom wall of the Beekman Tower Hotel in New York, a solemn buffalo head gravely watched the proceedings. At the stroke of 12, buffalo burgers were served to all present, along with Canadian cheese, cider and apples.

Not royalty, but definitely a VIP, was Ted Kennedy. A local Eastern newspaper reported in the Society Column that Senator Edward Kennedy celebrated his 41st birthday in New York at a square dance given by his sister and brother-in- law. It was reported that the hosts moved all the French antiques around in their apartment to make space for a real, country-style hoedown. One guest remarked, "It's so way out, it must be on its way back in." Perhaps someone should get the word to this segment of the population concerning square dancing and its popularity and scope.

Callers in the News:

Catch Arnie Kronenberger on the syndicated TV show "To Tell the Truth." Arnie gets little opportunity to talk but does some calling with a group of east coast dancers who open the show. You'll notice Al and Bea Brundage as members of the square.

CBS television covers the square dance scene: Kirkwood Lodge, well-known site of countless square dance vacations on the Lake of the Ozarks, was the location this past month of a "special" filmed on the spot to feature a generous portion of contemporary square dancing. The unique showing, which spotlights CBS regular, Dan Rather, along with Marshall Flippo and an abundance of happy dancers, was planned to coincide with the observance of Square Dance Week.

Certainly not least of the TV appearances was made by Bob Brundage. He took his exhibition group to Arthur Godfrey's studio to audition for a spot on the show. While they were waiting to go on they did one more quick run-through of their program. The next thing they knew is that the representative for Mr. Godfrey told them to report to such-and-such a stage. Bob asked about their audition. The answer was that they had already passed.

The longest square dance was held in Oregon. The hard working dancers who succeeded in getting square dancing recognized as the Official Dance of their state by the Oregon Legislature, have moved on to conduct a dance event which they hope to place in the Guinness World Book of Records as the "longest square dance." The Portland Area

Council was the official sponsor and the Lloyd Center Shopping Mall on an ice rink (temporarily without ice) was the place. It started at midnight, Saturday, September 8th, and continued non-stop until 8:00 o'clock Monday night, September 10th. 27 callers alternated in one hour segments with one PA playing continuously. Record book signatures showed 900 dancers from five states and Canada representing 77 clubs. There was always at least one square on the floor. Coverage by newspapers, radio and television publicized square dancing and the Mayor issued a proclamation about the event. A special badge was given commemorating the date.

The place is Diekirch in the Country of Luxembourg, that small European nation tucked in between France, Germany, and Belgium. The occasion was the International Folk Dance Festival.

Square dancers do not need to go to unusual places or greater heights to show off. Well, maybe not great heights in elevation, but they do go to great heights off the ground. One of the exhibition groups seemed to have the motto, "Anything you can do, I can do higher." This parody of a familiar Broadway tune seemed to sum up the enthusiasm of the 18 young members of the Mayfield, Ohio, Unicycle Square Dance Team. These two squares, and two alternates, make up what must be the world's most unusual square dance exhibition group. Not only can they "dance" virtually everything that is danced under normal conditions, they perform their act several feet off the ground on unicycles. Actually dancing on these one-wheelers may look simple as these young people do-sa-do, promenade and even do a partner swing, however, Bob Howell, veteran caller and one of the coaches of the group, says that it's a tricky operation and gets even trickier when dancers mount the tall, nine-foot unicycles.

Usually an exhibition will include two squares of unicycle dancers working simultaneously, sometimes as two independent groups, sometimes combined into a double square or Royal, which simply means that one square is working inside or beside the other. When watching the complex movements of the unicyclists, a spectator asked one of the coaches recently, what was the most complex movement for these dancers? Expecting the answer to be some complicated pattern, he was surprised to hear that the basic do-sa-do was perhaps the most difficult, primarily because switching from a forward motion to backing up takes far more years' experience than these performers have achieved. "Instead of a do-sa-do," the coach explained, "we use a right arm turn and manage to achieve just about the same results."

Square dancing tractors

Perhaps a little closer to the ground are square dancers who dance on ice skates or roller skates. Groups have formed all over the country just for the fun of dancing on blades or wheels. But not to be outdone by those tiny wheels on unicycles or roller skates are members of the Farmall Promenade.

Think nothing is as emblematic of the United States as apple pie? Or maybe baseball is the *ne plus ultra* of the American dream? You've clearly never seen a tractor square dance. The act is exactly what it sounds like. Four seated couples maneuver vintage tractors into daisy chains and do-sa-dos in front of a live audience. It would be hard to squeeze more nostalgia into a performance that combines made in America machines with our "National Folk Dance." Laurie Mason-Schmidt is the caller for Farmall Promenade, the most famous group of square dancing tractors. "We all have real jobs, believe it or not," she says during a show. "We farm. I teach school. And some days we dress up a little strangely and get on our tractors and square dance." The first tractor dance was part of a 1953 advertising campaign by International Harvester to show off the fast hitching abilities of their Farmall Super-C tractor. The (then) new technology allowed farmers to change implements as easily as switching dance partners. An ad from one of these performances describes the act as a "sensational never-to-be-forgotten act." The special touches that made Farmall Promenade a success have spread to other troupes. Tractor square dances always feature eight riders in their performances - four couples to make up the dance's traditional "square" - who often dress in exaggerated drag to play the male and female roles. Another important similarity between troupes is the colorful rhyming instructions of their caller, referred to as patter call.

Let's stay on the farm and take a look at square dancing on horse-back. Some square dancers are double-threat people, for they square dance afoot and on horseback as well. Over the border in Edmonton, Alberta, Jimmy Lindsay calls for a colorful group that exhibits square dancing on horseback for various Canadian functions and on television. The ladies have red saddle blankets and scrapes; the boys blue. They wear matching shirts, white western pants, white hats with matching ribbons. For a performance the riders are lined up outside, Jimmy starts the music and the eight mounted dancers come out at a canter, led by four standard bearers. They promenade to position and Jimmy starts off

311

with Honor Your Partner. The horse-borne dancers do Ends Turn In, Venus and Mars, Trailing Star, Allemande Thar, etc.

In the States, at Streator, Ill., the Red Arrow Riding Club members like to square dance on foot and have trained their horses so that they, too, can follow the dance routines. The group dances on horseback every Tuesday night at Fun and Frolics Acres with Vince Twang as regular caller. They have a record player with two speakers and use the popular records. Their routines are made up from the basics list in Sets in Order. They are arranged at a slower pace for the horses but riders and their mounts have become pretty proficient with Wheel and Deal, Do Si Do, Weave the Ring, Allemande Left, Grand Right and Left, etc. Apart from com-

bining their two hobbies, the Red Arrow dancers are beginning to be invited to exhibit square dancing on horseback at civic celebrations, fairs, etc., in their local area.

Perhaps the most daring and unique of all square dance demonstrations was performed by the United States Army. The Helicopter Square Dance Team was founded in the 1950's to help promote interest in the helicopter, the US Army's "new flying machine." This is their story. In the 1950's, the U.S. Army conceived of a way to promote helicopters at national air shows across America - by square dancing with helicopters! A team of expert pilots were assembled to perform these incredible dancing stunts. "Boy" helicopters were dressed in straw hats and corn-cob pipes

and "Girl" helicopters were dressed in skirts and long hair made from mops. They danced to classics such as "Turkey in the Straw" and "The Arkansas Traveler." This team's flagship performance at the 1956 National Air Show in Oklahoma wowed spectators as they danced their way into audience's hearts - and into aviation history! The retirement of the square dance team of the 1950s did not mean the end of helicopter square dancing. Several years later, flyers from the Naval Air Station, San Diego, Calif., demonstrated their skill at the manipulation of the whirlybirds in a square dance routine. This was a feature of Wide, Wide, World telecast, and Arnie Kronenberger called a square to the helicopters. The swooping and swirling of the midair dancing took place near NBC's television studios in Burbank, and created quite a spectacle.

Staff photographer Joe Fadler was on hand during the hours of rehearsal to capture and bring you the scenes.

Chapter 14. Asilomar

Through these gates pass the greatest people on earth:
square dancers

Back in 1948 we had set a couple of goals for ourselves. One, of course, was to hold classes for dancers so we could teach them how to dance well. That idea spread across the Los Angeles area and throughout the rest of the country as well. From the classes came clubs and dancer associations. The second goal was to start the magazine. We hoped that we might last a couple of years, but with the rate that subscriptions increased we knew that the magazine would have a longer run than that.

We saw the Santa Monica Diamond Jubilee with 15,000 dancers and 30,000 spectators. Also, exhibitions were staged at the Hollywood Bowl and at the Los Angeles Memorial Coliseum (built for the 1932 Olympics). The largest audience for a square dance was for the 1951 Tournament of Roses parade, with millions able to watch it on TV. Square dancing even had its own television programs.

The one goal that we had not achieved by 1951 was to give callers and dancers the Lloyd Shaw type experience. I had attended the Lloyd Shaw sessions in Colorado Springs in 1947, '48, '49, and '50 - I'm not sure how many of them. We had so much fun at these sessions we got the idea -- why couldn't we do something like this for dancers? As well as we could we taught people in the clubs and classes the way we had learned at Shaw's, but we kind of had the feeling that many callers who were now teaching classes were too far removed from the Shaw experience and therefore were maybe not teaching all the things which we thought were important. Things like how to dance smoothly, and the fun of after parties, and the fun of couple dancing, mixers, and contras - the whole ball of wax.

A square dance vacation institute would not be the first in the county, but it would be a new experience for us. We didn't have any guidelines to go by, but we knew that it was going to be important to have a good, well rounded faculty. Unlike Shaw's program where he was the only teacher, ours was going to be a staff situation with callers from different areas that could give a broad aspect of square dancing and round dancing.

And here, another element enriched the picture. Almost simultaneously, with the beginning of Sets in Order magazine, we started Rip 'n' Snort, an amazing square dance club which gave us the inspiration to combine both the local club concept and the magazine's broad perspective.

Going back to that time before the Second World War, I never forgot that wonderful facility where hundreds of students attended a week long college YM/YWCA conference and where I had first been bitten by the square dance bug. I hadn't planned to join in then, but it looked like fun and everyone was having a great time. "Captain Jinks and the Horse Marines" was done in a large circle, "Oh Susana" was a square and my first exposure to contras was when the

315

instructor/caller announced "Sir Roger de Coverly" which I later realized, despite its fancy name, was no more nor less than the "Virginia Reel." At any rate it was the result of that experience that I started thinking, years later, what a wonderful spot Asilomar would be for a square dance.

My memories of my college Asilomar experience thirteen years earlier were still very vivid, so why not combine the best club feeling of square dancing and the expansive outreach of the magazine with the unbeatable setting of Asilomar? This would be an opportunity to be with dancers from all over, and not just from our own community. It would provide us with the viewpoint we felt that we needed for publishing the monthly magazine, Sets in Order.

Jay Orem, our most capable, energetic business manager and friend, set out to tie-up the details. Working with the management of Asilomar (then owned privately and run by the YWCA), he buttoned down the dates and rates. Asilomar eventually became a State run conference grounds in Northern California, adjacent to Pebble Beach, Carmel, and Monterey. A quick trip up north, a visit to the conference grounds, and we had a complete package: meals, living accommodations, dancing and class facilities, all in one location, right on the beach overlooking the Pacific Ocean. Then with the support of our Rip 'n' Snort club members, a strong word-of-mouth campaign, and the promotion by the magazine, we encouraged some of the curious to come and see what a square dance vacation was all about.

Chuck Jones, President of Rip 'n Snort and unofficially the "voice of the dancer," summed up his reason for attending: "Somebody told me Sets in Order was going to sponsor a vacation institute. I thought they said 'Sex in Order.'"

There were other dance camps being held around the country. Jim Piper had a camp somewhere in the East, and

Herb Greggerson hosted week-long sessions on Texas style square dancing. Even in Stockton, California, just a couple of hundred miles north of Los Angeles, Lawton Harris had started a folk dance camp that featured international folk dance. In some ways it was similar to the Hollywood Peasants we had participated with in the late 1940s. Square dancing was an important part of the program at Stockton, but it was not the feature. Harris brought in folk dance teachers from around the world to teach their ethnic specialty. In 1950 I was on staff to introduce California style square dancing, and along with me was Jack McKay, a well-known caller from San Francisco. In contrast to the California style, Herb Greggerson was there to teach the old time Texas style square dances, and Ralph Page of New Hampshire smoothed us all out with his New England type quadrilles (Ralph was known at the time as the singing caller) and contra dances. The Stockton folk dance camp started in 1947, so it was already three years old when we started Asilomar.

We wanted to focus on Western style square dancing – the type we advocated in the magazine - and we also wanted to fully integrate the smoothness of contra dances and the grace of round dances. Contra dances are a great way to introduce people to dancing. We selected dances that used the simple Western square dance moves, but we kept the traditional timing. Contra dancing also expanded our music selection by using Scottish and Irish reels, jigs, and hornpipes. Round dances were similar to ballroom dancing, but without the anxiety. When you talk to most men about dancing usually they say they don't know their right from their left. Actually they were really afraid of making mistakes with their feet when their brains were trying to think of what to do next. Round dancing took away that anxiety by having the choreography worked out by professionals, then the dancers either had to memorize the dances, or a cuer could remind them of what to do. Round dances also got away from the usual

317

boom-chuck rhythm of squares and brought in two-steps and waltzes and fox-trots.

We invited several callers to be on our staff - they all agreed (more on them later). We set the dates from June 27th to July 2, 1951, and everything seemed to be in order. Now, would anybody come? We had hoped that we might entice 100 dancers to attend our initial program. We sent out brochures, advertised in Sets in Order, and talked it up among our club members. This was a first for us and we had to develop our own ideas of how this might work.

What exactly is Asilomar? ASILOMAR is a Latin word meaning "refuge by the sea." Philosophically, it was a place to think, to contemplate, to meditate. Physically, it was a conference center that thousands of groups found ideally suited for informative, inspirational, career-enhancing workshops and seminars.

The retreat was founded Aug. 7, 1913. The original thought was to build a retreat for young women attending West Coast colleges. Asilomar, at first, consisted of 10 tent houses, the Phoebe A. Hearst Social Hall, and a circus tent that served as the dining hall. Eventually Asilomar became the regional YWCA conference center. In 1956, it became part of the state parks network.

The secluded center has been compared architecturally with the Ahwahnee Hotel in Yosemite National Park because of the extensive use of native woods and stone. The 105 acre conference center, which was designed between 1913 and 1928 by Hearst Castle architect Julia Morgan, includes clusters of 32 conference and meeting areas that ranged from a 10-seat living room to a 850-capacity multiuse auditorium; a dining hall that could seat 500 in the main section and 150 more in each of the two wings: a 256-capacity chapel; and 313 guest rooms, some with wood-burning fireplaces. Each of the five main conference buildings was equipped for audio-visual presentations. There was a concert size electric organ in the chapel, and a grand piano in the auditorium.

What were the physical attributes of this place which has been described at times as a state of mind? Actually, Asilomar was and still is rich in comfortable accommodations for rest, food, and fun.

Among the living accommodations were, first, the Long House. This was a rustic building, long as its name implies - with small twin bedrooms opening on a central corridor. Community lavatories, showers, and toilets were provided separately for men and women. This building was for the budget-minded or for young people who found the feeling of a mountain camp in Long House.

Guest Inn, Scripps, and Lodge were three large rambling buildings of approximately the same type of housing. Each had a commodious living room with a rustic fireplace, comfortable chairs, tables, etc. In these three lodges, connecting baths served two rooms each and contained a shower and a toilet. Hot and cold running water was provided in the rooms designed for from one to three people. Hill Top had a charming living room with a fireplace and the bedrooms had private baths.

319

The great building for meals was called Crocker Dining Hall. There was nothing quite like the feeling of walking in to breakfast out of the crisp morning air and seeing the fires ablaze in the great stone fireplaces, smelling the wonderful and abundant food, and entering the clatter and clamor of the daily reunion with your dancing camp-mates. You found that meal time was the time when you could most easily chat with others and really get acquainted. Meals were served semi-cafeteria style, i.e., the first course was usually on the table, then you got up, table by table, to file out to the serving windows of the kitchen and pick up hot food.

What might be termed the "heart" of Asilomar was the Administration Building where people registered and the Sets in Order Institute office was located. There was a spacious lobby for lounging, reading, playing ping pong and pool, also a piano and a candy stand. The record store, designed as a service to participants, was in this building.

But, we wanted people to come here to dance. Most of the dancing was done in Merrill Hall, a big peaked-roof building that could dance 25 squares. By its capacity for dancing we decided the capacity of the camp. Daily classes were held there and the night dances as well as the after dinner Fireside Hour of singing and discussion.

So, Asilomar was geared up for the kind of thing where you could have any kind of meeting - business or educational or anything like that. Well, it happened to be just perfect for us because it had the large auditorium and it had meeting rooms where we could have classes for anybody who wanted to talk about square dancing. It was located in mid-California, right at Monterey just west of Salinas, at the north end of the 17-mile drive, adjacent to Pebble Beach Golf Course, with some of the most beautiful ocean shoreline I've ever seen. In our early sessions, sometimes we would go over to watch people like Bing Crosby and Bob Hope play - I think it was in February that they had some of the big matches then. So, a lot of the illustrious people were there.

There were other attractions at Asilomar too – including tennis courts and a heated swimming pool. Nearby are the famous 17-Mile Drive of the Monterey Peninsula, historic Monterey, and picturesque Carmel.

We had confidence in the facilities and the staff, but there was one thing, beforehand, that had worried us. With dancers coming from so many places, our concerns about getting people to mix grew as we saw reservations come not only from California, but from Oregon and Washington and Canada. We knew that we could have a problem in getting these people to be friendly with each other. So we spent time in figuring out mixers and everything else, but we didn't have to worry. Even as we were setting up for the first registration with staff members ready to introduce the dancers to each other, up comes Bud Blakey, a delightful square dancer from San Diego with the spontaneity of a person who just naturally is a friend to everyone and he became our unofficial greeter in a way that no preplanning could ever hope to accomplish.

The spirit was contagious and from that moment and for the balance of that first Asilomar, as well as for the Asilomars to come, we found that our job was simply to furnish the setting, the housing, the food and the place to dance and the "student body" would take care of the rest.

So, we were off to a good start. We had friends of ours who were part of our club (Chuck Jones, for example, who had such a talent for putting people at ease) and so many of the old timers who were part of setting up the camp. We planned the camp in a way that we figured might work knowing that we could change it later. If it went well the first time we might have another one. Something that really helped to meld the individuals into a group was that the first thing in the morning, after breakfast, we had one hour in which we taught styling. That way we got them off the boards dancing smoothly and that reflected during the whole balance of the day. Every dancer received a hard bound 3-ring notebook which included notes on procedures, schedules, etc. One of the most important hand-outs was a sheet on styling – one of our major goals for the Institute.

Square dancing is not unlike golf, tennis, bowling or many activities where there are a few essentials a player must know and can learn in a relatively short period of time. Then, once he has learned these, he works to improve his performance.

That is how we felt about square dancing. A person should always strive to be a better dancer. Unlike some activities where an individual is essentially involved with just his own game, square dancing, being a group or team activity, requires the participant to blend in well with the others in his unit (square, line, etc.). Because we are part of a team, standardization and styling plays an important role in our enjoyment of the activity.

When I first became interested in square dancing in the years just before the war, it was pretty much a hit-and-miss proposition as far as any uniform style of dancing was concerned. People skipped or ran or two-stepped, depending on their mood the type of music that was being played, and the area in which they danced.

Immediately following the war, I had an opportunity to travel through much of the United States and Canada on a series of business trips. During these trips I had occasions to drop in on square dance clubs, listen to callers and talk to dancers in areas that would one day form the nucleus of this fast-spreading American folk recreation.

I was amazed then at the variety of styles that existed. I counted some eight different ways to swing, four different styles of handholds for a promenade, and at least three different do-si-dos. Each area seemed perfectly happy in the style of dancing it practiced and it was only when dancers traveled to another area that any confusion arose. The wise dancers were those who adopted the policy of "when in Rome..." However, there was a strong feeling by every group that their particular style of square dancing was the way it should be done.

As I watched this variety of styles, I wondered how square dancing would ever resolve itself. I was particularly concerned when the first square dance festivals were held, drawing dancers from many areas -with many styles - into one hall.

We started Sets in Order Magazine with the idea that it might lend a helping hand in explaining these area differences and perhaps be able to come up with some form of standardization that would be acceptable to everyone. Our hope was that with some give-and-take in every area on the part of the dancers and the leaders, a formula might be developed where dancers could learn in one area and then enjoy their square dancing any place they visited. It wasn't so important what style of dancing was adopted as long as it was comfortable and intelligent. We felt that one standard style adopted and enjoyed by all would be a great assurance for the future of the activity. Somehow it all worked out, though not without a lot of patience and understanding.

Since the first issue of Sets in Order in November, 1948, we watched the slow transformation of the square dance, through usage, into one predominant style - a style of Promenading, a style of Swinging, a grip for an Allemande

323

Left, and a handhold for a Right and Left Grand - taught and practiced everywhere.

With patience and study and a great deal of give-and-take, callers discovered that this basic style can be danced comfortably. It can be executed to the beat and sometimes to the phrase of the music with sufficient time for each movement to be danced comfortably so that the different basics and figures are accomplished without jerking, yanking or pulling. And it can be done in such a way that dancers get the maximum joy from the figure without worrying about what unexpected twist, flip or twirl might send them scooting across the floor.

Since the beginning of Sets in Order's first Asilomar back in 1951, we have observed the policy of adhering to one style of dancing considered to be "the standard." Consequently, when the SIO/ASDS Illustrated Basic Movement Handbooks were first issued, these standard definitions were included. Then when CALLERLAB – The International Association of Square Dance Callers was born at Asilomar in 1971, the definitions endorsed by this group were included in the handbooks and a giant step was taken in international square dance standardization. I've got to admit that I don't know what I would have done if we hadn't had Shaw's back ground in that, because this made them feel sort of proud in dancing. They weren't just getting from Point A to Point C; they were doing it and enjoying the route as they went.

We were able to pull together an amazing staff for that first session at Asilomar. Ray Smith of Dallas, Texas, brought some six feet and more of excitement in calling in his unmistakable Texas accent. Ray had also recorded an album in his inimitable Texas style, authored two books on square dancing, and was a really colorful figure in the square dance world. Ray was scheduled to present some of the newer calls, plus basic figures. We also had Fenton 'Jonesy' Jones, the best known of all callers throughout the country, largely because of his splendid recordings on the MacGregor and Capitol labels. 'Jonesy' was famous for his singing calls and was the author of a new singing call book. Dale Garrett, another faculty member, was the first president of the Associated Square Dancers of Southern California. He brought much knowledge on the forming of square dance clubs and associations. Dale and his wife Ruth headed the classes on Round Dance Teaching Techniques. Ralph Maxheimer, well-known for his Round Dance instruction records on the MacGregor label, with his wife Eve, presented the daily sessions in American Round Dancing.

In addition, Ralph had extensive experience in leading Caller's Courses which made him the perfect choice to help with the Callers' Workshop Periods. From the earliest days, Asilomar included caller training courses. At first these daily sessions would be interspersed with the dancing and every staff member would take a turn at indoctrinating the aspiring callers. For a time, caller's schools at Asilomar became a prime attraction and as many as 30 or 40 student callers and their partners would enroll. Staff leaders such as Bob Van Antwerp, Lee Helsel, and Ed Gilmore did the bulk of the teaching and, over the years, many fine callers received their initial training here on these grounds.

It was a very popular staff for the day. They all had followings. I think we had 180 people for that first session. It was fun and we did lots and lots of things that became a permanent part of the program. That first summer we had one session and it had a waiting list.

When it came to making plans for the 1952 summer program, one problem stood out very plainly. If the policy was to keep the Institute at Asilomar to the comfortable size experienced in 1951, there would have to be one of two alternatives; either: (1) An awful lot of people who had missed last year's session and heard of its fun and achievements and expressed the wish to be enrolled in 1952 would have to be turned down; or (2) a second session, giving twice the number an opportunity to attend, would have to be arranged. The latter seemed to be the most feasible.

We decided that rather than have two identical sessions with the same staff, we would hold two entirely different Asilomars, with a different faculty for each session. The Early Summer Session (from June 29 through July 5, 1952) had exactly the same staff as 1951: Ray Smith; 'Jonesy'; Dale Garrett; Ralph Maxheimer, and we added Terry Golden, a folk singer. The Late Summer Session (August 24 - August 29) had a faculty of Al Brundage, Ed Gilmore, Frank Hamilton, and Arnie Kronenberger. We hit the jackpot by being able to contract Sam Hinton to be the folk singer for the late session. So in the second year we did two summer sessions. Then, a few years later, we were doing two sessions in the summer and one in the winter and a winter weekend.

We stopped doing all of them in the 1990s, after almost 40 years. That session of our life was over. We handed the program over to Frank Lane who kept Asilomar going for several more years.

Remember way back at the beginning of Sets in Order, two of the first people to come on staff were Jay and Helen Orem. When Jay introduced himself he said, "I'm Jay, and I sell things." Well, Jay started off selling subscriptions and advertising space, and he soon became the business manager for Sets in Order. He knew that to make a sale people needed to be exposed to a product many times before

326

they even noticed it. His belief in exposing products dominated our approach to advertising. Look back through old issues of Sets in Order and you will see we constantly mentioned the name of the magazine and products we offered. "Sets in Order" was on each page at least once. While the Record Square was still going, we made sure there were several ads that referred to it, and it always was in the record review.

At the same time, Jay knew that the ads had to be different in every issue or they just became background. So when we started Asilomar we began the advertising campaign early in the year and continued on through the year. First, a full page ad was run in Sets in Order and it gave just enough information to be a teaser, such as location, staff, etc. People had to write to us to get the full brochure that included more details on program and cost. Our first Sets in Order advertisements were an announcement, later we had artwork of the beach and the Asilomar setting. We moved on to promoting the staff at the first session.

Each year after that our advertising campaign became more sophisticated. For example, for 1952 we identified the potential customers and stated the benefits specifically for each group. The ad started with a call in general to dancers in general to attend. Then we defined the program for dancers – getting to dance to the best callers in the country and so forth. Callers were targeted by telling them of the training they could get. Adding the second session that year was a big draw also because dancers did not have to adjust their whole lives to a particular week. Finally, we pushed the music. Terry Golden, who had been at Asilomar in 1951, was returning and he was a big draw. We hustled and were able to contract Sam Hinton, one of America's best known folk singers to be at the late session. We also listed the names of the bands for live music.

In another issue of the magazine we ran a full page ad that was in the question/answer format.

QUESTION: Is Asilomar primarily for dancers or callers?

ANSWER: It is essentially for both. A good balance of old and new materials will be presented, with a great majority of all sessions designed for everyone.

QUESTION: Will there be mostly square dancing or round dancing taught at Asilomar?

Answer: Here again good balance and good judgment will be the prevailing factor. Frank and Carolyn Hamilton, long experienced in round dance instruction classes and Institutes, will not only stress basic fundamentals of couple dancing, but will also present those new and old round dances that have lasting characteristics.

QUESTION: Will there be special instruction for callers?

ANSWER: Definitely. A certain portion of every day will be devoted to caller help by Ed Gilmore, Al Brundage and Bob Osgood. A certain portion of the time will also be set aside for the callers for experience and guidance. In addition, the planning of all courses will provide particular emphasis on teaching techniques, new ideas on teaching and presenting the older and newer square dance figures.

QUESTION: Will we get to hear the faculty call?

ANSWER: You bet. Each night's program will be the responsibility of one of the faculty members, who will do the majority of the calling for that evening.

For 1953 we unveiled what goes on at the Institute. We figured that people were more likely to buy if they knew what was in the package.

What do you do at a Square Dance Summer Institute? You dance and dance. Basically, for a square dancer, a real honest-to-goodness square dancing vacation becomes an unbelievable paradise. Whether he's a caller, or whether he's just a dancer interested in the fun and enjoyment square dancing has brought and is continuing to bring him, a square dance camp, such as Asilomar, on the rugged, beautiful shores of the Monterey Peninsula in California, brings him new experiences in square dancing friendships compared to nothing he had dreamed imaginable.

What is an average day at the Asilomar Sets in Order Summer Institute? Well, aside from the "free time" which is generously given to those who wish to admire the beauties of the neighboring scenery, the morning starts after breakfast, at 9:00 o'clock, with a session of square dancing for comfort. This is the place where roughness is eliminated, where little tricks and helps on styling emphasize the fun, and yet bring out the considerate and more attractive forms of square dancing patters.

Following this, an hour of round dancing, with an emphasis on the fundamentals along with a good smattering of the old and some tasty samples of the new. Next it's time for an hour of square dancing for fun, with some of the best known callers in the country demonstrating what has proved to be a formula of enjoyable programming and fun dancing. By then it's lunch time.

Following lunch, another hour of round dancing; then some more time is spent on squares, new and old, with contra dancing, workshops, experimental sessions, all having their proper place.

Nineteen-fifty-six was a rough year, and perhaps it was good that I had Asilomar to keep my mind occupied. Ginger moved into her own apartment in July and so I had to host the Institute alone. But thank heaven for all the support, especially Jay and Helen Orem and Ruth Paul. Without them I don't know what would have happened. But with them Asilomar came off beautifully.

We still carefully structured the program so there was something special for everyone. For people who just came to dance we made sure they were exposed to the finest callers who worked on styling, smooth dancing, and the latest in choreography.

Callers, of course, got to observe first-hand how the best called; in addition, aspiring callers could get one-on-one instruction time. There were also special sessions on round dancing and clinics for round dance leaders.

We continued the contra dance program. We especially liked contras because they use a limited number of basics and most of them are danced in the same manner as in square dancing. The one basic difference is dancers move to the phrase of the music. Most of the movements are done in increments of eight beats. The Contra sessions were held the first thing each morning and started off with the very simplest contras. Contras were also featured somewhere during the evening programs.

Since many square dancers had young families, we started a program especially directed towards those square dancing parents who plan their vacations for the entire family. Bob and Babs Ruff of Whittier, California, set up and guided this special supervised recreation for the children of participating square dancers. Bob and Babs were well-qualified for this important post because of their experience in recreation work.

Hobbies and crafts, special games, swimming in a large heated pool, nature study hikes, glass bottom boat trips, etc., were just a few of the many outstanding recreational possibilities for the youngsters. There were also special parties and some square dancing for youngsters from the age of 5 through 18. We also made arrangements for baby-sitters for children under age five during the day and for the evening programs.

The 5th National Square Dance Convention was in San Diego in 1956, so our advertising sold California as much as it did Asilomar. We wanted to tap into the pool of dancers who were already planning on heading to California, so we touted the advantages of going to the National Square Dance Convention and tying into one of the Asilomar sessions. One way to do that was to point out the additional vacation opportunities between San Diego and Monterey, such as Hollywood, Disneyland, Knott's Berry Farm, Yosemite, the Golden Gate Bridge, and more. We also played some mental games to pique the interest

Asilomar (pronounced Ah-see-low-mar, accent on the see) is a place. It is a square dancer's Shangri-La (pronounced Asilomar). Its name means Near the Sea. You won't find it on your maps because it isn't a great big place. It's just the right size to accommodate 200 square and round dancers at Sets in Order's Summer Institutes. You'll find it sandwiched between beautiful Carmel on one side and California's first capital - Monterey – on the other. In terms of distance, it's about 120 miles South of San Francisco, 450 miles north of San Diego and about 3000 miles west of New York City. (You can't miss it.)

In terms of climate, it is ideal for square dancing. Even in the summertime, it is never hot! It's a cool and invigorating 60 or 70 degrees when temperatures in the rest of the country soar into those blistering 90's and 100s. You'll often need a sweater or jacket in the daytime and usually a light coat or shawl in the evening!

That last paragraph was intended to remind people from the mid-West and further east of what summer weather was like at home.

In 1957 we held a Sets in Order subscription dance with a theme I felt sure-would drive dancers away. Thank heavens I was wrong. We addressed a letter in Sets in Order to people who had attended Asilomar, and we sent out another letter to former attendees to come to my birthday party (number – gasp – 40!) The letter reminded them of some of the delights of being at Asilomar, such as: *And what would Asilomar be without that 9 AM session on "California Styling" by Osgood each morning before our eyes are open and the stiffness out of our joints. By the way, do you recall how Bob kept us up-to-date on Dick Tracy, Orphan Annie, and the weather (especially if hot) in our home towns?"* and *"We shall dance again, both squares and rounds, to music, calling, and cueing of the Asilomar Staffulty and be entertained by the Master Firesiders Hinton, Helsel, and Golden. The Staffulty is behind this and is contributing its efforts to make it a huge success. It will be a bawl! AND - to cap it off - Chuck "Bugs Bunny" Jones will MC in his own inimitable style.*

The advertising campaign for Asilomar over the years featured photos and drawings of the facilities and the natural beauty of the North Coast setting. We had aerial photographs and we had artistically done maps of the peninsula. Shortly after each session we posted pictures of dancers and staff having a good time. One of my favorites was a cartoon advertisement worked out by Frank Grundeen.

We even offered enticements to attract dancers. For example, we were told by a number of people that they just could not come up with the cash at once to enroll, so we started a layaway program. Dancers could choose which session they wanted to attend and we would set up an account and let them know how much per month to deposit to have the bill paid before their date. And to make it more attractive, we made it so they could withdraw their money if they found they had a conflict.

We got a boost from Square Dance Square, a retail shop near Santa Barbara. It ran a contest with the first prize being a scholarship for the dancer's caller to Asilomar. Whenever dancers purchased anything at Square Dance Square, they identified their caller and credit went into an account for the caller. At a certain date, they closed the voting and first prize went to the caller with the greatest number of votes. That caller received a scholarship for him-self and his partner to Asilomar and a cash prize equal to the tuition to pay for transportation. Second prize was for one person. However, there were no real losers in this. Any caller who received 500 votes or more was awarded a scholarship of room, board, and tuition for one.

The advertising was attractive and effective, but only as long as we kept up the quality of the Asilomar Institute. We worked even harder at developing good programs and finding the top square dance and round dance leaders to teach the classes. The emphasis had to be on what callers and dancers could get from the Institute.

As we have said before, square dancing is people. The atmosphere of Asilomar created some bonds between people that lasted long after the week was over. Asilomarites began to think of Asilomar as home and family. Highlighting one of the August sessions was a square dance wedding. The setting was the redwood chapel  in the pines on the lovely grounds, where Frances Carlson of Riverside and Harlan Sandusky of Colton, California, both participants at the Institute, were married. Guests were also participants and were attired in full square dance regalia, as were members of the wedding party, making it a most colorful occasion.

Rev. Harris Pillsbury of Pacific Grove officiated; Bob Osgood gave the bride in marriage; and the Ed Gilmores of Yucaipa, California, were the attendants. Music was furnished by Lunette Brezeale at the piano. At the reception following the ceremony, tables were decorated with the traditional white tapers, and bright blooms brought from homes on the Monterey Peninsula, where such beauties as giant begonias and fragile fuchsias are a specialty. The Institute was attended by some 136 persons from 16 states, with a faculty headed by Bob Osgood, with Ed Gilmore, Al Brundage,

Frank Hamilton, Arnie Kronenberger and Sam Hinton. At the end of the five busy and fun-filled days, the consensus; "I've never had more fun in such a short time in my life!" as one of the dancers expressed it.

In February of 1971, eleven members of the Square Dance Hall of Fame gathered during one of our regular sessions and made square dance history. In fact, square dancing would never be the same, because during three days of meetings they formed CALLERLAB: the International Association of Square Dance Callers, an organization which was to play a key role in the dancing and the calling of the future.

In 1990, after forty years of hosting the dance institute at Asilomar, it was time to retire. We had closed the magazine in 1985, but we continued Asilomar for another five years.

What else is there to say about these marvelous forty years. I think I will leave it to some of the attendees and Staffulty to explain what Asilomar means.

"I remember the early Asilomar sessions with live music by Jack and Lunette on the banjo and piano. Those two really stimulated the atmosphere. I remember one evening after the regular dance program when many of the dancers decided to go into Monterey for a snack. The only place open was an ice cream parlor called 'The Creamery.' Almost 100 dancers converged on the little shop that had only one young lady waiting tables. It became pure pandemonium. Some of the group got behind the counter, took orders, made the sundaes and milk shakes, collected the money and tips for the waitress and in about an hour left with the waitress shaking her head in a daze. Wonderful times!" - Jay Orem

"Florence and I thoroughly enjoyed our seven-year stint at Asilomar as members of the Staffulty. Looking back I recall with pleasure the following: The fireside gatherings each evening with Terry Golden singing; Chuck Jones' 'Voice of the People' sessions. I remember Chuck saying, 'The walls of our room are so thin I found myself shaving with another man's face.' Sharing our knowledge with others in a helpful manner was our purpose at Asilomar.

"Vaya con Dios" - Fenton 'Jonesy' Jones

"Asilomar has always been something very special in the square dance activity. I was thrilled when I was asked to become a member of the Staffulty many years ago and it was a great experience to participate with the fine leaders you had. I felt as though I had finally made it to the top. We wish you a happy and well-deserved retirement and are happy to hear that Frank Lane will be continuing with the institute as the high-quality square dance vacation it's always been for the past forty years."

- Al and Bea Brundage

336

"We were on the Staffulty at Asilomar from the first years until we retired in 1971. Those 11 summers and 10 winter sessions stand out as the happiest and most valuable of the many dance affairs we attended, and they provided, in our opinion, the ultimate in dancing enjoyment for many hundreds of dancers. For so many years and in many ways, Bob has done more to develop and guide the square dance activity than anyone since Dr. Lloyd Shaw. To us he has always been 'Mr. Square Dancer.' We wish Bob and Becky a happy retirement, and to all of you at Asilomar, the best of everything." - Frank and Carolyn Hamilton

"We remember square dancing at Asilomar in the fifties when our type of dancing was new, square dance vacations were new and it was exciting to be breaking new ground. It was square dancing when dancing was the capital word and we loved it. We look back with sadness and joy. Sadness because we miss the many friends we made at Asilomar but joyful to have been a part of it."

-Joe and Claire Lewis

"Bob Osgood is a very gentle but firm leader and a highly organized individual. Being such, he ran a highly organized institute. In the early days we had a staff meeting every day between 4:00 and 5:30 PM. Now this is the time when the lucky patrons get to shower and shave and clean up for the evening or take a short nap. These meetings created a horrendous rush between the evening meal and Fireside for the staff to clean up for the evening dance. Bob met his match when he assembled the first Winter Asilomar. Manning Smith and Lee Helsel had not worked together previously. Both were experienced institute men and had conducted their own successful camps. Both were *ad lib* types who often did their best work winging it, so to speak. The first night of this institute, the staff assembled in the living room of Tide Inn and proceeded to have an all-night after-party. Manning and Lee played their own version of 'Can You Top This?' going through category after category of jokes. Needless to say sessions that followed were more relaxed and less structured; the number of staff meetings were cut. Bob discovered Becky and they lived happily ever after and we all love each other to this day."

- Bruce Johnson

"We remember the many wonderful and unusual after-parties at Asilomar and especially the many things that didn't work: Bob's wig which wouldn't come off no matter how hard we pulled; the music for our Philharmonic orchestra that was heard only on stage but not by the audience. We remember the time the lights went off due to an electric failure and Flip and I called with a tape recorder and with battery light. We remember when Ed Gilmore refereed the Staffulty vs. the Participants volley ball game which included the staff being sprayed with whipped cream. We remember many learning times, the fun times, the surprise times, the essence of camaraderie and belonging. We were just better people for having happy times."

- Bob and Roberta Van Antwerp.

"To be on staff at Asilomar was a goal I set as a young caller some thirty years ago. When this goal was attained, I had the pleasure of working with Bob and Becky, Bob Van Antwerp and Mike Seastrom. This was one of the highlights of my career and I shall always be grateful for the opportunity." - Jon Jones

"ASILOMAR: A place I would have worked absolutely free (don't you wish you had known that 26 years ago?) A place where I have been privileged to stay in the 'Presidential Suite' in Tide Inn each year, never knowing what I might find when I returned to my room. A place where I have made some of the most endearing friendships in my calling career A place where I have served with a staff of the greatest square and round dance professionals in the world. To you, Bob and Becky (whom I consider the 'Pappy' and Dorothy Shaw of my era) a sincere appreciation for allowing me to be a part of your lives and a part of the fabulous excitement called Asilomar. I want you to know I will always treasure fond memories of working with you."

-Marshall Flippo

Chapter 15. Going National

Once we had completed Asilomar and the Diamond Jubilee in the early 1950s, things were happening so fast that it was one of those times when we'd barely get done with one job, say in our case, editing the magazine or finishing Asilomar or planning the next thing, and something else was starting.

I have to think back to over 50 years ago when the three late, greats Carl Anderson, Walt Bowman, and Ed Gilmore, who were the proud fathers of the National Convention, came into the office to talk about their brainchild. But let's back up a bit.

If you recall at first there were no classes as we know them today. Folks just joined a square dance group and learned to dance by dancing. For the most part, dancers "stayed put," dancing with just those who, like themselves, were members of the group. With the start of classes, groups usually became clubs, frequently organized and run by the dancers.

Then the growing square dance "explosion" reached boom proportions and by 1947 and 1948, club leaders saw the advantages of combining with other clubs and forming associations. These, in turn, offered, as one of the advantages, an opportunity for dancers in the area from various clubs to gather together for a big three-hour dance on a Sunday afternoon. These big dances - some were called festivals, others round-ups, stampedes or hoedowns - soon became the "frosting on the cake" for the dancers.

There were many of these big dances springing up across the country and for the first time, dancers began to experience the full scope of the activity - meeting dancers they had never met before and hearing callers who, amazingly enough, could be understood and followed, just as easily as they understood and followed their own home-club caller. This was a giant step for square dancing.

By 1950, the popularity of these festivals had grown to such proportions that they were attracting upwards of two to three thousand dancers for a single dance with multiple callers. The big events were becoming an accepted part of the activity and some areas were extending the festivals to two-day events, run by the local dancers and callers and by associations within the area.

Still high on the success of the Diamond Jubilee and Asilomar, it wasn't any surprise when early in 1952 we got a call from Ed Gilmore. He and Walt Bauman and Carl Anderson wanted to come over to the office and talk - and talk they did. We had a great time and they put forth an idea which was probably equally an idea of all three of them. It was to have a national square dance convention. Try it out and see if it would fly. They had no preconceived ideas except that they knew one thing they wanted was to have a convention and not just another square dance. Admittedly, they were very impressed by the crowds that had gathered for the Diamond Jubilee and they also were impressed with the other things that were happening successfully. They knew that in our area and throughout the country dances were cropping up - big ones - state conventions; sometimes tristate or regional conventions that were attracting good crowds. So, they said a national activity like square dancing rated a national convention. As we talked together, Carl, Walt, and Ed expanded on their plan. It had become obvious that with the rapid growth of square dancing there was an increased need for an exchange of ideas - a place to go, not only to dance, but to learn from each other how to dance more smoothly, how to recruit and retain dancers, and to discuss other important topics of the period.

It was one thing to learn from others within a single community. It would be quite another thing to share this knowledge on the broadest scale possible. The resulting plan was to produce a "Convention" - a word that separated itself from being just another festival where people came to dance. Here, participants would have the opportunity to take part in educational seminars along with the dancing.

The three of them formed a joint leadership council with the town leaders in Riverside, California. They discovered that if they called it a convention. they could get the support of the city of Riverside. If it were another big dance which would be just one of many that wanted to rent the Riverside Auditorium which had three floors of dance space, there would be a large fee. So, what they wanted to do was to have a large square dance that was not just dancing, but included training sessions; discussion by leaders; exhibits and things of what was happening in square dancing; and more or less a show case for the square dance activity.

They had set a date to run from early Friday May 30th thru late Sunday June 1st, Memorial Day weekend. And that was not a long time into the future. They didn't have much time to work on it, so they really set forth, incorporating ideas of participation that we had learned earlier from the Diamond Jubilee. They had a lot of people working for them in setting up this new baby. We, like everybody else in square dancing, cooperated all we could. The whole staff of Sets in Order took part in the first convention. We ran the program in our magazine and personally sent our invitations to some of our square dance caller friends and others to attend.

This had never been tried in square dancing that we knew of. Well, the thing was a success. They had 5200 people at this first one. But remember, this was the first of anything of this type, this was a great start. They say the first of anything is often the best simply because it is the "first." In their wildest imagination the dancers in the area hoped they might make a substantial contribution to the world of square dancing. Looking back, one can see that it was not only a substantial contribution, but one that set guidelines for the future. They discovered what they could do by working together.

Years later on the final evening of a National Square Dance Convention, several of us were seated up in the bleachers watching the parade of states. As the floor began to fill with thousands of dancers, a man seated behind us introduced himself and said that he was head of the convention bureau of that city. "How in the world do you folks do it?" he asked. "In working with the sponsors over these months we have yet to come across anyone that is a paid representative of the square dancers."

"That's right," we assured him, and explained that all of the labor was volunteered and when an area was given the nod to host a coming convention the workers in that community pledged their responsibility for no less than four years in preparation, organizing and planning the big event.

The professional sitting behind us was amazed. "Why, we pay thousands of dollars to experts to put together something that doesn't begin to rival the size and scope of one of your three day events. You must really have worked out something magical."

Magical is probably a pretty good word for it, for throughout North America and in more than 50 countries overseas square dancing subsists as a voluntary activity. The callers, teachers, cuers and prompters, who have invested in sound systems, records, schooling and research are paid, but not on the scope of an entertainer. The element of giving plays a major part in the enjoyment of square dancing.

For you who are, or may one day be, the club or association president, take a tip from Howard Thornton, former President of the National Square Dance Convention Executive Committee: "If you give a job to someone (1) tell him the job, (2) remind him and then (3) tell him that you reminded him." In other words, don't just tell him and then let it go, taking it for granted that it will be done, and don't do the job yourself.

.   Hoping for 3,000 attendees, dreaming they might reach 4,000, the sponsors in Riverside were overwhelmed when 5,200 eager square dancers stormed the city to be part of what was to become a yearly tradition. What started out as a dream had become a reality. Kansas City picked up the ball for National Number Two in March, 1953, and the story from that point is square dance history. Differing in many ways from "just another dance," the National has set guidelines for the activity. It has become the "showcase" for square dancing, looked upon with amazement by civic groups who can't understand how such a gigantic undertaking of this type could be accomplished by volunteers.

When you stop and think about it there are many things that are remarkable about our National. It does provide the opportunity for an area to offer square dance hospitality to dancers from all over the world. It gives callers and teachers an opportunity to be seen and heard by thousands who might otherwise never know of their existence. It gives dancers a chance to meet and dance with others and to experience at first hand, the broad scope of American Square Dancing.

In 1963 we (Becky and I) received a letter inviting us to take part in the Annual Fiesta de La Quadrilla down the coast in San Diego. This is one of the truly excellent square dancing events, and - according to the invitation - we were asked to provide an hour and a half long workshop. Shortly after we started to plan the session we received another hurry-up letter saying that it wasn't a *workshop* we were supposed to do, but rather a *clinic*. Now, we wondered, what is it that these folks really have in mind? What is the difference between a workshop and a clinic?

The whole field of definitions in square dancing is an interesting one. The same terms have taken on different meanings in various areas it seems. To us, a workshop and a clinic could very well be one and the same. In our mind we classify them this way: *Lecture Session*: One person addresses a group in a non-active "sitting" session. *Panel*: Two or more persons discuss a topic where the sitting audience may or may not ask questions and lend to the meeting. *Clinic or workshop*: there is dancing participation.

In a workshop (or clinic) as opposed to a regular dance, there is usually an object or 'theme' involved. The objective may be to learn a different or new movement or basic, or it could very well involve practice of some of the old dances. It could be work on styling or on any number of facets of the square dance picture.

We've heard the definition used that says a workshop is intended primarily for the introduction of new material, while a clinic is designed to review old material or improve on dancing style. Because of the fact that any dance movement - regardless of its actual age - when presented to a group of dancers for the first time is a new dance, we feel that these two definitions can be confusing. For that reason we prefer to classify both under the same listing.

As long as we're sticking our neck out on definitions, here's one that provokes a great deal of discussion. *Square Dancing*. This is not simply a type of dance; it is the name of an entire activity which encompasses dancing in various formations: *e.g.* squares, large circles, lines, and couples.

When we refer to square dancing generally we are not omitting round dances or contras but we include them all. When you speak of going to a square dance or to a square dance festival you would expect to see more than just the squares but would enjoy rounds and perhaps other forms of the activity as well. To change this and always refer to square and round dancing would tend to separate the activity and indicate that there are two separate activities where we definitely feel there is just the one. And in this one all the various forms are of equal importance.

What is the difference between a *festival, a round-up*, and a *jamboree?* These are just three of the common designations given to "big" dances. Those in charge of these large area functions usually decide on a title that seems to fit the occasion best. The actual format of these affairs varies from a three-hour afternoon or evening dance to a two or three-day event. One caller or a number of callers may be involved in any of these and it's quite natural to expect workshops, panels, exhibition shows and other things to be included as part of the program.

On the other hand, a convention – which is often confused with festivals, roundups, and jamborees - is a term usually reserved for the larger representative square dance gatherings with a regional (several states) or a national flavor. In the true sense of the word, a convention is designed to stimulate the thinking and encourage improvement in the activity and it serves as a showcase for the entire (or regional) square dance movement.

If you are looking for controversial terms to kick around, start with the word *leader.* All callers and teachers should be leaders. Not all of them are. On the other hand, quite a few dancers with no interest in becoming callers or teachers are actually leaders in the square dance movement. By simply being a caller, a person does not automatically become a leader. To lead requires something special of an individual and most especially indicates that the person must possess those unique qualities that invite others to follow.

And, while we're on the subject, what is meant by *national caller*? or *name caller*? Or *traveling caller*? We must assume here that a national caller is one who is referred to in this manner because his reputation or fame has spread across the country. Perhaps he has been a traveling caller, leaving his own home area to accept calling engagements in other communities. Perhaps he has made records which have been enjoyed across the country. A person considered a name caller is one who has developed a reputation for his particular talent.

Jim Mayo, the first chairman of CALLERLAB told of a discussion concerning scheduling callers for the National Square Dance Convention. Someone made a distinction between "national" and "local" callers. The problem was that there was no agreed upon definition of "national." Before there were NSDCs, shortly after WWII, there was no need to identify a "national" caller because square dancing was local. There were a handful who were known by reputation ('Pappy' Shaw, Benjamin Lovett), but it was rare for a caller to travel far from home. After WWII travel became easier, but callers were identified as "traveling." At first there were only a handful of traveling callers - Les Gotcher, Ed Gilmore, etc. - but the numbers grew. By 1960 there must have been hundreds of callers who traveled about the country. They relied on state festivals, commercial events, big regional festivals, etc. to pay their expenses. Some of the really best callers did not travel because they were completely booked in the home territory, but those who did travel got the name "national caller." Today "national callers" are likely to be recording artists or they have on-going contracts at big mobile-home parks.

While these terms have been frequently used to evaluate a caller's ability, they naturally only reflect upon those individuals who have wanted to "spread their wings." This is not to say that there are not dozens, and perhaps hundreds, of callers with equal ability whose desires or necessities require that they stay close to home, calling to local clubs and conducting square dance classes in their area. The label often put on a caller who travels is the indication that he is a professional or is commercial. So many times the insinuation is that this is something less than admirable.

Perhaps these terms need clearing up along with the others. To begin with, if there are any amateurs in square dancing they are the square dancers - either beginners, or experienced people - who are involved in the activity only as participants. The professional would be one engaged in conducting the activity for the benefit of others. While this most often refers to those receiving some remuneration for the tasks they perform, it does not necessarily eliminate those who spend the majority of their time in looking after the "business end" of square dancing even though they receive no pay.

The commercial side of square dancing contributes greatly to the progress of the activity. This phase would certainly include those with halls to rent. It would include those who manufacture, distribute, or sell public address equipment, microphones, clothing, records, books, and magazines. Many successful square dance commercial ventures have been responsible for thousands of dancers taking classes and being provided a place to dance.

The meaning of the terms professional and commercial, when applied to square dancing, should refer to phases of the activity designed to further the best interests of all concerned. It would truly be a poor commercial venture that set out to damage or misrepresent its particular specialty.

On the other hand, there is the exploiter who tends to misuse the activity and appropriate it for his own personal gain. Exploitation of square dancing in this way is a true stumbling block in the activity.

But back to the National. There had been no guarantee that the first National would be a success, so no plans were made for a second other than to allow cities to bid for it. The original organizing committee would go over any bids and make a decision. In spite of learning from their experience with the first national, planning the second was still like inventing the wheel, because the city was different as were the facilities. Arranging for housing and meals and music and sound systems had to be redesigned simply because of the change of location. One factor was in favor of a successful second convention, and that was that the organizers of the first shared their knowledge.

It was decided that Kansas City would host the 2nd National Square Dance Convention, and quickly we became aware of changes. For example, the 1st was held at the end of May, Memorial Day Weekend (in the days before the exact date for Memorial Day was set), but the 2nd chose to go in late March (27th through the 29th, and allowing registration on the 26th). There was a lot of discussion on ways and means for square dancers from out of the area to attend the 2nd National Convention in Kansas City. The committee considered approaching the Santa Fe railroad to furnish a special train as it serviced the most communities from which dancers would travel. Santa Fe agents in all towns affected were to be alerted to answer questions regarding the special train, which will probably feature a special floor laid in a baggage car for square dancing *en route*!

Kansas City did a lot right: Something was going on at all times in from four to eight halls, so it was impossible to attend all sessions. To me, the most important part of the whole affair was that the representative dancing from all areas was melding closer together. I felt that no particular area dominated, that there was an equal distribution of ideas from the whole United States, and that every area was deeply interested in what was going on in other parts of the country. Fewer extremes were to be noticed; callers who had had a slower tempo than average had picked up, and the fast ones had slowed down, giving every indication that square dancing is working towards a unified whole. The atmosphere, more so than ever before, was one like that of a big, happy family.

There was a huge welcoming committee in the station — men in their best Western clothes, complete with fancy suits and boots; ladies in long full square dance dresses, flowers in their hair — all of them complete with broad smiles of welcome and outstretched hands to greet us and badges from here to there telling us who they were! From that minute on Kansas City belonged to the square dancers from all over the country. Dancers from 28 states and 2 foreign countries, 149 callers among them, and 50 round dance teachers, converged for three days of institutes, dancing and friendship.

Special exhibition groups which came from a wide range of states were especially highlighted by such numbers as the Ozark Tap Dance Square from Camdenton, Missouri, which won over the audience the minute it appeared on the floor; the Y-Knot Twirlers from Los Angeles, California; the several groups of outstanding college age square dancers from Colorado and other parts of the country. The excellent couple dancing teams from Texas and Colorado, and the very excellent costumed group from Oklahoma City dancing "By the Sea," all added to the color. The special exhibition by the Waltz Quadrillers, with Homer Howell doing the calling, did a wonderful job on the Grand Square in three-quarter time. In all, there were 22 exhibition groups and each one of them contributed to making this the most successful portion of the festivities.

Approximately 5200 attended the gala three day affair, which attracted some of the best-known callers, exhibition groups and dance clubs in the nation. Workshops for callers and dancers took care of many of the daytime sessions and specialized in waltz quadrilles, contras, rounds and squares. Special panels were conducted for recreation leaders, club and association enthusiasts, and caller groups. And there was rarely a time where a square dance "just for fun" could not be found somewhere.

Big highlights of the session were the multitude of dances which were featured in ten different halls scattered over a wide area of Kansas City with transportation especially arranged by a series of shuttle busses constantly on the move. The big finale was held Sunday night at the Municipal Auditorium Arena. The floor handled two hundred eighty-five squares at one time - quite a sight to see. The live music was excellent and the sound system superb. It was no effort at all to call and cover that tremendous area. The non-participating audience itself numbered several thousand, who were completely captivated by the spectacle of the hundreds of enthusiastic dancers before them. Proceeds of the convention were given to the children of the cerebral palsy, diabetes, and heart disease camps in the Kansas City area.

Little things you see on the sidelines always stand out in your memory a long time after a big square dance jamboree or convention is over. Along the sidelines at the Kansas City Convention, keeping well out of the way of the swirling skirts and fast moving squares but still in view of the thousands seated in the balcony of the huge Municipal Auditorium was a young couple, gaily dressed in matching square dance togs. The green and yellow flowers on her dress were clearly of the same material that made up his western shirt. And as if that weren't enough, he had on one arm a basket

351

just about the size you use for picking up groceries in the supermarket, and in it, their baby, a young square dancer of approximately three or four months. And yes, you guessed it, the blankets and all the trimmings were of the same material as the shirt and dress!

By this time, there's every indication that this affair has been definitely established and would be held in some major city each year from now on. The folks who did such a wonderful job of organizing and carrying out this year's confab hold the responsibility for designating the site for 1954. Two bids, one from Denver and the other from Los Angeles have already been officially presented. Rumors are that Oklahoma City, Omaha, Chicago, St. Louis and Corpus Christi, Texas, are contemplating sending in their bids.

The National Square Dance Convention was not the only large dance festival going on. The 4th Annual International Square Dance Festival was held in Chicago at the International Amphitheatre, on Saturday, October 24, 1953, just months after the NSDC in Kansas City. The staff included such outstanding leaders as Dr. Lloyd 'Pappy' Shaw of Colorado Springs; Ralph Maxheimer, North Hollywood, Calif.; Al Brundage, Stepney, Conn.; Don Armstrong, New Port Richey, Fla.; Fred and Mary Collette, Atlanta, Ga.; Ed Gilmore, Yucaipa, California. The Chicago Park District, the Chicago Area Callers' Assn., and Prairie Farmer-WLS Radio Station were co-sponsors of the Festival, which featured simultaneous dances, clinics, lectures and discussions in three or more halls of the giant Amphitheatre. John Drake of WLS radio gave us an insight into running huge conventions in an article submitted to us.

TRIAL BY AUDITORIUM:
Or - How to and How Not to Stage Square Dance
Festivals in Chicago
By John C. Drake of WLS

To the two things they say are sure you can add one more - there is no one big book telling how to put on square dance festivals.

When we started, we thought we had all we needed: the Recreation Director of the Chicago Park District was our Chairman. The parks had piled up 15 years' experience in teaching and staging square dancing. One of our organizers had written one of the better-known books on square dancing. WLS had a quarter century of experience with our National Barn Dance show on stage and radio.

When we started talking International Festival, we called on leaders everywhere for counsel. How could we go wrong?

Everything went well; we sold 9,507 tickets; we had over 450 leaders registered for the clinic; the night spectacle was terrific. Georgia staged a beautiful demonstration of dancing in the southern tradition; Canada's French-Canadians typified the grace of skating transferred to square dancing; an Indiana county made a hit with their unique jig-dance.

And we lost over $6,000 ($54,000 in 2015 dollars).

From this and the second Festival a year later, we learned some things it might be well to put down here as briefly as possible. A square dance festival is not primarily a show.

• *You must have the local callers and dancers involved in a big way in your planning, ticket selling, hospitality activities and every other way. The assistance of the Chicago Area Callers' Association made a world of difference in 1952.*

353

•   *Spectators have their place but such a big activity must have the support of the dancers themselves.*

•   *Thorough organization is essential. With many diverse elements at work, it is easy, we found, to overlap on some functions and overlook others. Advance organization and committee structure, plus follow-through to see that all elements are working, are of first importance.*

•   *A big event must have a philosophy so that we have basic motives and a reason for doing what we do. Such words as "beauty," "democracy," "fun," "hospitality," "friendliness" take on real meaning in the light of this philosophy being actively expressed in a big event.*

•   *No one thing will make a growing event. This is why we must have a building combining a big hall with other smaller areas, so that jamboree dancing and exhibitions may be held.*

•   *Advance ticket selling is important; through it, the local dancers become the supporting agency, as they have done with our festival after three years; thus it is their activity, as it should be.*

•   *Do not depend on mass media to fill your hall. Radio stations, newspapers, TV, all play their part but they cannot reach the individual as he can be reached through his caller or his club.*

•   *Keep a fund of new thinking always on tap. Never simply repeat last year's event, no matter how successful. Bring in innovations, keeping ahead of the field, not behind it.*

The organizing committee for the NSDC chose Dallas, Texas, as the locale for the Third Annual National

354

Square Dance Convention. Dallas had a location for the Convention, but did not have dates at the time of being awarded the Convention. Later, the dates were confirmed as April 8, 9, and 10, 1954 – another shift on the calendar. The Southwestern Caller's Clinic, co-sponsors of the 3rd Annual National Square Dance Convention, brought 250 leaders from all over Texas. The General Chairman and the President of the callers explained that the State Fair Buildings had been secured; that sound engineers had been engaged to make the acoustics perfect; the Dallas Junior Chamber of Commerce would handle ticket sales and all proceeds will go to their fund for crippled and under-privileged children; there will be a luncheon each day at the Baker Hotel, official convention headquarters; after-parties each night; parade of the states on Saturday; a varied program is being worked out; and a new singing call, "It's Convention Time in Texas," written especially for the occasion by Richard Dick of Little Rock, Arkansas had been adopted to help advertise the Convention.

The callers and dancers in Texas recognized that there were regional differences in square dancing, and so to make people from other parts of the country feel comfortable about traveling to Dallas, they published articles about square dancing in Texas.

HOW WE DANCE IN TEXAS
By Tom Mullen, Houston, Texas

You out of state visitors to the Third National Convention, to be held in Dallas, April 8, 9, and 10, 1954, may be wondering about the so-called "Texas Style" of dancing you have heard so much about. You will be eager to know if you will feel comfortable in accepting an invitation to dance in a square predominantly made up of Texas folks.

355

You can fit, like a glove, into Texas dancing!

To make it easier, let me tell you a little about our traditional background. Texas Style might be defined as that degree of dancing proficiency to which the average Texas square dancer is willing to be elevated without doing violence to the traditions of the old West. While it may be said that there is no one Texas Style, because each area of this vast state has its differences, yet a traveling dancer can readily discern a basic, grass roots, old timey thread running thru all the calls.

Do-Si-Do: The much-discussed do-si-do (partner left, corner right, repeated until the caller runs out of rhymes!) is integrated with the history of square dancing in Texas and antedated what in some areas is called do-paso. Be alert for "Spread out wide like an old cowhide and do- si-do on all four sides." Some sections of the State, principally the northern, do only one change of the do-si-do regardless of what the caller tells them; elsewhere a longer do-si-do is enjoyed.

We seldom do "wrong way" square dancing, and an examination of 35 recent programs fails to reveal a single hash call. Box the Gnat and Box the Flea, as they are understood in some other spots, are seldom called, although Dallas has used a very enjoyable break by the same name for many years. Most calls consist of an introduction, two changes of the dance, a break, two more changes, and an ending.

Some Differences: With one exception, the differences in dancing within Texas may be relegated to foot work and hand grips. The exception first— Dallas and immediate vicinity do the dos-a-dos or All Around the Corner, left shoulder to left shoulder, to "see saw" their partners, they pass right shoulders. [Note: Texas had all around and see saw backwards from the rest of the country because Joe Lewis wrote his notes wrong from a Pappy Shaw clinic. Joe also exported the wrong

style to Australia during a tour he made there] Foot work
— the basic Texas two-step is gradually dying out. Cen-
tral and South Texas still cling to the step-close-step, but
only use it, unconsciously through habit, at various
points around the square. Elsewhere, throughout the
State, the straight walking step, not a shuffle, predomi-
nates. Hand grips vary between the conventional hand-
shake type, the forearm grip and the Houston preferred
pigeon wing "grabbing thumbs," them Yankees say.
Wherever you are, the first right and left grand will tell
you how to adjust.

Texas Style is a Texas Smile of welcome and
will be seen in profusion at the National Convention.
Why don't you come and visit us—we'd like the chance to
"dance Texas" with you all.

Advertising like this made more people feel comfortable about visiting Texas. And it worked. Square dancers
from 43 states and from Canada numbering in the thousands gathered to take part in the Third Annual National
Convention of their hobby and received a typical warm
Texas welcome. From nine in the morning until 2:00
A.M. the following day for three days straight, the two
great halls in the Dallas Fair Park were kept alive with
clinics, workshops, round dances, square dances, contras, and after parties. A parade of the states was part of
the climax on Saturday. Estimates of those actually registered at the convention ran somewhere between five
and six thousand.

Following the 3rd NSDC there were several changes
made in protocol. It only made sense that in the first couple
of years that planning extend only one year into the future.
But with the growing success of the National, the National

Executive Committee decided to announce the locations of the next two conventions. The 4th was to be in Oklahoma City, and the 5th would go to San Diego. Eventually Oklahoma City chose April 21-23, 1955 and San Diego went with June 22-24, 1956. The date for the Convention bounced around from April through late July (to some frustration on the part of dancers concerning travel plans) until the Convention was awarded more than a year or two in advance because the convention facilities in most cities were booked years in advance. This issue was not seriously pondered until after the San Diego convention in 1956.

The 5th NSDC came to the West Coast June 22-24,1956 in San Diego. San Diego is just a couple of hours south of Los Angeles, home to SIO, and we took advantage of the proximity to promote the magazine and Asilomar, though first we pushed the Convention itself. We touted the great things going on in San Diego, such as using the Balboa Bowl as the site for exhibitions. Then we invited people to drive north to visit us at the offices, then continue north to the Monterey Peninsula for the Asilomar Dance Institute.

Looking back over the first five Conventions, the 1st in Riverside attracted just over 5,000 dancers, and the total grew each year until 11,777 dancers registered for San Diego. And all of those dancers went home and became the best advertising for the big Convention. The increasing attendance created a problem in that not all cities had adequate facilities to host that many dancers. Because of the participation aspects of this type of gathering the Convention city not only must provide adequate housing and feeding facilities but it must furnish enough halls with good floors and passable sound for all those attending to dance with some degree of comfort.

Each year those responsible for selecting future sites found their task more difficult. Actually, I wondered if somewhere along the line the purpose of this whole thing hadn't been lost. It's true that the great size of the convention attracts much attention to the activity and possibly brings more newcomers into the field. However, aside from the thrill of the crowds and the natural excitement that goes along with such an affair, I wonder if it just isn't too big to accomplish real permanent good for the whole activity. Perhaps, with a sudden swing to local, state, and regional conventions each of which attracts some 5,000 participating delegates, the National could shift its emphasis and purpose. Looking back at the participation and attendance at workshops and clinics and the exchange of ideas and swapping of inspiration and material among the leaders once each year, I couldn't help but think of how much an Annual Leader's Confab could help stimulate these local festivals and therefore square dancing in general.

Because many cities felt that they didn't have adequate facilities to house, feed and dance a convention of this size (12,000 at San Diego in 1956), they were reluctant to bid for future conventions. The Executive Committee, which consists of the weary General Chairmen of the past conventions, gave much thought to this problem.

Some of them felt that since thousands of dancers from all parts of the Square Dancing World take active part in each National Convention, the answer might be to concentrate more on the "business" part, such as workshops, panels and teaching sessions and play down the mammoth dances operating continuously. Others felt that the solution would be to limit attendance by accepting only enough advance registrations to comfortably fill the dancing facilities, with preference given to out of town registrants and local dancers admitted on a first come first served basis.

Also, much discussion centered around the time of year best suited for the convention. Traditionally, it had been a springtime affair, sometimes extending into early summer. The largest attendances have been at summer conventions when it could be included in a family vacation. However, many of the national leaders and professional callers are otherwise occupied at that time with institutes and tours and many dancers felt that the quality of the convention programs would suffer without their participation. This question was not resolved until after the 1964 Convention in Long Beach, CA (July 23-25) when the date settled onto the fourth weekend in June.

To assure that bidding cities really could host such a large event, bids were accepted only from Associations or Federations of square dancers that showed support by local callers, Chamber of Commerce, Convention Bureau, Hotel Association, Restaurant Association and city, county and state officials. All of the information received was carefully studied by the Executive Committee and correlated with geographical location, proposed dates and activity in that area. The basic goal of the Executive Committee is to see that the national conventions help square dancing to grow as a healthy, non-commercial, fun-type hobby and recreation for everybody. To meet that goal, the NEC (National Executive Committee) issued guidelines for bids.

The guidelines specified that the Bid be submitted and the convention be sponsored by a recognized, active square dancers' association (preferably with past experience in the planning and staging of successful square dance festivals or jamborees), that the Bid show the level of support from local callers and musicians, and that there were adequate dining and housing facilities with rates agreed to by local hotels etc. to maintain standard rates. The Bid needed to include plans for any profits derived from the convention. And most importantly, the Bid needed to describe the dance facilities, including location, types of floors, acoustics, meeting rooms, and accessibility by air, rail, and automobile. The

Bid form was detailed enough to present some degree of assurance that the bidding committee could successfully host a Convention.

San Diego was the high point of attendance for several years, but each Convention had its special flavor. For example, Denver (May 28-30, 1959) offered child care and a midnight rodeo. It also featured dancing from 10:00am to 11:30pm, with many hours of workshops and clinics each day, including round dance and international folk dance, and special sessions for callers. The Committee worked hard to present the best callers and teachers available to cover topics such as smooth dancing, styling, gimmick dances, and more.

Perhaps the most memorable event at the Denver Convention was the historical Pageant of American Square Dancing designed by Dorothy Shaw. It had been planned to be a mutual production by Dorothy and 'Pappy' Shaw, but 'Pappy' passed away in 1958. Dorothy did not surrender; she contacted Chuck Jones who had become a close friend to the Shaws by his attendance at the Rocky Mountain workshops in Colorado Springs. The Pageant covered the history of square dance from Appalachian Mountain dances of the 1700s, the New England Quadrilles and longways sets with dancer appropriate costume, the beautiful Viennese waltzes that had just arrived in America, the Mexican influence with the varsouvienna and West Texas style dancing, and onwards through the influence of Henry Ford and the Rocky Mountain Dancers, and into the exhibitions done in front of the American Pavilion at the World's Fair in Brussels. Chuck Jones, with his captivating style, served as narrator for the Pageant.

Generally, we have been very supportive of the National and the local committees, but we can't help but look back at what went wrong. Before anything else is said, however, a few facts should be reviewed. Most of the experts making guesses a year ago would have bet that the Des Moines folk would be doing well if they attracted five thousand dancers. The fact was known that there just weren't the hotel accommodations that there were in some of the other Convention cities. Even more important was the fact that Iowa was a relatively new square dance community without the years of festival experience usually required to tackle the big square dance event.

Before the Convention started more than seven thousand had already preregistered, a number that almost equaled the number of dancers at most of the previous conventions. By the end of the last night 12,328 dancers had bought tickets and danced in at least one of the sessions (making this the largest NSDC to date). Hotels were loaded but university dormitories and homes were opened to the guests. The police, the townspeople and the hosting square dancers leaned over backwards to be hospitable and committees worked overtime to try to keep up with this tremendous throng.

What criticisms we may have are not then aimed at our hosting friends. We just wonder if the giant that has grown from this Convention idea hasn't gotten a bit out of control. In the general sense of the word, "convention" would have you believe that this is a time of evaluation, of exchanging ideas, of planning for continued growth. Instead we saw an almost complete lack of programming where the dance sessions were concerned. Half-hour and hour periods where one caller after another got up and called virtually the same material were the order of the day. Singing calls were infrequently interspersed and the tempos we clocked were up around 148 beats per minute.

Perhaps partly because of this the round dance sessions were extremely well attended. We also noted that the contra workshops attracted more and more dancers each day until at the final session the room was packed. When asked how many of those participating had never danced a contra before, a large majority raised their hands. Perhaps this too indicated a searching for comfortable dancing that couldn't be found "downstairs."

"Where are the old timers and the top names among our traveling and recording callers?" was a question most frequently asked during the three days. Of course, some were on hand but many were noticeably absent.

We still say that square dancing cannot exist as a competitive activity. Perhaps the absence of so many of these top-notch callers indicates their reluctance to be a part of the contest to see who can call the fastest and most complicated combinations of non-danceable material.

Originally the Convention idea started with co-chairmen, one being a dancer and one a caller. Perhaps this wasn't such a bad idea. Maybe in this way a balance of thinking would be reflected in spots where a caller's experience could ease the committee past some pitfalls obvious to a caller but not so evident to a dancer.

Undoubtedly there were many who enjoyed the dancing just as it was in Des Moines. That's fine. The fact that there were those who enjoy another style is also important. The Convention Executive Committee is certainly in a good position to sense this and to note the importance of good balance as future Conventions develop.

If this is going to continue to carry the name National Square Dance Convention let's stop long enough to take a look at what we're doing before we go a step further in this direction.

So, onward to Convention #10 in Detroit. How large can a square dance become – and still be called a square dance? This question has been in our mind for some time and it must have been in the minds of some of the 18,112 (6,000 more than any previous convention) who met in Detroit in June, 1961, to take part in the Tenth Annual National Square Dance Convention. The National Convention is an unusual outgrowth of a very remarkable hobby. When the first of these was conceived in 1952, the word convention was repeated in guarded tones and the title national was spoken only in whispers.

There were great differences in area styles of dancing in those days. People would promenade, swing and do-si-do in ways that changed from one state to another. Even the calls meant different things. How in the world, then, could square dancers ever bridge these and countless other difficulties in order that a get-together might be constructive enough to be called a convention and all-inclusive enough to be termed national?

As we have watched first-hand at each succeeding convention, we've found that many of the area differences have melted away and that the National has come to play a definite part in the activity. In this respect we've made these observations:

(1) The hosting square dancers can be greatly benefited by this opportunity of working together to produce this mammoth event.

(2) Non-dancers in the hosting city can become even more square dance conscious as a direct result of a National held in their area.

(3) Dancers can attend one of these affairs and get a feeling of the immensity of the activity. They can catch the friendliness in meeting old friends and acquiring new ones. They can hear callers they've never danced to before, see many leaders in action and learn new dances and, in general, be a part of a truly large spectacular.

Just what, you may ask, is the National? What makes it different from the great regional festivals and local jamborees? Perhaps the best way to find the answers is to take a close look at one National Square Dance Convention in action and trace its progress from the idea stage to completion.

Detroit initially had almost everything going against it. With optimism, enthusiasm, and selfless devotion Detroit literally built the 1961 National Square Dance Convention from a hole in the ground. Michigan's bid was accepted before Detroit had a place big enough to hold such a national gathering. Cobo Hall was under construction, but only concrete pilings had been poured, and the site was a muddy, yawning cavern. Few believed the building would be completed by 1961; some thought it might never be finished. As early as 1954 there had been talk of Detroit hosting a convention, but there was no facility in the city adequate. The idea was tabled until 1958 (with Cobo Hall still a riverfront skeleton) when the suggestion was passed along to the Detroit Convention and Tourist Bureau. A committee was formed, and the support of the Detroit Department of Parks & Recreation, as well as many of the square dance clubs throughout the state, was sought and secured.

A tentative reservation was made for Cobo Hall, and even at that early date the committee was turned down on the first date it sought, so great was the advance booking. However, they were able to book the hall for the end of June. The bid was elaborate, giving Detroit's qualifications, and was supported by a fine, large scale photograph of Cobo Hall, as well as an eager group of Detroit exhibition dancers who ably performed early American dance figures popularized by the late Henry Ford, and basic in square dancing.

Once the bid was awarded, committees worked endless hours, often neglecting other interests and businesses. Callers gave their time, and clubs financed committee work through benefit dances. Above all, there, was enthusiasm and energy: enthusiasm about the task, and energy in getting it done. Out of the muck and mire, piles of steel, and mountains of cement that so recently marked Cobo Hall's riverfront site - buoyed by hope, energy, fine direction, and hard driving work came a great Convention. Detroit hosted over 18,000 dancers.

Just as it did after the San Diego spike in attendance, the numbers at the National fell off substantially. And something similar had happened leading into the Detroit Convention. But, from 1962 (Miami Beach) through 1969 (Seattle) attendance hovered between 10,000 and 14,000. Then came the 19th held in Louisville, KY, in 1970. The previous year, Seattle had only 12,000 dancers, but the Convention went so well that word of mouth pumped up expectations. Louisville just was not ready for the 19,452 dancers.

Would you consider a single event that attracts upwards of 19,000 persons, that represents perhaps a composite expenditure of more than a quarter of a million dollars ($1,567,500 in 2015 dollars), as being representative of a *small* hobby? Or would you share the feelings of those who consider that the National Square Dance Convention has become Big *Business?* In the past we have shown reluctance to write critically of the National. We've felt that the unselfish donations of time and energy by so many have more than justified the inevitable errors in judgment that come with a one-time performance. We have marveled on many occasions that these big events have *come off* as well as they have and we have been generous, we feel, in "saluting" the jobs well done. Undoubtedly each convention has benefited from each of its past conventions. Obviously in many ways it has much more to learn. Let's take a look at the Louisville convention. We must start by saying that the success or failure of the Big event depends upon each individual's view point. If a dancer has a great time, personally, then the convention is a success in his eyes. If, on the other hand, he doesn't enjoy himself, his opinions will be that the event is less than successful.

Our analysis has been built on the assumption that the National Square Dance Convention should be a showcase and represent the best that this activity has to offer. On this basis we feel that 19,542 square dancers that came to Louisville from 50 states and the District of Columbia as well as several Canadian Provinces and countries overseas, expected the ultimate in intelligent programming, pleasant dancing, and satisfactory facilities.

Instead, they danced for three days and nights on cement floors in a huge barn-like structure, in temperatures and humidity we long since have decided were far less than passable for square dance enjoyment. As though this weren't enough, the large area was divided into smaller sections by cloth partitions that neither controlled the sound not the dust, and it was in each of these sections that hundreds of square dancers spent their time. Add to this a center passageway traversing the length of the building lined with booths and you have the rather ominous picture.

To be sure there was one area where the sound WAS good - and where there was modern air-conditioning - but this area was adequate to accommodate only a portion of the great throng. When it came to the panels the truly significant portion of any National - these, too, were "housed" in one large room. Sometimes three or more serious talk sessions, each with a seated audience of several hundred, were being conducted simultaneously. Only cloth partitions separated the "rooms" and the sound of many public address systems fighting each other created a din that was both discourteous to those serving on the panels and virtually "impossible" from the standpoint of those in the audience who had come to listen and to learn.

The fact that the sound was bad was not the fault of the technicians or the equipment, but it was merely an impossible situation to start with. It was almost as though years of experience and progress in square dance acoustical know-how were tossed out of the window and here, at what should have been the "show place" of modern square dancing, sound was at its unbelievable worst.

The National Convention affords an excellent opportunity to exhibit the ability of literally hundreds or men and women callers from all parts of the square dance world. Along with young newcomers are some of the finest and most experienced callers the activity has to offer. Dancing to as many of these callers as possible is an attraction to which many convention goers look forward. Here then is the opportunity for the National to show the best judgment in programming so that the callers supporting the Convention at great personal and financial sacrifice may be acceptably presented.

In a location such as Louisville, with only one air-conditioned hall, it became all too obvious that only a select few callers were given "key" Spots. Others, including some fine proven callers, drew assignments in out-of-the-way halls with poor acoustics, sometimes during the dinner hour when only one or two squares were in attendance. If we have learned anything from the past, perhaps it should be in the field of fair programming and the National is one place where this accomplishment should be displayed.

The goal of each succeeding National has seemed to be to beat the past attendance record! Previous to this year the record was held by Detroit whose 1961 mark reached

18,195. While Louisville did beat this we feel that the National has come close to proving that the useful purpose of this big event may no longer exist. If the National is to continue (and it would appear that it will, with the announcement of convention sites for the next four years) then we would like to make some suggestions. These, by the way, reflect the composite thinking of many leaders who have discussed this with us during recent years.

First: we suggest that the emphasis be shifted from "*size*" to "*quality*." People coming from other areas should be intrigued by local accomplishments and displays.

Second: we would suggest that programming become a function of a permanent committee or at least be supervised by those with previous experience so that some form of continuity be retained and constant improvement be realized.

Third: we would like to see a thorough study made of the panels to be covered at the National so that here too some form of continuity may be retained from one year to the next.

Fourth: we feel that a statement from the General Chairman, well in advance of each convention, should tell in detail what a convention goer may expect. This should include the air-conditioning (if in an area that is warm and humid); acoustics; the type of sound equipment to be used; dancing surfaces, etc.

Fifth: the financial situation of the National should be made known. With so many people donating time and effort to help make each yearly event a success, the net money result of each convention is of great interest. We feel it is unfortunate that, due to a ruling by the National Convention Board some years ago, the net financial outcome of the various conventions is not made public. Too many people play a part in all of this for it to be kept secret.

[Since this was written, there has been more transparency of the financial workings of the NSDC. The National Executive Committee, made of past chairpersons on NSDC, has released basic information on

total income and profit or loss. Included was how much the cities chipped in to help out. For example, the total income from the recent Birmingham Convention was $590,394, including $61,847 from the sale of shuttle bus passes (but this amounted to a loss of $16,945, part of which the Birmingham Metro Transit Authority and Convention groups have agreed to absorb). The 1983 Louisville Convention, second largest in history with 30,953, had many methods for use of its funds including expanding, improving and subsidizing the Kentuckiana publication, SQUARES AND ROUNDS (it's now free to all members); a free dance for all workers including paying for their Convention badges; all loans were repaid at 200%, and establishing a trust fund guided by a group of trustees with the interest going quarterly to the Association. Louisville offered to loan Indianapolis funds for their early expense, although this was not needed. The 1976 Anaheim Convention, perhaps, had the most financial problems, largely because of the all-time high attendance of 39,796 which required practically every available bus in southern California. This, as well as the expensive preparation of two movies covering the Convention and the historical pageant resulted in a very large loss. After several years these losses were finally covered largely through dances at Disneyland, sponsored by many of the Board members of the 1976 Convention.]

While there are undoubtedly many very worthy charities to which monies can be contributed, we would like to think that income from non-profit square dancing events can be most effectively used when plowed back into the activity, here are some suggestions for possible local use:

- Leadership seminars for training club officers,
- Halls - the leasing, purchasing and renovating of suitable places for square dancing,
- Area-wide promotional and advertising campaigns for new classes,
- A professional study of the area relative to its potential and ways of building its square dance program,
- Promotional materials, films, records, books, etc.,
- Caller/Teacher training,
- Underwriting the services of callers and teachers to conduct square dance programs in schools, institutions, etc.,

- Furnishing P.A. equipment where needed.

There are many more opportunities of course. Monies resulting from a National Convention, just as from local association functions, do little good while sitting in a bank. Their only true value is when they are wisely spent for the improvement of the activity.

Looking past the immediate area, there are many groups that are doing outstanding jobs in *preserving* and *building* and who will grow with financial support. One of these is the non-profit Lloyd Shaw Foundation, Colorado Springs, Colorado, with its school program and its library and archives that are being continually developed. Other reference libraries are cropping up in various areas. Here students of American Square Dancing may read and borrow books, tapes and records in their quest for knowledge of this activity,

The original goals of the National Convention set up in the early 1950's can be just as meaningful today as they were when they were conceived. No longer do we have to prove that we are a *Big* activity. Now we should settle for the words *"service"* and *"quality."* As a result of hosting a National an area should be stronger - not weaker, It should have far more local dancers, healthier clubs, larger classes, If any tensions or cliques existed prior to the process of producing a National these should have all disappeared as a result of dancers and leaders working closely together.

The National was never intended to be a showcase for just a few. Instead it is a testimonial to a truly great activity. Hosting a National should be one of this activity's great rewards.

"What a great convention" commented Laverne Maddux concerning the 1976 NSDC in Anaheim when she

371

saw us the other night. "I've never been a part of anything so exciting in my life."

"That sound had to be the world's worst!" The man on the other end of the telephone came close to being irate. "With all the know-how, you'd think that after these years they'd come out with good sound."

"I cried out of sheer delight, just watching the pageant portraying 200 years of square dance history."

In reading some of the letters since the Convention and listening to others as they extolled or condemned the recent big event, we were reminded of the three blind men who were taken to the zoo so that they could "see" an elephant.

It must have been a similar situation with those who attended the 1976 Convention in Anaheim. From one view point, a participant returned home with nothing but good things to say while another who may have had an unhappy experience with housing or with the crowds, or with some other phase that resulted in a negative reaction. Take these two varied viewpoints on the shuttle bus system which brought dancers from outlying areas to and from the Convention complex each day. "They were sheer disaster," said one man. "It was the best shuttle bus system we have run across at any of the Conventions," countered Herb Egender of Denver, Colorado, who went on to explain that the frequency of schedules, the convenience and the low cost made the shuttle bus a perfect solution.

On some occasions in the past, we've been critical toward certain aspects of a convention relative to the sound, programming or the handling of crowds. Of course, we've also handed out more than a fair share of bouquets.

We know that each convention is produced by a brand new committee of volunteers. A convention chairman, in day to day life may be an attorney. The program chair might be an architect and the person in charge of sound could be a first rate cabinet maker. In the beginning the convention assignments might be completely foreign to each of these chairmen but by the time the big event is over each will have become an expert in his own field of responsibility. Unfortunately, too often they earned their degree in the school of hard knocks. More than one past committee chairman on these past Nationals has stated, "By the time the convention was over, I had the knowledge necessary to put on a first rate convention if we had it to do again the following year"

Nobody questions the sincerity and devotion of these workers. It's because of them that this annual event is held. At the same time, we should see a steady improvement with each convention, so each year builds from the information gathered before. The convention is a show-case of square dancing and in every respect should present the best of what this activity has to offer.

As an example, in the case of sound - one of the prime ingredients of modern square dance program, if we learned at a National Convention 20 years ago that a huge hall divided into smaller halls by cloth curtains isn't a satisfactory acoustical arrangement, then the same arrangement should not be used in following years. Look for a solution.

While every caller is not necessarily a sound expert simply by virtue of his owning a public address system, he is in a better position to sound a hall than some willing soul with no calling experience. At a recent Convention, the sound in some halls was good, in others only passable and in many far less than adequate or, as a number of dancers expressed it, "Just plain bad." Could this have been improved? Definitely, if such sound experts as Jim Hilton and others who have had considerable experience in providing sound under less than ideal conditions were consulted.

Of course, it's not difficult to Monday morning quarterback these conventions and it's easy to be critical. Sometimes we don't know the whole story. In the case of Anaheim, for instance, the Facilities Chairman, who was in weekly personal contact with the head of facilities at the Anaheim Convention Center and had, to the best of his knowledge, worked out even the most minute details discovered that during the week of the Square Dance Convention itself, the Convention Center facilities expert left on vacation leaving behind instructions relative to the discussions made during the critical period of the planning years. These types of problems are not uncommon with all convention planners of the past and they will continue to be problems in the future unless someone comes up with a workable solution and an improved system of continuity.

The fact that many of the same problems arise year after year, problems with programming, various types of scheduling, sound, allotment of facilities, etc., would indicate the need of better coordinating from one convention to the next if these yearly conventions are to improve.

To be sure, a masterful attempt is made each year to pass along to future committee chairmen advice and suggestions arising from the convention just completed. To a degree this must help. But each convention has its own share of problems and individual circumstances which, in one way or another, differ from other conventions. So it's quite conceivable that each chairman starts out fresh with little or no experience in a field of events this large and must, through trial and error, learn the hard way.

Now (1976) that we have had 25 National Square Dance Conventions we wonder if it is not time to look realistically at some of the problems that occur over and over and determine if it's time to make some changes - changes that would be helpful to the sponsoring group and still prove acceptable to the governing board that makes the final decisions relative to policy. Here are four suggestions:

(1) Establish a continuity office. For lack of a better title, this is basically a "home office" location with a paid executive secretary working directly under and for the National Convention Executive Committee and with the upcoming convention leaders. The precedent for paid executive secretaries in the field of square dancing has already been established both in LEGACY, the organization of square dance leadership communication and in CALLERLAB, the International Association of Square Dance Callers. Neither of these groups will ever reach the size and scope of the National Convention but they do find a distinct advantage in running their affairs in a business-like manner with an office and a paid professional at the helm.

(2) Hire the services of a professional public relations person or organization. It is sometimes disturbing when a convention as large as the National is unable to get top coverage, not only in the local press and television but on a national and international scale. These "big ones" are real attention getters and the experiences of the past would indicate that it may take professional, established P. R. people on a continuing basis year after year with the National Convention directly and with square dancing in general to catch the attention of the news services, network television, etc.

(3) Take advantage of professional caller assistance on a continuing basis. This can can be an invaluable aid in improving the image of the National Conventions by assisting with programming and sound. An international organization of professionals, which could be CALLERLAB, with its composite technical knowledge of square dancing, can provide an invaluable service for this yearly event. As a vital cog in the square dance scene, the caller suffers or benefits

de-pending upon the outcome of each convention. He can benefit only if the dancers can hear and understand him. He can benefit only if programming is done intelligently. In the recent years since professional callers have been contracted to staff the caller's seminars produced as a part of National Convention, CALLERLAB members have made up 100% of all the staffs to date.

(4) Establish a think tank of knowledgeable individuals who can isolate themselves for a time and take a positive, constructive look at the National Convention, where it has been, where it is, and where it can be in the future. This group should represent a cross section of the activity as well as top leadership from other fields who might add fresh input to the meeting.

Nobody is suggesting that any of the vital decisions and directions of the National Convention idea should be taken away from members of the Executive Committee who have worked too hard over 25 years to develop the National. We feel that it's time that all those involved look more closely at the National and view it for what it is…one of the largest single participation events in the world, and see how it can be improved. As the showcase of square dancing, it should represent the very best the activity has to offer.

It's one thing to refer to square dancing as a folk activity, run at the club and association level by individual volunteers. It is another to suggest that annual big events should be run in any way but on a purely professional basis. To those reading this who may be disappointed that we haven't dwelled more strongly on the shortcomings of the conventions or that we should have passed out more orchids, we feel that those attending are fully aware of those things that went well and of those things that need improving.

We want only the best for this activity and we know that this view is shared by square dancers and callers and teachers. Undoubtedly our suggestions are not the only possible solutions but we would like to think that they will be considered and that definite strides will be taken to insure that problems which existed in Anaheim will not, if at all possible, be with us in the future.

The 1976 Anaheim Convention still is the largest ever held - 39,796 dancers in attendance for at least part of the time. The second largest was 1983 Louisville with 30,953, and third was 1988 Anaheim with 26,967. I think it is unlikely we will see numbers in excess of 10,000 again. Perhaps that is best. Smaller communities can host the Convention and put most of their energy into quality.

As I look back over 50 years of Nationals, I see mostly how each one was special. Perhaps the 50th held in Anaheim, CA, in 2001 had a particular effect on me. Simply that it was the 50th carried the significance of square dancers working together each year to share their love of the activity with no expectation of any personal gain. It was personally moving also. I can't remember how many groups I addressed over the weekend sharing my love of square dancing for over 50 years. One event I was a guest at was the press breakfast where I tried to impress representatives of the square dance publications from around to world. And later, a special session was set up where my dear friend Osa Matthews and I reminisced. Osa was one of only three callers alive at the time who had been on the program at the 1st NSDC. Known as the Palm Springs "Call Girl," Osa was also given the tribute of being asked to call at the trail end dance held in the original facility for the national – the Riverside Municipal Auditorium. They say that someone filmed that session at Anaheim, but I have not brought myself to watch it.

Chapter 16. National Folk Dance

Sets in Order was just a baby when the idea of an "official" square dance week was planted. The idea goes back almost to the start of square dancing's "big boom" period in the early 1950's, when it was noted that a mayor in Calgary, Alberta, Canada; a governor in Michigan; and a city council in Nebraska proclaimed an "official" square dance day in each of their respective areas.

By 1956 a number of state governors had set aside square dance weeks with accompanying documents and releases to the press. A newly-elected governor in the Lone Star State celebrated his inaugural, not only with an official square dance proclamation, but with a bona fide, genuine Texas style Square Dance Inaugural Ball. Governor Rosseline of Washington State declared the first week in September, 1958, to be State Square Dance Week. Then, in the Spring of 1959, the Narragansett Callers' Association of Rhode Island embarked on a campaign to advertise square dancing to the general public. A committee of five couples was appointed to study fund raising plans and the type of advertising to follow. "LEARN TO SQUARE DANCE WEEK" IN RHODE ISLAND. Consequently, on November 11, 1959, a statewide "Square-o-rama" of 7 square dances and 1 round dance was held. An M.C. was stationed at each hall and six teams of roving callers went from hall to hall, to call for the dancers. Three portable TV sets and 20 electrical appliances were given as door prizes. Funds realized from this opening gambit, along with donations from some of the clubs, were used to advertise square dancing during the week of January 10, 1960. This week was designated as "Learn to Square Dance Week" and was so proclaimed by Governor Christopher Del Sesto of Rhode Island.

The Governor's Proclamation was inserted in the *Providence Sunday Journal* of January 10. The *Journal* gave a very good write-up and pictures in the same edition. On Thursday night there was an appreciation dance for those who had worked so hard on the campaign. An NBC-TV affiliate station asked to have square dancing on one of their scheduled programs and the good response to this, a first for the station, resulted in a weekly square dance teaching show on the same station. A CBS-TV affiliate followed through with a similar request and one of the teenage callers was asked to call on a Rock `n' Roll show with Dick Clark.

These were big events in the local histories of square dancing and doubtless the impressions made within each particular area proved beneficial. However, as independent programs, what actual good they did was restricted to just the local areas where they occurred. It was a case of each area doing its own thing without any thought of coordinating ideas and dates. Eventually it became apparent how much more effective it would be if all areas joined together to celebrate the same dates and establish one Square Dance Week everywhere.

At about this same time the push to get a square dance commemorative stamp was started. In the January 1959 issue of Sets in Order we published an article about special stamps. This was of special interest to me because my dad was a stamp collector and I inherited his enthusiasm for it, plus his collection. One of the things that was fun for me as a collector was to find that in having a publication, with a 25,000 average circulation, that a lot of our subscribers were from overseas. I think we at one time had 50 countries represented in our subscription list. A number of times, people in different countries would send me new issues as they came out. After watching everything under sun being honored by our postal department, including chickens and truck drivers and actors, we couldn't see square dancing being left out of it. So, a number of organizations - dancer associations, etc. - started getting the word out to get petitions into the post Master General and the postal department or the committee in charge of selecting subjects for postage stamps or commemorative stamps.

We picked up the petition idea and publicized it in the magazine. Not really ashamed of our postal service for honoring all these other things, but noting that any number of countries like the Philippines and others all had stamps on dancing, why couldn't we have a square dance stamp. We thought that our thousands of signatures would have some impact on the selection. So we started "Operation Postage Stamp."

Every user of U.S. postage stamps must wonder at one time or another just where the ideas come from for the special commemorative issues we keep seeing on our letters. These are the stamps that pay tribute to some person, place, event, or activity. In the past few years there have been stamps for gardening, for teachers, for shipbuilding, and one for virtually every field — except square dancing.

With millions of copies of every new commemorative issue being printed and used on letters that circulate around the world they draw attention to many phases of American life while leaving out perhaps the most important one: that America, a happy nation, knows how to play. Other great nations and some small ones have issued stamps for the games and dances of their people - so why not America?

We decided to do something about it so we wrote the Postmaster General in Washington, D.C. First we received our own letter back with a note that we should see the enclosed literature. Then there was a two page printed "History of a Commemorative Stamp" and with it a small booklet "A Guide for the Selection of United States Commemorative

Postage Stamps." After going over it all quite thoroughly we were still enthused. Here is the general idea: all suggestions for the subject matter for these special stamps are carefully studied by the Citizens Stamp Advisory Committee before its recommendations for the Post Office Department's commemorative stamp program are submitted to the Postmaster General for final approval.

By law, the Postmaster General has the exclusive and final authority to determine which postage stamps shall be issued. Therefore, further legislation is not necessary. As a special service to individuals, organizations and groups who may wish to submit ideas for a commemorative postage stamp to the Post Office Department, the Citizens' Stamp Advisory Committee adopted a set of criteria to govern their issuance. Here, briefly are some of the points: No living person shall be honored nor shall any American citizen until 25 years after his death. Events having wide-spread national appeal and significance may receive consideration. Commemorative postage stamps shall not be issued to honor a fraternal, political, or religious organization, a commercial enterprise, or a specific product.

We felt that a stamp honoring the American Square Dance would be widely accepted and would be in exceptionally good taste. We can only surmise that if an anniversary to commemorate was needed, square dancing could easily be celebrating its 200th in this country. If an appropriate date of issue were needed — why not time it with the National Square Dance Convention? Because requests for such a stamp should be made 18 months prior to the date of issue, any hope for a stamp in 1960 would necessitate immediate action.

The stamp idea went into hibernation for a while, but then in June, 1964, Elmer Alford in The Dalles, Oregon, picked up the square dance stamp idea and had written the Post Office Department on the proposition of a square dance commemorative stamp. Hearing back from the post office people, he was told that his letter was on file and that it would be brought to the attention of those responsible for the 1965 commemorative stamp program. A large article in the local (The Dalles) newspaper ran an illustration and a story on the proposal.

Later, in October, 1964, the post office department took a positive step in releasing a new commemorative honoring "American Music." A second commemorative came out dedicated to "Modern American Art." If we can guess correctly, we might just assume that the next in the series would be the "American Dance."

One element that concerned us, however, was the way that our activity may be pictured on a stamp. Getting the stamp was one thing. It would certainly draw attention to American contemporary square dancing and would let the world know that the Americans do enjoy a great dance activity. However, it would be disappointing if the "American Dance" were depicted as one of the dozens of other dance forms existent in our country today.

We weren't naive enough to think that the others were unimportant or non-existent, but we felt that the American square dance was and will continue to be the true dance of our country. It was highly possible that the Post Office Department artists might see American Square Dancing as it was fifty, a hundred or a hundred and fifty years ago, so we wouldn't be surprised if such a stamp came out with an old time fiddler, a group of people in bib overalls, and a Virginia reel in progress.

Just because Sets in Order was focusing on the commemorative stamp, the initiative for a national square dance week did not stop. The second week in September of 1965 had become official Square Dance Week in Portland, Oregon, and with a purpose. Through public demonstrations hundreds of non-dancers had an opportunity to view modern American Square Dancing first hand just in time for the opening of fall beginner classes. The Portland Area Council of Square Dance Clubs decided that it was worthy of all-out support. The square dance clubs, the two callers' organizations, and eventually even the city government became involved.

Work started in May with the appointment of a general chairman, who happened to be a caller for two clubs and a member of both local callers' groups, with ideas about encouraging square dancing. A letter went out from the president of the Portland Council requesting co-operation from all clubs and callers in donating certificates good for five free beginners' lessons in square dancing to be used as door prizes. They were intended to tempt the public into the Fall classes. Also, three public demonstrations of square dancing were carefully scheduled so they did not conflict with the State Fair and the beginning of hunting season.

The celebration received good publicity. The Mayor of the city of Portland signed a proclamation naming this Square Dance Week. The metropolitan newspapers blanketed the state and the committee received interested comments from square dancers throughout that area who saw some of the 48 column inches of publicity, and the TV programs or heard the radio announcements. The theme for square dance week was: Let's Double The Dancers.

Then an even larger goal than a postage stamp or square dance week made its debut at the 1969 NSDC in Louisville: it was the movement to have square dancing declared the National Folk Dance of America. So many people had questions about the movement that it seems we should have some answers.

Q. What is behind the move? Who are the people involved?

A. Apparently the initial impetus for this movement originated by common agreement between Northern California Veterans' organizations and square dancer associations. The combination found common ground in the "typically American" nature of both. The Council of Square Dance Associations of California appointed the Santa Clara Valley Square Dance Association as a single point of contact for this joint effort.

Q. What do they think they can accomplish by this drive? How can they do it? Where will they get the money? What chance do they really have to succeed?

A. At the 19th National Convention in Louisville last summer a Five-Step Program was presented to delegates from 36 states.

1. Square Dancer Unity. Number One Priority. Each association was asked to endorse and return the Resolution to the Santa Clara organization.

2. Legislative Guidance Obtained. The National American Square Dance is not a political issue. Congressional contacts and/or contacts with the public news media are not recommended until requested as part of a unified national effort.

3. The National American Square Dance complements all square dance programs.

4. The National American Square Dance is a non-commercial program. Support is voluntary.

5. A Financial Support Program is organized around the National American Square Dance badge. Some contributions for initial publicity have come from California associations.

So, who paid for all this? The expenses are being financed by putting out badges reading, "Support the American Square Dance," showing two square dancers on a map of the United States, in red on white. They were available for a $1.00 donation. Of the money taken in 5% stayed with, or is returned to, the parent organization. 30% went into a National American Square Dance Trust Fund to transport and care for square dancers delegated to represent the square dance before Congress if Congress required this. 65% went for operational expenses, including making the badges, advertising, publicity, promotion, etc. Advertising went first into square dance media in order to involve that segment before hitting the outside world.

The first thing to do, then, was to get the word out that the movement was a-borning and see if the bulk of square dancers in the country agreed with the importance of the project and were willing to become involved to put it over.

The Resolution which had been drawn up explained the goal of the drive.

RESOLUTION

A National American Dance — The American Square Dance

WHEREAS, *love of Country and professions are enhanced by traditions that have become a part of our way of life and the customs of its people, and*

WHEREAS, *we have distinctive and meaning-ful symbols of our ideals in our National Flag, our National Anthem and in many cultural endeavors, but no official designation of our National Dance, and*

WHEREAS, *the "Square Dance," first histori-cally associated with our people and re-corded in history since 1651, has consistently been the one dance traditionally used by our people throughout our entire existence and is a dignified and enjoyable expression of folk dancing and is American in charac-ter, and*

WHEREAS, *official recognition after three hundred years will enhance the cultural sta-ture of the United States of America, na-tionally and internationally, and*

WHEREAS, *such national and international prestige will be in the best interest of all Americans at all levels of community, state, national and international cultural affairs, and*

WHEREAS, *The American Square Dance is of the American Peoples' Heritage, official recognition may be given by the Congress and the President of the United States with community, state, national, and internation-al pride.*

NOW, THEREFORE, BE IT RESOLVED BY
State of.., in regular assembly in that we urge the Congress of the United States to PROCLAIM The American Square Dance as the National American Folk Dance of the American People and the National Dance of America.

Beginning at the association level and going state by state, the first order of business was to have this resolution endorsed by an absolute minimum of three quarters of the country's associations. As of November 1, 1970, one third of the states, District of Columbia, and Guam had returned endorsed and dated resolutions. That was a good start, but we projected that it might take several years to manage the next item: the method of getting the Congressional Proclamation. The organization wanted it to have maximum fanfare with a possibility of national publicity from the Bicentennial Committee for two or three years before the nation's 200th birthday in 1976.

On April 19, 1971, Representative Gubser introduced H.J. RES. 555 to the 92nd Congress First Session in the House of Representatives: *Resolved by the Senate and House of Representatives of the United States of America in Congress assembled, that the dance known as the square dance is designated the national folk dance of the United States of America.* The resolution was then referred to the House Committee on the Judiciary.

In 1970, while working with the Gold Ribbon Committee and others on the idea of a national callers association, Sets in Order started a new publication. We felt that club officers needed information on how to be more effective leaders, so we started a free publication with pointers on how to keep the club together, etc. The newsletter was called *Gavel and Key*, and it lasted from 1970 to 1978.

Also around that time a handful of folks met at Copecrest to analyze what direction square dancing was taking. This Crossfire group did not last too long, but it did pave the ground for LEGACY. In 1971, Stan Burdick of *American Square Dance*, Charles Baldwin of *The New England Caller*, and I met at a New York airport hotel to discuss the scope and range of square dancing and how to improve communications among all the aspects of square dancing. We were the Editors/Publishers of the three major square dance publications in the country. Stan came up with the acronym LEGACY, for "LEaders GAthered for Commitment and Yak."

To be effective as a coordinator and problem solver for the entire activity, LEGACY, or whatever group took on the task of coordinating the various elements of square dancing, needed a direct pipeline into each of the segments. In the course of taking a close look at the part callers played in the world of square dancing, it became apparent that the callers and teachers formed only a portion of the package. There was much going on in square dancing beyond the role played by the callers and that any study would be incomplete without understanding the whole picture.

A good place to start studying contemporary square dancing was the Gold Ribbon Report that broke square dancing down into several segments. We focused on thirteen elements, which for the most part, covered the contemporary field of western square dancing. The thirteen groupings included the following: publications; callers associations (local), and CALLERLAB in the planning stages, the National Square Dance Convention in successful operation since its start in 1952; dancer associations (local) and perhaps an organization that would synchronize the activities of all existing dancer associations; suppliers (square dance clothing, books, shoes, etc.); archives center/history of the activity/Square Dance Hall of Fame (the Lloyd Shaw Foundation and Archives Center); square dance records (later to include licensing of using square dance music); and sound systems. Possible other units that might cover vacation institutes, square dance travel, square dancing in schools and colleges, etc., were discussed. All of the parts placed together formed a massive jigsaw puzzle and if any piece was missing our evaluation of square dancing would be incomplete. We published the Gold Ribbon Report in the January 1969 issue of Square Dancing (Sets in Order) magazine.

While the three of us were fairly well coordinated with our thoughts regarding the need of some coordinated effort (but not an organization) to care for the activity, we each had our own ideas concerning the direction square dancing was taking. I should mention here that over the years there had been numerous attempts by single individuals or groups of individuals to organize the activity. Among them were a number who were obviously out for a personal gain. All of them were defeated. The three of us believed that this would be a strictly democratic procedure, with the unselfish goal of protecting the future of square dancing.

The first LEGACY meeting was in May of 1973 in Cleveland, Ohio. The plan was for representatives to attend from all phases of square dancing. The members (called trustees) represented dancers, callers, round dance instructors, publishers, record producers, vendors and other interest groups. They represented all areas of the world (with trustees from 39 states, three Canadian provinces and two other countries). The trustees met in odd numbered years around the country to discuss square dancing. They sometimes found possible solutions to problems. These discussions often led to the passing of resolutions that were distributed to the general square dance world.

LEGACY met at the NSDC to discuss the state of square dancing locally, nationally, and internationally. At that first session, we were given ten areas to explore, each having a significant part of the square dance activity. We were assigned to groups to examine and determine what was wrong with that particular area. Later we attempted to find solutions for these distressed areas. After each of the brainstorming sessions, we gathered for a general session. There we heard reports of progress, if any, that had been made.

Among the goals of LEGACY was the desire to pass along the leadership experience to the state and area organizations. The strength of LEGACY, as in all organizations, came from the input of its component parts. We shared these things with one another through communication and cooperation, and these efforts needed to be coordinated. In some small respect, this was being accomplished through the Mini-LEGACY program, which was in the capable hands of Walt Cole of Salt Lake City, Utah. It was organized to coordinate our efforts by utilizing the material and leadership expertise to assist those attempting to accomplish the same ends.

There have been other very gratifying spinoffs from LEGACY, among which are the National Association of Square and Round Dance Suppliers, which offers its services to the consumer, as well as to the supplier. Roundalab, the International Association of Round Dance Teachers - I need not go into the service they provide for Round Dance Teachers and Cuers. A leadership manual, put together by John and Freddie Kaltenthaler and their very fine committee, was available through LEGACY. It was a great help to the new leader, as well as the more experienced, as a guide through the pitfalls of organized square dancing. And we now have an International Square Dance Week.

Starting in 1982, LEGACY, the international communications group for square dancing, spearheaded the Square Dance Week program. This meant, basically, that the program that had been officially in effect for well over ten years and even longer, unofficially, was greatly enhanced. Square Dance Week celebrated on an international basis should attract the attention of non-dancers, not only here in North America but throughout the square dancing world.

Meanwhile, in 1970 the first coordinated square dance week got off to a flying start. By the second year, in 1971, more than 49 States and Provinces had taken part in the unified celebration. That successful program more than proved that Square Dance Week was here to stay. What had been unrelated area programs became a large and effective international event. Because the dancers from British Columbia were coordinating their programs with the folks in Florida (and virtually everywhere else), the result took the shape of a great advertising campaign. Area radio and television shows and colorful picture spreads in the newspapers gave the impression of a concerted, unified campaign.

No effort is worthwhile unless it reaches its goals. Square Dance Week provided a means of "telling the world" about the pastime that was enjoyed by so many thousands everywhere. It paved the way for better community understanding, by showing what square dancing was really like. It became a showcase for square dancing at the precise time when people were searching for a wholesome and friendly couple activity.

Leaders on the west coast of Canada and on the east coast of the USA helped to determine the latter part of September, just preceding the start of new dancer classes, as the period that would accomplish the greatest good. The dates set continued from the third Monday each September through the following Sunday. Thus, with proclamations by mayors, provincial and state government officials and with the cooperation of the local press, an effective campaign could be waged.

A change of time and place: July, 1978. New York City, my birth place which has always held a rather magical, mythical spot in my memory. Not having visited the "Big Apple" for almost a dozen years, I had forgotten much of its appeal. But driving into Manhattan from the airport all the recollections started pouring back. The bridges, the rows and rows of skyscraper lights reflected in the river, the seeming thousands of taxis, and there was little doubt that we had arrived.

I had returned to the big city at the invitation of the U.S. Postal Service, to take part in the first-day ceremonies for the American Dance stamps being issued at the Lincoln Center. Thousands who shared in the pride of square dancing had waited for more than a dozen years for a U.S. stamp to commemorate the American folk dance. At last the dream was to become a reality.

For those of you who are not stamp collectors, we should fill you in. When the Post Office brings out a new postage stamp, its first day of issue is usually limited to one specific location which is associated with the new stamp. A ceremony is held, with representatives of the Post Office and guests connected with the subject of the stamp in attendance. Lincoln Center, with its Library for the Performing Arts, might very well be the hub of American Dance, insofar as theater, ballet, and modern forms of the art are concerned. And so it was chosen as the site of the first day celebration. A special branch post office was set up to sell the new quartet of stamps and to hand cancel them with first-day of issue.

In attendance were leaders of outstanding ballet companies, choreographers of Broadway's musicals and personalities such as Nancy Hanks, who heads up the government's cultural program, Walter Terry, dance editor of *Saturday Review*, the daughter of Ruth St. Denis, and others. While there was a noticeable rapport among these artists, it was apparent that no one was quite certain what to do with those of us called upon to represent the square dance. Perhaps they had expected bib overalls and hob-nailed boots, but it was clear that those present knew little of the current status of American Square Dancing.

This became even more apparent when they began taking credit for the issuance of the new stamps (which one speaker said they had worked on for the past five years). Had no one told them of the tens of thousands of signatures of square dancers on petitions that were on file with the Post-master General, and the campaign for the stamp that has lasted more than twelve years? Perhaps it didn't really matter, for now we had our stamp and the waiting was a thing of the past.

There were the usual speeches and each of us representing the four different aspects of American Dance, as portrayed on the stamps, received special albums commemorating the event and containing a sheet of the new stamps.

We were proud to have been a part of all of this, to enjoy the luncheon on the Grand Tier of the Metropolitan Opera Building and to hear from some of the "greats" in the field of dance. But we couldn't help but make some comparisons. At one point Murray Lewis and Jerome Robbins, the emcees, said something to the effect that "... if a bomb were to be dropped on the gathering, ballet, theater, and modern dance leadership would be wiped out for many years to come." In contrast, at one of the recent CALLERLAB conventions, with so many of the top caller/leaders sitting in the audience, one of the members jokingly said: "... if a bomb were to land on this gathering, it might set square dancing back fifteen minutes." A bit of wry humor, of course, but an indication of the depth of leadership in the square dance activity.

We enjoyed ourselves immensely during our brief stay and we did all the things expected of a tourist, But the great feeling of pride upon receiving the album on behalf of square dancers everywhere, and the realization that square dancers can accomplish so much by working together, overshadowed everything else...Still, we had our stamp and this was a giant step toward bringing square dancing, the American folk dance, to the attention of the world. The irony of the stamp story is that we spent a decade to get the stamp, but within a few months the US Postal Service changed the rates and so our 13¢ stamp was retired.

With our square dance stamp wetly applied to hundreds of first day envelopes and properly canceled, we put more effort into the movement to make square dance the national folk dance. Folk dancing is the oldest form of dance, and it is also the basis for all other dance forms, including ballet, ballroom, disco, modern, and jazz. Over the years it has come to reflect the life and times of a culture and has acquired the qualities of social recreation. Folk dance is distinguished by being participatory rather than a performing art, at least in a vast majority of situations. Square and line dances are part of the folk genre, and are not limited to the United States. The use of traditional costumes and accessories in folk dance aids in preserving a culture's link with its past.

Not to be confused with National Square Dance Week was the effort to have square dancing be declared the national folk dance. More than 200 square dancers and callers from 32 states "invaded" the Nation's Capitol on April 27, 1982, to lobby for passage of HJR 151, a bill before the House of Representatives which would designate square dancing as the National Folk Dance. SJR 59, a companion bill in the U.S. Senate, was passed on September 23, 1981.

It started with a phone call from Mabel H. Brandon, White House Social Secretary for President and Mrs. Ronald

Reagan. Would veteran caller Paul Hartman, along with several squares of dancers and a live band, be able to be a part of the President's annual Fourth of July picnic for the White House Staff and their families? After a full three seconds of deep deliberation caller Hartman allowed that he would be able. As you can well imagine, this was not your run of the mill square dance party. Where else are security checks required for all dancers and every detail cleared with an assistant to the President of the U.S. of A.? Two months of planning and the event came off without a hitch. A magnificent summer day, 2,000 picnickers, several squares of dancers, a great 7-piece square dance orchestra and fireworks! A truly glorious Fourth!

The following, from the Congressional Record of September 24th, 1981 was given by Majority Leader, Senator Howard Baker of Tennessee. It's delightful to discover a bit of humor being permanently recorded.

Mr. President (the Vice President of the US is the President of the Senate), yesterday, the Senate passed a joint resolution designating the square dance as the national folk dance of the United States. I was pleased that I was able to cosponsor this resolution with 27 of my colleagues. But today, I wish to express my admiration and commendation to my most distinguished colleague and friend, the minority leader, Senator Robert C. Byrd of West Virginia (Senator Byrd was noted for his playing the fiddle - well enough that he had an album released). For it is the distinguished minority leader, a geographic neighbor, a kindred spirit in the appreciation of American custom and folklore, and an erudite student of our history, who had brought this matter to my attention — through his sponsorship of Senate Joint Resolution 59.

Of course, I must admit, Mr. President, that my original intentions in cosponsoring this resolution was of a more dubious nature. Convinced, that a so lively and energetic expression of the American spirit most certainly would have had its origin in Tennessee rather than West Virginia, I was prepared to, shall we say, appropriate this resolution. I must say to the minority leader, however, in the spirit of historical accuracy, that my research in this regard has been disappointing. And it is a disappointment I fear I must deliver to Senator Byrd's State as well. My research indicates square dancing in this country has its roots in neither Tennessee nor West Virginia, but in New England of all places.

Rebuffed on that count, Mr. President, I have nonetheless comforted myself in the knowledge that the clog dancing form of the square dance, which as I am sure the minority leader will agree is most artfully performed in Tennessee, is now the vanguard of America's square dancing boom.

Seriously, Mr. President, the square dance is indeed a rich element of our heritage - a reflection of the vitality, resourcefulness, creativity and imagination of our people.

That its popularity is increasing throughout our land is as reassuring to me as any other symbol of the continued creativity and vitality in our country.

So finally, Mr. President, with the permission of Senator Byrd, I renew my request that my name be added to this resolution and I would say to my friend, the minority leader, `If he'll do the fiddlin', I'll do the callin' and perhaps we can persuade our friends from New England to do the dancin'."

"Why all the fuss? What difference will it make if square dancing is officially recognized or not?" you might ask.

"We care," said the sponsors — the square dancers who had been working on this project for a dozen years or so and who hoped they would soon witness a successful climax to the campaign. The sponsors of the bill believed that with official recognition, many doors would be opened for square dancing. It was hoped that there would be greater access to facilities in which to dance, a more general acceptance in our schools, and a greater public awareness of the activity which truly has been a part of American life since this country's birth more than 200 years ago.

Of course, when anything of this nature begins to attract attention, you're bound to hear rumbles of dissent. But who could object to legislation supporting square dancing? Perhaps those who feel other forms of dance are more deserving. One such objection surfaced in newspapers across the country and a stack of clippings covered our desk in short order. The column was by a William Raspberry, a syndicated columnist for the *Washington Post* writers' group. Tongue in cheek, perhaps, writer Raspberry referred to the bill as the major political-legislative-cultural story of the year

"It is impossible to suppose," says Raspberry "that people for whom folk dancing means an Irish jig could be happy with this bit of terpsichorean treachery. Partisans of the New Orleans' strut will see an official allemande as an attack on their culture "

To prove that square dancers cared, on the evening of April 27, 1982, square dancers from all over the country played host to our senators and congressmen at a reception that, naturally enough, included a square dance. Dave Taylor, Chairman of the Board of CALLERLAB, did a few tips to involve our lawmakers and convince them of the wholesome ness, joy and friendliness that this activity has to offer. It was all a part of seeking the affirmative support for HJR151

Square Dance at the U.S. Capitol building

and SJR59 which were bills that designated the square dance to be the national folk dance of the U.S.A. The latter companion bill passed the Senate the next September.

When the majority of the dancers arrived in Washington on Monday, April 26, 1982, there were 193 co-sponsors for HJR 151, with 218 needed for passage of the bill. By the end of Tuesday, after dancing on the Capitol steps, visiting the House gallery, and hosting a one-night stand for members of Congress, the dancers heard the good news from the organizer of the event, George Holser. "We are well over the magic number. All that remains is to get the bill scheduled on the floor of the House."

On Tuesday, at 11:00 AM, the dancers congregated on the west patio of the U. S. Capitol to demonstrate for the media what they hoped would soon be the National Folk Dance. Spectators, along with reporters, cameramen and technicians from PBS and the three major TV networks, braved rain to watch. Dave Taylor called several tips for the dancers. Special demonstrations were given by the Chattanooga Choo Choo Cloggers from Tennessee, and the Pensacola Special Steps, a group of handicapped dancers from Florida. Tuesday night the National Folk Dance Committee hosted a dance reception and one-night stand for Senators,

Representatives and their aides in the cafeteria in the Long-worth Office Building (one of the House office buildings on Capitol Hill). One hundred and twenty-three guests attended and many tried their hand at dancing or participating in a mixer.

The visit paid off. On May 11, 1982, the House passed the bill and on June 1, 1982, the President signed it into law. But, due to a last minute amendment by Senator Robert Garcia of New York, the designation was for only two years and would run out at the end of 1983. George Holser says, "Naturally we would be happier if there was no time limitation, but we have been told that usually there is no problem getting the designation extended, and, eventually, if there is no opposition, making the bill permanent."

So the sponsors turned to making the designation permanent. On February 28, 1983, Rep. Norman Y. Mineta of California introduced the bill in the House of Representatives, where it was referred to the House Committee on Post Office and Civil Service. On March 17 it was referred to the Subcommittee on Census and Population. That sub-committee scheduled hearings for June 28, 1984.

Meanwhile, Senator Robert Byrd of West Virginia introduced an identical bill in the Senate on June 10, 1983. Of course, no Senator can address the Senate without making a speech, and here is what Senator Byrd had to say, direct from the Congressional Record:

The PRESIDENT pro tempore. *(In the Senate the Vice-President of the United States is the President. If he does not preside, then another senator is named President pro tempore – for the time. – ed.)*

The minority leader is recognized [concerning] S. 1448 DESIGNATION OF THE SQUARE DANCE AS THE NATIONAL FOLK DANCE OF THE U.S.A.

Mr. Byrd: Mr. President, in the last Congress I introduced a Senate resolution to designate the square dance as the national folk dance. The resolution was adopted by the Congress with an amendment and signed into law by the President on June 1, 1982.

Since that time, the square dance has enjoyed an increase in popularity. Membership in the many square dance organizations formed over the years has grown, and new organizations have come into being since the enactment of the law... Here is a summary of square dance activities since last June which I have received from the National Folk Dance Committee.

The recent designation of the Square Dance as the National Folk Dance of the United States of America, by Congress, has resulted in a proud and positive reaction by millions of people, especially active dancers, all over the nation. The wide coverage by the media, focusing attention on the National Dance through television, radio, newspapers, and magazines has created an enormous interest and growth in square dancing which is overwhelming.

Clubs, churches, and social groups are clamoring for information about the dance. Square dancing is currently being taught in schools across the Nation, from elementary through high school, and many more schools are seeking ways to include the activity in their curriculum.

A number of universities, through their English Language Extension Course for foreign students, include students' participation in square dance parties so they may be aware of this part of our American heritage. Commercial concerns entertaining foreign customers use these square dance parties ... to treat them to a true part of America. The recognition, by Congress, has increased spectator attendance at square dance festivals and civic functions. Formal organizations have increased in number by twenty-five per-cent. Many who have ridiculed the Square Dance for being rough and hayseed are taking a second look, and finding square dancing to be modern, appealing to people of all ages, races and creeds. The Square Dance has been danced for more than two centuries, conforming with the ever-changing life style of the American people. Class distinction is forgotten when people join together to enjoy the true fellowship of the Square Dance. The calls are in the English language.

The Square Dance is recognized as the State Dance of Alabama, New Jersey, Oregon, Tennessee and Washington. It has been declared the official dance of Cook County, Illinois, and legislation is pending, according to reports in Alaska and Kentucky to designate the Square Dance as the official dance of those States. Everyone can enjoy the fun and fellowship of this wonderful part of our American heritage. We truly believe the Square Dance should have permanent designation, by the Congress, as the National Folk Dance of the United States of America.

Mr. President, the amendment to the square dance resolution limited the designation to two years. After reviewing the summary statement above, I hope that all of my colleagues in the Senate will agree that the enthusiasm with which the Nation has accepted the square dance as the national folk dance justifies a permanent designation.

I am pleased that I am supported in presenting this bill to the Senate by the distinguished majority leader, Senator Howard Baker, and the distinguished chairman of the Judiciary Committee, Senator Strom Thurmond, and many other Senators on both sides of the aisle who cosponsor this bill today, and I thank them for their interest.

Senate Bill 1448

*Be it enacted by the Senate and House of Represent-
atives of the United States of America in Congress assembled, that the Congress finds that*

*(1) square dancing has been a popular tradition in
America since early colonial times;*

*(2) square dancing is a joyful expression of the vi-
brant spirit of the people of the United States;*

*(3) the American people value the display of eti-
quette among men and women which is a major element
of square dancing;*

*(4) square dancing is a traditional form of family
recreation which symbolizes a basic strength of this
country, namely the unity of the family;*

*(5) square dancing epitomizes democracy because it
dissolves arbitrary social distinctions; and*

*(6) it is fitting that the square dance be added to the
array of symbols of our national character and pride.*

*Sec. 2. The square dance is designated as
the national folk dance of the United States.*

*Sec. 3. This Act shall take effect January 1,
1984*

The bill was referred to the Committee on Judiciary,
and on September 15, Senator Thurmond reported the bill
out of committee and to the Senate without amendment and
without a written report. The bill was passed by the Senate
on a voice vote on September 20, 1983. The same day it was
referred to the House Committee on Post Office and Civil
Service.

The word was sent out to square dancers all over the
country that September 21, 1983, was the date set for all

square dancers to call Western Union and send a public opinion message to congressmen asking co-sponsorship of HR 1706. The National Folk Dance Committee asked square dancers to indicate to the 98th Congress that there were millions of people looking forward to the permanent designation of the square dance as the Folk Dance of America.

Like most of you, we had done what we could to support the campaign. June 28 was the day members of the Subcommittee, chaired by Katie Hall of Indiana, would hear testimony on the bill, then send their report to the House of Representatives with a recommendation to approve or disapprove passage of the bill. It all sounded so simple.

The day preceding the hearings, an estimated 2,000 square dancers from all over the country gathered at the west side of the Capitol Building and for two hours put on a colorful demonstration of squares and rounds. The several tiers surrounding the dance area were filled with government employees and the dance, despite the heat of midday summer, went off without a hitch. Then, the half-dozen of us met with members of the work force who were planning the Thursday meeting.

Originally, there were to be three speakers in favor of the bill - Congressmen Leon Panetta and Norman Mineta and me - followed by three speakers opposing the bill. We had each been told to limit our talks from 7 to 10 minutes and, with an hour and a half scheduled for the meeting, this seemed reasonable.

Shortly before traveling to Washington, signals were changed. We were told that in addition to the two sponsoring congressmen, we would be allowed three others. So along with me, George Holser, vice chairman of the program supporting the bill, and Cathie Burdick, co-editor of *American Square Dance* Magazine, were added. The bill had 253 cosponsors, including 17 members of the Post Office and Civil

Service Committee, the group that holds much of the responsibility for bills of this type. In a letter, dated March 15, 1984, from the House of Representatives Committee, William D. Ford, chairman of the committee, wrote: "Questions have been raised about the representativeness of the square dance by experts in dance matters. They point out the difficulty in selecting one dance over another and praise the multiplicity of equally old national dances — clogging, soft shoe, tap, line dances, contra dances and solo dance traditions."

Three major concerns were expressed about designating the square dance (or any other dance) as this country's official dance. Essentially, they were: (1) The possibility of offending those who do not feel themselves to be a part of the America that is represented by square dancing. (2) The possibility of creating a perceived standard form of folk dance that will inhibit the natural, creative evolution of American dance traditions, and (3) The possibility of setting up barriers to our ability to represent the cultural diversity of America to audiences overseas.

Those who opposed the legislation included a caller whose background was strong in one night stands and who was a member of the Country Dance & Song Society, along with several scholarly types with lists of degrees behind their names representing such formidable organizations as The Smithsonian Institute, The National Council for the Traditional Arts and others.

Still confident that what we had to say would satisfactorily answer any possible objections, we made a request

404

that we be allowed to give our testimony following the opposition so we could reply to any points that might be raised. This request was granted. (Monday morning quarterbacking is an essential American quality and looking back, we realize now it would have been better if we had kept to our original slot).

Room 311 in the Cannon House Office Building is not a large one. Seating space for some 75 persons was filled with costumed square dancers and a few non-dancers intent on the goings-on. Chairwoman Hall's gavel came down about 10 minutes late and, after a brief introduction, Congressmen Mineta and Panetta gave their talks which were excellent. Dwelling on the heritage of the activity, stressing the friendliness, the family aspect and the size of the activity, they obviously made points. Following each presentation, Chairwoman Hall asked pertinent questions which were fielded well and those of us seated in the gallery felt comfortable — for the moment.

Then came the opposition. Each one speaking for what seemed like an eternity, the jist of their testimony covered, among other things, the following:

1. To select square dancing and eliminate rounds, clogging, contras and quadrilles, etc., would be doing an injustice to all other forms of American dance. (The Congressmen who had preceded them, had already pointed out that square dancing was a term that encompassed all of these forms.)

2. To select square dancing and overlook dances of so many of the ethnic groups would be a disservice to many Americans.

3. What about the Eskimo and Indian dances? Weren't these a part of America long before anyone ever dreamed up square dancing?

4. "According to my research," one witness testified "square dancing has been pointed up in the pulpits in certain parts of the country as a sensual, sex-ridden dance that should be frowned upon by good church-goers."

There were other points put forth by some who said that to pick a particular dance and make it the folk dance of America would open the door to all types of requests such as to make the hot dog "the official meat of America," volley ball, "the official sport of America," etc.

Following each speaker, the Chairwoman asked good questions and the answers, sometimes taking several minutes. It soon became evident that, with a number of interruptions, when the Chairwoman had to scoot across the street to the Capitol to vote on some bill, we were running out of time. The closing hour of eleven came and went.

The noon hour passed and still the balance of the supporting testimony had not been given. Somewhere after twelve, the Holsers and McClures were called up. Their testimony spelled out the efforts of more than 15 years and numerous bills to get this law passed. Both had their facts well in hand and largely supported the contemporary scene which, unfortunately, was the prime objection of many who spoke in opposition.

About this time, we were "warned" that the meeting had almost run out of time and that another hearing was scheduled in the same room at 2:00 PM. It was well after 1:00 PM when Cathie Burdick and I were called to testify. Cathie was approximately one minute into her talk when a recess was taken for the Chairwoman to go to the Capitol once more for a vote. It was at this point that both Cathie and I were told to limit our talks to just our summaries "because of time."

Picking up where she left off, Cathie pointed out very gently that the square dance dress she was wearing (a very attractive one) cost $5.00. (Chalk one up for our side.) Unfortunately, at this point Cathie was asked to conclude her testimony. Then it was my turn. Like the others, I had spent weeks planning what I would say. What do you do when they cut you down to three minutes? I'm still not sure what I said.

I know it didn't include what I planned. I'm sure those seated on the Subcommittee listening to all the testimony were tired by this time. All of us had submitted our talks in writing, but who in Congress was going to read?

I think now of things that should have, and perhaps could have, been done differently. We never imagined that attention to time schedules would be so disregarded, that those invited to testify would not be allowed their time "on the stand." Had we known earlier how the meeting was to go, we certainly would have spoken earlier. It was obvious that if the bill passes (this is being written early in July, 1984) or if it doesn't pass and if future efforts are to be made for permanent passage, we need to take a good, strong look at the activity as a whole.

The contemporary form of square dancing is indeed an offshoot a development of what has gone on over the past 200 years. To ignore the other phases of the activity, to overlook the traditional forms of our activity, spelled certain doom. Win, lose, or draw, we need to put the entire activity into perspective if we wish it to be recognized by our government as the Folk Dance of the USA.

There's much to be said in favor of introducing some of the traditional contras, quadrilles and early rounds to our new dancers and to remind them that what they are dancing is a part of our heritage. An emphasis on our roots and an ability to dance the dances of our ancestors could add that speck of variety, that enjoyment of dancing to music, that little extra push to dance smoothly and comfortably — dancing that many of us feel the activity needs.

In January, 1985, a letter from Congresswoman Katie Hall, Chairwoman of the sub-committee studying the bill said, in part, "Thank you for your testimony before the sub-committee on H.R. 1706, a bill to designate the square dance as the National Folk Dance. After discussing H.R. 1706 with the members of the sub-committee on Census and Population, it is the opinion of the chair that there is insufficient support to mark-up H.R. 1706 in its present form. The subcommittee will assist Congressman Mineta and Congressman Panetta with future legislation honoring the square dance, so that this great American folk dance will continue to be recognized for its contributions to the preservation of American folk culture. Again, thank you for your efforts during the sub-committee hearing on H.R. 1706."

While we still are not certain why anyone would want to deny square dancing its rightful place in this country's heritage, we should not be too concerned. Legislators probably have not had the opportunity nor taken the opportunity to become a part of the square dance program and recognize its significance. Someday, perhaps, this may change but in the meantime, our work is cut out for us. In building toward the future, let's put the emphasis back on those segments of square dancing that will attract those who cannot afford the time or expense of developing highly contemporary skills.

Let's think about the importance of the more casual dancer, the person who becomes involved in a one-night-stand and allow him a recreation of limited basics. Let's make sure that, once having completed a minimum number of lessons, he will be able to enjoy an on-going program, dancing only once or twice a month if he wishes with no hassle to move further. Let's assure him that he is square dancing and not hold over his head the feeling that"...if you really want to have fun, you have to move on into other programs and dance more frequently..."

Truthfully, with a good strong base of recreational square dancing, built on a foundation of just a few basics, there will be a far greater likelihood that some of these individuals, given the opportunity to take further classes, may do so, thereby enlarging the Plus and Advanced programs. Those wishing the recreational form will have no fear of their preferred program suddenly disappearing, and once we have accomplished this it may not be so difficult to impress others that this is, indeed America's folk dance.

Feeling somewhat like Jimmy Stewart in *Mr. Smith Goes to Washington*, I shared in the recent episode aiming for passage of H.R. 1706 — the bill to have Congress permanently recognize square dancing as the Official Folk Dance of the USA. After 48 hours in the Capitol, we returned home, frustrated, a bit unnerved and a little sadder-but-wiser about the goings-on of government.

Chapter 17. Traveling Caller

I am not including the times while still in the Navy that I had occasions to visit and sometimes call a tip in several cities across the nation, and I am not counting the several experiences while traveling for the Squirt company. Most of this started once Sets in Order began reaching out across the country. Except for Herb Greggerson and one or two other itinerant callers, this was an entirely new experience for me. At first invitations to call outside the area came from contacts made at the Lloyd Shaw summer schools in Colorado Springs. Then, after the introduction of Sets in Order in November 1948, I may have become the first "big name" caller, although many of those inviting me to call had never heard me call until the beginning of the National Square Dance Conventions and the release of early records.

The first "big dates" were single events - fly to the city, call the dance, and then return home. These first out of town engagements were experiments on my part and on the part of the sponsors, either club presidents or association sponsors for a festival or jamboree. By the early 1950's invitations started coming in on a regular basis, to the point where I found that by accepting several I could package them into a single trip. I soon discovered that calling one night in Kansas City, the next in Spokane, Washington, the third in Dallas, Texas, was a bit short on smarts. We found that by accepting a series of geographically located engagements made sense, and from that point on our travel ventures smoothed out.

1951 – The Eastern Trip

Did anybody ever hint to you that square dancing might be slowing down a bit? Well, Ginger and I wanted to see how things were, first hand. Here's a brief play-by-play account of what happened. [*Editor's Note : Because there isn't nearly enough room to say all the wonderful things we would like to say about this event, we will use a short-cut by referring to the following stock paragraph, wherever it applies:* **Paragraph A**: *The square dancers in this city were perhaps the finest people it's ever been our pleasure to meet. Their hospitality, their sense of humor, and their complete and overwhelming desire to pass this square dancing fun on to others not only made us feel welcome, but makes us want to return again. – Bob]*

Chicago: (See Par. A) —January 6th and 7th.

Brrrr. Square dancing in the Chicago area seems to have advanced quite steadily. Dancers use a combination of positions for the promenades and swings, and in some areas designate the No. 1 couples as facing the caller, while in other areas the No. 1 couples have their backs to the caller. The expression on dancers' faces is the same here as everywhere else. They danced for fun. Did two dance sessions and one caller's meeting, and of course the before and after dinners and parties.

Pittsburgh: (See Par. A)

Don't ever look like you're idle in Pittsburgh. Folks like Eero Davidson and his wife, Mimi Kirkell, Francis McNaught, and a bunch of the others will either find a dinner for you to attend, a television show to do or something else to keep you on the go. They don't sleep in this city. (Note: You don't wear "Western" clothes in the best cafes!)

Boston: (There's a right way to pronounce that, you know) (See Par. A)

This was the place we were warned we would need to be most careful of our manners and where folks would

411

wear tuxedos while square dancing. They don't, and we ceased being worried as soon as Charlie Baldwin picked us up at our hotel and took us to our Institute at the Boston "Y." There were a few slight differences between Boston dancing and Chicago dancing, Pittsburgh dancing and Cincinnati dancing. It was noted here in Boston that the normal speed of dancing was no less than in any other part of the country. I had a chance to watch Lawrence Loy call in his own wonderful style, and noticed how quickly the dancers adapted themselves to any type of calling.

Durham, N.H.: (Par A)

Dr. Schultz of Durham, New Hampshire, told us when we met him last summer that we hadn't lived until we took part in an old fashioned kitchen junket. On Friday, Jan. 19th, we were really indoctrinated. There is something about the old longways or contra dances that is completely unbeatable. We can't overlook the important fact that we spent as much time as we could work out with Ralph Page of Keene, New Hampshire. We attended some of his Institute sessions and had many a cup of coffee, just talking square dancing. When it comes to the old-time line dances and quadrilles, Ralph Page is truly a master

New York City and Area: (Par. A)

What names and what places! How we looked forward to New York, and how pleased we were, getting to know the Teffertellers at the Henry Street Settlement House. And, we mustn't forget the Michael Hermans! There is such a thing as taking a difficult dance and making it look difficult, but when you take a difficult dance, put it into a teaching technique in a huge circle and make it come out as the simplest type of dance form, then you are truly an artist. That is our impression of how the Hermans work.

Detroit, Michigan: (Par. A)

The home of a great many of our modern day motor cars is also the home of a lot of wonderful square dancers. And can they dance! There is very little difference in the dancing style in this area and back home in Los Angeles.

Phoenix, Arizona: (Par. A)

It was Valley of the Sun Festival time again; and Ginger and I, after five weeks of freezing weather, stepped into the 82° sunshine of this desert capitol. It was truly a wonderful dance. Phoenix square dancers showed us that square dancers are the nicest people you can find.

We got back to Los Angeles with just enough time to do the laundry, check in at the magazine and re-pack for another trip – back to Kansas City. There's nothing new under the sun, they say, but as far as we know Mission, Kansas, came out with a "first" on February 8th, 1951 when the Sunflower Squares presented the initial Sets in Order Square Dance Party. Admission charge was to show proof of being a subscriber to Sets in Order, plus $1.00; or a brand new subscription, plus $1.00. If those who attended were not subscribers, old or new, the regular admission price was $2.00. Those who wished to subscribe at the door were, however, admitted at the lesser rate of $1.00.

In 1952 I was the first American caller to visit Alberta, Canada. There were over 1400 people on the floor, the largest square dance to this time ever held in Canada. The record did not last long. 'Jonesy' Jones was brought to Edmonton by the Dancers and Callers Association and this dance held in the Prince of Wales Armories broke all existing records, with dancers driving up to 400 miles to be in attendance. (That hurt, but that was the drawing power of 'Jonesy'.)

In 1953 Ginger and I set our personal record for traveling. Our little notebook where we kept track of such things said we had made six square dance trips out of California, traveling some 32,000 miles. We had been to Alberta, Canada, and British Columbia. We saw some of the best organized institutes and jamborees in Tucson, Arizona, Sheridan, Wyoming, Missoula, Montana, and Kansas City. And of course we made another appearance at 'Pappy's' Cheyenne Mountain Callers School.

In Colorado Springs we met the Andersons. During the week we chatted with them quite a bit and got to know them pretty well. As we talked about square dancing we found that they came from Aruba, a small island in the Dutch West Indies, off the coast of Venezuela. Aruba was about the size of New Jersey and had a mammoth oil refinery run by Richfield of New Jersey. The plant was managed by a small group of Americans and was operated by several hundred island natives. In order to recruit the laborers they needed from the States, Richfield made every effort to provide ideal living and recreational facilities. An entire segment of the island had been made into a special complex and virtually every type of living necessity had been provided for. This included every type of recreation from gymnasiums, health spas, flying clubs (they even had their own Piper Cubs), golf (I think) and ballroom dancing. Only in the last year had a group started a square dance club. With no callers on the island, they depended upon records and the club officers to handle the programs.

Then came the question: Would we be interested in coming down for a couple of weeks? We could teach them dancing, squares, rounds, etc., and teach a few of the inhabitants how to call and teach. Explaining a bit further, the Andersons told us that they would keep us busy and we would be working on alternate days with two different groups. The one would be the American personnel and the other would be the natives of the island. Evidently, contracts with the island government required that it be done in this way. We were assured that we would be given every bit of assistance that we might need.

This would be our first calling/teaching venture outside of North America and obviously there was quite a bit to consider. I had only just recently resigned from the Squirt Company and being an independent caller/teacher seemed a little bit risky, but the lure of traveling abroad and spreading the activity to unknown regions was appealing.

We had been in the midst of planning a cross country calling/teaching tour that fall, and adding on a couple of weeks to the Caribbean meant a full month away from home, family, magazine, home club calling, etc. The Asilomar vacation institutes were already over for that year, but planning for the future year was in progress. The almost month long tour meant getting guest callers for the two existing clubs. With a bit of night work and pushing here and there, we got two issues of the magazine fairly well locked up before going. We set off in early October with a packed schedule, calling in such places as Dallas, Oklahoma City, Kansas City, Cincinnati, Detroit, Michigan and with scarcely a day of breathing time.

Like every traveling caller to follow in the next few years, we found that there was a bit of competition among the dancers, club officers, etc., to see who would house the visiting calling luminary. Well before we left home they told us in each area who would be picking us up and with whom we would be staying. In Detroit, one couple was picking us up at the airport, taking us to their home, feeding us, taking us to the dance and keeping us over night. Then, couple No. 2 would pick us up the next morning, take us home, have a dinner for us, take us to their dance that night, and take us home afterwards. Then, in the morning take us to the airport where we would head for the next city. We would have liked the time after the dances to just get some rest, rather than staying up half the night partying. But, we were younger then and all this was a bit exciting for us.

Following several days and nights like this, we were in Florida and headed for Aruba, a 21-mile island dotted with brightly colored plaster homes surrounded by Diwi trees, which appeared to be blowing in the wind. We were met by our friends from Shaw's caller school, and we got a view of the island as we headed to the far end. Always astounded by the welcome from square dancers wherever we turned up, the greeting here was phenomenal and for the next two weeks, we were treated like the Rajas of Rashapor (whatever and wherever that is.)

During the two weeks we were with them, we were guests at many parties, had many trips around the island, got acquainted not only with the mainland U.S. citizens, but with the oil company workers with whom we would split half our time. The goal was to spend alternate days and evenings with the American employees teaching rounds, squares, and con-tras, and with daytime sessions for the several who thought they might like to learn to call. Then we were to spend the alternate days with the natives of the island who had been doing some square dancing and wished to learn more. Alt-hough Dutch citizens, these folks spoke a language all their own, Papiamento, but they all understood English.

Somebody once referred to their square dance club as the Potluck of the Month Organization. "Square dancing was just part of the fun," they told us. "Enjoying supper and the spread of delicacies, almost beyond description, was in itself a highlight, too." The square dance club of Aruba had an unusual thought on the potluck picture. Whoever was to bring the hot dish was told to bring "more." Evidently over a period of years of having potlucks, sometimes experiencing rather doubtful concoctions, the members decided that a combination of spaghetti, cheese and meatballs prepared in a certain way was always the highlight that brought cries of "more" from the members. So, consequently, they settled on this one dish which they nick-named "more."

We returned from Aruba with an application for the Rip 'n' Snort Club of Aruba. Part of the dues were in square (Dutch) nickels – honest!

In 1954, we got an invitation to go in exactly the opposite direction from Aruba. The Central Alberta Callers Association wanted to promote a Square Dance Institute at Banff in the Canadian Rockies. The accommodation was at the Banff School of Fine Arts, a branch of the University of Alberta. The accommodations were good and were yearly getting better with additions to the campus. The scenery is unsurpassed by any place in the world: the heart of the Canadian Rockies near Lake Louise, only 70 miles from Calgary. This was the first Institute in Alberta and it set quite a precedent. We were thrilled to be invited especially because of the additional staff we got to work with: Ed & Dru Gilmore. Bob & Babs Ruff, Bruce & Shirley Johnson, Manning & Nita Smith, Lee & Mary Helsel, Joe & Claire Lewis, Marion & Bill Johnston, Al & Bea Brundage. Almost all of them ended up in the Callers Hall of Fame.

The Institute was an unusual setup. The class started at seven each evening and went to ten. Participants drove to our meeting place in Calgary from as far away as Edmonton to the north, and Lethbridge to the south. Since not all the callers could make the same night, they all needed to fit the caller training around their regular jobs, the callers were divided into two groups, each group coming on alternating nights. It was a good series and out of it came a number of callers who remained in the activity for thirty years and more.

Something "special" happened just prior to one of the sessions during our second week together. The classes were held in the sizable basement of the home of the people who were hosting me and just as we were finishing dinner one night the phone rang and after Bud (my host) hung up, he said as he hurried out of the room, "We've just had a call from the 'committee' and we have to be down at the station in ten minutes." I grabbed the box of records, Bud put the top on the PA system (just remembering in time to disengage the electric plug from the wall) and we rushed out to the car.

By the time we reached the station other cars were pulling up with square dancers getting their ties in place, square dance dresses zipped, etc. I followed along, not being sure just what we were getting into. Almost immediately a troop train, marked with Red Crosses on the side, had stopped at the loading docks. Grey ladies from the Red Cross and other volunteers who had reached the station ahead of us were doling out cups of hot chocolate, sandwiches, and small banners saying "Welcome to Calgary." By the time Bud had found a packing box on which he set the sound system and had it plugged in, the caller with his large white Stetson hat had arrived and at least a dozen squares had formed along the length of the track. The sounds of "Chinese Breakdown" got everybody's toe tapping and the caller started out with some simple square. In no time at all faces were pressed against the windows, bandages, casts, and slings visible. A few of the more ambulatory passengers made their way to the doors of the train to step outside and watch what was going on.

As the first tip ended and the caller began selecting his record for the singing call, you could see from the expressions on the faces of the onlookers that this was exactly the elixir they needed. About that time someone told me that this was a train load of casualties returning from the Korean battle fields and heading toward the northern provinces of Canada. Their unscheduled stop was a brief one but three station employees of the railroad, all of whom were square dancers, had started the communications network. Their routine: as soon as one learned that a train was coming in, they would call two phone numbers. Each of these dancers would call an additional three numbers and as the calls snowballed, as many as 150 couples could be rounded up, day or night, dressed for dancing and ready to say through their friendship, dance, and joy, "Welcome home, veterans. We're proud of you."

Oh yes, we forgot to mention. The caller was also the mayor of Calgary.

I thought the trip to Memphis, Tennessee, in 1955 was going to be just another dance festival. The wrinkle in that theory was that I was the first guest caller for their big festival. Before the plane landed I got into my square dance clothes, and once on the ground I waited for the aisle to clear before I collected my miscellaneous belongings and so I was the last one off. I remember that as I looked out the windows the stewardess said, "Apparently they're expecting the governor or some bigwig to come in on one of these flights." When the cabin door was opened and the steps rolled into place, I could hear a band but because of people in the aisle I couldn't see anything. Finally I picked up my bags and moved with the other passengers.

As I reached the top of the stairs, a man with a large key and a very beautiful young lady walked up. "We greet you on behalf of the Mayor of Memphis," said the man. "And I'm your hostess!" said the lady. Then he handed me the key to the city in one hand, and taking my brief case from the other replaced it with a microphone and said, "Will you call a dance for us?" Then I noticed about a dozen squares at the base of the stairs and that was perhaps, as difficult a dance as I ever tried to muster up. I remember they had a large convertible to take me wherever I was going, but I don't remember too much else about the evening or the weekend. However it certainly started with a bang!

In the years following WWII, square dancing took me to a number of countries, including several that had been our enemies only a few years earlier. I found that traveling takes its toll on a family. With my travel calling, working with the magazine, the Asilomar sessions and a young daughter, Linda, who needed more attention than a traveling father sometimes could give; it got to be rather hectic in the Osgood family. And so in 1956 Ginger and I were divorced. She continued her work as an artist and was extremely successful and we still see each other frequently and keep in touch. My work just seemed to enlarge. I had two or three beginner classes a year and called regularly for several clubs that I had started and were doing very well. I didn't think I needed anything else to keep me busy.

However, in 1957 the Air Force Special Services invited me to come to Europe and do some teaching and calling on bases in England, France, Germany, and North Africa. The funds for this were not from the taxpayer, but were from the money that came in from purchases at the PX. The invitation, incidentally, was instigated by Cal Golden, one of the leading instigators in square dancing in Europe at that time.

From the early days of the magazine we began to get reports, primarily from members of the military, from places in different parts of the earth, that square dancing was getting a toe hold. Among our many communicators was Cal Golden, who I had met for the first time at Lloyd Shaw's school in Colorado Springs. At that time he was in his early years of a life-long military career. Involved in square dancing for a number of years, he had somewhere along the line entered into a championship calling match and had become the "world champion." Introduced to the members of the class by 'Pappy,' Cal (the Kid from Arkansas) took a lot of kidding about his championship. Over the years that followed, Cal (remember he made an appearance at the Diamond Jubilee) was shipped to Europe where he eventually became a Chief Master Sergeant. He was heavily involved in running the enlisted men's mess with all its duties, while at the same time becoming a very important part of the square dance picture. While in Europe, Cal Golden devoted his spare hours to popularizing the robust art of Do-Si-Doing. He taught beginner dancers and conducted clinics for callers. He was featured at jamborees throughout Europe and gave forth with his infectious sense of humor and individual calling style. He also organized dances to benefit charities, such as the Air Force Aid Society and England's Home for the Blind.

Cal became an invaluable caller-coach as well as becoming one of the world's most colorful callers (you should have seen his outfits some of which were custom made by Nudie of Hollywood, the designer for the stars). About 1956, before the Air Force shipped Cal stateside, he used the special services branch of the Air Force to start a German callers association. Then in early 1957, he brought proven leaders from the states to spend time in England and France to call for the overseas dancers and to teach calling techniques to those who had already learned to dance and had a yearning to call. In early June I received an invitation: "Osgood, Robert L. and partner - you are invited to come to Europe to teach square dancing starting at the end of August…" But I did not have a partner.

The wives of one or two of our dancers graciously said that they would give up all and join me, but that really was not an option. So (partnerless) I went to the National Convention in St. Louis the last weekend of June where I met with Cal Golden and discussed the situation. When our conversation was over, I knew more than ever that I would like to make the trip.

Now people go to these national conventions (at least I do) not so much to dance, as to visit old friends. Somewhere in the previous years I had done a calling weekend for the Pat Patericks in the Washington, D.C. area. Running into them the first day at the convention, we set up dinner and in the process of the meal I mentioned my rather unusual dilemma.

Helen Davis

"Oh, as a matter of fact, we have someone that you might be interested in," chorused the Patericks. "She's been a friend of ours, a single lady, and very active in our square dance picture. As of next year she will be the program chairman for the first Washington D.C. area clinic. Would you like to meet her?" I would and I did meet Helen Davis later that evening. Breakfast with Helen the next morning, lunch whenever we could make connections, dinner that night and – and now that we were old friends, I offered her an invitation to join me on what was planned to be an eleven weeks tour visiting, calling, and teaching in Germany, France, England and North Africa. She said, "OK."

Having traveled quite a bit in the last few years, fly-ing itself was no novelty, but the MATS aircraft, a four prop transport job was different in a number of ways. First of all, they had all of the seats facing the rear of the plane (I guess

Me in my gift bowler

so that we could see where we had been). Actually it was quite comfortable and in ways of safety seemed to make sense. My contact with the Air Force said we were going to be on the "blue plate" spe-cial, but the cabin service was not what one might call "fancy": a paper sack for each one on the aircraft complete with a sandwich or two, a piece of pie, a piece of fruit and a carton of milk. That did not give the military many points as far as I was concerned, but - forget that. I was on my way!

Yes, I was headed for Europe. But, and I was con-vinced about this, I was not going as a tourist. I was going to have an opportunity to put to good use all that I had learned and all that had been happening to me over the recent years. How fortunate could I get?

The flight was good, and as we drew closer to France, our greeting of an amazing sunrise shook out whatever sleep was left in us. While the plane was descending it was easy to pick out the rivers and countryside. We had traveled all night and it was just daybreak when we got our first view of Paris. Here was the Seine and I could spot the Eiffel Tower. We could even see the Arc de Triomphe. Stopping just long enough at LeBourget Field to let off a few passengers, we took off for the final leg toward our destination, Am Main airport in Frankfurt, Germany.

We were met in the arrival area by several of the square dancers among the military and by Betsy Davison

423

who represented the branch of the Air Force that handles special arrangements. We had a short meeting for a briefing period, and then the Bill Brocketts and Fred Stabens put Helen and me and our luggage (PA system, etc.) into their car and headed for Ramstein Air Base.

This was just twelve years following the cessation of hostilities that ended WWII, and though much clean-up had been done, one didn't have to look far to find only remnants of homes and entire cities. The air-lift had occurred several years earlier and the infamous Berlin Wall was yet to be constructed.

The Brocketts and the Stabens housed us for the next two days. I wanted to see everything, and our hosts assured us that we would in due time have our eyes filled. In the meantime, the briefing sessions would go on. The next morning we met with Betty (I have forgotten her last name) who was to be our tour escort during the entire time we were on the project

The schedule for the next ten weeks looked like a grand battle plan. Starting out with bases in Germany, then swinging through France with several days in and around Paris, the Air Force would fly us to England and a full schedule had been laid on there. Following England, the project planners had answered a request from a square dance group in Casablanca to spend a week with them. Then, a return to Germany for a callers school and the annual winter square dance round-up. Possibly, if we were good, there would be some time off during the project and before heading home so we could visit places we would like to see while in Germany. It all sounded good and the next day following the briefings we were off and on our way.

My headquarters was located in Wiesbaden, Germany. Here was a beautiful city, which for a number of reasons, was spared from bombing by the allies. Whether or not it was declared an "open city" I don't recall. But I do remember being told that it suffered one bomb that was dropped by mistake. A short distance away, across the Rhine River, was Mainz – or Koblenz(?), a major industrial city which 12 years after the cessation of hostilities remained in rubble.

We took part in the annual square dance festival at Ramstein Air Base. What was really interesting to me about that particular square dance was the friendliness of all the people. I suddenly realized that in one square there was a corporal in the #1 man position; #2 man was a major; #3 was a civilian worker; and #4 was the general that ran the base. All these people had no concern about rank or anything else as long as you could do your part in the square. I have often thought that is the beauty of people in a square dance costume. It certainly makes everyone equal. It was a lesson I had felt before but I really saw the example here.

I think one of the greatest impressions that stuck with me for a long time was a lady and her husband who came up to me and said that I didn't know how much square dancing meant to them. They said that when they land in a new area and take on a new job and get into new quarters, they spend the next few weekends seeing the country, driving around visiting places they've heard about. And then when that is over they stay home and begin to accept some of the invitations - and they come continually - to cocktail parties. They were not teetotalers but doing this night after night was no fun. And then came square dancing. They said it had changed their lives and had really been a boon for them. Well, there was one more reason for square dancing, being there at the right place at the right time.

I called at the club for the service personnel. It had a good dance floor and the first night I was there they had eleven squares. Within the club they had four or five callers. It was very healthy and I had a ball not only calling for them but dancing with the people. They all seemed so appreciative that somebody would come across from the States to see what they were doing over there. I also remember that was at the beginning of the 11 weeks.

We left there and did the rest of the tour then came back there at the end. I went to that same club and there were three squares and one caller. I asked, "What happened?" They said it is called rotation. All the people that were there when I first arrived were not there now because they have been sent to other bases. Almost at the end of the evening, the caller asked everybody to come up to the stage. He took his hat and he said, "In this hat is everybody's name that is here tonight. I'm getting transferred tomorrow, I'm being rotated. I'd like to pull a name and that person is going to be the caller from now on." So a name was pulled and the guy darn near fainted. He had been square dancing for about three months and he was the next caller. But this was not unusual. Square dancing has survived with this type of situation many times. They just simply turned over the PA system and the records that the club owned and the club proceeded.

On one of my working days, I was driven out to Furstenfeldbruch Air Base to put on a one-night stand for young pilots in training for the new German Air Force. What a strange feeling to arrive at a German airfield and see large numbers of American fighter planes with Maltese crosses on their wings. The surprise (shock) soon disappeared when I was shown into the sizable gymnasium where the uniformed men and local girls, partners for the evening, were waiting for me.

Usually a one-night stand is a "one-night stand" anywhere. You can count on a number of Virginia Reels, simple squares and circle mixers. But, with a German speaking congregation and with little or no conversational German to draw upon, it was an interesting, but successful, fun evening.

A translator helped out, and that fact plus the "watch me, do it like this" paid off for me. It took a little while to get accustomed to the military, drill-like maneuvers these future fighter pilots put into the square dancing (very precise).

Well, outside of Germany and doing several jobs there, we went to France and we called at the NATO Headquarters. There were three generals on the floor at that time, but you couldn't tell because of the square dance costumes. We also did a callers school there. Our directors and guides asked us what we wanted to do along the way in our spare time. They tried to work us just six days and give us the seventh day off. I said I would love to see parts of France that were the big names during the First World War. And I will never forget Verdun. We're talking about well over 50 years after World War I and there was a countryside still chopped up, still messed up from months and years of bombing.

England was perhaps a highlight because they had quite a number of American personnel there. Square dancing had started in little bits during the War and they kept it up and it grew after the war. The British themselves were coming into the activity more. In 1952 American caller Mildred Buhler had moved to London to follow her husband and his career. She felt that her calling career was over, but not so. She was greeted with open arms, and she was instrumental in founding the British Association of American Square Dance Callers, which spread throughout Europe. In Germany it was to happen later on that the Germans really came in and became the moving force. But here in England it had been going for a while. I called for one or two of the air bases and had great dances. One thing I do remember was that at different times during the dance, the PA system would pick up the tower and we would get some of the directions from the tower. And we wondered how many pilots got directions to do an allemande left. We never did hear.

We were asked if we would like to do anything extra that they hadn't planned on before and that was travel down to North Africa and do some work at Casablanca. We went down there to the Nouasseur Air Base, North Africa and they had a real going square dance program. While we were there the Sheriffian Square Dance Club became officially one of

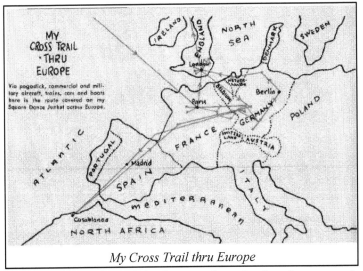

My Cross Trail thru Europe

the major activities of the base and we had a chance to do a callers' institute and also do some workshops with the dancers and call a dance or two. They too, were extremely appreciative of having the activity available to them.

Now, if you recall I had met Becky Smith and her daughter Wendy just a few months before the 1957 European trip. She had not taken square dance lessons yet, but I was smitten. The Rip 'n' Snort club was in the midst of planning the trip to Hawaii in the fall of 1958. I really do not recall if she hinted or if the idea just came to me, but in February I told her that if she wanted to go the Hawaii with the club she would have to marry me. I still do not know if it was me or Hawaii, but we did marry in March. Some members of the club took responsibility for helping her to learn to square dance as well as they could. Her first trip with a square dance club she made as a caller's wife.

When we got back from the Hawaii trip and saw how much fun that was; and planning it was fun - Becky and I decided that we would do an experiment and we would take a group, mostly from our club, but we would publicize it, and we would do a trip to Europe. Well, that was another experience. We did several things absolutely right, we worked with a travel wholesaler, which meant that we could set up a three-week trip, do everything we wanted, see what was fun, do all the tours, include three meals a day, have a group picture, have a square dance each week in a different country, and the whole cost from Los Angeles to England, Scandinavia, Germany, France and back home for under a thousand dollars a person (allowing for inflation, that would be over $8,000 now). The thing that we discovered in setting up the first trip, which became our program for trips after that, was Becky and I sat down and figured what we would like to see. We didn't ask a lot of people what they wanted to see; we figured if we could get something that we would enjoy and publicize it, there would be other people that would like doing the same things. So, we did just exactly that. We found the countries we wanted to go to. I think we went to Norway and I know we went to England and France and Germany, and we ended up in Switzerland. So, for 21 days that sounds like an awful lot of ground to cover but we did it leisurely enough with time off in every city and at least three nights off, and we did have square dances in every country where we could find square dances.

You all know the saying, "Getting there is half the fun?" We've managed to have our share of nerve racking experiences on some of these traveling junkets over the years. One of the craziest occurred when we tried to set some sort of a distance record in a pocket sized tour lasting just a week.

Usually calling tours can be stretched out sufficiently to permit plenty of time for travel. For some reason we allowed ourselves just 11 hours to get from Ottawa, Canada, to a dance in Lake Worth, Florida, (near West Palm Beach). But why worry? All our flights were confirmed and in good order. Then the phone rang. It was 6:15 AM and our host for the past three days, Angus McMorran, said it was the air lines.

"Your flight's been cancelled due to freezing conditions on the field."

"What," we asked, "are we supposed to do?"

With a little luck, we were informed, we could get a plane later in the day and get to New York by 6:00 PM. 6:00 PM! We were due at the Florida dance at 8:00! A quick call to Montreal airport and we found that we could catch a 10 A.M flight on Eastern Airlines. Next a check of the railroads and news that there was a train leaving at 7:05 A.M. that could get us into Montreal by 9:15 A.M..

By this time it was 6:40. We were still in our pajamas. Nothing was packed, and the station was on the other side of town. Shades of Patton's drive across France, Revere's ride and other similar dashes as Angus handled the car through icy streets with us trying to finish dressing in the front seat. We were at the station by 7:04 A.M.. Double parked in front of a line of taxis, a porter grabbed our bags while we bought our ticket, and the gate guard flashed the red light to hold the train a minute more. We were breathing hard but we were still in the race.

430

It was 9:20 A.M. when we stopped at Montreal. We were out looking for a taxi in no time flat. Finally one stopped. The French driver had a little trouble figuring where we wanted to go, but the five-dollar bill along with a bit of sign language did the trick. Slippery streets, early morning traffic, bucket loads of snow and distance were finally overcome in a mad race that put us in front of the Eastern Air Lines counter by 9:45 A.M.

All Eastern flights were cancelled.

Trans-Canada Air Lines came through with a substitution, and with the help of two porters and three airline employees we cleared customs, checked baggage, bought new tickets, and boarded our plane. Now we could rest for a bit. We missed our original flight from New York to Miami, but we were now scheduled on a National Airlines jet leaving New York at 1:55 P.M.. It was twelve noon when we landed. A short walk to the counter and we were ready to check in. "We're sorry, but starting today that flight leaves at 5:45 PM."

Another quick shuffle and we managed to shift to an immediate flight due into Miami at 6:00 P.M. Just time to phone Florida and then onto the plane. We were over the Miami Airport by 6:10, but circled the field for twenty minutes more. On the ground, a breathless committee of one grabbed us and our luggage, handed us a ham sandwich, pushed us into a car, and we were on our way to Lake Worth some 60 miles further on. There was no light in the back seat but we managed to dig out a reasonably clean western shirt, tie and pants and undergo a quick dressing operation reminiscent of "general quarters" back in the comparatively calm Navy days. With microphone in one hand and records in another, we catapulted out of the car as we came to the hall. It was just 8:30 P.M. and we started to call the first tip. We can only imagine how it sounded, but take our word for it — we were never so glad to get to a dance.

431

In July, 1959, just a year after Becky and I were married, we took a phenomenal trip to Alaska. We were invited to be the first invited caller team to the Annual Alaska Convention. We flew into Fairbanks, Alaska, arriving on July 3, just before the historical Fourth of July. We witnessed the 50 star flag being raised over the Alaska for the first time on the Fourth of July. (Alaska was the 49th State as of January 1959, and Hawaii became the 50th in March 1959. Our visit was in July, so it was appropriate that the new 50 star flag be raised.) The rather rustic hotel we stayed in hosted a square dance. I remember when the dance had ended, about 1:00 in the morning, we were heading toward our room and saw a small boy sitting on the steps of the porch grasping a paper sack filled with fireworks. He didn't look very happy so I asked him what was the matter. He said his folks said that he could set off the fireworks as soon as it got dark. The catch was that it didn't get dark until about 2:00 in the morning and then it stayed dark for less than an hour. We were above the Arctic circle at the time.

This being the first such event for the people in Alaska, they really went all out to make it super-special. Not only had Becky and I been married less than a year (and that was about the length of time she had been square dancing), but they counted on her, being the caller's wife, to do quite a bit of the presentation work. She helped me teach a couple of round dances, including "Battle of New Orleans." They also set up a sewing session for her to lead for the women in the group – now, Becky does not sew and did not look forward to the job, but, somehow she got through it.

We then moved on to Anchorage for more dancing and teaching. We discovered that this was also a big venture for our friends in Alaska. Square dancing was still in its infancy and raising the funds to bring up a couple of characters from the "lower 48" was no small undertaking. This became apparent to us when we went into a local supermarket in the center of Anchorage. There, just past the checkout stands, was a card table and behind it, a smiling square dancer busily engaged in selling cookies to a couple passing by. Taped to the front of the table in large letters:

> **BUY OUR CHOCOLATE CHIP COOKIES.**
> **HELP BRING BOB AND BECKY OSGOOD TO ALASKA.**

The money raising must have been successful for there we were having a great time with some mighty friendly dancers.

On the second afternoon that we were in Anchorage for the festival, we were picked up and taken out into the country to a little old wooden shack which turned out to be the television studio for the area. It was about that time they informed us that we were to do an interview about ourselves and about the festival. Our hosts dropped us off at the station where we were met by a very attractive lady, who said she would be our MC. She told us that she just wanted us to relax for a few minutes as we talked about square dancing before the camera. While a taped segment was being played she took us over to the "set," which was a large sofa, a large table, all made up to look like someone's living room. We met the cameraman who told us that the camera was in place and ready to go. There was no fuss, no muss, and no time for makeup —the three of us were seated on a sofa, the hostess in the middle and the camera facing us some six feet away. As we watched on a monitor, we could see the tail end of a commercial, then the red light went on and our interviewer started talking.

We don't remember a thing she said but it was something about our being in the area for a special square dance festival and "isn't this great!... and perhaps the Osgoods would like to tell you all about square dancing, so I'm just going to leave you for a minute or two, and you go right ahead and talk to the folks at home..." With that she got up, turning just long enough to motion with her hands that we should move a little closer together. Then she was gone.

"... Well, square dancing, uh, oh, Bob, you tell them. Well, let's see, did you know that square dancing was one of this country's favorite hobbies? Well, (gulp) it is."

About that time we both noticed that the man behind the camera had disappeared also, leaving his headphones hooked loosely to the side of the camera. The red light on the camera was shining bright and clear, indicating that we were beamed out into the community. There was no one to tell us what we should or shouldn't say. (Oh, what a temptation it was to sell subscriptions to the magazine.)

It seemed as though we were on camera forever. About the time we started describing the previous year's National Convention, having completed the story of Lloyd Shaw, the birth and growth of Sets in Order and what it takes to be a square dance caller, the cameraman returned to his post followed shortly by the hostess, carrying a partially drained cup of coffee.

The closing was almost as abrupt as the beginning and, in a flash, the red light had gone out and we could tell from the monitor that it was time for the afternoon reruns of "The Beverly Hillbillies." (A slight touch of irony.) We've sometimes thought that it would be interesting to have a tape of the show but, then again, maybe it's just as well we don't.

So we met the new kind of "49'er" – the square dancers of our 49th state. Alaska brought a whole new group of square dancers to become "stateside" dancers, too. Sets in

Order ran a lengthy article about our square dance experiences in the land of the Northern Lights.

The next stop was Ketchikan. Ketchikan is strung along the lower continental tip of Alaska for a distance of about 10 miles and supported three major square dance clubs. All three clubs participated in the Fifth Annual Southeastern Alaska Square Dance Jamboree held at the Eagle's Hall in downtown Ketchikan - an average of 6 squares dancing at all times to the calls of the 11 callers.

Most square dancing ends in Ketchikan, in common with other Alaskan areas, during the month of May and club members defect to the sport of salmon fishing during the summer. Dancing resumes in September. Contrary to the general concept of a frigid climate throughout Alaska, Ketchikan is said to have a "banana-belt climate," with an annual average rainfall of 12 to 13 feet per year. With the admission of Hawaii into the United States, the new geographical center of the States moved to just 90 miles south of Ketchikan, at Prince Rupert, B.C. Thus Ketchikan will be the closest American city to the geographical center.

Square dancing in Anchorage, as in all of Alaska, is not blessed with the powers of Old Sol. The long, confining winters demand that an individual have an outlet for his ambition and physical energy. Square dancing filled a basic need for "Something to do." The average age of Anchorage square dancers was around 30. New dancers were constantly being encouraged and the interest created a need for more and more dance instruction. But many of the instructors were in the military, and Anchorage hoped that the new dancers would be ready before they got hit with rotation. Dudes and Dames Club of Anchorage was the only military sanctioned square dance club in the Anchorage area but was not limited to military alone.

Alaskan square dancers don't come to the square dances on dogsleds, no matter what romantic notions readers may have. Instead we found everything from Volkswagens to Cadillacs parked outside the square dance hall and a lot of the dancers come in by plane or boat to Kodiak from the outlying villages. The dancers themselves were a cross-section of typical Americans: housewives, school teachers, nurses, office workers, cannery workers, carpenters, pilots, salesmen, doctors, heavy equipment operators, and a large number of professional Navy personnel.

Wherever we went, even in Valdez, Alaska, we were bound to run into square dancers. We had just finished a day's side trip by boat to visit the breath-taking Columbia Glacier and were registered at the Valdez Hotel for the night. Becky was busy addressing some postcards when Mr. Francis Krch, (pronounced Kirsh) the manager-owner of the hotel came up and asked her, a bit cautiously it seemed, if we might be the same Osgoods who square danced. Before we left the next morning we'd met just about the most frustrated seven square dancers we'd ever seen – they needed one more to make a square.

Our imaginations sometimes fool us. We had pictured Fairbanks as being a rather large semi/metropolitan city and Anchorage a sprawling frontier town. As it turned out we might have been more correct if we'd just switched the two descriptions. We visited Fairbanks over the Independence Day weekend and, after watching the ceremonies of the 49-star flag being raised for the first time at Ladd Airforce Base, we joined three carloads of square dancers for a trek up the graveled Steese Highway to Circle Hot Springs and Circle City, only a stone's throw from the Arctic Circle. What a time we had swimming in the hot mineral water pool and then square dancing in the lodge.

The dancing here was much like what we remembered of the first square dancing we'd ever seen, at Kohl's

436

Ranch, in Arizona's Tonto National Forest, quite a number of years ago. Here the youngsters played with their toys or watched along the side lines as their parents joined the one or two squares having a ball with "Birdie and 7" and "She'll be Comin' 'Round the Mountain." Just like at home, the young fry were undoubtedly told by their parents that they'd have to go to bed when it got dark. The only problem, up there it just doesn't get dark in the summer. We stopped dancing at 11 p.m. long enough to go outside and take some color movies. At 2 A.M. it was as bright as it would be at 2:00 in the afternoon.

In recent years there may have been many hundreds of tours, cruises and cruise/tours of square dancers heading to virtually every corner of the globe, but back in the late 1950's it was a different story.

Following WWII folks wanted to get out and see the world and tourist ventures became more and more common. Realizing the dollar advantage in group travel, agents began organizing tours to Europe and the Orient and the concept of traveling with others who shared the same or similar interests, church, fraternal, service organizations, etc. - became intensely popular.

Having gotten our feet wet in local square dance group travel culminating in a successful cruise of 53 square dancers to Hawaii in 1958, we began soon after to plan our first square dance junket to Europe. Remembering the many invitations to bring a group of dancers to Germany, France and England when we visited these countries in 1957, we felt we were ready to take the next step. A persistent stream of letters from the overseas dancers renewing the invitations and encouragement from our local dancers was all that was needed to start planning for our overseas venture in 1961.

We discovered many things. Travel was a specialized field and best handled by experts in the planning of programs of this type. Handling group air and ground arrangements, making deals with hotels, restaurants and special attractions was out of our league, so in a short time we had arranged for the services of a travel wholesaler. This was a specialist who was accustomed to handling large numbers of people traveling together.

Becky and I worked on plans for this project for many months. Believing that planning is half the fun, we sent out bulletins on a regular basis to those who signed up. We covered the historical and geographic descriptions of the cities and countries we would be visiting. We explained about the currency in each country and made suggestions regarding the weather and what to wear. And, by the starting date every one of our 30 square dance travelers was pretty well briefed on what was to happen.

This being the first time of anything quite like this for us, we had to use our imagination in doing the planning. In analyzing the trip once it was over, we realized that we had prepared more than enough. Before our initial overseas venture Becky and I decided that we would have a certain routine when arriving in any new country. One of us would lead the group through customs and the other would take the end making certain that no one strayed, nor that we overlooked any cameras, jackets, hats, or wives. As it turned out, we were perhaps a little too over ambitious.

Experimental European Trip - 1961

[Ed. Note – Bob was planning to guide a European trip in 1962 but in September 1961 he and Becky led a group of 32 dancers on a trial run.]

Gather 'round. As much as I might protest showing home travel movies, you must let me tell you about our safari—our 1961 square dance trip to Europe, that is. In case you haven't heard it before, Becky and I are quite strong advocates of the value of square dancers traveling together and this recent experience has served to underline our feeling even more

Junket to Europe

What a time we had! - 32 of us, all square dancers, all from California. We left Los Angeles via the Polar Route on an SAS jet bound for Copenhagen, Denmark. The trip was a success before it ever started. We'd been planning and talking and dreaming about the three-week junket for almost a year and as we left Los Angeles it seemed like just a continuation of an experience that had already given all of us so much pleasure.

On the arrival in Denmark, the first stop in our first visit to Europe, Becky was to gather the troops behind her and, single file, head off toward immigration and customs, while I, feeling that my job might be the most demanding, would be the last in line. Becky took the point and the "troops" having utmost confidence in her, followed closely behind.

Telling it as Becky recounted afterwards: "I led the group up to this shack where a man was sitting behind a counter. I was quite impressed when he reached his hand out (not knowing that he really wanted to see my passport). I

439

shook his hand (thinking this was a real nice greeting) and said, 'Good morning, sir. There are 32 of us.' A bit nonplused, I imagine, the man gave up on that and asked, 'cigarettes?' 'I don't smoke,' I told him. Not yet completely fazed, he then asked, 'liquor?' Admiring his friendliness, I smiled and said, 'I don't drink.' Then, as I remember it, the official just let us all through."

Copenhagen home of Hans Christian Anderson, the Little Mermaid statue, Tivoli Gardens; an impromptu square dance in a little tearoom on the rain and wind blown shores of the North Sea. Then on to Norway. Smorgasbord for breakfast, bright knitted woolen sweaters for almost everyone in the crew, three memorable days by boat and bus along the fjords, Bergen to Oslo.

Dancing? We were all dancers. Many of us danced at home from two to five nights each week, but this was our opportunity to see the world and to enjoy it even more because we could share it with a group of square dancing friends. But there were some unusual square dance occasions. With the cold wind coming down from the glaciers, those of us enjoying the beauty of the fjords found there was no better way to keep warm than by breaking out a fast paced bit of dancing on the deck of our steamer. Then, once, while being entertained by a group of Norwegian musicians and dancers in a small folk village, we had the double pleasure of dancing their dances with them, following that we included members of their group in a brief but enjoyable tip of American Square Dancing. The old gentleman playing the Hardanger violin spoke no English but came out with enough of Rakes of Mallow to give us a lot of fun.

Then we went by jet from Norway to England. We spent some time renewing acquaintance with members of the British square dance group and we began making rather elaborate plans for the junket next year. One of the delights of our entire trip was a surprise invitation into a lovely English country home where all of us were treated to afternoon tea and where we tried our best to say thank you and answer our host's request to see what American Square Dancing is like. Unthinkable, perhaps, by good old English standards, we managed to get the cook, the maid, our bus driver and the mistress of the household all in the same circle mixer. Unusual to say the least but heartily satisfying and long to be remembered by us all.

Over the Channel to France - with the Palace of Versailles, Paris at our feet from the top of the Eiffel Tower, the colorful artists of Montmartre, the Seine winding its lazy but captivating pattern, the chestnut trees heavy with fruit, escargots to be tasted and French nightlife to be enjoyed — who had time for square dancing?

However there was one episode in Paris that bears retelling. The group was hopelessly lost. The street signs made little sense and the old fable that everyone in France spoke English was a bit exaggerated. Anyway, about this time, all eyes on Becky. "Don't worry," she said, or words to that effect, "Let me take care of it." About that time they spotted a policeman. Not sure what she was doing but undaunted by the challenge, Becky strode up to him, and in her best school French, caught his attention, held out a card with the name of the hotel, and clearly as her admiring followers watched (and listened) said, "Monsieur?" He turned to face her as she inquired, "Voulez-vous…avec moi?" Smiling broadly, as only an official of the Paris police might do, he said in perfect English, "Madame - it is but two blocks away - just turn left at next corner and you can't miss it." To the sixteen or twenty with Becky during the adventure, Becky was their most competent leader; not realizing, of course, she had asked the friendly gendarme if he would go ice skating with her.

The Rhine River in Germany could never have been lovelier. It was almost impossible to see all the castles as we looked from one bank of the river to the other. Here, as before, members of our group had occasion to make good friends of folks native to the country. We sang with them on the boat; we sang with them in the Hofbrauhaus in Munich; we shared a picnic with them in the Bavarian Alps and we danced with them whenever we had the opportunity. How could we ever equal such happenings?

A most fitting climax to the tour was the big square dance, the Seventh Annual Roundup of the European Association of American Square Dance Clubs held in Bad Kreuznach, Germany. All of us enjoyed mixing into the squares so that we could be with as many of the overseas dancers as possible.

Interesting to note as the trip neared its completion was the fact that for every spot visited there were those among the group who said, "That was our favorite country. That is the place to which we would most like to return."

Now comes the fun of thinking back, of reliving these experiences that happened so fast that we could only store them away until we had a more leisurely opportunity to take them out and think them over. There is no doubt that, had just Becky and I made the trip alone, we would have enjoyed the experience, seeing the wondrous lands, meeting new friends, and eating delicious and unknown foods. However with 32 sets of eyes, almost as many diaries and 27 cameras I feel that the greatest pleasure will come in sharing and reliving this square dance junket together for many years to come.

European Trip - 1962

Nineteen-sixty-one passed, and we were involved in our second (not experimental) square dance tour to Europe. A group of 90 square dancers from twelve states and Canada took off by jet from the United States and flew to England to begin a 24-day trek through Europe. With Becky and me serving in a leadership capacity, were Jay and Helen Orem of our Sets in Order staff and Bob and Roberta Van Antwerp.

We began in England, and since we had learned from previous tours that it was best to rely on professionals, we planned a dance in cooperation with Tommy Cavanaugh, one of Britain's finest. We had asked Tommy to invite the British square dancers to join us and instructed him to hire a suitable hall and put on whatever touches might add to the pleasure of the evening.

The big night arrived. Our dancers, coming down for dinner in the hotel dressed in the finest square dance attire, caused quite a bit of comment as they moved through the lobby. Dinner completed, the evening of surprises started when, instead of the regular coaches usually used for such occasions, our dancers found two giant, double-decker busses, ready and waiting to take them to the dance. Arriving at Victoria Hall (which turned out to be one of the most plush dance places in all of London), the busses were met by English lackeys (substitute "footman" for "lackey"), knee breeches, buckled shoes, purple waistcoats, and (get this) powdered wigs. Arriving at the giant doors of the hall a second lackey opened them and our people passed through a large marbled mezzanine to a second set of doors opened by yet a third lackey who loudly announced the name of each arriving guest.

"Golly, these Britishers really know how to put on a dance," was the general reaction. To say that the evening was a success would be the understatement of the year. Each round and each brace of squares was announced by one of the costumed footmen (who it turned out were actor friends of Tommy Cavanaugh).

Midway through the evening there was an outstanding exhibition of Morris Dancing, lots of mixing with the British dancers, who it turned out were even more impressed with the goings on than their American counterparts. "Golly (if the English used that word), the colonists really know how to put on a bash!" It wasn't until well into the dance and during the conversation between the English and Americans that most of our people discovered that this was not exactly "normal," and that the English, who took part in regular American Square Dancing on a regular basis, utilized gymnasiums, armories, basements, church halls, etc., just as did their friends from across the Atlantic. Regardless, it was an evening with beautiful chandeliers, gold drapes and hardwood floor, plus perfect sound that was not soon to be forgotten.

Paris in the spring may be wonderful, but Paris in the fall, we have come to agree, is unbeatable. The Eiffel Tower, Arc de Triomphe, Montmartre district, the Seine, Notre Dame, and our trip out into the French countryside to see the Palace of Versailles, formed memories for us that for some I am sure will become the most valued and long lasting. The beautiful thing about traveling with 90 people (who after the first 24 hours seemed to have been lifetime friends) is that even in a city the size of Paris you cannot walk down the main boulevards without bumping into someone, somewhere along the way, that you know. Though Paris was not scheduled as a square dance stop, a good portion of our group accepted the invitation of American square dancers stationed in Paris to dance with the Paris Squares at one of their regular Tuesday night get-togethers. A great time was enjoyed by both guests and hosts.

Among our many lasting recollections of Paris was the scene that greeted us on the day we finally left our hotel and headed for the airport. Thousands of soldiers and gendarmes with machines guns lined the various avenues and it was only by serious talking that we were able to convince some of our people that this was not in our honor, but was rather a safety precaution for French President DeGaulle who passed us on the way.

Then on to Germany where we chartered a Rhine River boat for 90 traveling square dancers. Because we had been told that the capacity of the craft was 180 persons, the night before at a square dance in Heidelberg Castle each of us invited one of the local dancers to be our guest for the cruise. So, there we were on a warm autumn morning, 180 of us waiting for our craft. Imagine, if you can, our amazement when the boat pulled up at the Wiesbaden dock. There had been one small error. The capacity of the boat was not 180. It was 1,800! And there we were for the next five hours, with a German Oompah band playing Deep in the Heart of Texas (the only almost square dance tune they knew), with miles of castles on either bank of the river, and we had one of the grandest almost unplanned, floating square dances you can imagine. That was a first — and only.

It is often most revealing to see square dancing thru the eyes of someone outside the activity. In this case we present a story on square dancing in Heidelberg, Germany, as it looked to a reporter for the Heidelberger *Lokalnachrichten* newspaper, translated from the German. We hope you will find it as delightful reading as we did.

AND LISELOTTE LOOKED AROUND SILENTLY
FORWARD, BACKWARD, ROUND ABOUT
Liselotte of Palatinate and several electors looked
down indignantly from their picture frames on the gay playing
that had taken place to their feet on Sunday evening in the

kings' hall of the Heidelberg castle: American square dance groups from all parts of the Federal Republic, some of them came from the French town Metz, had come together to a folk-dance evening and amused themselves without taking care of the traditional frame of the castle, as their pioneer ancestors had done.

As one stated: the gay liveliness of the American folklore suited the kings' hall magnificently. One has to imagine the picture: tables and chairs have been put to the utmost edge of the dance hall and show a gigantic parquet on which phantastically dressed dancers of both sexes move: men in cowboy costumes, closely worn trousers colored (red or turquoise) or also black shirts, with the typical tie loops; some of them had even brought a pair of cowboy boots from the "Wild West," another one wears a waistcoat made out of brocade, which were formerly worn by the gamblers, the professional players, who went from town to town and played with the cowboys for high profits. We know this already from American pictures. Instead of the pistol bag, however, they wear an essentially more peaceful handkerchief at their belt and they had not brought their large hat with them.

And finally, south to grand, magnificent, marble Italy. Italy left us with a multitude of impressions that only time will allow us to unravel and enjoy to the fullest. Venice — the gondolas and St. Mark's Square with its thousands of pigeons. Then Florence — magnificent home of Michelangelo. Eventually Rome

Rome, we all agreed, was like no other place in the whole world. If you, like us, grew up with an etching of the Roman Forum or the great Colosseum hanging above the sideboard in your dining room, then you would feel strangely at home in this oldest of cities. I still can't get over the feeling of walking through streets and buildings erected more than

2000 years ago or the pleasure we had traveling along the Appian Way or wandering through the ruins of Palatine Hill.

The only square dance we had in Italy was an impromptu affair. A group of Italian students in a bus parked alongside ours managed, in broken English, to ask us what this *balio del quadrato Americano* (their way of saying American Square Dancing) was all about, and it didn't take long to form a couple of squares.

Illustration by Chuck Jones ©SIO/ASDS

Square dancing is indeed the great international language. Wherever we went members of our Junket made friends with the people of that country. We can't help but believe that we also made many friends for America.

In the summer of 1964, after the National Convention in Minnesota, we headed up north through the Great Lakes country and took a week out to serve on the staff of Pairs 'n' Squares, a Canadian square dance camp some 100 miles north of Toronto. The camp itself was beautifully situated on the shores of a lake and it didn't take us long to get to know the wonderful group of Canadians and the proportionately smaller number of U.S. citizens who had enrolled.

Camp commenced officially on July 1, and the Canadians, in exuberant respect to their Nation's Dominion

Day, shook us loose from our dreams quite early with a P.A. system turned loud to march music and strains of "The Maple Leaf Forever."

All during that day we were reminded that this was the big day for the Canadians. And somehow we had the feeling that they were also saying, "We just dare you Yanks to show us up on this one." Two days later on July 3, we'd come to believe that these folks expected us to do something on the Fourth. Little huddles here and there indicated countermoves were ready for anything that we might dream up. Undoubtedly, they would be ready for us from breakfast time on.

We finished the dance at eleven that July 3, had a fine after party and then sat rehashing the day's events with Don and Marie Armstrong of Florida who were with us on the staff. It was inevitable that talk should be directed to plans for the following morning. Certainly there were plans, but nothing out of the ordinary. There'd be a few flags, and perhaps some singing, but actually nothing that our Canadian friends hadn't already anticipated.

By that time it was ten minutes to midnight and the thought came to us all at the same time. Why wait? Why not start the Fourth of July now, in a few minutes, just as the clock told us that the Fourth had arrived?

Out of hiding came a paper sack filled with firecrackers. Aha, we thought, this is going to be the real thing! Next we carried the 56 watt amplifier out to the grass terrace facing the rows of housing units now dark, where the entire student body of the camp was fast asleep. Spreading the Jensen speakers as far away from the set as we could and aiming them directly at the housing units, we started things off exactly at midnight.

We'd thought perhaps that the sound effects record we'd brought would come in handy. Now the wail of a dive

448

bomber with machine guns going full blast was aimed at the dancers. With volume up, we next put on sounds of city traffic and the scream of a siren on a police car. (One or two windows lit up showing that we were beginning to take effect.) Next came the sound of a barking dog. (More lights.) And finally, full volume, the sound effects of a baby crying. (That did it — more than half of the lights were on now — two doors had been opened — and one lady stumbled out looking for her baby who was probably safely tucked in bed at home some fifty or a hundred miles away.)

Now it was time for the Star Spangled Banner. We put the record on and, as we rebels set off firecrackers to emphasize the words of the anthem, our square dancing friend, Ed Moody from New England, in pajamas, with his hair in his eyes like some youngster just pulled out of bed, came staggering out to greet us. His arms were filled with skyrockets and more firecrackers.

In a way, it probably wasn't a nice thing to do. We undoubtedly disappointed our Canadian friends horribly. I imagine more than one of them agreed that some Americans just don't grow up. However, we must admit that smell of punk and the sound of each firecracker going off, did something to us. For a short time we had that feeling we used to get when we clutched that bag of firecrackers in our hand and shot them off one at a time from our curb at home.

We had to leave our own country to get the old feeling back again and, though they seemed a little upset at the time, we can't help but think that our Canadian friends must have understood. And, being good square dancers, probably nodded their heads by way of saying, "There's a nutty streak in all of us!"

A little earlier that summer, in early May, we traveled with seventy-eight square dancers throughout one corner of our world – Asia.

We'd flown more than 6,000 miles from the United States to Tokyo in a matter of hours. We'd visited the major sights of this fabulous capital city of Japan, traveled into the cherry blossom land around Nikko, and had an opportunity to shop in Tokyo's leading department stores. The time was just right for a square dance.

Three large busses painted olive drab with the initials U.S.A. printed on the side of each one picked us up at the entrance of the Imperial Hotel that Tuesday, May 5. We drove through the downtown sections of Tokyo, past parks and industrial districts and through the suburbs, and some forty-five minutes later we pulled up to the Green Park School, for our first square dance of our Orient Junket.

As we crossed the school grounds, we could hear the sounds of a large gathering of dancers. When we stepped into the main gymnasium-type building, we were greeted.by hundreds of square dancers forming a huge double lane that snaked back and forth across the entire length and breadth of the hall. This formed a gauntlet for each of our dancers to walk through as he was greeted personally by the Japanese and Americans who were to be our dancing hosts for the evening. Never have we had a more warm welcome than this. Finally, when the last of our dancers passed through the reception line and the Grand March started, there was hardly an empty spot on the huge floor, so great was the number of dancers.

The dancing ability of the Japanese was amazing. Most of these young people were in their late teens or early twenties. Some did not speak or understand English (any announcements were translated into Japanese) and it will always amaze us how perfectly they followed every call. We gave them no walk-thrus, but soon discovered that they were up to date on anything and everything and were exceptionally smooth and comfortable in their dancing.

When it came to doing the rounds, we were amazed to find that although they had not previously done some of the dances on our list, they would simply follow close behind one of our couples and do the waltz and two-step routines simply by watching and following. Before the evening was over, we had an opportunity to dance to some of their callers and were quite enthused with the ability they demonstrated.

One gets an over whelming feeling of appreciation coupled with amazement and satisfaction when he realizes that he is in an activity that cuts across all language barriers and allows him to feel completely at home even though he may be thousands of miles from his home club area. There is much to tell and so much to remember concerning our American Square Dance Workshop Junket to the Orient.

Together we traveled for ten days through Japan, then flew to Bangkok, Thailand and enjoyed the sights of ancient Siam and modern Thailand. We even had an opportunity to square dance with representatives of the SEATO nations who were gathered in Bangkok to hold meetings on explosive Far East problems. These men and women, some of them sitting on opposite sides of the conference table, left their concerns for a brief time while they square danced with members of our group to Bob Van Antwerp's calling.

From Bangkok, our jet flew us by the way of Kuala Lumpur to Singapore, land of Somerset Maugham and the wonderful old-world luxuries of the Raffles Hotel, and on to Hong Kong. In Hong Kong the majority of our members discovered that prices on cameras, tailored suits, tape recorders, etc., were so low that they kept extremely busy buying things in order to "save money." Hong Kong harbor, the floating cities of junks, a view from a hill across the rice paddies into

Red China, and one fantastic experience after another, made Hong Kong one of the highlights of our square dance junket.

Next came Manila and our trip by hydrofoil to Corregidor where McArthur had his headquarters before he escaped to Australia. He did return. Though it was hot in the Philippines, the huge open air ballroom of the Manila Hotel housed a hundred or more square dancers from many parts of the country. Foremost among our recollections will be the appearance of the famed Baranggay dancers who put on a performance of Philippine dances in our honor.

Our stopover in Hawaii meant we were almost home. A banquet and square dance with members of all the clubs in Hawaii at the elegant Meeting House of the Princess Kaiulani Hotel was the happy conclusion to our tour of the Far East.

In 1966 we were off to Europe again. To say that the seventy-six of us who left the States on June 2 had a wonderful time would be a gross understatement. First, it was Portugal with its magnificent coastline. Its windmills and its unique form of bull fighting. They don't kill the bull but eight completely unarmed and unpadded "football players" come into the ring and attempt to wrestle the bull to its knees.

A highlight, of course, would be our visit to Spain and our unforgettable Moron Air Force Base dancing with 150 square dancers coming from all parts of Spain. Here, once again, we had an opportunity to see firsthand just how much square dancing means to these people overseas.

Athens with its Acropolis just a short distance from our hotel, and a cruise through the clear, blue waters of the Aegean, stopping at the legendary Greek Islands and Istanbul, supplies us with memories enough for several lifetimes. At one stop we found a most unlikely place for a square

452

dance. The floor was a bit uneven (rough might be a better description), and the area showed very few signs of having been swept up or cared for. That was the least of the problems however, as the acoustics were good and there was plenty of room. That was most important!

The setting was the centuries old Greek ruins at Efesos on the Turkish mainland and as we stood in the stage section of the ancient amphitheater, some bright soul came up with the idea: "Hey, this is a good place for a square dance." It didn't much matter that minutes before folks were complaining of being foot-weary or that centuries ago, John and other apostles had preached on this very spot. It just seemed that this was a proper place and time for a dance.

Among the thousand-and-one unforgettable incidents is the recollection of Bob Van Antwerp electric megaphone in one hand accompanied by music on a small battery-powered record player - as nine squares took part in perhaps the first square dancing ever held on shipboard in the harbor of the island of Rhodes. This was a wonderful trip from beginning to end, and one which makes us repeat again, "square dancers, without a doubt make the best traveling companions!"

Another change of time and place: June 1968. There was something vaguely familiar about the sounds and the action that warm Monday afternoon. But if it was square dancing, it was unlike anything we'd seen or heard before. "Heads pass thru, separate, go round one. Into the center, star thru, pass thru..."Bob Van Antwerp was doing the calling. He was standing (in walking shorts) and calling through cupped hands so the dancers could hear. He seemed "less at home" than at one of his regular club dances in California.

The place was Nakamakama Village on the banks of the river bearing the same name, just an hour's drive from Suva, the capital city of the British Island of Fiji. This was but one of the "memories" that 66 of us have brought home after a remarkable tour covering Tahiti, Fiji, Australia and New Zealand. As in our other "see-the-world with square dancers" experiences, we square danced only on a few occasions, but these were memorable ones indeed.

Take the dance in the native Fijian village, for instance. We had been treated to the songs and dances of the young warriors and the belles. We had sat with them on the floor in the large thatched roof meeting house and enjoyed the feast spread before us. When they asked us to dance for them we had no time to worry that we weren't costumed correctly, that the grass matted floor might be less smooth than hardwood, or that there was no sound system.

Perhaps you've noticed that in a pinch it's not impossible to improvise some rather passable square dancing under almost any conditions. In this case the local musicians seemed only too willing to take part, and it was surprising how quickly hollow bamboo poles pounded against the ground, wooden sticks hit against each other, and a few miscellaneous musical instruments could turn out chords and phrases which accompanied our dancing.

Following a brief demonstration the locals expressed their desire to give American-style square dancing a try. We doubt if we ever again will see such an exhibition. Young girls in their traditional costumes who a few moments ago were showing us the intricacies of the ancient "Canoe" dance now giggled their way into our squares. An old chieftan, almost toothless, and bare from the waist up and "dressed" in a bright red lava lava, took number four spot in one of the groups.

If you ask us what we enjoyed the most during our several weeks in the South Pacific, we'd have to say in all honesty that we enjoyed it all. From the standpoint of square dancing it was a great pleasure to meet so many of the square dancers both in Australia and New Zealand.

Our first meeting with our Australian counterparts took place when a large contingent greeted us at Sydney Airport. The square dance in Sydney was nothing less than fantastic with dancers coming from areas as far as several hundred miles away. We had an opportunity to dance to many of Australia's fine callers and to share squares with some of the friendliest folks you'd ever want to meet.

The style of dancing in Australia differs a bit from that which is considered "standard" in other places. The Promenade is in skater's position, and Allemande Left is done with the hands held up. In a Box the Gnat both the man and lady turn under in a dishrag-type of movement, and the figure "All Around Your Left Hand Lady, See Saw your Pretty Little Taw" is done just in reverse with the men passing to the inside, left shoulder to left shoulder around his corner and then again on the inside, right shoulder to right shoulder around his partner, a variation attributed to the first trip to Australia made by Joe and Claire Lewis in the early 1950's and reminiscent of a style of dancing enjoyed in Dallas, Texas at that time.

Never to be forgotten was a "barbecue tea" given for the 66 American square dancers in the Melbourne home of Ron and Ella Whyte. Such hospitality! And if you wonder about the significance of a "barbecue tea" you'll be pleased to know that it involves big thick juicy steaks and sausages, a half dozen varieties of salads and a spread of delicious food that almost defies description. This, topped off with a square dance in the 12-square "playroom" of the Whyte home, made this just one more unforgettable evening.

Our "big dance" in Melbourne was fun for all of us with more than 300 area dancers taking part. The climax was the playing of the Star Spangled Banner and then the singing by everyone present of Auld Lang Syne as the Americans made their way out of the hall to the waiting buses.

The final square dancing on the trip was held on a Saturday evening in Christchurch, New Zealand. Art and Blanche Shepherd along with many square dancers and callers from New Zealand's South Island took part. The mayor who started off the festivities said that he felt square dancers "made the best possible ambassadors" and wished us all a happy evening of dancing.

There was just no one phase of this South Pacific Holiday that overshadowed any of the others. Perhaps of all the events we most enjoyed the opportunity of meeting these people from other countries who share the same enthusiasm for square dancing that we enjoy. Square dancers are indeed a dedicated lot wherever you may find them.

Early in 1981, I was invited by the Government of India to be that country's guest at its cultural pageant and Republic Day celebration, being held in the capital city of Delhi. On January 22, after a connecting flight from Los Angeles, I boarded an Air India 747 out of New York on a flight that would eventually take me through 13 time zones, more than halfway around the world. The purpose of my visit was to observe some of India's folk dances and to sample some of the many faces of India.

The trip lasted a week but in that short period of time, I saw much of the old and new sections of Delhi, visited the Taj Mahal in Agra and paid a very informative visit to Bombay. In so short a time, one sees only a small part of such a large country.

456

If you were to take a typical, old-fashioned American Fourth of July celebration, mix it with the crowds at the annual homecoming football game and toss in a bit of the Pasadena New Year's Day Tournament of Roses' Parade, you would get a fair idea of the size, scope and excitement of Republic Day in India. The focal point of the celebration took place down the main street of Delhi. This was the grand parade, led by Prime Minister, Mrs. Indira Gandhi.

At the start helicopters flew over the parade route showering the more than a million spectators with rose petals. Next came a lone helicopter dressed up like a gigantic elephant, trunk, tusk and all, lumbering from one side to the other. It delighted the young as well as those of us who had never seen a costumed helicopter before. Then the parade began in earnest.

A dozen giant elephants, real ones this time, led the procession. Next was a display of military might (mostly Russian equipment) and marching units from all of India's varied military divisions. Then came the unusual: a file of some two dozen flag bearers, waving brightly colored banners, led the contingent of folk dancers. They came from 13 of India's states, each unit breathtakingly costumed in the native garb of its area. The dancing units, some of them numbering more than one hundred, would move fifty yards or so, then, while the parade stopped briefly, they would each perform a small portion of their regional dance and then move on. Accompanied by drums and a varied assortment of pipes and horns many of the dancers sang as they performed.

One unit of men from the shepherd communities of Southern Orissa came down the parade route on stilts, dancing to the accompaniment of instruments known as the Dhol and the Mohure, while a drummer sang as he beat his drum. A few of the dance groups were on floats accompanied by fairly large musical ensembles. All the dancers seemed to be

457

enjoying themselves and the crowds stacked up along the curbs reacted spontaneously to their performances.

Once the parade was over, I spoke with the cultural minister of the country. As he started talking about the folk dances of India, it was easy to see that he was launched on one of his favorite topics. "The dances from each of our regions are essentially distinct and different from each other," he said. He told about the natives of one community, whose unique folk dance is done to the accompaniment of a waterfall. Their footwork is a gliding step that interprets the falling water and the rhythm is that of the water hitting the rocks at the base of the falls.

Another special form of dance is done by the tribesmen in a northern section of the country. As it was described, the males of the community would occasionally have a night on the town. Then, after tearing things up a bit, they would wander boisterously back to their own community. Not yet ready to call it a night, someone would suggest a bit of dancing. The more prudent, aware that the authorities might be looking for them to curb their rowdyism, would caution the group to be quiet. Each time one of the members would start to speak loudly or let out a cry, others would go "shh." This would be repeated over and over, shh, shh, shh. As the dance moved on in virtual silence, but not without enthusiasm, the shh, shh, shh, shh, shh rhythm would increase in tempo, though not in volume, and this shhing sound became the accompaniment of the dance.

One night we saw samples of folk dances from some of these tribal societies at the Republic Day Folk Dance Festival. Presented in a large arena, dance groups from 13 states put on a strikingly colorful pageant with each unit unique in its costume, music and dance. Many of the dances featured men only and as folk dances are intended to do, they told stories of battles and wild game hunts and imitated the skills of farm folk and village dwellers. Spears and shields from one of India's states reminded us of African tribal dances. In one number the male dancers attacked each other with sticks, setting up a rhythm that increased as the dance went on, not totally unlike the Morris dancers we enjoyed in England.

Equally as important as the choreography and the dancing were the costumes. And here the Indian performers shone — bright colors, subtle colors, animal skins and bird feathers. Amazingly beautiful!

We must admit that not all of our trips were to the far corners of the earth – some of the best were day trips, and did not even involve square dancing. One was a journey on the Southern Pacific to the desert in California to see the a-mazing colors of the spring wildflowers. Encouraged by the success of that train trip the Rip 'n' Snorts took the train to Cheyenne, Wyoming – in the winter! Having traveled to-gether by bus, by train, it was time to try out RIPs' sea legs. Chartering a boat out of one of the harbor cities near Santa Barbara, RIP turned out early one Saturday morning, boarded a craft and ventured to "capture" (cruise?) an island. Boarding small boats, the whole contingent made the voyage out to one of the Channel Islands. Setting ashore, club mem-bers with the Rip n' Snort flag in hand, proclaimed the island belonged to the land of RIP.

Just a short way up the coast from Los Angeles is the beautiful, historic city of Santa Barbara. RIPs built close ties with members of the Fairs 'n' Squares square dance club of Santa Barbara. RIP members would become close friends with the Santa Barbarians, and either coming or going to Asilomar, they made a number of bus and private car side trips to Santa Barbara to dance to the calling of Bruce John-son.

Several times over the years RIP members set out by bus to visit the sites and activities of San Diego. Again, great opportunities for close association with fellow members and great fun. But after a trip to the world-renowned San Diego Zoo we wondered who was on which side of the fences and cages.

We have always felt that for a square dance club to be really strong, the members must bond in friendship with each other, and what better way than sharing a fun day or weekend or week traveling together. The shared experiences and time over meals made our club extend beyond the dance floor.

In recent years the role of the traveling caller has been played up as a rather glamorous phase of the square dance activity. This has not always been the case. Our recollections go back to the time when contemporary square dancing was new in most areas and where often as not someone would forget to come and open the hall for the visiting caller or, as on one occasion, the hall was already booked for a women's club meeting. We recall the time when a member came to open the hall and turn on the lights. Then he left with the cheerful words that only guests would be present. The members would be off somewhere attending another dance.

Every traveling caller is loaded with stories of experiences while on the road. His job is not necessarily an easy or predictable one. The person who travels from one city to the next calling his 2 to 3 hour program and then moving on to the next city is often touted as a "star" in the giant theater of square dancing. And there is good reason for this. Those sponsoring the visitor are faced with heavy expenses, costs of the hall, printing of tickets, etc. and only by all intentional effort to attract the dancing public will the expenses be met.

The local caller calling for the same home clubs week after week has an equally challenging job, but, because he is established in the community he seldom gets the "star" treatment. Let him get out on the road, however, and call for clubs five or six hundred miles from home and overnight he too becomes a "star."

Travel calling is not an easy life, and while it has its glamorous aspects, it is also a case of living out of a suitcase, of driving sometimes 8, 10 or 12 hours in order to make the next engagement.

And so, we salute the traveling callers.

Chapter 18. Prelude

"I don't know what you mean by 'glory,' Alice said.

> *Humpty Dumpty smiled contemptuously. "Of course you don't—'till I tell you. I mean, 'There's a nice knock-down argument for you.' "*

"But glory doesn't mean 'a nice knock-down argument, " Alice objected.

> *"When I use a word," Humpty Dumpty said in a rather scornful tone, "it means just what I choose it to mean-neither more nor less."*

"The question is," said Alice, "whether you can make words mean so many different things."

> *"The question is," said Humpty Dumpty, "who is to be master, that's all."*
>
> *-Lewis Carroll, Through the Looking Glass.*

Since the summer two more serious attempts have come to my attention to start a National Association of Square Dancers or of Callers, and I am sorry but both attempts are being made by very good friends of mine. I hope to retain their friendship but I still feel that it will be terribly dangerous for the good of the movement, as do many of our alarmed correspondents, who have written me about it and feel that we must all fight it. But probably someone will soon get such an organization started for the glory and profit of his own city, and for the glory of himself. And there will probably be enough of you, flattered by being asked to represent your state or your community, that will join the thing in order to inflate your own ego and to increase your own prestige.

462

The rest of us must kid the life out of you. If you do, we must be ready to immediately start that super-duper association we have promised, with "every member a President" and dedicated to combating any self-appointed group who tries to destroy all our rich folk variations and to kill square dancing by codifying it as an organization dedicated to "kidding the pants off the pretenders."

I hope you keep yourselves free, so you can join the jolly fellowship and the laughter of the other free folk who refuse to fall for, or to recognize any such organization.

-Lloyd Shaw to his 1947 Caller's Class

It has often been feared that standardization will retard development and cramp initiative in design. Standards should, however, always represent, and often do represent, the best known way of getting something done, and should be used until a better way has been developed. When this has been done, the standard should be changed appropriately. Standards should not be static but progressive in character. - If a progressive policy is adopted towards standardization, there need never be any fear of retarding the development of new ideas, and the many advantages of standardization can be enjoyed to the full. It is hoped that leaders in the standards field will fully evaluate the potential of this method.

-Bob Osgood

The three quotations above seem to be in total conflict with each other. The first one from Humpty Dumpty describes what was going on in square dancing in the late 1940s. The activity was a free for all; every caller had his favorite list of calls, and some of the names were identical to

463

what other callers used, but the figures were completely different. Or a dance may have 4 or 5 different names but still be an old, familiar classic. The second was Lloyd Shaw's warning about square dancing becoming so over-organized that we lose the folk tradition and democracy of square dancing. And the third refers to standards that are used to assure product quality. There was also the complication of callers who chose to do their own programs specifically so dancers he taught could not dance anywhere else.

Caller's associations, such as the Callers Pow-Wow were formed to train new callers in the basics of timing and choreography and how to teach new dancers, etc. The Callers Pow-Wow became so popular that it became the Southern California Callers Association. SCCA existed to educate all callers on topics from new choreography to how to use a microphone. But what really made SCCA grow was selling liability insurance at a low cost – something that no other agency at the time could provide.

But, as mentioned above, there were some callers who were intent on promoting themselves and not to promoting square dancing. SCCA adopted a code of ethics in 1949 (see Chapter 7) in an attempt to get callers to have professional standards.

The major push was to keep square dancing fun and to have callers be concerned with the square dance image. Only item eight in the code (nomenclature) dealt with the technique of calling, but soon it dominated the dialogue. Having the same name for specific movements drew everyone's attention and used up a lot of time and energy. SCCA, hoping to make square dancing simpler and available to everyone no matter their address, came up with a list of dances and figures that were in common use.

1951 SoCal Callers Basics

Every square dance contains one or more movements which require little or no teaching. These movements are listed below and for convenience and reference are called Group A.

Group A
1. Honors right and left (Bow to partner and corner)
2. Circle left and right
3. Right and left turns (facing)
4. Twirl

Basics

These next movements require more teaching than those listed above. These are grouped below as Fundamental and Basic Figures. These figures were the building blocks of square dancing. They are all calls that could not be cued in English in the time allotted.

1. Allemande left or right
2. Grand right and left, half or all the way around
3. Promenade by two or in single file
4. Swings: (a) walk-around, (b) buzz, (c) two-hand
5. Do-Sa-Do, All Around, See-Saw
6. Do-Si-Do, also Mountain style
7. Ladies Chain, two, three, four, Grand Chain
8. Right and Left thru, and pass Right Thru
9. Do-Pas-o
10. Star by the Right or Left, 2, 4, 6, 8; Star Promenade

Additional movements which comprise the complete square dance and all beginning groups should know are grouped as Beginning Breaks. These movements teach the fundamentals indicated by the numerals to the right.

Beginning Breaks:
1. Turn back Group A, 1, 2, 3, 4
2. Once and a half A, 1, 3, 4

3. Double Elbow A, 1, 4
4. Allemande Left Just One A, 1, 3, 4
5. All Around Left Hand Lady & See Saw A, 4, 5;
   and a number of others

Basic Dances
Square Dances in which the fundamental and Basic Figures
are used are listed below.

Arkansas Traveler	Bird in the Cage (7 Hands)
Dive for the Oyster	Figure Eight
Irish Washer Woman	Lady Half -Way 'Round
Oh,-Johnny	Again
Pistol Packin' Mama	Pop Goes the Weasel
Roll the Barrel	Solomon Levi
Lady 'Round Lady,	Forward Six & Back Blunder
Gent 'Round Gent	

Since the list goes on for several pages, adding more individual and complex figures and dances by name, it is hard to believe that the goal of the committee was to simplify square dancing. These lists all deal with choreography, which is undoubtedly important, but Association lists left out what Lloyd Shaw saw as the most important elements of calling: Clarity, Rhythm, and Command.

We were told for many years that these techniques were the prime essentials for any square dance caller. Just think about these three for a minute. If a caller does not possess Clarity he simply cannot be understood. Without a sense of Rhythm, the caller's delivery grates on one's nerves making it difficult, if not impossible, to move to the music. And, Command. Without the ability to differentiate between the all-important directional commands and the frills of non-essential (though colorful) bits of patter, the caller is simply not in control. Dr. Shaw knew that the techniques of calling could never be supplanted by choreography.

Since the early 1950s a grocery list of factors worked together to force the creation of a national association. One of these factors was our belief that people who stood out from the ordinary in terms of service to square dancing should be recognized. In March 1956 we announced the beginning of the SILVER SPUR award. Another way that we recognized merit was printing articles on all aspects of square dancing with the author's by-line. We also highlighted callers who had written some especially well done choreography or who had attained a level of fame in their section of the country. In 1961 we featured some of these callers on the cover of Sets in Order Magazine with oil portraits by the noted artist Gene Anthony. The paintings eventually were hung at the Sets in Order offices (later known as Sets In Order Hall), and the collection of paintings became fondly called the Square Dance Hall of Fame, though at first we did not call it that (in fact it was not until the 1970s that we called it the Hall of Fame.). It seemed appropriate that since Lloyd Shaw was the first one honored with a Silver Spur that a portrait of his wife, Dorothy Stott Shaw, should be the first to grace the cover.

Each month during 1961 another caller appeared on the cover of SIO. Each of them had been nominated by a member of the Sets in Order/American Square Dance Society. Over the following decades a number of outstanding individuals were added to the list. Anyone looking at these names would recognize them as representing the ultimate composite of square dance leadership of the time. Any single one of these men might not alone be able to capture the respect of all callers, but, with all Hall of Famers working together, they presented a "body of knowledge" that a great percentage of callers could respect and follow. Their backgrounds and accomplishments formed an impressive foundation for square dance caller/leadership.

In the summer of 1961 square dance leaders of the day recognized the need to establish a means of preserving and promulgating square dancing and passing on the leadership principles of some of the old timers like 'Pappy' Shaw, Jimmy Clossin, Herb Greggerson and others. It was then that Ed and Dru Gilmore, Don and Marie Armstrong, Jim and Ginny Brooks, Frank and Barbara Lane, Bruce and Shirley Johnson, and Bob and Becky Osgood met in the mountains of Colorado to discuss forming a callers' federation for that purpose. The seed for CALLERLAB was planted then and was nurtured during the decade of the 1960s through informal meetings, opinion gathering, and various expressions of concern for the direction square dancing was taking. Sets in Order provided the friendly umbrella for these activities and, in the 1960s, established a group to provide a foundation of credibility for the proposed callers' federation.

In 1963, Arnie Kronenberger and I set up a Southern California caller leadership breakfast meeting. We wanted to see the callers' reaction to a moderately dressed up session - business suits and ties and the ladies in go-to-church get up. We arranged to have as our speaker a Carnegie lecturer, with the subject - leadership. The session was held in the down town Los Angeles Athletic Club. The message was that calling and square dancing was a respected business and we were respected business men and women. This was another step away from the old barn dance image.

These trial conferences must have had their counterparts in other areas in North America because the feed-back encouraging more of the same was extremely encouraging. Reports on the various sessions were carried in the square dance press. In 1970 we estimated there were close to 6 million active square dancers and perhaps somewhere between 4,000 and 5,000 callers world-wide, and that number included only callers who had joined a local association.

The guiding lights of the activity had pretty much eradicated the view that square dancing was done in barns (with the jug on the floor nearby). It was no longer considered a "hick" activity, particularly so by those who were involved in it. Some of the festivals and weekend sessions were being held in fine hotels: Ed Gilmore, Bruce Johnson and others held a 3-day dancer conclave in the famous Mission Inn in Riverside, California. Al Brundage and others utilized the hotel at West Point. A memorable three days of dancing took over Lovett Hall, originally constructed for this purpose by Henry Ford. You could expect to square dance in some of the finest clubs, hotels and convention centers, a long way from the old proverbial barn. Square dancing had reached a high plateau, was done by the finest of people (everyone), and was treated as an activity of quality, while still retaining the basic elements of providing friendliness and sociability.

In 1964, I gathered a group of local Los Angeles area callers (Ed Gilmore, Bob Van Antwerp, Arnie Kronenberger, Bob Ruff, Lee Helsel, etc.), and we laid out a plan for a several day callers seminar. Taking the idea to the directors of UCLA's Extension Department, we found a ready group of faculty members who seemed excited to work with us on a proposed 3-day program. They suggested that the imminent lecturer and producer Eva Schindler-Rainman work with a faculty of experienced caller/leaders. The session would be open to fifty callers and their partners and one square dancer (owner at one time of Kirkwood Lodge).

The UCLA conference went very well. Dr. Schindler-Rainman led off by saying, "Successful leadership depends in part on helping group members achieve their goal...a leader who connects with the group, helping them to achieve their goals and their desires and their needs is one who is much more likely to be successful."

This was to be the first of a series of hoped for conferences dedicated to developing stronger leadership and an awareness of the principles of teaching. The two-day meeting attracted participants from many sections of the United States, including the East Coast, the Midwestern States, the Pacific Coast area, and Canada.

Dr. Alma Hawkins, Chairman of the Department of Dance at the University, addressed the group in the initial session. Her topic, "Dance, Today and Tomorrow." At one point in her speech, Dr. Hawkins said, "I sincerely believe that if square dancing is guided wisely that it can be one of the very important avenues through which the individual can renew his sense of wholeness, find a satisfaction, and help to live a more fruitful life."

Following Dr. Hawkins, Caller Bob Van Antwerp of the Long Beach Recreation Department tied the remarks of the speaker closely to the current square dance picture. Following him and interspersed with the talks made by Dr. Rainman, were short talks by members of the Caller Advsory Committee, made up of Ed Gilmore, Lee Helsel, Bruce Johnson, Arnie Kronenberger, Bob Osgood, Bob Page and Bob Ruff.

In 1965 we followed up on the UCLA conference by holding the University Leadership Conferences for Square Dance Callers on the campuses of Southern Methodist University (SMU) Dallas, Texas, and University of California, Los Angeles (UCLA) Westwood, California. The agenda for these two meetings was again to focus on leadership.

How much do you know about leadership? How much do you know about teaching? These are fields which, up until recently, received little or no attention in the training of callers. Today, however, to be successful, a caller must be a leader. He must be sensitive to the needs of the people he works with and he must concern himself with the basic requirements of being a teacher.

The two university conferences had these three fundamental objectives :

1. To increase the skill of the square dance caller as a teacher and leader.

2. To provide the caller with some insight into his relationship as teacher to the group.

3. To expose the caller to ideas, techniques and methods of adult learning.

When neither of these conferences attracted a large audience, we let our attention on training callers in leadership skills shift to what many callers perceived as a more pressing issue.

A letter from Wayne Foster of Glen Oaks, Michigan summarized the subject.

Dear Editor:

I hope I'm not a voice crying in the wilderness of call-patterns when I say, meekly, Can't help but wish we had more directional calls:

If the caller tells me what to do and gives me sufficient time to do it, I feel I can cope with about any of the figures. However, my day-job is a demanding one and when I go out in the evening I don't want to have to memorize routines incorporating the basic figures. It's just too much work.

My wife and I like square dancing immensely — have been at it for the past 5 years—but— well, like I say, I

*wish they'd tell me just what to do and then give me time
to do it.   Signed...*

Wayne Foster pointed out the burden of learning all
of the new patterns that were being written and expressed a
wish for a simpler method of dancing. The new trend of hash
calling versus memorized patterns was putting pressure on
everyone to change. Our focus now became choreography
and how it affected the individual caller and square dancing
in general. I recall that in those early days if you went to a
square dance for the first time you'd get into the Number
Four spot and by the time the dance progressed to you, you
had already memorized everything that was being done, and
you had a ball.

It seemed to me that a lot of people like Herb Greggerson, Jimmy Clossin, Les Gotcher, and Al Brundage
played a part in the development of the modern method of
teaching and calling. I'm sure that somewhere along the line
Sets in Order, also, had something to do with it, probably
when we started to break down the basics for analysis in the
square dance publication.

I was once asked if I knew when the grid or posting
formation began. The first routine of grid dancing I did was
about 1947. Formerly, we had number one couple go down
the center, split those two, separate, and go around the outside, back to home. Eventually, we got to the place where
more than one couple worked. Instead of just number one
couple going down the center, we had numbers one and three
doing the movement. Thus, instead of one couple splitting
the opposite, both couples had to pass thru. Not only was the
grid born, but other formations as well. We already used circles and lines of three, but with the new choreography callers
invented lines of four (facing in or out), ocean waves, and
two couple boxes. Old standard figures could now be done

from multiple formations, and greater variety and complexity was added to square dancing.

Directional calling, or calling a series of basics rather than a pattern, helped to free callers from memorizing long patterns. The trick was to learn formations and how each of the basics affected the squares. However, the new/old problem of defining calls and agreeing on names for them came roaring back. The only way we could see to deal with the problem was through an association of callers who would agree on terminology, etc.

Nineteen sixty-four was an election year with two widely separated candidates: Lyndon Johnson and Barry Goldwater. They were selected at their respective party conventions which occurred at almost the same time as the National Square Dance Convention in Long Beach. The three conventions provided an opportunity to do some good comparative thinking.

What is different between a political convention and its square dance counterpart? One thing came to mind as we watched the politicians present their platforms—why not a platform for square dancing? We had our hopes and plans for the future; we saw opportunities for this activity that would allow it to grow and be enjoyed by more and more people everywhere. Why not put these thoughts down as a platform?

We began jotting down ideas on odd pieces of paper - backs of envelopes and old paper napkins - thoughts that might fit into a national square dance platform: Just what are our goals for 1964, 1965, and on into the future?

Being daydreamers from away back, it wasn't difficult for us to recall some of the hopes we've had for this activity. If we were to spell them out, perhaps they would appear something like this:

We see a strong square dance movement, in cluding as it should, all of its many elements such as rounds, squares, contras, quadrilles, etc., that go into making up the complete square dance picture.

We see every community, big or small, enjoying a healthy square dance activity. We see the emphasis being placed on the home club, the home club dancer and the home club caller. We see the club as being the hub and center of the square dance activity, with every dancer having an opportunity to "belong."

We see the callers within any given area working closely together, developing their own leadership improvement programs and taking part in regular courses designed to improve their ability as teachers. We see them doing all of this in order that they can learn how to avoid the pitfalls of getting on the microphone untrained and unqualified.

We see square dance associations formed only where definite needs for them exist — and when formed, we see them as efficient, well run, organizations dedicated to the dance, the dancer, and the club. We like to think that the time for associations existing only to perpetuate themselves is at an end.

We see a time when a square dance class is not regulated by a desire to "rush 'em thru"- get 'em out of classes and into clubs. And we see time given in classes where folks can learn the value of friendliness and where they can learn to dance and not just maneuver from one spot to the next with no regard to the music.

And we see classes taking thirty weeks if it takes thirty weeks — or forty weeks — if it takes that long — or a year of class if it means that the dancer will stay with the activity for a good long time and not be a "dropout" after the first exposure to club dancing. Classes that take only ten to twelve weekly three-hour lessons can never hope to develop a strong, friendly, enthusiastic future dancer.

We see a time when the emphasis will be on the quality of dancing and not on the quantity of dances taught; a time when challenge will mean true variety, utilizing all the forms of square dancing. And when moving to music will be enjoyed by all rather than a few.

What about these thoughts? Was it too impossible to think that these things might come to be, not just in one or two areas but in all respects and in all parts of the square dancing world?

Perhaps these would have all remained just unwritten "daydreams" for us had it not been that I was asked to deliver the keynote speech at the National Square Dance Convention in Long Beach. And remembering the two political conventions then in progress, I attempted to see how our day dreams might be presented as a platform for square dancers.

Here, briefly, are seven points I suggested as a starting place for local square dance associations, caller associations, national convention organizations, and others who may wish to use them or adopt them as a pattern in helping to plan for a secure square dancing future.

I. Develop a Caller/Leadership Program: It is essential that those desiring to call have an opportunity to study the art of calling, not only from those proficient in the field but from leaders in other fields of business, as well.

II. Develop a Dancer Awareness Program: A dancer progressing through beginners' class has infinitely more to learn than the simple basic square dance movements. He should be aware of the activity as a whole and most especially of how it affects him and his association with other dancers and with his club.

III. Develop a Dancer Conservation Program: It's not enough to bring a new dancer into the activity. We must learn how to keep him there. A study of the reasons why a person comes into square dancing in the first place and the careful analysis of various reasons why he drops out can be of great help in keeping those dancers an active and happy part of square dancing.

IV. Develop a Product Control Program: The manufacturer of a nationally distributed product makes certain that wherever that product is available it will be of highest quality, for the product in any area reflects back on the product as a whole in all areas. In the case of square dancing, an emphasis on the quality of dancing rather than the quantity of material used, is a step in the right direction.

V. Develop a Public Relations Program: Our public image—the impression we create upon others — is vitally important to our future. There is little we can do to erase a bad impression that others may have concerning the activity. If we produce a good healthy program in every area, we will attract others and create a good impression for our square dancing upon the community as a whole.

VI. Develop a General Cooperation Program: There is a crying need for coordination, cooperation, and understanding among all the various units that play a part in the square dance activity. If the combined efforts of all dancers, callers, associations, manufacturers, and producers of square dance equipment, owners of square dance halls, etc., channeled their efforts in a common direction, square dancing would indeed benefit.

VII. Develop a Sales Program: Throughout the country there is a great untapped potential of folks who have never been introduced to today's form of square dancing.

We needed to look seriously at Item IV. Few businesses can survive without some form of product quality control. One bad bottle of a soft drink can ruin sales in an entire region. Auto manufacturers spend thousands to assure the quality of their products. One lemon can set them back much time and many dollars.

Product control is important in square dancing too. One hundred callers in an area doing a completely satisfactory job can be "hurt" seriously by one caller misrepresenting the activity. Each person picking up a microphone is actually representing square dancing to all the people with whom he comes in contact. The impression he leaves with the people he works with must reflect not only on the activity but on all other serious minded teachers and callers.

One unusual facet of square dancing is that anyone, whether he has ten years of active participation in square dancing behind him or whether he knows little or nothing about the activity, can pick up a microphone, purchase a public address system, advertise for classes and attract people simply by advertising that "square dancing is available."

For years people have been concerned that the responsibility of being a caller can automatically belong to anyone who desires to take it. Those most interested in doing something about this felt that in order to retain respect there should be some standards achieved before a person is to be recognized as a caller

And so it was that for many years those concerned about the future of square dancing felt there should be some criteria, some standards, that would indicate a qualified caller.

Some of the proponents of this idea felt that this should be set up on a national basis with testing and controls put in the hands of a few who would serve as judges. We disagreed with this procedure.

First: The dangers of allowing a few "judges" (selected how or by whom no one knows) to pass on the capability of all square dance callers far outweigh the glories of a certificate which rates an individual as either a master caller or an apprentice caller or something in between. This would take us back to the days of square dance contests when judges declared dancers winners and thus the best square dancers in a given area. These contests literally killed square dancing for many, many people and it took years to revive the activity in some locales.

A caller's ability on timing and phrasing might be able to be judged. However, callers' classes all over the United States have been doing this and, were helping callers to improve. A caller might be graded on how many thousands of calls he has memorized, but what had this proved? A caller might even be tested on his ability to meet a given set of circumstances or tests with a floor filled with dancers, but would this prove his ability to handle ten or twenty or a hundred different sets of circumstances each caller faces continuously when he calls for so many dancers in many different halls and cities?

And how could you possibly rate loyalty, honesty, understanding, and yes, even that unbeatable person-to-person necessity — a sense of humor?

We don't need judges and certificates; we do need communications and of this every worthwhile caller is aware. Communication doesn't come from an individual or an association telling someone what to do. Communication comes from a sharing of ideas; a little of the best from one person added to the best from his neighbor. Each time a group of callers gets together to talk, each time a local callers' association holds a discussion meeting, each time a caller/leader shares his experience personally or via the news media — this communication has a starting place. We would be the last to claim that the square dance world has reached its desired goal in the field of communicating and that there are not miles of room for improvement, but we seriously doubt that judges and certificates are the answer.

Second: We questioned that the problems of local callers can be answered completely on a national basis. True, similar standards might be adapted by groups throughout the world, but standards and problems are two different animals. Standards of values are items that all persons of integrity are willing to accept and try their level best to abide by. Problems generally arise from local sources and are best answered on the local level by local associations familiar with the background.

Almost without exception every callers' association had a set of standards or a code of ethics to which its members subscribe. Those few individual callers not interested in accepting such a code are certainly not going to be interested in accepting a national code. And how in the world can a national association administer a national set of standards or enforce it beyond what the local associations are doing unless it is interested in national controls? Square dancing simply did not fall into such a category!

Third: We readily admitted that square dancing was no longer a baby. It had discarded the fad garments and we, too, were interested and concerned that its future be a healthy, growing one. But we also knew that we can never completely disregard the fact that this hobby is a folk activity, a recreation giving people pleasure through their own response and ability to enjoy what the caller (or the record with calls) has to present.

There must be a sense of pride in the activity, a sense of responsibility to help keep square dancing wholesome and alive, which can be shared by every successful caller. Whether or not a caller has a fancy badge, a license or a certificate that says he is qualified, he must still prove himself among his peers, to the members of his local calling society and to his dancers. There is no other judge. To believe there is a magic reaction simply by joining a national association is pure myth and fantasy.

Almost as soon as the December 1966 issue of Sets in Order began to reach their destinations, we started to get feedback on that month's "As I See It" column (about setting standards in square dancing). From the response, it was soon apparent that what square dancers and callers did not want were national controls. Instead, there seemed to be a great deal of interest in the establishment of guidelines for callers in the form of a code of ethics. It was felt that by leaving the option up to local square dance callers' associations, where they existed, and up to the individual when no associations were available, that a moral responsibility shared by all leaders would have a tremendous advantage at the present time.

It was easy for readers to get the impression that we sat in our offices in Los Angeles and relied only on receiving written material. Nothing could be further from the truth. Everyone at Sets in Order was an avid square dancer, and many of us traveled around the country to attend festivals, conventions, and conferences. For example, in May, 1967, we had an occasion to be at a meeting of representatives of some 70 different square dance clubs and we couldn't help but be agreeably surprised at their serious concern over the "...apparent damage caused by the unrestricted use of new, non-descriptive basics..." We were agreeably surprised because this was a gathering of dancer leaders and these folks seemed dedicated to do something about the situation—now!

Let's take this one step further and actually pin down what they may mean by new material. We feel that they refer

480

to new language. Everyone enjoys variety. Not everyone wants to dance the same old dances all the time—and so the need for variety is not the culprit. It's how this need is interpreted.

Every month there are new singing calls being written and released on records. If the caller uses one of these and if you find it a nice figure to a toe/tapping tune, great! You have your variety.

Suppose that by using just the names of basics you already know, your caller blends three movements into one satisfying composite. If you are able to follow all three, you are flattered. The caller has complimented you by leading you through an extremely difficult combination of maneuvers. You have proved that, because you know where each of these movements starts and stops, you are properly set for each subsequent new call, that you are a competent dancer.

This is challenge — both for the caller and for the dancer. It requires a great deal of ability for a caller to plan ahead those movements that will work in this way. It takes real ability on the part of the dancer not only to listen to each call but to retain it and to execute it properly in time with the music and in the proper sequence in which it is given.

Now, let's suppose that the caller takes these same three standard basic movements and gives them a name. Let's say he calls it "Slipinthegrease." What has he accomplished? For one thing, he's given himself one call to remember rather than three. More significant, however, is the fact that while you (the dancer) could quite ably do each of the three standard basics if called by their familiar titles, now you must commit an entire routine, plus a new term, to memory.

With those movements that are already known as basics, there is unlimited variety in the number of combinations that can be composed. Without adding another new term,

481

there is sufficient ammunition for any inventive composer to work with indefinitely.

There seemed to be no way to control the flood of newly named calls through callers' associations. In some areas they tried by introducing one new "approved" term each month. Other new terms "leaked" in, and a dancer could be faced with the prospect of one new term to memorize each time he goes out to dance.

"Let them dance" is a slogan that should become the motto of every caller. And we're not talking about "Bird in the Cage." We're referring to dancing which can get just as difficult and just as challenging as anyone would want — but not with the artificial challenge that comes from inventing new terms.

The callers to be congratulated are those who can use simple English together with a vocabulary of already existing basics and come up with almost any combination you could hope for. This knack of calling takes practice. It doesn't come easily and not everyone can master it. It is, however, the mark of a professional who can control the movements of a group of dancers without having to invent a new movement with a brand new name which must be memorized before it can be enjoyed.

Somebody once said that square dancing is a paradox because it's the only activity where folks try hard to sell new people on coming in and then invent hurdles to get them to drop out. No phase of square dancing does more to discourage a dancer than the needless addition of new terms. And, bear this in mind, we're not just talking about poor movements— we're referring to all new non-descriptive language which adds one more hurdle for the dancer.

482

Before you can fix something, you really ought to know what it is you are trying to fix. And you should anticipate the consequences of making changes. In other words, you need to know where you are and where you want to go.

To see where square dancing was headed we needed to establish a starting point. I suggested that the square dance activity be theoretically divided into these major areas: (1) The one-night stand or the purely recreational square dance which utilizes plain English which anyone can follow and which can be taught in just a few minutes; (2) A Limited Basics Square Dance Program for the square dancer who wishes to dance regularly but only 3 or 4 times each month and for whom a list of twenty basics would be adequate; (3) A Full Program Utilizing Existing Basics for the enthusiastic dancer who may be able to dance two or more times each week and who will attend a full learner's course and absorb all of the accepted basic movements. Finally, (4) Exploratory Dancing for the person who has an unlimited amount of time and energy to devote to workshops where the experimental movements are tried out.

Of the four categories, number one will reach the greatest number of people. It is possible that it will, at one time or another, touch a good fifty per cent of the population. The second, or limited basics group, will appeal to many people who do not have a place in the program as it is today. The full basics group, represented in the third category, will draw those with the time to devote to several active clubs. The fourth or exploratory group may be of primary interest to callers.

In addition, groups should be set aside for Teaching Square Dancing in the Schools and for Research and Tradition.

Second, I proposed this as a solution to the language problem: Consider adopting a list of basics— and not add to it. Go with this list for a certain period of time and then, if there are changes — old movements to drop, or new ones to add— take the action at the end of that time. And then, hold off on any new language.

In lieu of the constant new language, teach callers how to get variety from the existing basics. Encourage callers' groups, schools and colleges, to sponsor institutes where leaders among the callers teach others how to be resourceful and how to develop calls without having to stoop to the invention of new names. Develop tools to help the callers— books with course outlines—collections of calls that fit each category— and incentives to help encourage all callers to participate. And find a way to instill the need for all of this in the minds of our dancer organizations.

To those who scream, "Lack of progress — you're going to stifle the activity without the new," make this one thing clear. We do need fresh good new material. New singing calls, new patter calls, new rounds will probably always be with us. A great number of the most popular singing call records have been created using the already existing basics. Many of those singing calls would surprise you with their simplicity, and yet their popularity results from the intelligent combining of compatible movements already in existence. We can have all the new, danceable material anyone will need, without resorting to new terms.

That column drew a lot of responses from dancers and callers alike. Several people wrote in asking for our definition of a "Basic" as opposed to a "Gimmick." Here is our often repeated definition of a Basic: A necessary movement with a short clear call that cannot otherwise be given descriptively in the time needed. The call should not be confused with the sound of other calls. The movement itself should not be one that could he called just as well with existing Basics. The movement should be smooth-flowing (not erratic or awkward) and should lend itself to rapid teaching. Lastly, to be considered a Basic, a movement must prove its ability to withstand the test of time through continued usage.

A "Gimmick," on the other hand, is a novelty figure or a combination of figures such as the Grand Square, the Grand Prowl, Tea Cup Chain, etc. It's important as a part of variety but usually must be explained before being called. Quite frequently a "Gimmick" cannot be called descriptively in a completely satisfactory manner.

In an attempt to encourage some good solid guidelines, we formed a "gold ribbon committee" made up of leaders of long standing who have proven their marked talents in at least one specialized field. The initial categories that were studied and a partial list of leaders who accepted the committee assignments follows:

One Night Stands: Jerry Helt, Ohio.
A Full Program of Existing Basics: Ed Gilmore,
     California;
Exploratory Dancing: Willard Orlich, Ohio;
Research and Tradition: Dorothy Shaw, Colorado;
Square Dancing in the Schools: Jack Murtha,
     California;.
Recreation: Bob Van Antwerp, California;
Square Dance Publications: Charlie Baldwin,
     Massachusetts;
Dancer Associations : Chet Ferguson, Oklahoma;
Caller Associations: Lee Helsel, California,
Round Dance Leaders Associations: Dorothea
     Brammeier, Florida;
Commercial Square Dance Suppliers: Jay Orem,
     California;

Our next step was to bring about some discussions among the members of this committee. These eventually resulted in a series of suggestions or a "master plan" which we all seriously hoped would help in forming guidelines for square dancing's future.

The Gold Ribbon Project was anything but a hurry-up project. Given the number of people involved and the time it took to share ideas, the report was not ready to publish until September 1969. During much of 1968 and '69 we held our own miniature think tanks, endeavoring to determine what steps to take and if taken, who would we select to help in determining the groundwork and possibly establishing an organization. Input from these earlier sessions, interest stirred up in making the Gold Ribbon report, plus considerable communications from individual callers and callers associations told us that the time was ripe to determine the possible need for a professional establishment of callers. At the speed things seemed to be traveling, it was becoming more and more apparent that a recognized combined voice of caller/leaders could be of great help in planning the future of the activity.

In May, 1969, we asked members of the callers' association committee to give an interim report. If it were possible to summarize the reasons for forming an effective caller/ teacher association, the following might be considered a fairly sensitive statement of purpose:

- To encourage high standards in ability and attitude among the callers and teachers in the area.
- To induce a spirit of cooperation rather than competition among the members.
- To encourage the training of new callers.
- To serve as a public relations force to help project the proper image of square dancing.

- To adopt, along with other similar callers associations, a universal code of ethics.
- To work closely with the individual callers, the clubs and the local dancer associations to perpetuate square dancing.
- To encourage high moral standards, self-control and a continuing desire for improvement.
- And finally, to be prepared to meet the individual needs of the area as they arise.

We did not know what percentage of the existing callers' associations had accomplished the list of "responsibilities." It was a matter of speculation how much of it was actually put into practice. The fact remains that these goals are important. The problem faced by many caller' groups, that of attracting greater participation by the caller/leaders in the area, would possibly best be solved by setting up worthwhile projects for the association and thereby establishing a meaningful purpose for the group. The success of any callers' association seems to be directly related to the active participation of the more successful caller/leaders in the area.

The entire Gold Ribbon Report still makes an excellent study project for current callers' associations wishing to be of even greater value to their members. The Gold Ribbon Committee suggests that the various area associations work together for common goals.

Here are the initial suggestions:

- Instigate a drive to bring every caller into his local square dance association.
- Focus the attention upon "Standardization without Regimentation." The striving for quality in dancing and for a standard style of dancing that will allow dancers to enjoy their

hobby anywhere in the world" has great merit.

- Establish a "Guest Speaker Bureau," a central registry of caller/leadership talent available to area associations for lectures, etc.
- Produce a formula for local "University Leadership Conferences."
- Arrange for an exchange of ideas between existing callers' associations. This could serve an extremely useful purpose

As stated earlier, the responsibility of the callers association is to establish standards of leadership, to plan ahead, to share in the progress and to help develop a strong, healthy attitude among dancers and callers that will lead to a stronger square dancing future.

In 1969, while holding planning sessions with three of these Hall of Famers, Lee Helsel, Arnie Kronenberger, and Bob van Antwerp, the hoped-for meeting was laid out and it was decided that a logical meeting place would be at Asilomar to coincide with the weekend when the annual Sets in Order weekend and week-long vacation institutes would be taking over the grounds.

We knew that if we wanted to get anybody to follow us that we should start out with the top known people in the business. So, we looked at our list of 14 or 15 who were members of the Square Dance Hall of Fame and said okay - here is a group that could start such a thing. So, we set a date and American Square Dance Society paid for everybody who could get to the meeting at Asilomar. We told everybody this was going to be an honors meeting for those people who are in the Hall of Fame so that we could recognize them openly, not just through mail. Well, out of the 14 or 15, whatever it was, 11 came. As Lee Helsel put it, the Hall of Fame callers represented a body of knowledge and that if anything were to develop from it, certainly the names and reputations of this group would attract attention.

"Body of Knowledge" is the keystone of any profession. It must be unique to the field and is the basis on which a profession is formed. The "Unique Body of Knowledge" is that which distinguishes one profession from another and therefore one activity from another. Plans for a meeting of the members of the Hall of Fame were begun in 1970 with a founding committee made up of Lee Helsel, Arnie Kronenberger, Bob Osgood, and Bob Van Antwerp. Summaries from the past ventures were studied and, following a lengthy preparation period, eight major discussion topics regarding the nature and needs of the activity were prepared as a partial charter framework for the potential new organization. These were the topics: (1) Let's put the dance back into square dancing; (2) An accepted form of standardization is vital to the growth and continuation of this activity; (3) Caller/teacher leadership training is the responsibility of the callers and teachers; (4) Professional standards for callers and teachers need to be established and maintained; (5) Today's square dancing is due for a reappraisal; (6) The combination of the various parts of the square dance activity (squares, rounds, circle mixers, quadrilles, contras and related forms) should be encouraged; (7) The selfish exploitation of square dancing should be vigorously discouraged and (8) The over organization of dancer/leader groups can pose a problem to the future progress of the activity.

We had prepared the square dance world for the next step – the formation of a national callers' association.

Chapter 19. The Kick-Off

Invitations were mailed to fifteen members of the Square Dance Hall of Fame to attend a meeting in February 1971, as guests of The Sets in Order/American Square Dance Society, to take part in an "Honors Banquet" and to discuss the "State of the Square Dance Nation." Eleven of the invitees were able to attend: Marshall Flippo, Ed Gilmore, Lee Helsel, Bruce Johnson, Arnie Kronenberger, Frank Lane, Joe Lewis, Bob Osgood, Bob Page, Dave Taylor and Bob Van Antwerp.

The purpose of that initial get together was to objectively discuss the trends of the activity and the role of the caller.

We did not need to have a get acquainted session with this group - they all had known each other for years. But we did start with a session in the afternoon of the first day just to say, "Ya know, while we're here, let's talk about a bunch of things, including the possibility starting a group that might be helpful to the rest of the callers in the world." Those of us who had been working on the plan for the weekend knew that we needed to get the others in the mood for the tough discussions to come, so that first night we had a banquet…and a roast. We had brought all the oil paintings from the Hall of Fame and spread them out in the dining room. Joe Lewis as Master of Ceremonies then led the roast of the members. By the end of that dinner we were a laughing, friendly group that was geared up for anything that might happen. The next morning, we got together and we told the people we had eight or nine points we believed were important to discuss. If the group agreed, we might have reason to form an organization. Each one of the callers was given a copy of these points; and when the meeting concluded, the group enthusiastically and unanimously signed the eight point charter and began planning for the future.

Statement One — Let's Put the Dance Back into Square Dancing. In order to insure a healthy, continuing activity, an emphasis must be placed on quality of dancing, on dance styling, on material used and on comfortable dancing.

Statement Two — An Accepted Form of Standardization is vital to the growth and continuation of this activity. So that dancers may dance anywhere, with anyone, a uniform method of dancing each basic movement should be encouraged.

Statement Three — Caller/Teacher Leadership Training is the responsibility of the Callers and Teachers. A continuous program of leadership training should establish values, implant firm foundations and build leadership.

Statement Four — Professional Standards for Callers and Teachers need to be established and maintained. A caller's character and actions must be professional and in the best interest of the activity as a whole,

Statement Five — Today's Square Dancing is due for a reappraisal. An educational program should be created to provide an activity for the greatest possible number of people.

Statement Six — The combination of the various parts of the square dance activity should be encouraged. Squares, rounds, circle mixers, quadrilles, contras and related forms all contribute to the maximum enjoyment of the activity.

Statement Seven — The selfish exploitation of square dancing should be vigorously discouraged.

491

> Any attempt to misrepresent or exploit square danc-
> ing should be opposed. Square dancing belongs to
> everyone.
>
> **Statement Eight** — The over organization of
> Dancer/Leader Groups can pose a problem to the fu-
> ture progress of the activity. Any organization that
> exists solely to perpetuate itself is of questionable
> value. The dancer, the caller, the clubs are the im-
> portant trio in square dancing.

*CALLERLAB FOUNDERS: Seated: Bob Page,
Marshal Flippo. Standing: Ed Gilmore, Lee Helsel,
Bob Osgood, Arnie Kronenberger, Bruce Johnson, Joe
Lewis, Bob VanAntwerp, Dave Taylor. Frank Lane*

One of the first actions we had to take was to give us
an identity. Arnie Kronenberger, our president *pro tem*,
came up with the name CALLERLAB (always all caps). Arnie explained that it was an association of square dance callers who met to explore, discuss, and make suggestions for
the improvement of square dancing, just as scientists work
in a laboratory. DIRECTION, the official publication of

CALLERLAB, was established at the same time. With Bob Osgood as Executive Secretary - then an unpaid, volunteer position - the organization continued to operate under the benevolent cover of the Sets in Order/American Square Dance Society, with CALLERLAB's home office and staff provided by SIO/ASDS, without cost to CALLERLAB until after a 1974 convention.

During our time at Asilomar we had several short meetings and talked about what the needs were. It was decided that initial growth of the organization would be on a gradual basis. Each person selected for membership would be personally invited to attend one of the meetings and, having attended, would be included as a member.

We held a second meeting in July of that same year. Don Armstrong and Earl Johnston were included as new members at that session. The total membership had now reached thirteen. Meeting number three was held in February, 1972, with Jerry Haag, Jerry Helt, and Jim Mayo present as new members. The fourth meeting was held in July, 1972, when Al Brundage and Manning Smith became members. The total membership had reached eighteen.

We decided at this meeting to increase the size of membership while still retaining the personal invitation method. The February, 1973, meeting included seven new members: Stan Burdick, Cal Golden, CO Guest, Jack Lasry, Johnny LeClair, Melton Luttrell and Bill Peters.

Back in October of 1971, with just two CALLERLAB meetings under our belts, we knew that we had to prepare the square dance community for the ideas that we were proposing. SQUARE DANCING (formerly Sets in Order) published an article that was attributed to the Sets in Order/ American Square Dance Society, the parent of the magazine and the Foundation. One of the ideas was to establish several different square dance programs.

We started promoting CALLERLAB in Sets in Order in March 1971, or at least we started letting the rest of the square dance world know that CALLERLAB existed. In February 1972 CALLERLAB held its third meeting so in November of that year Sets in Order ran a story to pique the interest of callers and dancers.

The article was to let the square dancers and callers know that the formation of CALLERLAB was not a recent event with no history. Everyone could see that some of the best known callers in the country had been working on the idea for a minimum of ten years. We also wanted people to know that we were not some hidden group that was trying to take over square dancing. We showed that membership was growing and that CALLERLAB was opening up membership to the best talent

In the time period of 1971 through 1973 the members worked to define the building blocks that had been signed at the first meeting at Asilomar. The board began the task of organizing the structure of CALLERLAB. Lee Helsel, who worked in the health field, suggested we follow the structure of the American Medical Association: Have a Board of Governors; Require attendance at annual meetings on a regular interval; Have a means of communications between the Board and the members; Have an Executive Secretary whose duties were to carry out the direction of the Board; Establish professional standards (which included methods of disciplining members; the disciplinary code was later modified); Incorporate the organization to provide liability protection for the Board and members and for tax purposes.

Committees were formed at that first meeting at Asilomar, and members were assigned to fourteen working committees. Almost everyone who was invited joined, and the membership grew to 24 by the end of 1973.

With the help of a professional artist, the CALLERLAB logo, DIRECTION newsletter heading, and other artwork was created, approved, and put into use. The legal firm of Paul, Hastings, Janofsky and Walker, prepared by-laws and papers of incorporation for CALLERLAB. The gradual growth, the in-depth planning of goals, and the strength of its leadership propelled CALLERLAB securely into its next big step, a full convention: the groundwork would be tested, its membership would be quadrupled, and the "baby" would be ready to stamp its mark on the future of caller/leadership.

A major concern in square dancing was a lack of an agreed upon list of basics for club dancing. But even more important was finding a way to slow down the bombardment of new undanceable basics. By the end of 1973 the preliminary work of establishing the credibility and structure of CALLERLAB, and looking forward to the first CALLERLAB Convention in the Spring of 1974, we approached one of the most pressing problems in square dancing. We had received countless letters from dancers complaining about the avalanche of new figures. We had set three major topics for the 1974 convention, one of them being "What We Dance." That led to the November 1973 publication of an extensive article on the topic. *[The full article is in Appendix #1 Standardization – ed.]* To increase awareness of what CALLERLAB was working on and to make the issues more immediate and pressing, SIO/ASDS published a number of articles leading up to the first convention. One of the early committees formed was "How We Dance."

As April 8, 1974 approached, there were lumps in the throats of at least twenty-three people (probably 46 counting partners). Would callers really come to a non-dancing, non-calling convention to talk about organizing and about improving square dancing? If they came, what would they expect? Could a large group of callers with large egos really be expected to sit down and agree on various aspects of square dancing? Would they get enough out of the convention that they would come back? That first convention was a real leap in faith-for the calling profession.

The fears were soon laid to rest. They did come to St. Louis and converged upon the Marriott for long sessions and much hard work from April 8th to April 10th. Over 100 callers and 60 partners from 33 states, 2 Canadian Provinces, plus Australia and New Zealand responded to their personal invitations to the first CALLERLAB convention, and they all came prepared to work.

Bob Van Antwerp welcomed all the delegates and then gave me the floor for my Key Note Speech [*see Appendix #4 – Ed.*]

Bob Van, as chairman of the convention, explained where the name came from and what work had been done by whom to prepare for this first annual CALLERLAB Convention. The goal of CALLERLAB was to look at ways to improve square dancing, and in no way were we a union. We all needed to get past our personal problems and focus on the activity as a whole. *[see Appendix #2 for Van Antwerp's opening speech – Ed.]*

He told the delegates that CALLERLAB started with 15 Hall of Fame members who saw that square dancing was being detoured by a lack of standardization and the use of so many non-descriptive calls. Too many callers and clubs were taking individual action that had no widespread effect. Therefore we need a group that represented a body of knowledge. We consciously decided to build the CALLERLAB membership slowly. At first each of the original attendees could invite one more for the next meeting. Finally, in 1973 we allowed members to invite several callers each. The one on one invitation system was our way of selecting the best, and it assured that a sudden influx of too many people would not upset the planning done by the founding members.

When we hit 25 members, we declared them to be the Board of Governors. After much discussion, we selected three goals for this convention:

1. How We Dance: Develop the plans for a caller /teacher basic manual with accurate naming and description of the calls. Also set a base list to work from.

2. What We Dance: Create a committee to review new movements.

3. What Is a Caller: Establish a means for accrediting callers and caller schools.

From 1971 through 1973 the first members of CALLERLAB had worked to identify problems and established committees to address those areas. Initially there were eight statements that the founders agreed to, and since then 7 more have been added.

9. Encourage the club caller system
10. National Square Dance Convention is missing the boat.
11. Identify what CALLERLAB can do to help caller/teachers in the future.
12. Open communications
13. An experimental moves clearing house
14. Fee structure for callers
15. Caller registry – a means to accredit callers.

Bob explained that committees for each of these topics have been formed, and we urged everyone to sign up for a committee. There was a lot of work to be done which would affect approximately 9,000 callers world-wide.

The Convention was organized to deal with three major topic areas in round-robin sessions: "How we dance," "Accreditation," and "New movements." All of the delegates were assigned to one of the three smaller groups. Each group was then presented the themes one after another, while a recorder and three judges monitored the discussion and recorded the vote on their findings. Each group heard the proposal on each of the topics by the same presenter so the in-put would be consistent. Then the floor was open to questions and discussion, after which the judges and the recorder retired to discuss how each group reacted to the presentation. At the end of each presentation, the presenters would rotate to a new group. The convention theme "Working Together" was most appropriate. In spite of some initial misgivings, it was far beyond a doubt that a large group of so-called *prima donna* callers can work together for the common good for the whole calling profession and square dancing. The friendly arguing, give-and-take, compromise, and camaraderie was inspiring and set the tone for all future conventions

Before breaking into the groups, Bob Van Antwerp introduced the Board Members who were also Committee Chairmen and asked each one to make a short report on progress and needs. The reports were also a way to recruit people for each of the committees. *[The Committee Reports are in Appendix #3 – Ed.]*

One of the big hurdles for the newly formed association was the idea of standardization. Each of the callers in attendance had been calling for years and had his own list of figures he liked to use…and in some cases, callers used the same figure but with a different name. To gain acceptance of the idea of standardization, Sets in Order had published a series of three articles on what the word "standardization" did and didn't mean. The recommendations of the Gold Ribbon

Committee from 1969 and the discussions of the founding members helped alleviate the resistance to standardizing the lists. Also, because the Board accepted the Sets in Order basic list as a place to start, there was a solid base for establishing the new lists.

In the years leading up to the first CALLERLAB Convention, square dancing had been overwhelmed by new calls. A caller would invent something – maybe something entirely new, sometimes just a combination of existing calls – give it a name, and send it off to one of the more popular callers' notes services. The editors of the notes did not evaluate the calls, they just printed them. There could be as many as a dozen or more new calls in each edition…that means that the four major note services, sending out a new edition each quarter, could publish a total of somewhere around 200 new figures a year.

But even before CALLERLAB could do something about the onslaught of new stuff, it had to standardize the lists (what calls were accepted as square dance basics) and the definition of each call. That was the top priority.

Standardizing the list of calls with their styling was the top priority of CALLERLAB. The Board had chosen the Sets in Order Basic 50 and the Extended 25 as the lists. SIO/ASDS has put in a lot of effort with the help of callers across the country giving input to develop the lists. It is one thing to have 25 callers approve the list and yet another to have over a hundred callers agree to do the same.

Frank Lane presented the CALLERLAB position on "How We Dance." One of Frank's first points was to equate discussing how we dance with the focus on quality control. If a product is not consistently made to a high standard, sales of that product fall off, and the product gains a bad reputation. He shifted gears and gave a detailed analysis of how we dance, focusing on five areas he felt we needed to work on: Rough Dancing, Poor Timing, Lack of Standardization, Inadequate Teaching, and Non-Descriptive or Awkward New Movements.

All of these point to a lack of proper training of callers, which leads to a lack of proper training of dancers. Dancers can be rough partly out of not enough floor time to smooth things out, but they can also be rough because they see callers let the experienced dancers get away with improvised but rough movements, such as high kicks. Also, a number of the new calls that are coming out indicate that the author had no knowledge of body mechanics; the movements are jerky, do not take into account hand availability, etc. Many callers do not know the actual definition of at least the 75 basics, therefore they teach them incorrectly, or they call them from positions that don't work. Also, many callers do not know how long each call should take, so they cannot give the next call at the right time. The solution seems to be better caller training, a standardized calling list, and note services and record producers issuing material that works.

Most of the callers at this session agreed to the resolution to use the SIO/ASDS basics with definitions and styling. Then questions came up that still seem to be hot potatoes: in ocean waves are hands up or down; how to do a Cross Trail vs. Cross Trail Thru; in stars do the men use a 'pack saddle' grip, or just touch hands at about shoulder height? Eventually the callers settled down and said that CALLERLAB should make a recommendation, and whatever that was, they would go along with it. Furthermore, any caller who wished to join CALLERLAB would have to agree to those standards as well.

Remember now, that the callers were in three different groups and each group would hear the same presentation of the three topics. After each group held their discussion and took a vote, the judges took that group's response back to the resolution committee, where the opinions of the three groups were discussed further. Later in the convention the resolution committee presented the final wording of the res- olutions. As each group finished its discussion of a topic, they knew only the opinions of the people in the session they attended.

The second topic, "What We Dance," was presented by Jack Lasry, who clearly stated that he was presenting his ideas, not the ideas of CALLERLAB. Callers and dancers are aware of the influx of new movements, and that is not necessarily bad. Square dance has always been in a state of change. For example, John Playford published *The English Dancing Master* in 1651, it contained 90 dances. In 1686 he published a new version of his book with over 900 dances. The difference between then and now is that in Playford's day, those were complete dances; in our time, they are ba- sics. Either way, dancers are exposed to too many dances and figures to learn.

This is the American way. We are always up-dating what is old, such as cars. But part of that up-dating is also disposal of what is old. In square dancing we need to be aware of tradition and present what the dancers like and are used to. So often now, at a Saturday night dance, which is supposed to be based on a known set of figures, callers call a new figure or one that is popular somewhere else in the country. If the dancers cannot do the figure or are rough while doing it, the caller may stop the dance and smooth the figure out. Now, instead of a relaxing evening of dancing known material, the dancer is faced with another workshop. The framework of a Saturday night dance should be the friendship, fellowship, and dancing with excitement to the creative square dance moves that fall in a framework he knows.

The problem is not just that the Saturday night has turned into the Tuesday night workshop, but that the guest caller moves on but leaves the figures behind. Also there are the note services which keep producing new material at a rate that no one can keep up with. Even if the local callers' association tried to evaluate the new movements, they could not get through them all in a Sunday afternoon, let alone evaluate them. There needs to be a way that the Saturday night dancer can go to a dance and feel assured that he will know what is being called. At the same time, there must be a place for the gung-ho, three nights a week dancer who wants constantly to be challenged with new material.

CALLERLAB should promote a program that brings mainstream dancing back to Friday and Saturday night but still allows for the introduction of new material at workshops or challenge dances. Jack Lasry then proposed that "CALL-ERLAB select a cross section of callers that represent coast-to-coast and border-to-border, and interest levels within the total picture, a committee of callers who are active in the picture and who are interested in participating in this committee. The committee would select one or two mainstream experimental ideas on a quarterly basis, based on their experimentation in their workshop programs, based on their observations as travelling callers, and based on the fact that they are the true leaders. Not challenge ideas, not fun level ideas, but experimental ideas that would fit within the mainstream program that we use so much today for the average mainstream dancer."

Bob Yerrington pretty much summed up what the majority of the callers believed. There must be new material, otherwise we would not get some of the really good calls we now consider as standards, such as Square Thru, Star Thru, and Spin the Top. We cannot put a moratorium on new material. Unfortunately, there is a lot of junk too.

Part of the problem is that callers are lazy, and they find it easier to present a new figure than to work on finding new combinations of the existing calls. The committee to help sort through all of the new stuff is a good idea. If an experimental workshop group spent a half hour per new call at the every other week sessions, it could cover 120 new calls in a year. That does not match the 200 calls that come out in just one of the note services.

After much discussion, we were back at the beginning: agreement that there needed to be a way to limit the number of new or experimental calls introduced to dancers in general, but there also needed to be a way to allow new material into the program. Most callers agreed that the Saturday night dances should be framed around an agreed upon list, but the job of selecting the list of movements needed to be done and definitions and styling agreed to. On the other hand, there were traveling callers whose reputation was built upon their introduction of new calls and they would feel unfairly restrained if they had to stay in the limited list.

The point that led to an agreement was that callers should use good judgment, as should the dancers. The dancers should be aware of the type of program a caller used and therefore not be surprised when they got to the dance. The club that booked the caller could do a lot to inform the local dancers on the type of program to expect. When we understood that idea about programming and lists, the members of CALLERLAB agreed to keeping the Saturday dances to the mainstream list plus the active quarterly selections. What was called at workshop or challenge groups was left entirely to the judgement of the caller. The approved list of movements at that time was the SIO/ASDS basic 50 plus 25, with the recommended timing and styling. For a while, at least,

503

the controversy on hand position was resolved by the SIO/ASDS handbooks.

The third topic that went through the thorough analysis process was accrediting callers. The debate went two directions: 1) What is a caller and who says so? And 2) Who can train new callers and accredit them?

Dealing with the first question, does a caller need to do everything? That is, must he be able to call contras and teach rounds? If so, at what level? Can a caller who exclusively does one-night stands qualify as a caller? Then, who signs off that the new caller is competent? If a new caller chooses to attend a caller's school, does he need to take an entrance exam? CALLERLAB has suggested a curriculum for caller's schools, so if a new caller goes through the class, is he automatically certified as a caller? Does going through a class qualify him for membership in CALLERLAB?

As for the second question, CALLERLAB has the caller training curriculum and should be able to identify callers who had the knowledge to coach new callers. Also recommended was that schools be taught by multiple callers so that all subjects were covered by qualified teachers. Within this discussion came up the question of what to do with students who show absolutely no chance of becoming callers because they had no sense of rhythm or they had tin ears. The solution here was that though the school is accredited by CALLERLAB, the students are not. Also, it was up to the school either to keep the student (and his money) or to tell the student early that he had no chance. The consensus was that even if a student showed no promise as a caller, he would be a better dancer, and perhaps even a better dancer leader, for having gone through the class. It was still up to the teachers of the school to certify the students, as qualified to be callers, or not.

During the round robin sessions on each of the three topics, more questions than answers came up, and that was true also when the recommendation committee made their report after reviewing the notes of each of the three sections on the three topics. In the end, however, CALLERLAB did pass resolutions on all three topics, and pretty much unanimously.

Now the work could begin. The committees each had their assignments of what to work on over the next year. The lists for mainstream dances were set, the Sets in Order Basic 50 and Extended 25, but the names of the calls, the definitions, and the styling needed to be reviewed and agreed to. New and Experimental movements were assigned to be reviewed by the New Movement committee, who then could recommend up to two calls per quarter for temporary addition to the lists. A committee was assigned to refine the curriculum for caller's schools and a way to certify the teachers of the schools. Also, a committee was assigned the task of approving callers for membership in CALLERLAB. All callers had to go home and convince the local dancers and callers that CALLERLAB and its resolutions should be accepted. Membership was opened up to more callers. And an agenda for 1975 had to be developed and publicized.

The most valuable accomplishment of CALLER-LAB 1974 was that we now had a viable organization that took leadership in square dancing. The strength of the founding and charter members and all of the callers who joined us in St. Louis almost immediately changed the direction of square dancing.

(All photos by Dan Sokolove, St. Louis, Missouri)

By just looking at the agendas and results of the following Conventions we can see the influence that CALLERLAB had on square dancing – not just the figures, but the professionalism of callers as well.

Chapter 20. The Aftermath of 1974

We started getting feedback from the square dance world pretty quickly. The initial Convention of The International Association of Square Dance Callers—the new and more formal name of CALLERLAB—was no sooner over than square dancers, callers, and association members everywhere began asking "What is it all about?" In my "As I See It" column in the July 1974 issue of Square Dancing I responded to that dominating question. Here is a summary:

> At this writing it is far too early to determine the significance of the First Convention, but put in the briefest of terms, it might be said that CALLERLAB represents the voice of many square dance callers who desire to work more closely together to accomplish specific goals for square dancing as a whole and for the elevation of professional callers' standards in particular.
>
> Going into the Convention there were three topics that were set as priorities. First, we had needed some form of control on the flood of non-descriptive new movements. Second, the activity suffered when the emphasis moved from quality in dancing to the need for standardization. And third, callers have needed some form of an accreditation program for years.
>
> Furthermore, various CALLERLAB committees undertook the study of these topics: 1) How to create some form of helpful coordination with more than 150 callers' associations around the world; 2) How to create a program of benefits for callers (insurance, retirement plans, etc.); 3) How to establish some means of helpful coordination with the Annual National Square Dance Convention; 4) How to address the need for a universal, professional, Code of Ethics for callers; 5) How to develop some form of

tune clearing house for those who produce square dance recordings.

During the course of the convention a platform for CALLERLAB was presented which included many of the points just mentioned and made the following recommendations: CALLERLAB should: 1) Develop an effective program of public relations; Find some method of effectively tapping the talent resources of the hundreds of callers in the activity today; 2) Create a center for reflective and advance thinking for the square dance activity; Concentrate on the two basic programs of American Square Dancing as a point of reference for the activity and finally; 3) CALLERLAB should become a body of knowledge for the square dance caller/teacher.

LEGACY and CALLERLAB are in a position to coordinate efforts for the benefit of the entire square dance movement. We are confident that the results will show a more healthy and enduring square dance activity emerging.

However, it was necessary to keep responding to questions about what CALLERLAB was about. We needed to consider how and what we dance. A few years back the Gold Ribbon Committee determined that one of the prime reasons people gave for dropping out of this activity was that there was just too much language, too many terms for the dancer to memorize.

The new dancer, in going through beginners' class, would be taught the 75 basics, then, thinking the learning period was over, he'd move into club dancing only to discover that the learning process would continue on and on. Because there appeared to be so much to learn, the emphasis went from quality to quantity, and while there were great numbers of dancers who could do hundreds of movements,

508

there were also great numbers who couldn't do too many of the movements with any semblance of good styling.

At the initial Convention in St. Louis, CALLER-LAB provided a clearing house as a means of screening the several hundred terms being "invented" each year; and as a result, CALLERLAB suggested no more than a total of eight experimental moves for "mainstream" club dancing during any given year. These "quarterly selections" would allow callers and dancers a chance to give input on what calls would be regularly used.

To augment the quarterly selections program, The American Square Dance Society, by way of a special poll taken of a large number of caller/leaders, produced a list of Ten PLUS Basics which, when added to the 75 Basics taught to beginners, pretty well summed up what "mainstream" club dancers were doing at that time. The idea was to update the Ten PLUS list once each year, using the CALLERLAB recommendations, but at the same time, holding the PLUS list at ten. We hoped this would be a "giant" step in the right direction.

Step number two followed closely. Being among those who were concerned with the lack of current styling and standardization, SIO/ASDS published a new picture series the following year to point out ways of becoming a better dancer. Body mechanics, arm and hand holds, correct timing - all were entered into the series. After these two programs have been in use for a year we proposed to evaluate their effectiveness, and then institute any necessary changes.

In order to arrive at a list of the most used basics, research and the questioning of a large number of callers resulted in 21 terms as a starter. A questionnaire was sent out to a representative list of callers in North America and overseas. Callers voted for any one of the terms by simply leaving it on his list, and crossing out any of those that he felt did not belong in the list. In addition, the callers being polled were asked to add any additional movements which they felt should be on the list. In all, 43 terms were considered. The response by deadline time was extremely impressive. The research proved that those movements which were favorites appeared on better than 80% of the questionnaires tabulated. The balance seemed to thin out rather rapidly.

With such a list of ten additional movements, mainstream dancing had established a reference point. As a means of feeding new material into this plateau, callers could avail themselves of the new clearinghouse service being offered by a special committee of CALLERLAB. In this program, a number of callers regularly screened the new experimental movements. At the end of each three month period, they balloted and determined which, if any, of the movements should be suggested by them for mainstream dancing for the upcoming three months. If, in the evaluation of the committee, there were not two movements that fit their definition then one, or possibly none, would be suggested for the up-coming quarter. Using the combination of the 75 basics, the list of TEN PLUS basics and the CALLERLAB quarterly suggestions, there was a workable system for mainstream club dancing everywhere.

The adoption of such a program meant that dancers traveling from one area to another, either as visitors or in making a permanent move, had no difficulty in being able to dance what was being called at any mainstream club dance. Festivals, attracting dancers from wide areas, had no trouble in programming dances that everybody could dance. Traveling callers, touring across the country, had little trouble in planning programs that the majority in attendance could follow.

Much of the success of this program depended upon the availability of a good selection of dances containing these TEN PLUS basics chosen by the SIO/ASDS survey and the current quarterly selections made by the CALLERLAB committee. The beauty of the entire program was that there were no limitations on variety, challenge, or choice. At the end of each year the TEN PLUS list was to be updated. Movements not in use were eliminated, while those that became more popular moved nearer the top of the list. After the CALLERLAB chosen quarterly movements has been in use for a minimum of six months, some will be added to the TEN PLUS list replacing ones that had to be dropped. To be effective, the TEN PLUS list would be maintained at a total of ten. When one TEN PLUS movement is added to the SIO/ASDS list, one will be dropped.

Remember too, that what we were discussing was just mainstream club dancing. The workshop groups and challenge clubs operate differently. However, if this single phase of square dancing had a definite direction - and a simple set of ground rules - many square dancers everywhere benefitted.

I was given the honor to present the Key Note Address at that first CALLERLAB convention. This, I think, was my opportunity to set forth the goals and the tone of the new organization. *[The complete address is in Appendix #4 – Ed.]*

March 1974, the first CALLERLAB convention was over, and Becky and I were exhausted. We had been working non-stop in high gear since we married in 1958: we were part of the team that met in Glenwood Springs, Colorado, in 1961 to create some form of standardization and a system for callers to communicate with each other; we had hosted two callers' workshops at UCLA; we had kept on schedule with publishing Sets in Order. Sets in Order had taken polls of callers to decide what figures should be included in recommended lists of calls to be used, which led to the Gold Ribbon Report. We had published the handbooks with definitions and pictures of how to do the basics; we kept up a frantic pace on producing square dance music; and we had maintained the Asilomar Institutes (three sessions a year). Then we had done the ground work to get CALLERLAB off the ground. We even used the Sets in Order offices and staff to have a place to give CALLERLAB a location. We then took on the job of Executive Secretary for CALLERLAB as well as chair of the Membership committee. On occasion, when CALLERLAB fell short of needed funding, we hit the Sets in Order accounts. We asked for, and were granted, a much needed year's leave to get rested.

I think the Board of Governors imagined Becky and me heading to some tropical island for a year because Al Brundage and Bob Van Antwerp presented us a set of matched luggage. The accompanying scroll read: "CALLERLAB and the First International Convention of Square Dance Callers is the result of the combined efforts of many; but one among them has been indispensable. Throughout the life of this organization he has worked selflessly and with unquestioning dedication. He has used the wisdom of his many years of experience and the full range of his considerable skills to lead us carefully and encourage us diplomatically. He has accomplished a monumental task when there was no one else to do it. Without his help there would be no CALLERLAB and there would be no International Callers Convention. The CALLERLAB Board of Governors meeting in St. Louis in April, 1974, thank you, Bob Osgood, for making this dream that we shared come true." (We used the luggage on the next Sets in Order jaunt.)

Headquarters for CALLERLAB moved from Los Angeles to Sandusky, Ohio, the home office of *American Square Dance* Magazine. Stan Burdick became the Executive Secretary for the 1974-75 year. A new work team (Advisory Board) made up of Stan Burdick, Marshall Flippo, Frank Lane, and Dave Taylor was appointed.

I did stay on as chairman of the Membership committee. Membership in CALLERLAB was by personal invitation. In February, 1971, CALLERLAB was started with 14 of the Hall of Fame members. These 14 wanted to share what they felt was the start of something meaningful with others, so at the end of that first meeting, an additional number of callers were invited to participate. Those who had been invited to the first meeting but could not attend were automatically included. At each meeting, additional members were added by personal invitation. At the 1973 session the number increased to 23. The Board of Governors was comprised of the original 14, and the additional members who were present at either the 1972 or 1973 annual meetings. Then we decided to increase in size, and hold the first International (Invitational) Callers Convention. Each Board of Governors member submitted the names of several who could contribute, as well as benefit, by being a part of the group. Those who attended the 1974 Convention were invited to pay their 1974-75 dues and become a member. In turn, these members were asked to nominate others whom they felt would make good members. Then, these people were invited to attend the 1975 Convention. Those who had been invited to the 1974 CALLERLAB Convention but were unable to attend, and who indicated an interest in being invited again, were kept on the active list and were invited to attend the following year. CALLERLAB was looking for good thinkers and good and willing workers.

The second CALLERLAB convention theme was "Time For Action." Under the able leadership of convention Chairman Dave Taylor, 565 callers and partners came to Chicago to deal with three major areas of discussion and ten "thrust" groups. The major areas of consideration were: The Basics - The Tools of our Trade, Dance Standards, and Dance Level Identification.

As in the 1974 convention, discussion was spirited. There was much give and take, and a great deal was accomplished. A highlight of the 1975 convention was the establishment of the prestigious Milestone Award to honor those who have made unusual and significant contributions to calling and square dancing. This award had its roots in the honors given the previous year, and in 1975, went to Al Brundage, Les Gotcher, Joe Lewis, and Lloyd Litman. A formal organization for CALLERLAB was adopted by the Board of Governors on March 23rd, 1975. In June of that year, articles of incorporation were filed in the state of California. Most of the invitees who attended the 1975 convention joined CALLERLAB, and membership grew to 379.

Following its first convention, CALLERLAB set up a clearing house to sort through the vast accumulation of new calls to come up with the first quarterly selections. In 1975, with more than 600 attending the CALLERLAB Convention in Chicago, an assessment was made of the total basics program used in mainstream dancing. It was apparent from the reaction of the group that an updating of the basics was in order and, by the end of the Convention, those gathered had decided on a one-year testing period for a list revised from the 75 basics, and the PLUS Ten basics.

The time had come for the first suggested revision of the Sets in Order Basic Lists on an international scale, something that could bring together all the independent callers' groups, and encourage callers everywhere to teach by one standard list. CALLERLAB, at its 1975 Convention, presented such a list that its members hoped would be tested on a temporary basis during the coming year. With few exceptions, the list closely paralleled the Sets in Order list.

At the 1975 convention, the reins of leadership were turned over to a newly created Executive Committee composed of Jim Mayo, Johnny LeClair, Arnie Kronenberger, Stan Burdick, Jack Lasry, and Angus McMorran (as Canadian representative), with Jim Mayo as chairman. After a year off, and feeling much refreshed, I returned as Executive Secretary for the 1975-76 year. The Quarterly Selection Program (formerly "New Movements Committee") became operational during this period. After publishing the suggested list of mainstream basics movements that CALLERLAB suggested for those who dance at least once each week, and who have been dancing for some time - in the June and July issues of 1975, we heard quite a bit on the subject. Most of it was good, praising CALLERLAB for taking the initiative to analyze square dancing, and to come out with what appears to be a good list.

Some of the comments had to do with the omission from the CALLERLAB list of some of the basics that appear on the basic 50 and extended basics (51-75) lists. As an example, Rowan H. Voss in Rockford, Illinois wrote, "How could we dance without a Dixie Chain?" Other letters said "What do you mean by substituting Zoom for Substitute?" And, they went on to point out that the two movements, while accomplishing virtually the same end result, each had their place, and each one fits best under differing circumstances. "I seldom go to a dance that doesn't include `Arch in the Middle and the Ends Dive In'," wrote one reader. This was echoed by any number of dancers, and substantiated by callers who felt that the basic created by Ed Gilmore more than twenty years before was established as a firm foundation basic.

515

Some other comments had to do with the order in which the basics were presented. "The list should either be alphabetical, in family groupings, or in a suggested order of teaching. It can't be all three," was a typical comment. As some of you remember, the list started out with relatively easy material, corresponding in a way to the suggested order of teaching in the SIO/ASDS basic and extended basics list. However, in several instances, when it hit a specific movement that was part of a "family" grouping, the teaching order was disregarded. For example, while it's quite conceivable that Two Ladies Chain and Four Ladies Chain might be taught during the same class lesson, 3/4 Chain, which is part of CALLERLAB'S family grouping, would be taught at some later time. Another example of this was the Circulate movement. While it was quite feasible for a caller to present all the standard forms of Circulate in one lesson, he would probably wait until the dancers have had several lessons to practice the movement before introducing Box Circulate and Single File Circulate.

"Professional Responsibility" was the theme of the 1976 convention which returned to Chicago and the Marriott in April. The two major topics of discussion were Accreditation and the Mainstream Basics. Additionally, four other areas received close attention. They were: National Square Dance Convention Liaison, Ways and Means, Dance Level Identification, and Quarterly Movements. Among other accomplishments at this convention was the major step of adopting the caller accreditation program. Many of those in attendance at the convention were displaying a CALLERLAB identification pin which was available for the first time.

516

Again, one of the highlights was honoring those whose contributions to square dancing were above the ordinary. Milestone Awards went to Herb Greggerson, Fenton 'Jonesy' Jones, and Jimmy Clossin (not present). Vaughn Parrish and Angus McMorrann were elected in the first election for seats on the Board or Governors. The Board then consisted of the twenty-five authorized by the Bylaws. Those Bylaws were formally adopted on April 11, 1976.

One action taken by the Board of Governors was to formalize and make a matter of record the rules and regulations governing the corporation to assure a turnover of members of the Board, and to provide an opportunity for any CALLERLAB member to run and be elected democratically by a vote of the membership. Lots were drawn for terms of office of from one to five years, beginning with the 1976-77 year. Jim Mayo continued as Chairman for the 1976-77 year with other Executive Committee members Frank Lane, Jack Lasry, Angus McMorran, and Bob Osgood.

In 1976, CALLERLAB also passed a resolution providing for the accreditation of all callers. The CALLERLAB Committee, chaired by Bill Peters, provided the administrative detail necessary for the implementation of the Accreditation program. The procedure was as follows: A caller desiring to be accredited, must first seek an application from the Executive Secretary of CALLERLAB. The caller then must obtain three accreditors in each of several categories to achieve a total of 20 points. Points are obtained in the following categories: General calling skills (teaching, timing, music, diction, choreography and figure construction, command techniques, programming, etc.); Specialty calling skills (One Night Stands, Round Dancing, Contra Dancing, Advanced Dancing). Training and Experience Points were awarded for successful completion of an appropriate caller training program, and points per year of active calling. The signature of three accreditors was required in each category except the Training category. There was no "grandfather clause" in the resolution. The accreditation procedure was not limited to CALLERLAB members, but rather, was for all callers everywhere. Any caller who becomes accredited would automatically be invited, by a present member, to attend a CALLERLAB convention. Having attended a convention, he will then be invited to join CALLERLAB.

A major change was made in the structure of CALL-ERLAB. The Board realized that the job of Executive Secretary was too big to rely on volunteer work, so they created the paid position with allowances for office expenses and additional staff. On July 1, 1976, the office of CALLERLAB moved from Los Angeles, California, to Pocono Pines, Pennsylvania. John Kaltenthaler was appointed by the Board of Governors to fill the post of Executive Secretary I had vacated

I had enjoyed the years serving as Executive Secretary, work horse, and custodian. I had seen the idea of CALLERLAB grow from a dream more than fifteen years ago, to mold into an actual organization in 1971, and to develop into an effective, professional leadership organization during the following three years. In the Convention "Flash" issue of DIRECTION I wrote in "A PARTING SHOT"

> *On the shoulders of the Executive Secretary rests the responsibility of keeping all of the members informed of those important happenings within the square dance caller fraternity, of making sure that committees are functioning, and that our annual CALLERLAB Convention comes off each spring with as few hitches as possible.*
>
> *In order to accomplish all of this, the Executive Secretary needs to communicate with you. But that is a two-way street. It's easy to say, "They won't need my feed-back; I'm just one of many members."*

518

Don't kid yourself. It's quite possible that all of the members could take this stand and consequently CALLERLAB would not be representing you, your wishes, and your thoughts. It will be more important than ever in the coming year to keep John, and the CALLERLAB office, informed, even though briefly, on a regular basis.

We look forward to the months ahead, to serving on your Executive Committee, and of spending some much needed time on our magazine and on the various projects of the Sets in Order American Square Dance Society. My particular thanks to our office crew, to Sharon Kernen, our girl Friday, and to Becky. Also, from all of us a "well done" to the outgoing members of the Executive Committee for 1975-76, Stan Burdick, Arnie Kronenberger, Angus McMorran, Jack Lasry and Johnny LeClair, with whom we worked this past year. Finally, an expression of personal pleasure that Mayo is once again our Chairman. His deep and sincere interest, not only in square dancing and the calling profession, but most especially, in the growth and development of CALLERLAB, has been demonstrated over and over again in our close association with him during the past twelve months.

I was re-elected to a five year term on the Board in 1976.

The 1977 Convention had a spirited debate on whether CALLERLAB should support the National Square Dance Convention. The end result was essentially for status quo: Whether or not to support the National Square Dance Convention is an individual decision of each caller.

A total of 930 people attended this convention: Membership increased to 595, and questions were being asked about what to do about conducting a convention if we got any larger. "This gathering," said Bob Augustin from Louisiana in his opening talk, "reflects 8,394 years of calling experience — an average of 13.9 years for every caller in attendance." With representatives from 48 States, seven Canadian Provinces, from England, Australia, New Zealand, and the Canal Zone, the group wasted little time in getting down to business.

The Board of Governors also passed this resolution: Resolved that CALLERLAB go on record as being opposed to contests in square dancing. In the conviction that square dancing is founded on cooperation between dancers and among callers, any attempts to pit dancers against each other, or caller against caller, could detract from this spirit of friendly cooperation, and should be discouraged.

In July 1977, CALLERLAB presented the updated list of programs. In order to provide additional plateaus for those wishing to move past the mainstream of square dancing, CALLERLAB committees came out with other lists. These were presented in order, starting with the Mainstream, Plus One, which would be the next step after Mainstream Experimental (including the Quarterly Movements). It is assumed that to move from one plateau to the next, a dancer will exhibit proficiency in handling the Basic, Extended Basic and Mainstream Basic plateaus. Then, after mastering these programs, dancers could move on to the following: Mainstream Plus One (4 movements that were also called Mainstream Experimentals). After the Plus One came figures that would eventually be added to the Plus One list (8 movements). Then a dancer could move on to Plus Two (an additional 12 movements). These comprised the total suggested by the CALLERLAB committees.

The need for a universally acceptable system of labeling levels, or plateaus of dancing, had grown increasingly apparent. For years the activity struggled with such terms as high level, low level, and intermediate level, Such labels as fun level, workshop, and advanced have proven to be fairly meaningless, as these phrases indicate different things in different areas.

Growing out of the CALLERLAB designation of various programs or plateaus, came a logical system of identification by the arrangement of basics into programs, each program dependent upon the basic movements utilized in the programs before it. It became possible to label a club dance in such a way that a dancer coming into one area from another would know what to expect if the program system were carried out in a dedicated fashion. Halls at a National Convention no longer needed to post the names or numbers of basics, but accomplished the task by simply identifying the program.

The programs were fairly well established by 1977, and while we knew that there would be changes in specific calls within a specific program, the name of the program would be consistent. It was hoped that by using this system of named programs there would be less connotation of ability, of high level, or low level dancing. The choice was up to each individual dancer. Each individual would then be able to select a plateau, or program where he is familiar with the basics it contains.

At the 1978 Convention, Cal Golden surprised the heck out of me by presenting me with the Milestone Award. Cal was a bit effusive in his presentation speech, but it touched me deeply.

The 1978 convention included a session for the caller's partner for the first time under the leadership of Erna Egender and Sharon Golden. New grievance and complaint procedures were developed and adopted, and received wide publicity during the year. That part of the bylaws which requires attendance at an annual convention at least every three years for continuing membership was changed to require attendance only every six years for those members outside North America. Breakfast was included as a part of the convention package that year to keep people from having to stand in long lines at the coffee shop, and was thought by all to be a good addition. John Kaltenthaler continued as Executive Secretary. The name of the committee to select experimental movements for use at the Mainstream level was changed to the Quarterly Selection Committee, and the committee was charged to select only those movements which were truly experimental, i.e., to avoid choosing movements which were on other lists

One of the original statements from CALLERLAB was that the National Square Dance Convention was missing the boat. As we saw it, the Convention served as a showcase for all the various parts of the square dance activity. More than a giant dance or just another festival, this once-yearly event was in a position to say to the dancing, as well as to the non-dancing world, this is what square dancing is all about. Since its inception in 1952, more than 250,000 dancers have participated in at least one of these big events. Countless thousands, perhaps millions, have become aware of square dancing because of the National. Newspapers, magazine articles, and television have all been quick to realize the news value of a participation convention of this magnitude.

Also, at the 1978 convention, the Advanced list of calls were selected by vote of a variety of Advanced level callers throughout the country, and the list was approved by CALLERLAB. The All Position Concept, which was an option for Mainstream, was considered automatic for Advanced Level. This does not mean that a dancer is required to be an All Position Dancer in order to begin learning the

Advanced Dancing's Basic Calls. However, as dancers progress within the Advanced Level program, they are expected to become comfortable with All Position dancing.

By December of 1978, it was evident that many dancers were starting to climb the ladder from Mainstream to Plus One. The chairman of the Advanced and Experimental Committees, Jack Lasry, addressed the situation directly to members of CALLERLAB: "It is normal for square dancers, who have had several years of Mainstream experience, to reach up into the next plateau of dancing: the Plus Programs — One and Two (established by CALLERLAB to allow greater variety in choreography). Only time will tell if these Plus One and Plus Two dance plateaus will become popular, but the early signs are quite positive on their acceptance."

There were 12 calls on the Plus One Program so an introduction to Plus One dancing can easily be done in a five to six week workshop of two to two and one-half hours. Some important questions were asked: Should we introduce one Plus One call per month to our Mainstream club and raise the plateau of dancing? If we raise the Mainstream club to a Plus One level, how will this affect bringing new graduates into the club?

Through negotiation with the Executive Board of the National Square Dance Convention, CALLERLAB agreed to assume full responsibility for the Callers' Seminar at the National Convention in Milwaukee in June of 1979, with expenses to be reimbursed by the NSDC. That seminar was highly successful, with the result that CALLERLAB was asked to continue its role. With 1027 members, CALLERLAB quickly was coming of age, and was gaining increasing acceptance by callers and dancers alike.

It was the turn of the East Coast in 1980, and over 940 members, invitees, and partners converged on Miami Beach. They came from 47 states, 6 Canadian Provinces, and 5 foreign countries other than Canada. After a misunderstanding with the hotel originally contracted for because of the Jewish high holy days, and severe heart palpitations on the part of the Executive Secretary John Kaltenthaler, we squeezed into the Americana Hotel on Miami Beach. Our theme was "Leadership and Judgement" and, for the first time, we hired a keynote speaker, an expert in the field of motivation, Bjorn Secfrer, who gave a rousing speech at the Monday evening banquet. This hiring of an "outside expert" was a most successful experiment which provided a basis for making decisions on future conventions. The Miami convention was the occasion for other firsts which proved quite successful. A professional tape service was engaged to tape selected sessions of the convention, and to provide tapes for purchase at a reduced price. The tapes proved to be a very popular item, and sales were brisk. It was decided that this service should be continued at future conventions. Those who arrived in Miami on Sunday were able to participate in another first - a social hour on Sunday evening. It was a welcome opportunity to meet and talk with people one might not get to see during the hectic working part of the convention. A number of guests from other square dance oriented groups were invited and attended the 1980 convention, including representatives of the Executive Board of the National Square Dance Convention, ROUNDALAB, and LEGACY. Their letters of appreciation after the convention indicated that they were greatly pleased and impressed. The value of promoting close working relationships among various organizations concerned with square and round dancing, became even more evident from this experience.

The Board of Governors had considered for several years the need for an assistant to help the Executive Secretary. The intention to hire such a person was publicized in

524

the December 1979 issue of DIRECTION, and letters of application were solicited. In Miami, seven applicants were interviewed, and Herb Egender was chosen as the Assistant Executive Secretary. The duties of the position were the publication of a quarterly newsletter "Guidelines," preparing public relations materials, assisting with convention arrangements, and other tasks prescribed by the Executive Secretary and the Board of Governors through the Chairman. The Assistant serves at the pleasure of the Executive Secretary and, like him, is a non-voting member at Executive Committee meetings.

The baby was born and was thriving. Each year there were tweaks to the organization, but most of the work of CALLERLAB turned to specific areas of calling. We found that many clubs throughout the country were pushing their dancers to learn not just Mainstream in a single season, but they were adding Plus 1 figures. CALLERLAB figured that this push of additional figures to be learned in a single season was brought on by a desire of clubs and dancers to be known as "higher level" dancers, and, since Plus 1 only added another 14 figures or so, it was easy to take dancers from Circle Left through Plus 1. To try to head off this "rush to Plus," CALLERLAB decided to combine Plus 1 and Plus 2 into a single list. The belief was that adding 30 calls to be learned in class would encourage clubs to stay at the Mainstream program. It did not work.

CALLERLAB also initiated a standard applications committee whose job was to make rulings on how various calls were used: for example, could Anything and Roll be used after Pass the Ocean? Later the role of the committee grew to cover not just standard applications, but extended applications as well.

BMI/ASCAP made their presence known again when they discovered how many callers and clubs were using copyrighted music. Their initial step to enforcing copyright was to require clubs to purchase the license. Instead, CALLERLAB negotiated a deal whereby the callers, the actual users of the music, could purchase the license one year at a time through CALLERLAB. CALLERLAB also offered liability and equipment insurance at a nominal rate. But the combination of dues, insurance, and licensing seemed to be too large an investment for some callers. The American Callers Association was created to provide insurance and music licensing with no convention attendance requirement, and substantially lower dues.

In June of 1981, I had to make an extremely difficult decision. My term on the Board was up at the next convention, in the spring of 1982. But, since I was no longer an "active" caller – that is calling 50 dances a year (I was doing just my once a month contra dances), I was no longer eligible for membership in CALLERLAB, let alone to serve on the Board. I had to withdraw my petition to be on the ballot.

In no way did that decision affect my commitment to CALLERLAB. In 1982, we offered a plan whereby CALLERLAB, Sets in Order/American Square Dance Society, and individual callers could have a benefit. The Board of Governors approved a plan whereby each member of CALLERLAB was encouraged to promote SQUARE DANCING Magazine. In return for this promotion, we would credit the individual selling a new subscription with $1.00 worth of literature published by SIO/ASDS, and also a direct donation to CALLERLAB of 50¢ per new subscription.

In June 1982, CALLERLAB surprised me again. (By the way, the magazine promotion was not intended to benefit me, other than increase circulation.) I was given the Gold

Card. Only two other callers had received the Gold Card, which represents lifetime membership in CALLERLAB. Since I had reduced my calling to less than 50 times each year, the Board of Governors honored me with this special presentation. CALLERLAB omitted this announcement in the Convention press release so I would not know of the award before the actual presentation.

The executive committee also proposed two changes in the by-laws, both of them dealing with full membership.

Article II, Section 7. Additional Continuing Require-ments for Membership: The following sentence has been added "Any member who has been a member in good stand-ing for a consecutive period of eight (8) years will be exempt from the Active Calling requirement in order to maintain full membership." This was approved to take advantage of the years of experience and leadership of callers who have re-duced their calling to fewer than fifty (50) dances per year.

Article II, Section 9. Gold Card Membership: This is an additional membership category and is intended to ena-ble CALLERLAB to avail itself of the expertise of those, who for one reason or another are no longer presently calling.

The Gold Card Award was first awarded in 1978, and we did not have a wording within the by-laws. This wording parallels the words inscribed on the "Gold Card".

With the change in the by-laws, I was again eligible to serve on the Board of Governors. I had to scramble to get the signatures on my petition, and then write a brief biog-raphy of my qualifications for the position. I have always found it a little embarrassing to write about myself (I was pretty good about promoting square dancing and the maga-zine, but promoting myself was a challenge. One way to do it was write the article in third person.)

527

I was elected to the Board (it felt so good to be involved again, and not just going along for the ride). The first year on the Board I worked mostly as an advisor, but then in 1985, I was appointed chairman of the contra committee.

In the midst of this all, Becky and I decided that it was time to close down the magazine. We offered this press release to the public.

The December, 1985, issue of SQUARE DANCING will bring to a close 37 years of continuous publication. As you can imagine, reaching this major decision has taken a great deal of thought and contemplation. In weighing this change, we have determined that rather than transfer the ownership/editorship to someone else, we would simply ring down the curtain on a magazine that has chronicled a vast era of square dancing history.

After having personally nursed 444 issues from concept through mailing, both Becky and I feel we will have said what we've had to say, helped where we could and supported, to the best of our ability, this activity which we have enjoyed for 47 years, and in which we expect to be active for a long time yet to come.

This change won't mean a complete retirement for us. It will take at least a couple of years to get our archives in order, and to wrap up projects that have been on the back burner. We'll continue to handle the sales of our products and to operate The American Square Dance Society, which maintains the Hall of Fame, the Silver Spur Awards, and the Scholarship Program. We will remain active with

CALLERLAB, and continue the various leadership conferences we handle each year.

The American Square Dance Society, which served as the home office for CALLERLAB in its early stages, produces and sells *The Caller Text*, *The Caller/Teacher Manual*, the *Basic/Mainstream*, *Plus,* and *Indoctrination Handbooks* among other specialized square dance items. We plan to continue our winter and Summer Asilomar Vacation Institutes which we've produced since 1951, as well as a few square dance tours, something we've been doing since 1961. We can be reached at the same address with the same telephone number as in the past.

And so it is that we bow out of one era of our lives and into another phase which will allow us greater time with family and friends, and an opportunity to do those things we've wanted to do for so long. Thank you for your continued interest in square dancing, and your support of SQUARE DANCING Magazine. We hope to keep in touch."

A couple of months before closing the magazine we made an agreement with Stan and Cathie Burdick of *American Square Dance* magazine. We gave them the subscription list to SQUARE DANCING Magazine in return for their promise to fill the subscription contracts with copies of *American Square Dance*. That way our subscribers did not miss out on a magazine, and Stan and Cathie had access to many more people who did not know about *American Square Dance*. It was an amicable agreement among friends.

The February 1986 edition of DIRECTION, which included the call to convention, notified the membership that we were going to have to change some parts of our by-laws because of a change in the California Corporations Code for Non-Profit Organizations. While we were redoing the by-laws, we rearranged some of the sections to place related items together.

Perhaps the most significant change was in terms for members of the Board. In general, most states require that the term of office for Directors or members of the Board one year. Our practice had been for five year terms. California adopted a slightly more lenient ruling for non-profit Organizations permitting three year terms. The revision reflected this change. All of those elected to the Board on the November 1985 ballot were be assigned three year terms, the maximum allowed by law. The remaining terms of Board members were to be drawn by lot to comply with the California Corporations Code, and the desires of the members of the Board.

Other changes included clarification of the types of membership. We also had to change when membership dues were due. Prior to this revision, the way, in which dues, notices, and assessments were handled could technically permit a caller who had become a member to receive all rights and privileges of membership for a period of up to seven months of our 12-month year without being a member in good standing. In order to be fair to all and to keep the dues at the minimum to enable us to operate on a "pay-as-you-go-basis," the Executive Committee recommended, and the Board of Governors concurred, that all dues would be due on or before the annual convention or the 1st of April of each year. This action was similar to what we did when we reorganized Sets in Order.

In 1986, I surrendered the chairmanship of the contra committee to Mona Cannell because I was elected to be vice-chairman for the 1986-87 term. The election to vice-chair carried with it the sentence of becoming Chairman of the Board starting at the end of the convention in 1987 through the convention in 1988. It was kind of a strange feeling having been involved with CALLERLAB for so many years, but never being an elected officer.

After looking over back copies of DIRECTION, I feel I must have sounded like a broken record to many CALLERLAB members. I kept pounding away at increasing membership, increasing membership involvement in CALLERLAB, and getting involved by joining a committee, or at least sending callers' thoughts to CALLERLAB. My first column for DIRECTION commented on what a good convention we just had, and that I was impressed with how CALLERLAB had matured since the first convention back in 1974. But I also emphasized the importance of communications by everyone. Even if a caller did not have a specific assignment, it was important for callers to talk with each other, and to share their thoughts with the Board.

The call for increased communication seemed to have prodded more callers to write, or even phone Board members. We were able to put together a consensus of the major goals for the year. Almost all members agreed that the most important thrust for the year was to increase membership. Also, high on the list of priorities was the goal of improving the teaching skills of all callers, members, and nonmembers alike. And of course, not to be overlooked on the list of priorities was fund raising. People get tired of hearing the message 'we should do this,' or 'you must do that.' People need praise in order to operate well. Back when we started the magazine, we always made it a point to recognize people who had done more than the ordinary for square dancing. We had the Caller of the Month column, and we gave credit to callers who submitted especially good bits of choreography. The big recognitions came with the Silver Spur and the Hall of Fame Awards. CALLERLAB continued this tradition of praise with the Milestone Award, Board

531

Recognition, the Chairman's Award, etc. In one of my chairman's columns, I talked about co-operation and mutual help in a specific instance.

> *I'm always impressed when I hear of instances of a caller stepping in to help another caller when a problem has made it impossible for him to meet an assignment, and I'm encouraged by reports of callers working together unselfishly for the good of the activity. One instance which stands out in my mind was the time an area, which had over 100 callers, presented a gigantic square dance with slots for only 30 callers on the program. The callers, themselves, selected who would represent them, and virtually all other callers showed up with their dancers to participate. That's cooperation!*

In the late 1980's, there was a drop off in the number of dancers, and a number of old time callers were retiring. We were really encouraged when we heard from callers working through their local callers' association striving to meet the needs of the dancers by soliciting the opinion of the local dancers about what they wanted as a good dance program. That's putting the dancers first.

I expressed my appreciation of what members were doing, especially when they sent not just complaints, but suggested solutions. We knew that communication was going to be especially important that year with discussions and possible decisions made at the Reno Convention regarding CALLERLAB's' next steps. The Executive Committee met in early December, and planned to telephone a random cross-section of CALLERLAB members to get their views on the following three questions:

1. What do you feel should be the major thrust of
   CALLERLAB?
2. What may we have overlooked in recent years?
3. How do you think we can attract new members and
   bring back those who have dropped out?

We, the Board, knew that we could reach only a small number of the total membership, so we called on members to write. To emphasize the importance of the issue, I listed my home address and phone number, not the home office, so members would feel they were writing to a real person, not just some anonymous body in an office.

When a problem arises, or when something does not go as we wished it had, it is easy to find someone to blame. That began to happen as more people saw that the dancer population was decreasing. "Of course, the problem must lie with CALLERLAB. There were huge numbers of people before CALLERLAB started meddling." All of us at some time has been faced by a critic of CALLERLAB, someone who claims that our organization is responsible for the problems facing square dancing today. When this happens, it is an opportunity for each of us, as well as our responsibility, to set the record straight. CALLERLAB is not responsible for these difficulties, nor is it a cure-all for them, but it has provided many solutions and directions, and continues to work for others.

This responsibility to "set the record straight" was a call for all CALLERLAB members to take assessment of the accomplishments of CALLERLAB and be prepared to explain them to fellow members, non-members, as well as dancers, should they take critical aim at CALLERLAB. Today, via our organization, there are communications between callers beyond the local range, which allow worldwide goals to be set. We have a system of accreditation for callers, an established caller training curriculum, and a universally recognized system of dance programs to be used wisely as the needs of our various communities dictate.

CALLERLAB will always have more to accomplish and, within its democratic framework, we can agree to disagree with each other. But by working together, great strides can continue to be taken. What we have is something very special. CALLERLAB is working, and it will continue to work as each of us recognizes that we must do our part in supporting it, and keeping it well and prosperous.

If you want someone to remember something, or, if you want someone to get something done, you must remind them in as positive a way as possible. Facing the criticism that "it's all CALLERLAB's fault," the critics need to be reminded of the other side of the story. So, support CALLERLAB by pointing out the positive. "If membership involvement is any measurement of success for any organization, then consider these indicators: (1) a significant percentage of our members are actively involved in one or more of our almost 30 on-going committees; (2) more than 100 members will be working on the giant post-National Convention Fund Raising Dance in Anaheim, California, June 26, 1988; (3) several hundred are already tied into the CALLERLAB around-the-world fund raising dances that will be taking place in the next few months and, (4) an estimated 180 members are presently involved in our Study Group projects created as information gathering programs vital to CALLERLAB's future."

According to tradition, the out-going chairman gives the opening speech at the new convention – sort of a last chance to make a point before the new chairman and board start disassembling everything you did. Well, not really. There is sufficient carryover on the Board, and the new chairman has spent a year in training, so there is a lot of continuity in the direction CALLERLAB goes.

534

I finished my term on the Board in 1991, and, like others, I continued to attend the Conventions. CALL-ERLAB has always been good at recognizing people who go the extra step, and at the 1991 convention, those of us with perfect attendance were: Stan Burdick, Bill Davis, Herb Egender, Marshall Flippo, Bob Howell, Jon Jones, John Kaltenthaler, Dick Leger, Melton Luttrell, Martin Mallard, Jim Mayo, Jack Murtha, Bob Osgood, Don Williamson, and Francis Zeller. Norm Cross, Cal Golden, Jon Jones, Jim Mayo, Bob Osgood, Dave Taylor, and Bob Van Antwerp, all former Chairmen of the Board, were also given a round of applause.

I think I mentioned that one of the highlights for me at the 50th National Square Dance Convention was being asked to be on a panel with my good friend, Osa Matthews. At that time there were only a couple of callers still alive who had been on the program at the first National Square Dance Convention – I was not because I was already booked for a dance in Northern California. Osa was on that program. Between us, we had well over a hundred years of calling experience. We had an enthusiastic crowd of dancers and callers who came to hear us two old timers. We played off each other in terms of our memories of square dancing, and we got some folks up to demonstrate some squares and contras. Then came the open question period, which was briefly interrupted by the announcement that the hall was booked for another session. The Convention people took a quick look at the crowd and decided to move the next session to another hall.

But, as heart-warming as that session with Osa was, a bigger thrill was yet to come. Before we got out of the hall, some representatives of CALLERLAB asked me to stay behind for a moment because they had something for me.

CALLERLAB's Chairman of the Board, Jim Mayo (do you remember Jim? He was the first Chairman of CALLERLAB back in 1974.) presented the Millennium Award to me. The following is the speech Jim made at the presentation:

As chairman of CALLERLAB, I am privileged to be here to make a presentation to a man to whom the whole of our activity owes more than will ever be measured. He has dedicated more than 60 years to the development, support, promotion and protection of square dancing in all its many forms. He is a one-man foundation who has committed his talent, his energy, his resources and his love to this activity. He has been at the core of our communication. He has guided us with his wisdom and experience. He has led us down exciting new paths to wonderful success.

He has been a caller, a cuer, a prompter, an editor, a movie performer and publisher. He has traveled the world spreading the joy of square dancing. He was a disciple of Lloyd 'Pappy' Shaw and has spread his philosophy to all who would listen. He has been a part of nearly every important thing that has happened in square dancing including the first of these National Conven-

You can barely see the clear glass Millennium Award I am holding

tions. The importance of his contributions is underscored by the fact that most of you have known almost from my first words who I am describing.

Bob Osgood has dedicated his life to square danc-ing. CALLERLAB now recognizes his dedication with the ONLY Millennium Award.

I think I have said enough.

Chapter 21. BECKY

I started writing this book in the 1950s, sort of. In those days I called it "The F-U-Ndamentals of Square Dancin'"

INTRODUCTION

One thing you can't say to folks about square dancing is "you're doing it all wrong!"

There just doesn't seem to be any really authentic way of doing any part of square dancing. Like "Topsy," square dancing has just grown, and though different in every portion of the country it's all correct. After dancing quite a bit in Southern California for several years I considered myself somewhat of an accomplished square dancer. You can imagine how I felt when visiting groups in Chicago, Wisconsin, New York, Virginia, and Washington, D.C., that I found myself completely baffled on almost every turn.

The swinging, the promenading, yes even the simple little do-si-do was a bit different in almost every place I went. One thing I learned from all this was that "When in Rome, do as the Romans do" and I began to enjoy the extra brain work that it required in adapting myself to the different types of American square dancing.

There was, with all this change, however, one universal similarity. "Just look at that dancer's face," one little old lady by-stander said to me in Virginia not very long ago. The dancer that was pointed out was certainly not what I would considered a champion or even an average dancer. Her feet were all over the floor and she bounced with a sort of skipping gazelle-like motion that was far from graceful. However, as my friend had pointed out – upon looking at her face - I discovered that over-bubbling, exuberant expression of joy that was identical with the expression I'd seen a few nights before in New York, or before that in Chicago, in Wisconsin, and, yes, even in my own state of California. Yes, the one thing in common was the fun.

There was no doubt about it. Fun was the keynote and fun was what all the dancers were having. So actually, with all the fine points that can be named about square dancing the little things that make dancing important to all of us are the sometimes overlooked elements in our everyday living. Very little in this book or in any other book on the subject is worth a good red cent if it isn't mixed with that one all-important quality of enjoyment and fun.

I had the temerity of youth to think I knew enough to explain square dancing to the world. I talked about formations and the basic moves, such as Right and Left Grand and Allemande Left. Then I presented hundreds of named square dances: Birdie in the Cage, Lady 'Round the Lady, Texas Star, etc.

The book got only so far as a clean type copy of chapter one.

As the years passed the focus of the book changed, as square dancing changed. The named dances lost their place to more and more basics. The increasing number of calls forced me to look at square dancing in general and where it was heading. Finally, after CALLERLAB and LEGACY were established, I looked again at writing a book, but then it was about the development of Modern Western Square Dancing. But again, the book was about the details, not the meaning of square dancing. There were very few smiles and laughs in the book.

Now in my fading years I look back and see what role I played in square dancing. I do want to be remembered for my place in square dancing while it went through its boom period through to the multi-level dancing of the 21st Century. I also want to be remembered for the fun I was able to share with so many people for so many years.

I have tried throughout my career to give credit to people who helped change the face of square dancing. Sets in Order had the Silver Spur and the Callers' Hall of Fame. So now, in September of 2002, I must give more specific credit to the person who was my support.

Square dancing and square dance calling is, and for the purposes of this book, always will be a couple activity. And while Ginger will be noticeable in the early parts of the book, so will Helen Davis, who spent eleven weeks with me, someone she hardly knew at all, to be a part of it. Becky, on the other hand, will have a key role with some complete segments about her and with her showing up from time to time to play an important part in my life story. Here are a few bits. Not knowing just what I will find already written, and in what condition when I start bringing the material together, I may do a few segments in detail, while others I may just mention the incident when the book is nearing its complete outline, some of these thoughts may have turned up or will be unwritten at that time.

The "As I See It" column published in April, 1969 featured Becky.

A revolution of a type has hit the Osgood house-hold. The discovery of gold in Alaska, the conquering of Mt. Everest, the initial running of the four minute mile and the invention of the telephone could not singly nor collectively have received greater excitement than that shown by Becky recently with her discovery of the game of golf.

Gently at first — a borrowed club, a half dozen tired golf balls, a miserable old golf bag heralded the discovery. These gave way in rather rapid succession to a matched set of clubs, a practice putting device on the living room floor, golf balls under the bed, golf cart, golf shoes, golf clothes, etc. Ah well, if the same cyclone has hit your home you know the picture.

The reason for mentioning this earth-shattering event is to point up an analogy. Becky and her "fearless-foursome" have discovered the fun of an occasional game on a not too difficult course. Some weeks they attempt eighteen holes; on others only nine. Apparently the exhilaration of getting out in the open to beat the little white pill around the golf links is just what the doctor ordered and seems to satisfy whatever urge started it all in the first place.

Apparently, this golf bug has hit many of our friends. Arnie, for example, thinks nothing of going out a couple of times a week and shooting thirty-six holes at a time. By contrast "Doc" gets his kicks out of the little three-par course over in the valley and Nadeen and Jack are apparently perfectly happy with pitch and putt adventures on a Sunday afternoon.

So here comes the analogy. What might please one of these friends of ours, undoubtedly would be too much — or too little — for one of the others. Certainly they all have golf for a hobby, but how it differs! The obvious "duffer" has his opportunity and so does the serious-minded low-handicapper.

Perhaps because of this "choice," golf is becoming more and more popular for more and more people today. The beauty is that the "duffer" in no way is ridiculed by the person like Arnie who enjoys a more serious game of golf. On the contrary, there seems to be a bond of appreciation and understanding between all who play the game regardless of the phase they select. (I watched one day as Arnie was giving a few putting tips and suggestions to Becky and I marveled another time when one of those I considered to be an expert golfer appeared to have a wonderful golfing morning with a trio of our square dancing friends — all new at the golf game — on one of the local three-par courses.)

The similarity between the game of golf and square dancing may be remote. The complete involvement of eight people within a square is a bit different from the solo endeavors of the individual golfer. However, the big point is that here there are no "levels. "The golfer, no matter how he might classify himself, will find others that share his same interest classification.

In square dancing there can just as easily be a place for everyone who wants to square dance. The person who square dances twice a month is as much a square dancer as the person who square dances six times a week. Level and ability have nothing to do with the choice. It is strictly up to the desire of each individual which plateau he chooses.

Frequently Sets in Order has been asked to develop a code of ethics for square dancers to be used as a measuring stick in the future development of this activity. Because of the folk-nature of square dancing and because a code of ethics often sounds like a set of hard and fast rules, we would like to present instead this little pledge which, by its very nature, puts the responsibility of square dancing's future squarely on the shoulder of every dancer - right where it belongs.

THE SQUARE DANCER'S PLEDGE

WITH ALL MY ABILITY I will do my best to help keep square dancing the enjoyable, wholesome, friendly and inspiring activity I know it to be. This I pledge in the sincere desire that it may grow naturally and unexploited in the coming years and be available to all those who seek the opportunity for friendship, fun and harmony — through square dancing.

-- by Becky Osgood

One time, not so long ago, Sets in Order published these lines about a square dancer. They are reprinted here in answer to a number of requests and because they seemed to belong as a part of indoctrination.

WHO IS A SQUARE DANCER?

Is he young . . . or is he old? Is he tall or short? . . . Have you ever really noticed? Is he the corner grocer or the engineer deeply involved in the next space flight? Does he belong to the church you attend? Did he vote for your candidate? You say, "I don't know," and what you mean is that it doesn't matter. Well then — what does matter? And who is he?

He's that hand — stretched out in friendship to you. He's that friendly smile — encouraging you on. He's that link that makes a square of dancers complete. He's a part of that class you started with. He's a part of that club you've danced with all these years. He's a part of that group of friends who travel together to festivals. He's the joy — the rhythm — the love that makes square dancing.

Who then is a square dancer? Look closely — for he is the most important part of square dancing — YOU.

Becky Osgood

For years after closing down the magazine, I continued to write or re-submit articles to *American Square Dance Magazine*. In September 1998 I submitted the following article.

The old Beverly Hillbillies Square Dance Club, which danced out here in Westwood, California for more than 30 years, was not necessarily a large one and you certainly wouldn't classify it as high level dancing but it was a high level fun group. Meeting twice a month, each evening had a special theme and each dance ended with refreshments and some form of entertainment. In that way over the years the club members had a good opportunity to know each other quite well and the Hillbillies became more like a family than just a group coming to dance.

Some of the stunts they dreamed up or borrowed and adapted to their own talents were nothing short of spectacular— at least we felt they were. Becky got in the habit of writing up some of these skits and stunts and sharing them with others. She also wrote down some of the after party guidelines followed by the club. Here's her list:

When planning games, stunts or skits for any square dance affair, it is always well to keep a few basic points in mind.
1. Be certain the stunt is suitable to present to a square dance group. If you can conscientiously present it to your own family, it's probably all right, but keep it clean.
2. Weigh the appropriateness of the stunt with the particular occasion. Each club is different; what works well for one group may flop for another. Think ahead and consider who will be there.

3. Don't take advantage of your caller or put him in an awkward situation. If he is to be included in a particular skit, check with him ahead of time. Or if you plan to "surprise" him, at least clear it with his wife.

4. Be aware of timing. A short, snappy skit or game will be the most appreciated.

5. Courtesy and thoughtfulness work both ways—from leader to audience and return. Practice them regardless of which side of the stage you are sitting.

6. Be prepared. Don't experiment with a new idea on a captive audience. Work it out ahead of time.

That article was one way to help me cope with my situation: it was written only six months after my Becky's passing. Thousands of people contacted us to tell us of the special place of Becky in square dancing and in our hearts.

We asked a close friend of Becky's to share her thoughts.

BECKY OSGOOD –

A friend, forever a part of our hearts. Wife, Mother, Grandmother, Tour Leader, Writer, Counselor, Student and Dancer, all roles that have been part of Becky's life, which she blended and rotated her priorities effortlessly as needed. The most significant role for Becky has been "Friend." The personification of the "Good Heart," she is the truest of friends to all who share her world of joy and balance.

She has understood that friendship and love occupy a central place in thought and tradition. Her friendship has never been diluted in any way. Friendship, as the perfection of human nature, has and always lives in Becky.

St. Aelred had written that "A truly loyal friend sees nothing in his friend but his heart." What Becky has seen in your heart, through her own spiritual maturity, has always remained meaningful to her, always open to your needs, beliefs, and with an understanding of your humanness and fears. She has exhibited the most graceful and loving way of disagreeing with you when necessary, a quality to be admired and imitated.

Square dancing, and the fellowship at the heart of it, has been a pivotal point in Becky's life. She has been the unobtrusive presence, always supporting, defining and guiding the activity through wisdom and love.

Becky does not need to be present in your space to influence your life for the best. Her true concern spans the miles and the lifetimes between you effortlessly. "Becky is the person I want to be when I grow up."

She died as she lived, never intrusive, always supportive.

-Sharon Kernen, published in American Square Dance, Aug. 1998

The Square Dance community lost a valued friend on April 6th, when Becky Osgood, the wife of Bob Osgood, passed away. Becky has been an important part of the Osgood calling partnership for many years. Becky and Bob were residing in Beverly Hills, CA at the time of her death. Bob has been an active CALLERLAB member for many years and served as Vice Chairman of the Board of CALLERLAB in 1986 and Chairman in 1987. Becky was endeared by everyone she met. Never intrusive, always supportive. She will be greatly missed.

–CALLERLAB DIRECTION,

Square dancing has always been and forever will be a couple activity. And ours, Becky's and mine, has been the perfect square dance partnership.

Not a square dancer until we were married forty years ago this past March, Becky was rapidly thrust into the role of caller's wife. Before our first anniversary, she found herself (along with fifty club friends she had inherited) on a combined cruise/ honeymoon to Hawaii. A short time later she became the first caller's wife to be invited as a part of a caller/teacher team to Alaska's inaugural State Festival.

Bob and Becky

In the years that followed she played an invaluable role as caller's partner in conducting square dance and contra classes and caller institutes. Becky participated in managing the twice-yearly Asilomar Square Dance Institutes, in planning and conducting more than twenty-five tours of square dancers to fifty countries overseas. She played a major role in the publishing of Sets in Order (SQUARE DANCING) Magazine and served as President of The Sets in Order/American Square Dance Society. A proud parent - two daughters, three grandchildren and two great grand-children - she was active in her church and managed a game of golf on Thursdays.

On learning of Becky's passing, dancers and friends around the world responded with phone calls, letters and cards. Their expressions of friendship and sorrow said it well: Becky was one of the dearest people we have ever known...there will be a great void in the dance community without her; she was truly a role model. She was loving, supportive, creative and very much her own person in a world that was always changing...had the ability to always be composed and ready with just the right words at the right time. She had a rare talent to make everyone around her feel good and feel important...A world without Becky is not at all like a world with Becky...

Her family and I thank you all for your good thoughts. - Bob Osgood

APPENDICES

APPENDIX #1: Standardization

WHAT WE DANCE

Needed: a method of evaluation, a clearing house of new movements

There is, in modern square dancing, no topic more controversial than that of new movements. There are those who feel strongly that these "inventions" are the heart and soul of the activity and that without a steady flow of this material square dancing would simply cease to hold its fascination. At the other extreme are those dancers who have been through classes, learned a certain number of basics, and now simply want to dance, enjoying what they know and not being involved with a continuing learning program. Then there are those somewhere in the middle, and perhaps this is the largest group, who would like their square dancing fashioned primarily on the seventy-five basics plus an exposure to a limited number of new, tested, danceable movements.

How to Decide?

With this latter group in mind, there appears to be a need for some method of screening or deciding upon which of the more than 200 experimental movements created each year shall be the ones selected for use. Our study shows that perhaps one new movement each month might fill the bill. A total of twenty-five somehow "approved" movements would comprise the PLUS list, over and above the basic 75. In other words, each month possibly one new movement would be added to the PLUS list and one would be dropped. Of course, if each area sets out to decide on a new movement to add to its own PLUS-25 list, it's possible that throughout the country there could be as many as thirty or fifty different selections every month. Apparently that is, in essence, what is happening today.

There needs to be some universal method of selection, some way to agree on what to add and what to subtract in order that the list be maintained at 25. First, of course, there must be some basis for judgment. Second, there must be some form of universally agreed upon clearing house to come up with the decisions. We have today four privately conducted caller note services that are in an excellent position to study this situation and suggest possible solutions. We have CALLERLAB, a growing group of concerned caller/leaders, who will be meeting next Spring and who are ideally equipped to come up with a workable program— soon.

We would like to suggest that these individuals accept the challenge and come up with a plan that can be put into effect in the coming year. We invite individuals, callers groups and others who have thoughts concerning such a program to send them in to The American Square Dance Society for circulation to the members of CALLERLAB and to others working on the project.

What's in a Name? We've always called it Square Dancing

Since our first issue we've referred to this activity as "Square Dancing." And what have we meant? We've always thought of it as an all-inclusive title—the name of a complete program involving singing call squares, patter calls and quadrilles, all done in square formation; round dances (both the not too involved current sequence rounds and the traditional free-style couple dances), mixers and called circle dances, the contras or line dances and several other miscellaneous related forms. We've realized that people in one area may say "square dancing" and spend all evening doing their "squares" in large circle sets. Others do their square dancing in lines. But, it's all square dancing. Thank goodness no attempt has been made to call this the American Square, Round, Contra, Quadrille and Circle program—that would be a mouthful.

Just call it Square Dancing and it says it all!

HOW WE DANCE

Needed: a better understanding of Standardization

Today callers and dancers everywhere are coming face to face with the problem of an acceptable standard for executing some of the basic movements. Perhaps a prime target for friendly arguments is the handhold to be used in the Swing Thru family. Which is more frequently taught, most comfortably executed, a forearm turn or the "hands up" position? Our study shows that both are being used. What's the problem, as long as each area uses what it wants to use? That's the problem. Areas themselves seem to be divided. Apparently, in some square dance communities, the "hands up" is popular in an Alamo Style where a balance forward and back is used. However, when this alternate facing circle is used only for swing thru types of movements, dancers almost automatically forget the "hands up" and go to forearm. The same thing is true with the four person swing thru. When swing thru starts with two facing couples who move forward and directly into the swing thru or spin chain thru or spin the top type of turning movement, the tendency is to go to forearms. If, however, used as originally presented from an established ocean wave formation with a balance forward and back, the "hands up" position seems to have the edge. (Those reporting say that it's virtually impossible to comfortably execute a balance forward and back in alternate facing lines when the dancers are "locked" by forearm grips. The alternative is usually a "grunt" forward and a kick.)

SEVERAL PROBLEMS

Other "standard" basics suffering from nonstandard treatment are the promenade (hands held in front, Varsouvianna position, skirt skaters position and loose escort position), the circle to a line, and one or two others. We also seem to be faced, as we always have been, with a number of individual or "fad" interpretations, patty cake clappings, unorthodox do-sa-dos and others. The decision of "Just how important is standardization and smooth dancing?" should be faced with an eye not just to the local scenes but to the universal picture. With more and more dancers traveling to dance with other clubs and at big State and National Conventions, their ability to mix with everyone, not just with others from their own areas, is important.

LEGACY and CALLERLAB, as well as callers associations everywhere, are in a good position to study the styling and standardization situations and to come up with some good workable solutions during the coming year.

We'll keep you current on the progress.

APPENDIX #2: Opening Address

by Bob Van Antwerp

These next few days are short days we have together. Let's not forget that this is a first for all of us, and with dedicated effort it will not be our last. We've only scratched the surface of some of the major problems confronting new callers today, but with a little trial and error, give and take, listen and speak and really communicate with each other, we will leave here with some positive commitments that each of us can and should resort to in order to have this recreational activity of ours progress forward with strength and unity by all, instead of a few sharing the burden for so many .

Square dancing has taken a new direction in the last few years and each one of us who is part of this movement has an important part to play in that direction. Those who are here today, have been selected for their loyalty to the dance movement, their willingness to help and their true sense of purpose. Above all you have demonstrated in the past your dedication to the square dance activity.

We have a great deal to accomplish and I do not intend to concern you with trivial matters. (Banner falls) Now that's a trivial matter.) I do not consider this a unionized type of group nor do we have any selfish motives in mind, rather we are dedicated to the good of the entire square dance activity. Each of us has his own beliefs on how the activity should expand and exist, but by working together we can form a bond of unity for the betterment of CALLERLAB with no intentions of control or monopoly. We need to approach the affirmative rather than the negative; approach and aim toward specifics rather than piddling generalities; to set deadlines for implementations and strive to meet them. Because we have all profited from this activity, I feel it is our devotion and feeling of responsibility that will say to each one of us that we put something back into it.

The need exists for direction and redirection if the activity is to flourish. We should set our sights high toward accomplishment, being careful not to set them so high that the time-tables for completion are impractical or should we accept assignments that cannot be accomplished. Goals should aim toward the purpose of establishing national unity in our activity and we should believe in what we are endeavoring to do to this group of respected individuals.

While we're here together we should enjoy this time with each other as we act out to accomplish something tangible. Your involvement, cooperation and willingness to share as we embark on this tremendous task of ours can only be attributed to the professionalism we all attest to. In short, I say let's get down to the business at hand, let's throw our personal whims to the wind and arrive at some sound conclusions that we can take back to our local groups, communities, and cities. Square dancing needs us as a team and we need it not only for the personal satisfaction but for what it offers to so many participants as their outlet to leisure time enrichment.

I had the opportunity to see the multitude of work, sweat, and almost tears that have gone into this First International Square Dance Convention, and I only ask that as one person as I finalize this opening portion that each of us must consider the fact that this function has been in the working stages for quite some time and appreciate the fact that many miles have separated the working forces and bodies who put this convention together. You may complain and criticize but to me it will only hinder the forward progress that the present members have pressed into action for the benefit of so many. I do urge you to consider, critique, and discuss changes and ask yourself individually what can I give as well as accept from my constituents.

Now to the immediate business at hand. The sessions planned have been given strong emphasis and are going to touch on many points of the square dance calling and teaching activity. I hope each of you will offer guidance when and where you can to make this encompass total involvement.

It is my privilege to introduce the delegates. But before I take off on this enjoyable assignment let me give you a few interesting facts on the delegates attending. First, counting all the registered callers we can account for approximately 1,695 years of square dance calling experience being present with us. That is equivalent to approximately 91,250 weeks or 638, 750 days of calling or teaching. Using an average of 9 hours a week, which is less for many and more for others, we can account for 641,250 hours behind that microphone and that's a lot of mike time. Our largest representation of registered callers are in the age bracket of 46 to 50. Our second largest participation are in the 41 to 45 age bracket. Also, you may be interested in knowing that our youngest caller delegate is 19 years of age and our oldest is 66 unless he lied. What other professional organization can attest to that age span. Next we have representation from 33 states. We have six callers representing two provinces of Canada. Two of our callers are attending from exceptionally great distances to be a part of this convention, one all the way from Australia and one from New Zealand and what a tribute to have these two callers present.

We are graciously blessed to have approximately 10 wives of our callers with us today. We thank you wives for being with us. The contribution that you make to us is endless and I'll say something else, thanks for just putting up with us and the support you always are ready to offer. Having some lady callers present I will not try to break it down as male or female counterparts but you know who you are and we appreciate your just being here. This has been a very special and memorable occasion for me to be allowed the opportunity to meet and greet all of you on behalf of some of the 9,000 callers that are teaching and calling in our profession.

I would like to now bring you up to date on the some of the projects that the members of CALLERLAB have been concerning themselves with for the past 2 to 3 years. Just what is meant by CALLERLAB? As you may know, CALLERLAB started out as an affiliation of a number of established callers and leaders. The group laid its initial ground work in Colorado as long ago as the summer of 1961, however, not until February of 1971 did 14 members of the Callers' Hall of Fame gather ln California for a meeting, then the group realistically went into action. It was the feeling of those who attended this session that the direction square

555

dancing was taking appeared to be loaded with detours. The lack of standardization and an uncontrolled flood of non-descriptive, frequently awkward experimental movements was one source of confusion. It appeared instead of working together for the common interest of the activity callers were for the most part endeavoring to lick the problem on an individual basis. It also was apparent that square dancing needed the benefit of coordinated caller/leadership direction. In forming the group to be known as CALLERLAB, the objectives were to determine ways to solve these various problems and to accomplish by working together the many projects that simply could not be accomplished by the individual working alone. Rather than immediately opening the doors to all callers everywhere it was decided that expansion of CALLERLAB membership would be on a gradual, personal invitation basis and that in this way a firm foundation could be built and maintained. A report, later on this afternoon, will give you more information as to the membership but I thought you might be interested as to how CALLERLAB started.

Some of the goals accepted by members of CALLERLAB the past 2 to 2 1/2 years are the endorsement of a caller/teacher manual for the basic program of American square dancing, as an accurate description of the terms that form the foundation of American square dancing. Number two, the endorsement of a caller/teacher manual for the extended basics program of American square dancing. Number three, the appointment of a committee to prepare a recommended curriculum for an approved five day caller/leader institute. It was at that time approved that Bob Osgood would carry out the functions of CALLERLAB as a wing of the SIO/ASDS and serve as Executive Secretary to the group at that time. It was approved that a $25 annual membership fee be established for CALLERLAB. It was approved that the Executive Secretary be instructed to establish a CALLERLAB archive and files starting prior to the Colorado meeting of 1961. Some of the statements that were presented during these many meetings that we had were: Number one, let's put the dance back into square dancing. Number two, an accepted form of standardization is vital to the continuation and growth of this activity. Number three, that caller/teacher leadership training is the responsibility of the callers and teachers. Number four, professional standards for callers and teachers need to be established. Number Five, today's square dancing is due for a reappraisal. Number six, the combination of the various parts of the square dance activity should be encouraged such as rounds, contras, quadrilles. Number seven, the selfish exploitation of square dancing should be vigorously discouraged. Number eight, the over organization of dancer/leader groups can pose a problem to the future progress of the activity. Number nine, the importance of the club caller system. Number ten, the National Square Dance Convention is missing the boat. Number eleven, what can CALLERLAB do to be of help to caller/leaders in the future. Another topic was communications. Number thirteen, the need for an experimental movements clearing house. Number fourteen, fees for callers. The last one was caller registry, a means of accrediting callers.

In order to establish just what CALLERLAB is involved in, working committees have been established for quite some time. In order to represent total involvement in our CALLERLAB, you have been given a committee assignment form. The intent of this form is to allow you as a delegate to select a committee you would prefer to work on. Give this your close consideration and be prepared to involve yourself in one of our important committees. Some of these committees have been endeavoring to operate in your behalf to make an initial report today but they still need your input on the committee you select, to make it as representative as possible for all of our approximately 9,000 callers. Now, as I lead into the different gentlemen who will be making the reports today, each one of them will be making a report as the chairman of his particular committee.

APPENDIX #3 Committee Reports

The Convention was organized to deal with three major problem areas in round-robin sessions: "How we dance," "Accreditation," and "New movements." All of the delegates were assigned to one of the three smaller groups which would be presented the themes, one after another, while a recorder and three judges would monitor the discussion and vote on their findings. Each group would hear the proposal on each of the topics by the same presenter so the input would be consistent. Then the floor was open to questions and discussion, after which the judges and the recorder would retire to discuss how each group reacted to the presentation. At the end of each presentation, the presenters would rotate to a new group, round robin fashion. The convention theme "Working Together" was most appropriate. In spite of some initial misgivings, it was far beyond a doubt that a large group of so-called *prima donna* callers can, in fact, work together for the common good for the whole calling profession and square dancing. The friendly arguing, give and take, compromise, and camaraderie was inspiring and set the tone for all future conventions

Before breaking into the groups, Bob Van Antwerp introduced the Board Members who were Committee Chairmen and asked each one to make a short report on progress and needs. The reports were also a way to recruit people for each of the committees:

1) Communications – Stan Burdick

How to communicate effectively – there are three national magazines, plus notes from associations all over the country. How can CALLERLAB help upgrade these publications? Also, CALLERLAB has its own newsletter, DIRECTION, and American Square Dance Society publishes the *Gavel and Key*. A suggestion for all callers is: Please respond quickly to communications…do not let them age on your desk top. Furthermore, there are the "listening posts" which will take comments and complaints and send them on.

2) NSDC Liaison – Dave Taylor

One of the CALLERLAB points is that the National Square Dance Convention is missing the boat. A poll found many callers felt the only reason to attend NSDC was to socialize. The NSDC was not a showpiece of square dance as it should be. CALLERLAB should have some role in NSDC, which is a dancer run activity. We need open communications with the National Executive Committee.

3) Rounds – Manning Smith

Reminded people that though he was more a caller than a cuer, he believed that callers should teach simple rounds – higher levels can be taught by the specialist.

4) Area callers groups – Vaughn Parrish

CALLERLAB has an obligation to build communications and have liaison with local associations, and that it needs to be a two way communication of CALLERLAB to local associations and back. CALLERLAB should be open to at least one member of each local callers association. There is a wealth of information that CALLERLAB should share with caller's partners. CALLERLAB should take advantage of openings in other publications, for example, *RV Magazine* is going to include square dances in its calendar – how can we help? Membership in CALLERLAB is prestigious and gives a caller "standing" in the dance community. And CALLERLAB should have caller clinics at the National Square Dance Convention.

5) Membership – Bob Osgood

You are here by personal invitation – get your invitation from your sponsor, go to the sign in table and pay membership dues of $25 and get your membership card. There is a form for you to make recommendations of new

members. Do not tell people you have recommended them…we will review the recommendations and notify.
6) Canada/US relations – Earle Park

Political red-tape makes it difficult for Canadian callers to work in the US. Going from US to Canada is easier. By a caller declaring himself as an entertainer, the border patrol generally allows people across. CALLERLAB should push for the US to change its policies.
7) Benefits for Callers – Bruce Johnson

Callers generally work for cash with no benefits. We need to look into pensions, insurance, etc. And we need people who understand negotiating. Perhaps CALLERLAB could negotiate contracts with hotels, etc., for reduced rates for members. Use CALLERLAB to solve the border problem with Canada
8) Caller's contracts – Marshall Flippo

CALLERLAB should develop forms that cover fees, date, dance level, and location (and how to get there). Make it a friendly letter of understanding
9) Basics – Johnny LeClair

Lists built on many surveys, but this committee needs relevant lists. Currently we are using the Sets in Order Basic list.
10) Record clearing house – CO Guest

There are big problems involving duplication of titles. The previous attempt at a record clearing house did not work because producers felt there were too many restrictions already, the clearing house could not regulate unscrupulous producers, and the clearing house really did not want the responsibility – they just wanted to make money off the producers.

CALLERLAB recommends that record companies let others know what they recorded. And producers should let others know if they decide not to release a particular tune.
11) Halls – Melton Luttrell

Halls have become expensive. One plan is to get plans on building halls. But if someone decides to build a hall, there are some necessities: a) accessibility, b) size planned around realistic number of dancers to use the hall, c) there are prefab buildings, but make sure they have 1) good floor, 2) good sound, 3) air conditioning and heating, 4.) kitchen, 5) adequate RR, 6) adequate parking, 7) consider babysitting space and office space. DO NOT build if there are affordable buildings in your area. And there are serious problems with ownership.

12) New Dancers – Jerry Helt

There is a lot of information on recruiting new dancers and how to publicize classes and square dancing in general. CALLERLAB can help with sharing that information. There are also many ways to help clubs retain dancers.

13) LEGACY – Charlie Baldwin

Reported on 1973 meeting – LEGACY covers all aspects of dancing from record producers to publishers to clothing outlets. LEGACY's goal is to discuss and evaluate the state of square dancing. It is a very informal 'organization.' There must be some coordination of the goals of LEGACY and CALLERLAB. We need to reinject vitality into square dance.

14) Ethics – Bob Van Antwerp

We have gathered codes from all over, but we want to create our own, not just duplicate what others have done. The rough is started but there is still a lot to do.

Appendix #4: Osgood Keynote Address at CALLERLAB 1974

Bob Van Antwerp: It's really my pleasure, it is a pleasant responsibility to present to you a friend in the first degree to the square dance movement and a real pro in heart and spirit and a personal associate, Bob Osgood.

Bob Osgood: A number of years ago the well-known television and radio personality, Ralph Edwards, was serving as master of ceremonies for a home talent show at the church where he attends.

About midway into the program, following a musical group which had just performed and with the curtain closed they were moving the piano from the stage for a square dance exhibition that was to follow. Using up the time, Ralph Edwards was interviewing the dignified, gray-haired minister of the church.

"Sir," said Ralph, "when I was a young man we wouldn't think of dancing, particularly square dancing, in a church. How do you feel about it? And the minister, tilting his head slightly, thought for a minute, then with a twinkle in his eye, turned to Ralph and said, "You know, of all the ways I can think of to get to heaven. I think I would like to square dance there best!"

Over the past three decades we have come in contact with literally thousands of men and women who have reached their heaven here on earth through square dancing. "Heaven," by the way, is defined in Webster's Third International Dictionary as ... a place or condition or period of utmost happiness, comfort or delight....

How many people moving into a strange neighborhood have found themselves among friends thanks to square dancing? How many times we've heard of marriages virtu-

ally on the rocks that have been rejuvenated through participation in this joy-filled activity? And we can think of the
many men and women in the Armed Forces stationed overseas for whom square dancing has meant a whole new way
of life, an escape from what sometimes amounts to a dreary
military existence away from home. To be sure, square dancing has provided a sense of "heaven on earth" for hundreds
of thousands throughout the world. This fact we accept when
we first pick up the microphone to call.

And so, as we begin this new adventure, this first
callers' convention, let's remember our responsibility to the
dancer. That's what this is all about! You know, whenever I
get puffed up over a particularly fine dance I may have
thought I called, I bring myself back to earth with the rather
sobering realization that it's not me they're applauding - it's
the dance. And my responsibility as a caller - my job, if you
will is to bring the two, the dance and the dancer together.

One of the reasons for our being here then is to find
ways for us to meet our responsibility to do a better job as
professionals in the field of calling.

We've come to the conclusion that one way to do a
better, more effective job, is to compare notes on a broad
basis with other callers...many callers from all over the
world. This then, is a reason for the CALLERLAB organization to come into existence.

For years many of us here have been opposed to the
thought of organization. We have felt that the very nature of
this activity raises it beyond the scope of organizational controls or organizational restrictions. But today it seems that
the patients are trying to do the doctor's work for them. You
heard a report earlier today regarding the Annual National
Square Dance Convention. One of the points here that
seemed a bit incongruous is that this group of dancers has
felt it necessary to set up a school for callers. It's a bit like
the patients putting on a medical convention for doctors. And

563

yet, you don't criticize them entirely. They saw a need that obviously wasn't being met and they set out to meet it.

Just a week ago a friend who is president of a large state council of square dance associations called to say that because the callers were not able to control the tremendous influx of new, non-descriptive experimental movements, he and a group of dancers were setting out to do the job themselves. They would decide on a list of calls a caller would be permitted to use and the caller will use these or not be allowed to call for these groups. Now, I'm not being critical here of the plan. But I am concerned that this task would have to fall to the customer, to our clients, to the dancers.

I'm reminded of a situation that used to exist in Oklahoma. When a club caller, or any caller for that matter, would show up at a dance he would be handed the program he was to call that evening. That's right. Each dance, patter call, singing call, and round would be listed on the program and that was his assignment. As far as I know this situation no longer exists but it indeed points up a lack of definite caller/leadership.

Maybe what we're looking for at this Convention is an opportunity to consolidate our leadership. To establish some guidelines. To put our best foot forward and to prove that by working together we can accomplish much more than we could ever hope to accomplish by working alone.

How many have ever been to the 17 mile drive near Monterey, California? One day out on the coast a number of years ago, I was standing on the beach watching the waves and just enjoying the spray and the fresh sea air, when I became aware of someone standing beside me. Another man had come up, unnoticed, and he too was watching the ocean, absorbed in its beauty. Neither of us said anything for a long time. Then the other man said, "This is a wonderful country. You know, I'm from the Philippines, and I'm proud of my country too. But right now we're having problems at home." And he continued, "You know, it's funny, but after the war when it became time for us to build a new government, we patterned our constitution after the Constitution of your country. However, having had the advantage of almost 200 years of history, we corrected many of the errors we felt existed in your constitution and when we were through, we felt we had a constitution that was as nearly perfect as man could make it." He paused for what seemed like a long time while he was obviously deep in thought. Then he continued again, "But do you know, it hasn't worked. There, on paper, is everything that a perfect government should be. And do you know what the problem I think is. I think that we have the words all right. We simply don't have the heart that goes along with it."

I think that we here at CALLERLAB 1974 do have the heart. I think we have the sincerity of purpose that is so necessary for us to be organizationally successful.

I feel that we are sufficiently mature to realize that it isn't we, by ourselves, that are the huge successes that make square dancing popular. Square dancing itself is the success. As callers, it is merely our responsibility, or our obligation, our privilege, to serve as the go-between, that is, to bring the dancer and the dance together.

Today CALLERLAB is a baby. Like all parents, we want our "baby" to be beautiful, talented and successful. Most of all, like all parents, we love it and we are learning to be patient as we watch it grow step by step. We have only the desire that it succeed in being an influence of good in the square dance activity.

We see this as a means of insuring that the square dance calling profession will become more deeply dedicated, more sensitive to the needs of the individual dancers, clubs and home club callers, more realistic in its approach to the activity as a whole.

What we have at the moment is our combined personal desires and objectives. As members of this profession we need to study our present programs and practices and determine if we are meeting our activity's needs. For this convention and for the coming year I would like to suggest this 10 point platform.

I feel that we should:

1. Establish some immediate working method of evaluating new experimental movements. According to a consensus of all our personal feelings of urgency there is no more important subject on our docket here at CALLERLAB for us to tackle than this. There is no problem that more logically fits into this realm of caller leadership than this and there is no subject that will be afforded more time and attention here at CALLERLAB, than this.

Perhaps, aside from the rather amazing fact that we have actually met here, I doubt if there is any subject of greater urgency facing caller leadership today, than this. And I might add, a great number of people all over are anxiously waiting to see just what we do on this subject.

2. We should recognize and encourage quality in dancing. There was a time when everyone learned all of the basics in a relatively short period of time and then concentrated on learning to dance them better putting the emphasis on correct timing, smoothness and intelligent body mechanics.

I'm sure that I'm not alone in feeling that it's about time that we return to this practice, and, as caller/teachers, build back into our teaching programs a better sense of styling and comfortable dancing,

3. We need some workable system of accrediting our callers and our teachers. Perhaps the only way we can effectively accomplish this is thru a leadership concentration such as CALLERLAB. Now, these three topics have been selected by you as the most urgent on our list of targets for this convention. Because of their relevance to the present and future of square dancing we have given them key positions in

our program here and you will be hearing a great deal more about them as the program unfolds.

The following I add to the platform because these points are of significant importance to all of us if CALLERLAB is to function as a meaningful organization. You'll recognize some of these as already assigned to CALLERLAB working committees.

4. If we are going to be involved, as the sign says, in WORKING TOGETHER then we need a workable code of behavior as our guide. Any professional society that's worth its salt has a code of ethics which its members find acceptable .

To be rightly labeled a profession requires the establishment of and the compliance with such a code. In the field of square dance calling, a code of ethics should define our relationship first with those we teach, with those for whom we call and with those who employ the use of our professional services. Second, with our colleagues, with each other, with our peers in the calling field, and third with the public in general. Such a code would also point out the primary obligations of the square dance caller and stress his role of service and of public trust.

But having a code of ethics is not enough. The necessary machinery should be developed to see that it is adequately publicized.

5. We need to develop an effective program of public relations. This area needs considerable attention, for there are many misunderstandings about square dancing in general and the square dance calling profession in particular that need to be corrected.

Melton Luttrell told us earlier today about a hall that he was building and from Joe Lewis I gained a different side of the same story. Here is a real unselfish project going on in an area.

A councilman in one of the districts, being obviously aware of what's going on and perhaps is being helped a little bit by some people in the area, is radically opposed to this building that is going to bring drunks and disorderly conduct and the use of many additional police in the area.

I think this is ridiculous and I think that one of these days we are going to be in a place with our publicity where people will begin to understand what this is all about and not get the feeling that we might have faced 20 or 30 or 40 years ago. We need to project the image of a caller and we need to project a correct image of this activity.

So public relations calls for a period of reevaluation of just what it is that we are offering the public and perhaps a period when the image of the caller and the activity can be radically improved and correctly publicized.

As a prime function of CALLERLAB I would like to see us develop the following projects.

First, the creation of a master roster of all callers everywhere on IBM cards is being developed in our office. Every time you send us the name of a new caller, or a roster from your area callers' association it is checked against the current list. This list will be a ready guide to our CALLERLAB potential.

Second, an individual file of every caller everywhere has also been started. You each have your own file folder which contains (we hope) your most recent publicity picture and another with you and your wife or husband together. Plus your personal information questionnaire and any additional biographical information you may have sent to us.

We and others in CALLERLAB who get this responsibility will have these ready to turn out whenever publicity stories seem appropriate. Having them is half the job. Putting them into print and getting them out to different publications and newspapers is not the problem once you have the information handy.

Third, a CALLERLAB bureau of publicity and advertising should be set up and manned by a square dance oriented public relations specialist, This bureau would give counsel to publications, develop special news projects, prepare newspaper, radio and television information, particularly where an inaccurate representation of square dancing and square dance callers has been made to the public.

And, as a matter of course it would cooperate in the currently effective Listening Post project. This is the HOT LINE operation set up by Charlie Baldwin of the New England caller, Stan Burdick of American Square Dance, and me, as a means of quickly passing along word of some impending problem that needs the quick action of square dance groups. It has been most effective.

6. We need to become aware of what talent lies here among the members of CALLERLAB. Or in more high falutin' words we need to conduct an inventory of our human resources.

In the roll call made by our Chairman earlier this afternoon, we met many men and women of great knowledge and background. Some represented here have life-long careers in business, teaching, professional and organizational skills. At the present time, even with our limited membership, we have among our members an almost unlimited storehouse of talent and skill.

A CALLERLAB human resources file has been started. We should, from the standpoint of the calling profession, be in a position to tap this reservoir of knowledge. And, just as important, we should as a professional in this activity, be willing to contribute our skills where they are needed.

7. We should create a center for reflective and advanced thinking for the square dance activity.

How I wish that we had with us in CALLERLAB such leaders as Dr. Lloyd Shaw, Ed Gilmore, Jack Hoheisel, Jim York and others who are no longer available to us. How much they could offer us in advice and direction and in knowledge of this activity.

There are others who are available today and we should devise means of tapping their knowledge and wisdom.

Many of those on the CALLERLAB Board of Governors, many of you here among the delegates, and still others out in the field have much to offer. We should tap the experience of these leaders while we can, so their wisdom can help this profession to grow and prosper.

A center for reflective and advanced thinking in the field of square dance calling should be established where these leaders would periodically congregate, exchange views, mull over the problems facing the profession, impart their wisdom and give those of us, who are still on the action front, the benefit of their thinking. Our profession could be much better for having created such an institute.

8. We should concentrate on our two basics programs as a Point of Reference for the square dance activity.

This is a project of CALLERLAB and has been since our first meetings.

In accepting these programs we have paved the way for tens of thousands of people to learn to square dance on a uniform program, safe in the knowledge that if they ever find they must drop out for a time, there is always a familiar, non-changing basic foundation for them to return to.

9. We should look for ways that CALLERLAB can complement the tasks being undertaken by its individual members.

By establishing clinics and a tune registration system to help those callers who record, by setting up a workable curriculum for callers' schools, by helping those callers in the business of publishing monthly Callers' notes, or by helping to promote international or regional publications, CALLERLAB will offer a useful service to its members and to all of square dancing without infringing on private enterprise and without competing with its own members.

10. And finally, CALLERLAB should become a body of knowledge for this phase of the activity.

When someone asks, "What is the thought on some particular problem or situation?" you will be able to say, "This is the stand that CALLERLAB has taken on the subject." You will know that this reflects the thinking of many fine callers.

How great it will be to know that as an individual caller you are alone no longer. This platform may seem far too ambitious an undertaking at this early stage of CALLERLAB. It is the essence of leadership, however, that our reach must exceed our grasp. Carl Schulz, an immigrant to this country, pointed out long ago, "Ideals are like stars. You'll not succeed in touching them with your hands. But, like the seafaring man on the desert of water you choose them as your guides, and following them you will reach your destiny."

Somebody may say of CALLERLAB, "This is fine, but it should have been done 15 years ago." Nonsense. We know things today that we never knew before and we can benefit from the experience of all of us here today in this room. Certainly we have some problems to overcome. We must learn to be patient. If the goals are important enough we can achieve them.

We all have strong feeling about what is right and what is wrong in square dancing. Here is our opportunity to listen to what others feel. At home we may be the sole leader among callers, but here (and this is one of the wonderful things that CALLERLAB is providing) we are among our peers. We can hear many points of view expressed. We can realize that we are not alone.

Don't be upset if things don't turn out just exactly the way you would like to have them turn out in every instance. For if this group is to be successful there must be much give

571

and take. We realize that in many instances some may be talking about apples while others are talking about oranges. Some of us may have difficulty in understanding the things being said by others, but let's listen and attempt to understand. And if we are successful in the next few years, in building a useful organization of several thousand members let us never misuse this sense of power. Rightly directed, it can benefit us all. Incorrectly guided, it can tear down some of the very goals we are trying to establish.

CALLERLAB should not be a union. It should, however, contain in its makeup some of the professional dedication that is to be found in some of the effective and healthy unions of today. It should not be a fraternity. Although the camaraderie, fellowship, friendliness, and protection that come with such a group must be visible in CALLERLAB in order for it prove its usefulness.

Will this convention be a success? It depends on what we mean by success. It has already brought together 110 callers and 60 of their wives. It has provided an opportunity for all of us to discuss the things that callers have wanted to discuss together for a long time. It is providing the setting and atmosphere for a meaningful discussion.

It is a solution oriented meeting. By that I mean, that from this meeting should come some definite directions which we all voluntarily and enthusiastically will want to support.

This is not a time to say yes, yes, we agree, and then go home to our clubs and do otherwise. If we believe that a caller should be a professional, then we agree together that each one of us should keep scheduled appointments, should speak in a professional manner concerning other callers, should adhere to the majority decisions made at meetings like this one so that we can all say, "We worked these problems out together and we're going to see them through to a successful conclusion."

Only through mutual respect and cooperation can callers prove to the rest of the square dancing world that they are leaders, that they are thinking of the good of the entire activity, that they are thinking of more than just themselves.

If we are as interested and as pleased and as satisfied with the success of another caller as we are with our own success, then this attitude will become contagious and the Spirit of St. Louis that has brought us together will spread throughout the world.

APPENDIX #5: My Eye

 Following a LEGACY meeting in Arkansas, I spent a delightful three days with my friends, Charlie and Marybelle Robbins, who lived in nearby Rogers, Arkansas. Knowing of my interest in the Civil War they took me to the site of the Battle of Pea Ridge. Leaving our car in the almost empty parking lot near the headquarters building, we walked up to the Ranger Station to get information about the area. Outside the building we passed a lone couple seated on a bench. As we approached them the lady waved, "Hi Bob! How's square dancing going in Southern California?" I was drawing a blank. "You don't remember us, but my husband and I danced to your calling in the San Fernando Valley about two years ago."

While Marybelle and Charlie may have been impressed, I realized it was just one more instance of my recognition signal ringing a bell. There's something about wearing a black eye patch that sets one apart.

I have joined the company of World War I newspaper journalist, Floyd Gibbons, Will Rogers' friend and pilot,

Wiley Post, and the man from Hathaway shirts as a patch wearer. Following World War II when I lost the sight of my left eye due to a service-incurred injury, the patch became more or less a part of me.

It's really not much of an inconvenience even though people do mistake me for someone else. More than once I'm pointed out to others as the Jewish fighter Moshe Dayan, also an "eye-patcher." It's strange but not everyone knows how to handle a person in this predicament. They never mention it, and some find it easier to look away or pretend nothing is out of the ordinary - which is fine.

Kids present a different situation altogether. They want to know, "What's wrong with the man's eye?" which is only natural. A three or four year old will stop and look - then turn to a parent and ask for an explanation. Obviously embarrassed, the mother or father will haul junior off in some other direction, leaving the youngster's curiosity unanswered, or perhaps partially answer with an "Oh, he's got a boo-boo."

None of this bothers me, except the youngster is truly curious and wants to know "what," "why," which I'd be glad to tell him in a way that would stem his curiosity and let him know that it's not all that bad a situation.

I remember one small tyke who had obviously asked his mother, "Why is that man wearing a pirate's eye patch?" I was pleased with her answer. "I don't know Billy. Why don't you ask him?" It was simple to answer his question. "I was hit in the eye during the war and now I need to keep the eye protected, so I wear this bandage." Or, depending upon the situation, the story may vary some, but usually when this happens the youngster is satisfied with the answer and goes on with whatever he was doing, thinking no more about it.

Over the years the black patch has brought about some interesting adventures.

During one of our Sets in Order tours our group of ninety was in Thailand. As a part of the sightseeing we took the group in small boats on one of the klongs. The dancers each got into the narrow, outboard powered craft one at a time. As each boat filled up with its three or four passengers, it scooted off and a new boat took its place, loaded, and went on its way. It took a while for all of the people to get on the boats, and with Becky and me at the tail end, we had an opportunity to enjoy watching the men on the dock help the passengers to board.

One of the helpers was a small boy, not more than five or six years old who kept looking over at me, obviously fascinated by the eye patch and by the moustache I sported at that time. When it was our turn to board, this small boy ran over to us, reached into his pants pocket and whipped out a miniature eye patch and small moustache which he quickly donned. Treasures perhaps gathered from Cracker Jack boxes. Needless to say, his ingenuity brought him a generous tip. He had probably waited a long time to find a visitor to match his "disguises".

And then there was the time when traveling from one area to another, I was calling a large dance in the Midwest somewhere. During the evening, I noticed a couple of small boys standing down at the foot of the stage occasionally looking up at me. When the dance ended and I had put the microphone down, I couldn't help overhearing them as one boy was saying to the other, "Oh, there's nothing wrong with his eye. He just can't remember the calls so he has them written and pasted on the inside of that patch."

A few years back, the Osgoods had a family reunion - the first ever for some 35 to 40 relatives. On the second morning of our weekend visit we lined up on the steps of the Administration Building and one of the groundsmen took a group picture, which would be a souvenir for all of us. As is a custom of photographers, he asked for a second shot. Looking around after the picture was taken, I couldn't help but be a bit flabbergasted to realize that not me alone, but every one of the relatives was wearing a black eye patch over his or her left eye. That's the way we Osgoods are.

Appendix #6: Floors We Have Danced On

SETS IN ORDER Front Door

SETS IN ORDER HALL: the dance floor upstairs

Over the years square dancers have done "their thing" on just about every imaginable dance surface there is. From ideal hardwood to less-than-ideal concrete with its tendency to wear out the soles of a lady's dance slippers in a single evening.

We were taught, when we were just learning to dance, that the way to move was with a smooth, gliding step, the feet being only slightly above the dancing surface and making a swish-swishing sound as one moved across the floor.

Now, that's no problem on maple or oak, but have you ever tried it dancing on grass? A football field is about as bad as it gets, especially at a half-time performance when the turf is badly bruised from 250 pound guards and tackles wrestling on it for the past thirty minutes. And, it's even worse when it's been raining. That swish-swishing sound becomes a slop-slopping distortion that changes its characteristics, depending on the depth and sloppiness of the water.

Our dancers out here have weathered the handicap of lawn-dancing any number of times, but the rain-soaked gridiron incident happened as the halftime entertainment on the "floor" of the Los Angeles Olympic Coliseum a number of years ago. As I remember, even though it was a play-off game for the pros, the spectators were smarter than the costumed dancers. Most of the rooters left the stadium sometime between the starting whistle and the end of the first period. Or they may have stayed home in the first place. But the dancers, sturdy souls that we were, sat through it all, waiting to perform. Then onto the muddy turf. And we danced! Until that time I don't believe any of us really knew the meaning of the word "soggy."

A good friend of ours, Chuck Pratt, remembers square dances on his family's farm many years ago. It was an annual event and, when the barn was empty, it was time to invite the neighbors and get things ready for the big party. As the youngest of his siblings, it was Chuck's job to get the rough barn floor in shape for the hoedown. He'd tie a piece of rope to a bale of hay and, starting out early in the morning, he'd drag the hay long-ways, against the grain, along the boards, pulling out the splinters and eventually coming up with a moderately smooth and serviceable dance floor.

Of course, over the years, we printed many articles about strange surfaces to dance on and about special places built for dancing. Here are a handful of samples.

In case you cannot read the text, it is reprinted here:
big tree stump: Dance Floor of Calaveras County California: Cotillion party of 40 persons dances on the stump of the Mammoth Sequoia Tree

The original tree was 302 feet high and 2000 years old! 1864 The Big Tree Stump of Calaveras County, California. The 18 inch bark of the original tree was removed by some vandals to a height of 20 feet. Out of the bark a house was built which was exhibited at the Crystal Palace Convention in London. The mutilated tree had to be chopped down, and on the remaining stump 49 people (including musicians and onlookers) danced at a cotillion on July 4, 1864. The original tree was 302 feet high, 96 feet in circumference,

2,000 years old. For many years dances were performed on this tree every Saturday night, religious services were held on it on Sundays, and a newspaper called "The Big Tree Bulletin" was printed and published on it.

I suppose we should remember that Mark Twain set one of his most marvelous stories in the same area: "The Notorious Jumping Frog of Calaveras County."

The picture to the right is of the notorious "Promenade Hall" in Rialto, California. It was above Johnnie's Market and was accessed by steep staircases either from the street or the alley. The front stairs were fitted with a system attached to the wall to carry people or goods up

Promenade Hall, Rialto, California

to the second floor. The hall itself, as you can see, was outfitted with posts to catch the unwary dancers.

Theme parks throughout the country caught the square dance fad and made space available for dancers. Disneyland also used to have dances, but even more, it put on square dance shows with live dancers and callers. However, "Farley the Fiddler" is still featured with his corny jokes and great old time fiddling.

The first time we ever saw a temporary wooden surface laid out on a grass area, was at the annual Penticton (Canada) Peach Festival. An arrangement was made with a local lumber yard to furnish and buy back hundreds of square feet of plywood. These sheets were mounted on stringers and the results were amazing.

Since that time there have been many successful jamborees featuring plywood or particle board flooring. We understand that some of the organizations store their portable floors from one year to the next while others resell the lumber at a reduced rate to the suppliers. This type of temporary flooring has also been used successfully in indoor structures to transfer rough concrete or carpeted surfaces into very satisfactory, danceable flooring.

There are times, however, when the dancers have to create their own hall, or at least a floor. Here is the story of the outdoor wooden floor.

Dancers in many areas may have been bemoaning the fact that, while they would like to play host to square dancers for some large dance affair, they just can't do it because there is no hall big enough. They may take heart from what was accomplished by square dancers working together in Oregon.

A specific example was the preparation of a huge outdoor wooden square dance floor for the 2nd Far Western Regional Square Dance Convention in Eugene. Members from 50 different clubs gathered to work together to lay what proved to be a dance floor covering 120,000 square feet. The clubs represented most of the areas in the Oregon State Federation of Square Dance Clubs.

This project was no spur-of-the-moment thing, having been planned for months by Buddy Randall, General Chairman of the Convention. Milo Mathews, Eugene contractor, was given the heavy responsibility for drafting the laying of the floor. And at the Mid-Winter Clinic held in Eugene about six months prior to the Convention the particleboard, Duraflake, was tried out to see if the surface was danceable. The material was also tested for warping by leaving it exposed to the elements for weeks at a time.

Mathews also had to keep in mind the wide range of temperature to which the floor would be exposed — the sun of August noons and the cool Oregon evenings.

The actual location was the campus of the University of Oregon, site of the Convention activities, and on the Saturday morning before the Convention was to begin volunteer workers showed up at daybreak, bringing their hammers with them. Daybreak means 3 o'clock at that time of year and some of the workers had driven great distances.

The ground, which had been leveled as much as the University would permit, was raked. A crew followed, laying 120,000 square feet of plastic to keep the dust and moisture from seeping through from the ground. A 3-inch thick wood shim under each joint allowed each panel of pressed wood to lock properly. A number of lift trucks distributed the panels one by one to the busy men who swarmed over the working area. Two hundred thousand metal staples were used to keep the 4' x 8' panels together.

If the volunteers asked for accommodations they and their wives were put up for two nights in the homes of Eugene square dancers. As the men helped with the floor-laying, their taws manned the coffee urns, made hamburgers and hot dogs.

The floor wasn't only pre-tested. After it was down, did the tired men start for home and their waiting beds? If you know square dancers you know better. That evening when the hoedown music started they were back, not with hammers in hand, but to dance and find that their work had been good.

The whole project was in the tradition of the old-fashioned barn-raising, where pioneers got together to help each other out when that help was needed — and had a whale of a time doing it! In our present age of what seems at times "total indifference," it is heartening to report an accomplishment like this—but then, "square dancers are wonderful people!"

Powder Mill Barn around 1900 when it was still used to lodge horses hauling gunpowder.

The next story is about one of the most unique conversions of a building from its original business into a square dance hall.

A real New England Landmark is the Powder Mill Barn in Hazardville, Connecticut, where Ralph and Betty Sweet, its owners, conduct a busy and successful square and round dance program. The Barn is located on South Maple Street in Hazardville and may be reached by driving about 6 miles south of Springfield, Mass., on Conn. Rt. 20. By turning at the traffic light in the center of town and driving 1/4 mile to the right, you reach this interesting spot.

The Barn was built by the Hazard Powder Company well over a hundred years ago, about 1845, as nearly as can be determined. The company owned over 400 acres on which were some 220 buildings. During the Civil War, the company was the Union's largest supplier of gunpowder and was purchased by the DuPonts in the 1880's.

Operations continued until 1913, when antitrust action, along with the high cost of transportation, caused it to fold. The Barn was used to keep the company horses, which hauled powder between buildings; and powder and saltpeter to and from the railroad and the Connecticut River.

The Barn was used intermittently for a riding academy and in 1959, caller Ralph Sweet and his wife Betty bought it to be converted for square dancing. This was done with the help of dozens of area square dancers, especially from the Enfield Square Dance Club.

By working at the Barn, the dancers earned a "Woodpecker" badge, shaped like Woody Woodpecker and bearing the words, Powder Mill Barn. The Enfield Club has held classes and club dances in the Barn since the Fall of 1959.

In March, 1961, a new maple floor was put down and in May, 1961, the Sweets moved into the upstairs with their four children. The Barn has a kitchen downstairs and the walls are lined with framed pictures of the powder making industry. The hall will hold 20 sets of square dancers. At present there are dances scheduled almost every night, including square and round dance classes, club and teen age dances.

The week of August 5-11 has been set for an exhibit on the powder-making industry to be held at the Barn. Pictures, powder cans, kegs, etc., will be on display—but no real gunpowder!

Square Dance day at Dodger Stadium

Appendix #7: Terry Golden and American Folk Music

At Asilomar we were blessed to have two of the best folk singers in the country join us. Not only did Terry Golden and Sam Hinton provide great leadership in getting people to sing out, they also gave us some of the Americana that goes along with the folk tunes. A number of these tunes were picked up by recording companies and became standards on the radio as well as in the square dance hall. At the time when we held the Asilomar sessions, many people knew these melodies but they had long forgotten – if they ever knew – the lyrics. We always had sheets of lyrics at Asilomar so there was no excuse for not lending your voice to the merriment of the evening.

Later on, Terry wrote a series of columns about folk tunes, where they came from, how they changed, how they were used in square dance, etc. Here are two that I think are particularly good.

Everybody is probably familiar with the song of the Erie Canal that warns "low bridge, everybody down/low bridge we're comin' to a town." Terry used to sing a satirical song

By Terry Golden – Colorado Springs, Colo.

of the Erie Canal that made the canal seem like one of the Great Lakes.

The Erie Canal, of the days when this song originated, wasn't a very frightening waterway. For the most part it was little over four feet deep — all that was needed for the barges of those days to clear the bottom — and the locks were only wide enough to admit barges something like ten or twelve feet wide.

Most of the time the canal was about the width of an ordinary two lane highway. Nothing went very fast. Horses and mules were the fastest animals that pulled the barges. Many barges were pulled by oxen. The small entrepreneur who was short on capital pulled his own. Considerable time was spent in "Locking through" — (going through the locks). The man in a hurry just had to fidget. Sometimes the berm would break, all the water would run out of the canal, and the barges would be ignominiously "mudlarked" until things were repaired and the water restored to the canal. Canallers bartered farm produce with farmers along the way, and hunted in the wilder areas. The barges were home for many of the canallers. Many were brightly painted and decorated.

The E-ri-e Canal - transcribed by Terry Golden, Rancho de Taos, NM

We were forty miles from Albany, Forget it I never shall
What a terrible storm we had one night on the E-ri-e Canal

Chorus:
Oh the E-ri-e was a-risin, And the gin was a-gettin low,
And I scarcely think we'll get a drink 'Til we get to Buffalo-
oh-oh,

'Til we get to Buffalo.

Two days out from Syracuse And the vessel struck a shoal,
And we like to foundered on a chunk Of Lackawanna coal.

The Captain he came up on deck With a spy-glass in his
      hand;
But the fog it was so 'tarnal thick That he couldn't spy the
      land.

The cook, she was a grand old gal; She wore a ragged
      dress;
We h'isted her upon a pole As a signal of distress!

The winds began to whistle, And the waves began to roll,
And we had to reef our royals On the ra-gi-ing canawl!

The captain, he got married, And the cook, she went to jail;
So I'm the only son of a gun That's left to tell the tale.

    The window curtains and flower pots told whether the captain was married or a bachelor. The greatest danger was probably from getting kicked by one of your own mules or getting into a scrap with another canaller.

    The Erie Canal was one of the most important forward steps in American transportation history, probably more important for its time than is the St. Lawrence Seaway today. 425 miles long, it was called Clinton's Ditch, for De-Witt Clinton, Governor of New York, who was largely responsible for pushing the project through to completion in 1825. You could now travel by water, in ease and comfort, from the Atlantic to the Great Lakes, from New York City up the Hudson River to Albany, then westward up the Mohawk, over the divide and down the western slope to Lake Erie at Buffalo.

It sure beat hauling the stuff by freight wagon, and it sure beat having to sail around Florida and up the Mississippi and its tributaries to Lake Michigan at Chicago. The Erie became the main stem of a complex system of canals that extended all over the Atlantic states. In those days Peter Cooper's "Tom Thumb" was about the only visible means of support in favor of railroading, and everyone got fired up about canals. There was even an absurd proposal for a canal through the deserts of the Southwest, showing that Western politicians then, as now, had imaginations transcending the public pocketbook.

It was all over almost as quickly as it began. Peter Cooper's toy grew into a ferocious haunching-faunching cast iron dragon that breathed fire and smoke and belched steam and glowing cinders. It tore across the pampas like a scalded dog. Its brash clanging tolled the knell of the canals.

But Ah! The pendulum swings back. Canalling is coming back — in a way. The old Erie canal now accommodates barges at least twice as wide as they were in DeWitt Clinton's day, and they draw as much as fourteen feet of water. The brawlers will be over their heads if they're fighting in the canals now. And the barges are like icebergs: a foot or two above water and fourteen feet below. Instead of the puffing of horses you hear the thump-thump-thump-thump of Diesels. And, with the private boat becoming increasingly a status symbol, some of the canals are heavily travelled by pleasure yachts and skittery craft with outboards, and maybe the occasional non-conformist who wants to be the first to go from here to there by canal in a wash-tub — with or without outboard. It's not even called The Erie Canal anymore; it's The Barge Canal now.

Music and background commentaries on the song may be found in The Burl Ives Song Book, (Ballantine Books); Carl Sandburg's The American Songbag, (Harcourt-Brace) ; Lomax's Folk Song USA, (Duell, Sloan, and Pearce); and many other folk song collections.

There were many songs that were tops for dancing to, but many people never heard the words to them. "Old Joe Clark" is a great banjo tune that Terry presented in his unique style.

Find one article on the history of the banjo, read it, and go no further. You'll feel the warm gratifying glow of authoritarian self-assuredness. If you do more, you'll fall into confusion.

The distinguishing feature of the banjo is the skin tightly stretched over a hoop, bowl, or gourd. This produces the characteristic dry, brittle, snappy tone quality that is so suitable for our fast-moving southern hoedowns. Instruments using this basic principle were developed in the Arabic countries and in India, long, long ago. Africans picked it up, probably from the Arabs, and probably it first came to this country with the African slaves and was developed from the negro's instrument into the modern form in the white man's minstrel shows.

Thomas Jefferson mentions it, calling it a "banger," (soft "g"). It was also called banjar, banja, banshaw, and bonja, before acquiring the present name. Most scholarly writings on the banjo have been done by long-hairs, and they take the instrument only a little more seriously than they do  the kazoo and ukelele. British writers convey the impression that the instrument is almost an English invention and certainly reached its most glorious flowering at English fingertips. It seems that in England the banjo usually had 6, 7 or 9 strings, while this country was working up a four-stringed instrument.

Then came the glorious day when, according to Lomax, a Tar Heel named Joe Sweeney, in 1840 added the fifth string, much shorter than the other four. It resulted in the peculiar technique that fits together with southern folk music like limestone, corn, and mint fit together in Kentucky.

In addition to the five-string, the commonest instruments in this country today are the short-necked four-string tenor, and the long-necked, deeper toned, four-string "plectrum" banjo, very like a five-string only without the fifth string. Some players used to wear "thimbles" on thumb and some of the fingers, and would strike the strings, Today, most players use a pick, or "plectrum," held between thumb and forefinger. The five-string banjo, though, calls for the finger picking technique, with, or without "finger picks."

Today, tunings have become fairly standardized, but some individualists persist who work out their own tunings and techniques. The Square Dance Revival helped bring back the banjo. Jack Hawes, whose flawless rhythm is recorded on SIO records, played the longneck four-string. Harry Raby, who recorded for Hoedown label, is a banjo expert, but always seems to be playing some other instrument.

589

I don't know who that old boy is who does banjo for Mac-Gregor, but he can fairly call forth the spirits from under the calfskin. Folkraft and later Folkways made recordings of Pete Seeger, one of the best men on the five-string, and one of the men who did most to bring back the old Southern finger technique. Cliffie Stone's old Capitol records featured another top five-string man, Bearded Herman, Cliffie Stone's dad.

"Old Joe Clark" is a superb fiddle and banjo tune. One of the best records is Folkraft's 12-incher by Shorty Warren's orchestra. Nice swing; clean snappy rhythm. Then, on an old 12-inch Intro record, is Joe Lewis's record of "Joe Clark," with that hypnotic rhythm that has already made the name of Joe Lewis more durable than the name of Joe Louis. But neither of these exploits the brilliant possibilities of the banjo. Dig out another 12-incher, Cliffie Stone's orchestra on Capitol, with "Devil's Dream" and "Old Joe Clark," both on the same side, Bearded Herman, five-string picker supreme, alternating with one Hensley, fiddle-scratcher par-excellence. Trouble with that whole series was they put two tunes together on each side, and most callers never went for the arrangement.

"Old Joe Clark" is one of those southern breakdowns with more verses than anyone will ever know, most of them non-sequiturs, many unprintable. Joe was a salty cuss, anyway:

Old Joe Clark a fine ole man, tell you the reason why:
He keeps good likker 'round the house, good old Rock &
    Rye.

Chorus: Fare thee well, Old Joe Clark, Fare thee well I say;
Fare the well, Old Joe Clark, I'm a goin' away.

Old Joe Clark the preacher's son, preached all over the
      plain;
The only text he ever knew was "High, low, jack & the
      game.

Well, I never did like Old Joe Clark, I'll tell you the reason
      why:
He tore down my rail fence, So his cattle could eat my rye.

I went down to Old Joe's house; Old Joe was not at home;
I ate all the meat that Old Joe had and left Old Joe the bone.

Old Joe Clark was a salty cuss, and guilty was of sin;
He made a Salty Dog with Rye when he knowed it oughtta
      been gin.

I went down to Old Joe's house and found him sick in bed;
I jabbed my finger down his throat and pulled out a pole-
      cat's head.

Old Joe Clark's a mean old man; I'll tell you the reason
      why:
My hogs got into his garden patch and stomped out all of
      his rye.

I won't go down to Old Joe's house; I done been there
      before.
He fed me in a hog-trough, and I won't go there anymore.

I went down to Old Joe's house; Joe was eatin' supper;
I stumped my toes on a table leg and rammed my nose in
      the butter.

Last time I seen Old Joe Clark He was settin' on a rail,
Jug of whisky under his arm and a possum by the tail.

And so, on, and on. Make up your own.

APPENDIX #8 - Keokuk

It was just a regular dance with perhaps a little more gaiety than usual due to the Thanksgiving holiday coming the next day - but of course, all of the Swing-Ezy dances were special affairs. Kenny Anderson, the caller for the group since it started as a class back in September of 1960, had set up his equipment as usual and the dancers were still coming into the hall during that first tip - just as they always did on past Wednesdays.

This could have been a dance in any of several thousand halls in any one of several thousand cities in the world. The calls, the rounds and the chatter between the tips would seem familiar to any one of us who share in this activity.

Suddenly at 9:35 p.m., as Kenny was calling "King of the Road," without warning, the sounds of the square dance changed. With a roar, a tremendous explosion lifted the roof, collapsed the walls and trapped the dancers below the debris.

What happened next became the subject of newspaper headlines and television and radio broadcasts around the world.

(News lead story - November 25,1965) "KEOKUK, Iowa –

An explosion in the National Guard Armory late last night killed and injured a great many of the 70 square dancers taking part in their weekly dance. The blast, apparently coming from the basement as the result of an accumulation of gas, completely destroyed the reinforced concrete building... "

It didn't take long for the statistics to come in: The total number of those who lost their lives reached 21.

Twenty-eight of the injured were in hospitals and burn centers in three states and 21 children were completely or partially orphaned by the disaster.

Less than twelve hours after the fateful explosion that killed or critically injured a large percentage of the Swing Ezy club, calls began filtering in. From Massachusetts, Washington, California, Kansas, Toronto, from almost everywhere came the question: "How can we help?"

The answer was not long in coming. Plasma and first aid were needed for the burn victims themselves and financial assistance for their families. Benefit dances, personal donations and many programs were started for the purpose of raising money for the relief of those injured and for the children who were orphaned. Within two days of the explosion five couples of those Swing-Ezy members who survived established the "Swing-Ezy Disaster Fund" to oversee the disposition of money that started pouring in.

The trust department of a local bank, a lawyer and an accountant donated their services and, within a few short weeks, more than $90,000 had been received.

A square dance club in Germany sent its entire receipts from a dance. The Northern Lights square dancers in Anchorage, Alaska, rushed their donation in. The fund received donations from every state in the union as well as from Canada, Germany, England, France, the Philippines, Vietnam and other countries around the world. Within the next three years a quarter of a million dollars had been received.

Because of the generosity of so many, a number of the young people received educations. Funds were made available to assist with the costly hospital bills. Children who had lost parents were provided for and a wide variety of help was made available.

The Swing-Ezy Square Dance Club no longer exists, although a number of its survivors continue to dance with clubs in the area and the members of the "Swing-Ezy Disaster Fund" meet on a regular basis.

Nola (Bennett) Joy, who survived the explosion but spent several years recovering from her injuries, lost her husband and small son in the disaster. In talking to her recently, she expressed her gratitude, not only for her local square dance friends who stood by her during the many months of recovery, but for the thousands of square dancers around the world whose contributions made it possible for her and the other survivors to receive the quality care that was required. As a means of showing her gratitude and appreciation, Nola has occupied her time in ways to benefit those in hospitals and needing help. "This is my way of saying 'thank you' to all those who helped me!"

And what of the caller, Ken Anderson? We understand that he lives in Florida and recently retired from calling. On that fateful night almost three decades ago, Kenny received second degree burns when the blast carried him through another room and out a window. His newly purchased car was totaled as was his sound equipment and all of his records.

In talking with him shortly after the accident, Kenny expressed the feelings that would come from any caller who had been with a club from the time it started as a square dance class more than three years earlier. "It's hard to believe what happened to all these friends, people that I knew so well and have called to for so many years. Oh, you know how close you get to your dancers, especially when you call to them every week."

When asked about the outpouring of offers of assistance from square dancers around the world, Kenny said: "I never realized how closely knit together all square dancers are. This is tremendous. It's as though we're all a part of one big family. I have never seen anything like it."

And Kenny had a personal reason to feel grateful. His sound system, a complete loss in the explosion, was replaced without charge by its manufacturer, Jim Hilton.

And so it is that the Keokuk disaster, despite all of its unhappiness, has once again underscored for all to see, what a tremendous fraternal attraction square dancing is.

The story from another side: Keokuk – aid from Canada
Ottawa Square Dance Association Presents Successful
KEOKUK KAN-KAN-KAPERS
By Bud Mayo — Ottawa, Ont., Canada

The Ottawa Square Dance Association and its member clubs made extensive plans since the first word of the disaster in Keokuk, Iowa, reached Ottawa. Many of our dancers have enjoyed countless happy square dance hours while guests of numerous square dance clubs in your country. Good fellowship and fun have prevailed in all our gatherings. I am sure I speak for all square dancers in this area when I say that we sincerely felt a sense of personal loss in this unfortunate tragedy.

Our first thought was to hold some sort of benefit dance for the Iowans and what evolved was our first Keokuk Kan-Kan Kapers dance. Sponsored by the Ottawa Square Dance Association, the dance was held — very successfully — on February 26. By all accounts and from the compliments of the dancers, this was a unique and enjoyable dance. Even the name was unusual and gives a clue as to what took place.

Realizing that our main purpose was to raise as much money as possible, we hit upon a plan which we think is new and asked each club member to bring to the weekly club dance two weeks before the event, one tin of canned goods. These were collected at a central location and put in bushel baskets which were to be raffled off at $2.50 a ticket during the evening of the Kapers.

We filled nine such baskets with some 52 cans per basket. The basket filled with soups was called the Soup Spoon; the one with tinned vegetables was the Vegetable Bin; the one with fruits the Fruit Bowl, etc. There was no extra time taken up with these raffles which were held between tips when people were on the floor. Value of the baskets was approximately $13.00. We also received square dance shirts,

"The winners." Happy square dancers not only help the folks in Keokuk but go home with a bundle of groceries, pants, dress material, etc., from our local stores and these were also raffled. Dancers were sold a ticket perforated in the middle and numbered at each end. Tables were set up along one side of the school gym and dancers could put one half of their ticket into a slotted shoebox for the basket, etc., of their choice. One box at a time was brought up and a dancer from the floor was asked to pull out the lucky number.

This pilot idea of ours added much zest to the dance. Over 500 tickets were sold, realizing close to $125.00. Keith Watters and Art Wilson, two area callers, gave of their time and talents and more than 30 squares helped to raise the total to $400.00.

Another highlight of this event was the presence as guests of Mr. and Mrs. J. L. Gawf, First Secretary to the United States Ambassador to Canada. Mr. Gawf accepted our cheque on behalf of the Keokuk Chamber of Commerce, making a very impressive acceptance speech. Excerpts from this speech follow.

...I would like to say that this kind act by the members of the Ottawa Square Dance Association conveys a degree

of sympathy and compassion which is somehow more moving and more heartwarming than any ordinary expression of condolence.

We in the United States like to believe that when tragedy strikes a particularly   cruel blow against an American community, nearby neighboring communities will lend a helping hand and in fact, they usually do.

However, it is quite another matter for a group of citizens of another country, in a community many miles away spontaneously to extend not only their sympathy but their tangible help as well to ease the suffering of people whom they have never known...

It has just been explained to me that square dancers everywhere are, in a sense, kindred spirits and that the bond between them is completely irrespective of distance and nationality. I must say that this is an example of international relations worthy of emulation everywhere; I think all of us in the United States and Canada can take pride in what you have done...

KEOKUK THREE YEARS LATER
By Evelyn Johnson, Long Beach, Calif.
Date Line, November 25, 1965 Keokuk, Iowa

AN EXPLOSION in the National Guard Armory late last night killed and injured a great many of the 70 square dancers taking part in their weekly dance. The blast, apparently coming from the basement as the result of an accumulation of gas, completely destroyed the reinforced concrete building

Three years ago this month, square dancers all over the world were shocked and saddened when the news of this disaster reached them. They lived with their sadness but their shock gave way to, "what can we do – how can we help?" Benefit dances, personal donations, many activities were started for the purpose of raising money for the relief of those injured and for the children orphaned. The Swing-Ezy Benefit Fund Foundation was soon established, to act as executors for this money.

To present a follow-up story on the progress of these dancers for their friends around the world, we sent a letter of inquiry and received the following information from Richard E. Denly, president of the executive committee of the Swing-Ezy Benefit Fund Foundation. The survivors are all doing extremely well. There are some who are still receiving therapy treatments and medical attention in the form of corrective surgery, mostly of scar tissue remaining from the most serious burns. Six of the survivors have remarried and are building new lives for themselves. Out of these six, one man and one woman, both of whom lost their mates, are now married to each other.

The caller, Kenny Anderson, is still active in square dancing and lives in the state of New York, a move that he was planning at the time of the accident. As to the children orphaned... they are adjusting well. The Goodrich children, four in number, are living with their maternal grandparents, with support checks from the fund foundation each month. The second family that lost both parents, the Becketts, are being cared for through the Foundation; the smallest child is living with his maternal grandmother, a retarded boy is in a home, the daughter is now married.

The older Beckett boy has returned to college to finish work on his degree, which was interrupted by the disaster. The Fund is paying his college costs. Of the other children, all had one surviving parent. While the Fund has not supported these children on a month-to- month basis, it has provided a number of things such as medical and dental aid and other necessities. When these children reach college age, and most of them are still quite young, the Fund intends to see to their education

.   The Swing-Ezy Club has been active since approximately six months following the accident. It was necessary for the club to move their dance location to Hamilton, Illinois, a town just across the Mississippi river from Keokuk as they were unable to find a suitable hall in Keokuk. The president of the club for 1967 was one who lost his wife in the disaster and he has since remarried. There are some of those injured who are still active in the club, but not too many.

The Fund received donations from every state in the union, as well as from Germany, Canada, England, France, the Philippines, Vietnam, and other countries around the world. Total contributions exceeded $230,000 before they stopped coming. Mr. Denly writes, "The response of square dancers has been overwhelming and exceedingly gratifying. The Fund has sufficient money to meet any and all needs of the injured and to provide college educations for the orphans, barring unforeseen circumstances."

The executive committee of the Fund Foundation is made up of square dancers in Keokuk. They have had the services of an attorney, a certified accountant, and the trust department of the State Central Savings Bank all donated free of charge. The monies in the fund not immediately needed have been invested in government notes and long term securities and are earning a safe 4% return. In this way, the fund will continue to grow in the years ahead.

These people serve as an inspiration to all of us in the courage they have shown, their adjustment to the radical changes in their lives, their victory over the disaster. We can all be proud of them and pray that square dancers will never again have to suffer such a disaster.

APPENDIX #9: "Pomes"

It seems that from the beginning, Sets in Order received poems (of varying quality – therefore the title of this chapter: Pomes, not poems) from all over the country and further. Some are paeans to Square Dancing, while others denigrate some of the peccadilloes of particular dancers.

One of the files in the SIO/ASDS archives holds a twenty-five year collection dating from the early 1960's through to the last issue of SQUARE DANCING (Sets in Order) Magazine in 1985. The writer, Beryl Frank, from Pikesville, Maryland, did the bulk of her corresponding with me in four line verse.

Beryl, as it turned out, was a long-time square dancer. Over the years her experiences took her, along with her husband, Louis, through all the normal stages of the activity from beginner's class into normal club responsibilities. Over the years she expressed her views, likes and occasional (but always humorous) concerns about the world of square dancing - and always in rhyme.

We've lost track of the Franks over the past ten years. I can't seem to even find an address. So, I'll never know if Beryl gets to see this, but here, for a new generation of square dancers to enjoy is a sampling of Beryl's "square verse" selected from the more than two hundred rhymes I have in the file.

> She wears a badge upon her blouse
> Or sometimes on her skirt

But mine must stay here to hide
The worn spot on my shirt!

On the subject of the square dance costume Beryl has this
to say:
They did not know just who she was
Or that she danced with grace
But they sure knew her pettipants
Were trimmed in purple lace.

A crowd is not the people
Who have come from near and far
A crowd is when three crinolines
Are squeezed into one car.

Here are some typical thoughts of the new square dancer:
I only have one problem
Can you help me with my plight?
And find a way for me to learn
My left hand from my right!

Searching, seeking madly
I ran around the square
No matter where I seemed to go
My corner was not there.

And, yes, the veteran dancer has thoughts, too:

Seven people demonstrate
The basics and the breaks
So how come all I demonstrate
Is how to make mistakes?

And a couple for the caller:
Be late for your dinner
Or miss it perchance

But never oh never
Be late for my dance.

The record is scratched
And my mike seems to scream
And nobody shows up –
How's that for a dream?

A Caller's Prayer By J. Edward Johnston, Kensington, Md.

"Square dancing is a lot of fun," one heard the dancers say
Let my job add much to this, but not to take away.
And though my contribution to square dancing be so small
Let that contribution provide joy and fun for all.

And when before the microphone my voice soars in the
        breeze
Let simplicity guide my calling and the dancers dance with
        ease.
When someone says that I'm all right but you ought to hear
        old Joe
Don't let my feelings turn flip-flops and hurt my ego so.

I'm not out front competing, hand claps are not for me;
It's because those folks enjoyed the dance their hearts are
        full of glee.
Other callers are all swell guys, some better on the old
        hoedown
But as long as I can serve at all I'll still be hanging 'round.

Let me not stoop to quibbling when dance clubs rip and
     snort;
Little can be added if I, too, blow my cork.
My job now as I see it, is not for the halls of fame
It's just to fill a humble spot, so gents can dance their
     dames.

And when the evening's over and the last call has been
     sung,
I hope that I will merit the words, "That's a job well done."

Square Dance Flu

Choose your partners, one and all,
Aspirin, Advil, or Tylenol!
Now fling those covers with all you've got,
One minute cold, the next minute hot,
Circle right to the side of the bed,
Grab the tissues and Sudafed.
Back to the middle and don't goof off;
Hold your stomach and cough, cough, cough.
Forget about slippers, dash down the hall,
Toss your cookies in the shower stall.
Remember others on the brink;
Wash your hands; wash the sink.
Wipe the doorknob, light switch too,
By George, you've got it, you're doing the Flu!
Some like it cold, some like it hot;
If you like neither, get the shot.

Big Cowboy Ball

The Cowboys of Springer, New Mexico, gave their fourth annual ball in that city. They sent something like eight hundred invitations at home, and abroad, inscribed with appropriate verse, as follows:

"Caller, let no echo slumber,
Fiddler sweatin' like a steer,
Huffs a-poundin' at the lumber,
Makin' music the stars could hear;
Hug the gals up when we swing 'em,
Raise them plum off their feet.
Balance, all ye saddle warmers,
Rag a little, shake your feet,
On to next 'un, and repeat it,
Balance to the next in waitin',
Promenade, and off you go,
Seat your pards, and let 'em blow."

SHAKE IT, WILL: The Hokey-Pokey by the Bard

O proud left foot, that ventures quick within
Then soon upon a backward journey lithe.
Anon, once more the gesture, then begin:

Command sinistral pedestal to writhe.
Commence thou then the fervid Hokey-Poke,
A mad gyration, hips is wanton swirl.
To spin! A wilde release from
Heaven's yoke.
Blessed dervish! Surely canst go, girl.
The Hoke, the poke – o banish now thy doubt
Verily, I say, 'tis what it's all about.
                    -author unknown

Virginia's Reel by Bill Staines

Gents to the middle, let the young girl fiddle,
And you ain't got nothin' to lose.
Allemande right, she could play all night
She could fiddle off the bottom of your shoes
Oh me, oh my, how she makes that bow hair fly.
How she hangs that music in the air.

Promenade down to the lonesome sound
Of the whippoorwill in the night.
Sashay back, look at ol' man Jack,
Well he's huggin' everything in sight.
Oh me, oh my, how she makes that bow hair fly.
How she hangs the music in the air.

Banjo Bill, well he stopped stock still,
As the notes came rollin' by.
They filled his ears and eased his fears,
And the tears come to his eyes.
Oh me, oh my, how she makes that bow hair fly.

605

How she hangs that music in the air.

The old string bass, he's lost his place
And his arms just fell like steel.
The guitar man dropped both his hands,
And he swore it was not real.
Oh me, oh my, how she makes that bow hair fly.
How she hangs that music in the air.

It's golden strings on Eden's wings
At the calling of the squares.
There's fiddle tunes, and there' fiddle tunes,
But Virginia's splittin' hairs.
Oh me, oh my, how she makes that bow hair fly.
How she hangs that music in the air.

She cast a spell no tongue could tell,
No prophet can reveal.
It's as quiet as death, just hold your breath,
As she plays Virginia's Reel.
Oh me, oh my, how she makes that bow hair fly.
How she hangs that music in the air.

Appendix #10 – SIO/ASDS

The American Square Dance Society is a non-profit service organization originated by the Sets in Order and probably known best as the publisher of SQUARE DANC-ING Magazine (first published in November 1948 as Sets in Order). The Society serves as a nerve center for square danc-ing, providing information, technical advice, and materials for radio, television, motion pictures, the press and independent authors as well as for college and high school students, seeking background assistance.

The Society is dedicated to the promotion, protection, and perpetuation of American Square Dancing. It has done what it could to lend support to on-going independent and organizational projects, including the annual National Square Dance Convention, the Lloyd Shaw Foundation, the Overseas Dancer Association, and many others. The society played a prime part in the formation of both LEGACY and CALLERLAB. Members of the Society who get the SQUARE DANCING Magazine each month are located in more than 50 countries overseas as well as in every Canadian Province and every one of the United States.

Since before Convention One, the Society has played various roles in the growth of the annual National Square Dance Convention. Through its magazine, the Society has donated an estimated $60,000 worth of publicity and advertising to the Convention since its inception. 462 North Robertson Blvd., Los Angeles is the home of the Society. Although the magazine isn't printed there, almost all of the Society's functions are carried on there. The Society-sponsored Square Dance Hall of Fame Gallery is located in the Hall and is open to visitors. [*The Sets in Order Hall closed about 1990, and the Hall of Fame portraits now hang in the Lloyd Shaw Foundation Hall in Albuquerque, NM. – ed.*)

The Society also awards the Silver Spur (created in 1956) for excellence in the field of square dance leadership. The award honors those who have devoted much of their lives, time, and energies to the promotion, protection, and perpetuation of American Square Dancing. The many other functions performed by the Society include:

- Awarding scholarships each year to aid aspiring callers wishing to attend callers' schools.

- Encouraging archive centers and augmenting many with complete sets of SQUARE DANCING Magazine.
- Publishing in its magazine directories of: Special events that are larger than normal square dance activities; square dance vacation institutes; callers' schools; square dance travel, cruises, and tours; publications; and a master directory of all square dancer, round dance leader, and caller associations, plus square dance information volunteers in almost every area throughout the square dance world.
- Publishing the Gavel & Key News Letter which is directed to leaders in square dancing and editors of square dance publications. Included in the Society's magazine, its purpose is to brief those who are interested in the present and future of square dancing on what is happening.
- Publishing a handbook series that covers: Square Dancing Indoctrination, Basic Movements, Mainstream/Plus Movements, The Story of Square Dancing, Club Organization,
- SD Publicity, Youth In Square Dancing, Party Fun, and One-Night Stands.
- Publishing Caller/Teacher Manuals for: Basics, Extended Basics, Contra Dancing, and Round Dancing.
- Producing school aids in the form of teaching records with calls and written instructions which are used to introduce contemporary American Square Dancing to the dancers of the future.

The Society worked in the background of Sets in Order before it was reorganized and became a membership organization much like the National Geographic. The idea was to make available to all square dancers all the benefits of belonging to the Society, such as subscription to SQUARE DANCING Magazine and special travel opportunities. Prior to the reorganization, Sets in Order Magazine operated a foundation that sponsored action and other groups to promote square dancing.

For example: Back in 1972, on our 23rd Anniversary we asked "why" relative to the various segments of square dancing. Why, we asked, do people square dance? Why do some dancers become callers? Why do we have conventions and why do we have associations? From that issue stemmed a suggestion of responsibility placement and into focus came the many service groups dedicated to perpetuate American square dancing. Why, we asked, couldn't all these groups take a share of the total responsibility in promoting, perpetuating and protecting this activity? Our suggestion was that each of these groups play a part in the total picture and that each segment, working together, could accomplish great things for this activity. It's like a giant jig saw puzzle. The 13 parts were all needed to make up the whole of square dancing and then once put together our picture was complete. The result of our questions was LEGACY.

The drive that started years ago for a U. S. stamp commemorating square dancing culminated in a stamp that honored four major areas of dance in America. Unfortunately, shortly after the stamp was released, postal rates changed and the stamp was priced so that it was not used.

A square dance float in the 1977 Tournament of Roses Parade, Pasadena, California will be seen by many millions of viewers around the world. Coordinated by a group in California, American square dancers everywhere have an opportunity to help make the float a reality. Square dancers made the float a reality for several years by raising funds (benefit dances and the sale of rose shaped embroidered stickers) and volunteering in the actual construction of the float.

Square Dance Week, at one time celebrated at many different seasons of the year, was coordinated a few years

609

back. The common time to celebrate Square Dance week is in September to accompany the beginning of classes.

Each year one or more caller candidates are selected for partial or full scholarships to some of the nation's leading callers' schools through our SIO/ASDS Scholarship program.

Gavel and Key is a newsletter for current presidents of square dancer, round dancer and caller associations, editors of area publication, members of the National Square Dance Convention Executive Committee and Board of Governor members of CALLERLAB which is published periodically. Serving as a communications publication directed to the leadership of square dancing, Gavel and Key indirectly reaches the several million in the activity today.

SIO/ASDS records public service announcements especially for use with local radio stations. These records include, on one side, four introductory announcements concerning square dancing and invite the listeners to join a beginner class. The announcements are l0, 20, 30 seconds and one minute in duration and time is provided for the local announcer to fill in with pertinent area club and class information. The reverse side contains square dance music only of varying lengths for tailor made radio spots. A printed sheet describing use of the record is included.

Recognition is an important service of the American Square Dance Society and over the years and throughout the pages of SQUARE DANCING Magazine, more than 498 individuals have been recognized as Callers of the Month. Additionally, some 304 couples have been featured in Paging the Round Dancers. Include the hundreds who have appeared as authors of various chapters of the magazine over 35 years and a reader will get a fair idea of the men and women who have maintained the responsibility of leadership during the growth of this activity. As these features continue, others will be spotlighted in coming issues.

There are other areas in which the SIO/ASDS encourages, supports and honors men and women in the activity. Here is a rundown:

For service to mankind the knights of centuries past were said to "win their spurs." In square dancing today there are many individuals who through inspiration, toil, and unselfishness have helped bring the true spirit of square dancing to their fellow men. Through this service they have also "won their spurs." In recognition of this service, Sets in Order Foundation wishes to honor certain individuals or groups of individuals at various times with the "Silver Spur" award. It is the hope of the Foundation that in this way many individuals may receive recognition of their contributions to square dancing and that many more will be inspired to give even more generously of their time, skill, and efforts.

It is pointed out that no award such as this can touch every deserving individual. For every recipient there will be hundreds, whose contributions are equally noteworthy and deserving but who will not be officially recognized.

We stress, however, that the true reward for accomplished services in this great activity is the joy of "giving." No material trophy will equal this satisfaction.

Recipients of the Sets in Order Foundation's Silver Spurs awards will be chosen by an impartial selection board appointed by the Foundation. Nominations may be submitted at any time by anyone and should be sent to Sets in Order Foundation. Reasons for nominations should be clearly stated. No discussion will be carried on relative to the nominations and, except for questions thought necessary from time to time by the selection board, those making the nominations will receive no acknowledgement.

Recipients for these awards can be professionals, non-professionals, teachers, callers, dancers, or enthusiasts of the great square dancing activity anywhere in the world who have done much, unselfishly, for square dancing.

The first Silver Spur was awarded in 1956. The most recent in 1983. Here are the names of the 18 individuals (or couples) who, to date, have received the Silver Spur: Carl and Varene Anderson ('72), Charlie and Bertha Baldwin ('76), Dick and Jan Brown ('83), Stan and Cathie Burdick ('79). Harold and Thelma Deane ('57), Ed Gilmore ('67), John Kaltenthaler ('79), Lawrence Loy ('56), Gwen Manning ('82). Jay Metcalf ('81), John Mooney ('58), Corky and Paulette Pell ('77), Dorothy Stott Shaw ('72).Dr. Lloyd 'Pappy' Shaw ('56), Ted and Gladys Sparshatt ('81), Steve and Fran Stephens ('74), Howard Thornton ('56), Dale Wagner ('81). [One more was added after this list was printed: Dr. William Litchman ('03).]

The Square Dance Hall of Fame

In any activity the size and vastness of square dancing, there emerge great leaders. There are a number of these individuals who have contributed something extra, not just to their own community, for which they may have been appropriately and adequately applauded by friends and neighbors. These are well-established leaders who were able to add their experience and expertise to help strengthen the activity. From 1961 to the present, 34 leaders (including five couples) have been inducted into the Square Dance Hall of Fame. Here, arranged alphabetically, are their names: Carl and Varene Anderson ('81), Don Armstrong ('70), Charlie Baldwin ('81), Al Brundage ('70), Bill Castner ('83). Jimmy Clossin ('61), Marshall Flippo ('70), Ed Gilmore ('61), Cal Golden ('78), Les Gotcher ('79). Herb Greggerson ('61), Frank and Carolyn Hamilton ('71), Lee Helsel ('70), Jerry

Helt ('79), Bruce Johnson ('70). Earl Johnston ('70), Fenton 'Jonesy' Jones ('61), Arnie Kronenberger ('70), Frank Lane ('70), Johnny LeClair ('70). Dick Leger ('78), Joe Lewis ('61), Melton Luttrell ('77), Jim Mayo ('78), Ralph and Eve Maxheimer ('81). Bob Osgood ('72), Bob Page ('70), Ralph Page ('61), Bob Ruff ('81), Dr. Lloyd 'Pappy' and Dorothy Shaw ('61). Manning and Nita Smith ('71), Ray Smith ('61), Dave Taylor ('71), Bob Van Antwerp ('70).

Each inductee into the Hall of Fame had an oil portrait painted which was hung in the Sets in Order Hall. Upon closing the magazine the portraits were all sent to the Lloyd Shaw Foundation archive and dance center in Albuquerque, New Mexico, where they still hang.

CALLERLAB Milestone Award

The CALLERLAB Milestone Award is the highest award CALLERLAB can bestow on any individual. The nominee must meet the criteria in all five categories to receive the award. The primary purpose of this award is to recognize those individuals, whether CALLERLAB members or not, who have made outstanding and significant contributions to the field of square dancing. This is often a difficult decision, for there are many outstanding callers in our activity.

The Milestone Award is a recognition by an individual's peers, which sets the recipient apart from the ordinary as follows:

- Outstanding and significant contributions to the field of square dancing.
- The contributions must have stood the Test of Time.

- Relates to unselfish contribution - divorced from personal gain and monetary rewards - requires attitude that thinks of others first.
- Recipient must maintain and conduct self in professional leadership capacity – professionalism reflecting high standards of leadership to which we have dedicated ourselves in our day to day actions.
- Recipient must have exercised broad influence in the square dance activity - although local geographic and highly specialized activity may lead to recognition

1975	Al Brundage		1984	Jim Mayo
1975	Les Gotcher		1984	Jim York
1975	Joe Lewis		1985	Jon Jones
1975	Lloyd Litman		1985	Dick Leger
1976	Herb Greggerson		1986	Melton Luttrell
1976	Fenton 'Jonesy' Jones		1986	Bill Peters
1976	Jimmy Clossin		1986	Dave Taylor
1978	Bob Osgood		1988	Bruce Johnson
1978	Manning Smith		1989	Bill Davis
1979	Doc Alumbaugh		1989	Decko Deck
1979	Ed Gilmore		1991	Herb Egender
1979	Lee Helsel		1992	Jerry Haag
1979	Bob Van Antwerp		1992	Jerry Helt
1980	Don Armstrong		1992	Stan & Cathy Burdick
1980	Charlie Baldwin		1992	Lee Kopman
1980	Jack Lasry		1993	Earl Johnston
1980	Benjamin Lovett		1994	Martin Mallard
1980	Ralph Page		1994	Bob Ruff
1981	Marshall Flippo		1996	Osa Matthews
1981	Cal Golden		1997	Ralph Piper
1981	Frank Lane		1998	Bob Howell
1982	Art Shepherd		1998	John Kaltenthaler
1982	Jim Hilton		1999	Gloria Rios Roth
1982	Johnny LeClair		2000	Tony Oxendine
1983	Arnie Kronenberger		2001	Jack Murtha
1983	Lloyd 'Pappy' Shaw		2001	Mike Seastrom
1983	Ray Smith		2002	Bill Heyman
			2002	Vaughn Parrish
			2002	Al Stevens

614

2003	Stew Shacklette	2012	Bob Brundage
2004	Wade Driver	2012	Mr. Tatsuzo Takase
2006	Betsy Gotta	2012	Don Williamson
2006	Cal Campbell	2013	Mike Jacobs
2008	Ed Foote	2016	Gardner Patton
2010	Masaru Wada	2016	Carl Sims

And just one more.

Millennium Award

The CALLERLAB Millennium Award is a one-time award presented to the late Bob Osgood, the primary force in the formation of CALLERLAB and one of our most influential Founding Members. The Millennium Award was presented to Bob during the 50th National Square Dance Convention in Anaheim, California in June 2001. The inscription reads:

Presented To Bob Osgood in appreciation of more than 60 years of dedication and service to Square, Round, and Contra dancing in all its many wonderful forms CALLERLAB presents to Bob Osgood the MILLENNIUM AWARD June 30, 2001

INDEX

INDEX

INDEX

INDEX

INDEX

INDEX

INDEX

INDEX

Made in the USA
Middletown, DE
29 May 2017